OXFORD WORLD'S CLASSICS

DHARMASŪṬRAS

PATRICK OLIVELLE is the Chair, Department of Asian Studies, and Director, Center for Asian Studies, at the University of Texas at Austin, where he is the Professor of Sanskrit and Indian Religions. Among his recent publications are *The Saṃnyāsa Upaniṣads: Hindu Scriptures on Asceticism and Renunciation* (Oxford, 1992), *The Āśrama System: History and Hermeneutics of a Religious Institution* (Oxford, 1993), *Rules and Regulations of Brahmanical Asceticism* (State University of New York Press, 1994), and *The Early Upaniṣads: Annotated Text and Translation* (Oxford, 1998). His translations of *Upaniṣads* and *Pañcatantra* were published in Oxford World's Classics in 1996 and 1997.

OXFORD WORLD'S CLASSICS

For almost 100 years Oxford World's Classics have brought readers closer to the world's great literature. Now with over 700 titles—from the 4,000-year-old myths of Mesopotamia to the twentieth century's greatest novels—the series makes available lesser-known as well as celebrated writing.

The pocket-sized hardbacks of the early years contained introductions by Virginia Woolf, T. S. Eliot, Graham Greene, and other literary figures which enriched the experience of reading. Today the series is recognized for its fine scholarship and reliability in texts that span world literature, drama and poetry, religion, philosophy and politics. Each edition includes perceptive commentary and essential background information to meet the changing needs of readers.

OXFORD WORLD'S CLASSICS

Dharmasūtras

The Law Codes of Āpastamba, Gautama, Baudhāyana, and Vasiṣṭha

Translated from the Original Sanskrit and Edited by

PATRICK OLIVELLE

OXFORD
UNIVERSITY PRESS

OXFORD
UNIVERSITY PRESS

Great Clarendon Street, Oxford OX2 6DP

Oxford University Press is a department of the University of Oxford.
It furthers the University's objective of excellence in research, scholarship,
and education by publishing worldwide in

Oxford New York

Athens Auckland Bangkok Bogotá Buenos Aires Calcutta
Cape Town Chennai Dar es Salaam Delhi Florence Hong Kong Istanbul
Karachi Kuala Lumpur Madrid Melbourne Mexico City Mumbai
Nairobi Paris São Paulo Singapore Taipei Tokyo Toronto Warsaw

with associated companies in Berlin Ibadan

Oxford is a registered trade mark of Oxford University Press
in the UK and in certain other countries

Published in the United States
by Oxford University Press Inc., New York

First published as an Oxford World's Classics paperback 1999

British Library Cataloguing in Publication Data
Data available

Library of Congress Cataloging in Publication Data
Data available

ISBN 0–19–283882–2

1 3 5 7 9 10 8 6 4 2

Typeset by RefineCatch Limited, Bungay, Suffolk
Printed in Great Britain by
Cox & Wyman Ltd., Reading, Berkshire

For

Anne, Gregory, and Richard

kalyāṇamitrebhyaḥ

PREFACE

In 1879 George Bühler published his English translation of the Dharmasūtras of Āpastamba and Gautama under the title *The Sacred Laws of the Āryas* as the second volume of the *Sacred Books of the East* edited by Max Müller. Three years later he brought out the translations of Vasiṣṭha and Baudhāyana, and in 1886 he published the translation of the law book of Manu (*Manu Smṛti*) in the same series. With the benefit of a hundred years of scholarship and numerous printed editions of the Dharmasūtras to work from, it is easy to find fault with his pioneering translations. But Bühler had to work directly from manuscripts and without the benefit of much that scholars today take for granted. I have benefited enormously from his translation and from his thorough and detailed comments in the introductions and notes. I want to acknowledge my deep debt of gratitude to Bühler's pioneering work.

There are many individuals and institutions that helped me during the years when I was preparing this translation. A Guggenheim Fellowship and a faculty research assignment from the University of Texas in 1996–7 allowed me a year's freedom to concentrate on several research projects, including this translation. Ludo Rocher came to the rescue and made sense of several difficult and corrupt passages, as did Richard Lariviere. Gregory Schopen read the introduction and much of the translation and as usual made wise and judicious suggestions. Their input has made this work better and the translations more accurate and accessible.

My wife, Suman, read the entire work several times and caught numerous errors and lapses. I want to thank her and my daughter, Meera, for their love and support. The editorial staff in Oxford, especially Judith Luna, Joanna Rabiger, and Elizabeth Stratford, have been friendly, efficient, and generous. Thanks to all of them.

CONTENTS

ABBREVIATIONS

A	Āpastamba Dharmasūtra
AA	Aitareya Āraṇyaka
AB	Aitareya Brāhmaṇa
AG	Āpastamba Gṛhyasūtra, tr. Oldenberg (1878–86)
AnSS	Ānandāśrama Sanskrit Series
ĀrṣB	Ārṣeya Brāhmaṇa
B	Baudhāyana Dharmasūtra
BU	Bṛhadāraṇyaka Upaniṣad, tr. Olivelle (1996)
CU	Chāndogya Upaniṣad, tr. Olivelle (1996)
G	Gautama Dharmasūtra
GoB	Gopatha Brāhmaṇa
HOS	Harvard Oriental Series
KaU	Kaṭha Upaniṣad, tr. Olivelle (1996)
KS	Kāthaka Samhitā
M	Manu Smṛti
MNU	Mahānārāyaṇa Upaniṣad
MuU	Muṇḍaka Upaniṣad, tr. Olivelle (1996)
MS	Maitrāyani Samhitā
PG	Pāraskara Gṛhyasūtra, tr. Oldenberg (1878–86)
PMS	Pūrvamīmāṃsā Sūtra
RV	Ṛgveda
ṢaḍB	Ṣaḍviṃśa Brāhmaṇa
SāmB	Sāmavidhāna Brāhmaṇa
SB	Śatapatha Brāhmaṇa
SBE	Sacred Books of the East
SG	Śāṅkhāyana Gṛhyasūtra, tr. Oldenberg (1878–86)
SV	Sāmaveda
TA	Taittirīya Āraṇyaka
TB	Taittirīya Brāhmaṇa
TS	Taittirīya Saṃhitā
TU	Taittirīya Upaniṣad, tr. Olivelle (1996)
Va	Vasiṣṭha Dharmasūtra
Vi	Viṣṇu Smṛti
Vkh	Vaikhānasa Dharmasūtra, tr. Caland (1929)

VkhG	Vaikhānasa Gṛhyasūtra, tr. Caland (1929)
VS	Vājasaneyi Saṃhitā
WZKSA	Wiener Zeitschrift für die Kunde Südasiens
Y	Yājñavalkya Smṛti
ZDMG	Zeitschrift der Deutschen Morgenländischen Gesellschaft

GUIDE TO THE PRONUNCIATION OF SANSKRIT WORDS

SANSKRIT words, including proper names, are printed here with diacritical marks. Sanskrit diacritics are simple and, with a minimum of effort, should enable the reader to pronounce these words properly. A general rule is that an 'h' after a consonant is *not* a separate letter but merely represents the aspirated version of a consonant. Thus 'bh' is pronounced somewhat as in 'a*bh*or', and 'ph' not as in '*ph*ysics' but as in 'she*ph*erd'. The dental group of consonants (t, th, d, dh, n) are distinguished from the retroflex group indicated by a dot placed beneath (ṭ, ṭh, ḍ, ḍh, ṇ). The distinction in their pronunciation is somewhat difficult for the Western ear. The dentals are pronounced with the tip of the tongue placed behind the upper front teeth, and the sound is similar to the way these letters are pronounced in Romance languages such as French (e.g. toi, de). The English pronunciation of these letters is closer to the Sanskrit retroflex, but the latter is pronounced with the tip of the tongue striking the roof of the mouth further back. Thus 'ṭ' is somewhat like *t* in '*t*ry', and 'ḍ' is like *d* in *d*ental. The difference between the dental 'n' and retroflex 'ṇ' is very difficult for untrained ears to distinguish and is better ignored. The same applies to the palatal sibilant 'ś' and the retroflex 'ṣ'; both may be pronounced as *sh* in '*sh*ame'. 'ṃ' nasalizes the preceding vowel sound, as in French *bon*. 'ḥ', with a dot underneath and most frequently at the end of a word, is a pure aspiration and is to be distinguished from the consonant 'h'. In practice, the vowel sound preceding it is pronounced faintly; thus 'ḥ' of *bhuvoḥ* is pronounced like the *ho* in Soho when it is pronounced with the accent on the first syllable and the second shortened. Finally, an apostrophe before a word indicates an elided 'a', which is not pronounced.

Guide to the Pronunciation of Sanskrit Words

Pronounce Sanskrit	as in English
a	c*u*t
ā	f*a*r
i	s*i*t
ī	m*e*
u	p*u*t
ū	t*oo*
ṛ	*ri*sk
e	pr*ay*
o	h*o*pe
ai	s*igh*
au	s*ou*nd
c	*ch*urch
g	*g*ive
ṅ	a*n*ger
ñ	pu*n*ching

BIBLIOGRAPHY

Primary Sources

Aitareya Āraṇyaka, ed. A. B. Keith (reprint, Oxford: Clarendon Press, 1969).

Aitareya Brāhmaṇa, ed. with Sāyaṇa's commentary by Kāśīnātha Śāstrī Āgāśe (2 vols., ĀnSS 32, Poona, 1896; tr. A. B. Keith, HOS 25, Cambridge, Mass., 1920).

Āpastamba Dharmasūtra, ed. G. Bühler, (3rd. edn., Bombay Sanskrit and Prakrit Series, 44, 50, Poona: Bhandarkar Oriental Research Institute, 1932). Ed. with Haradatta's commentary *Ujjvalā* by U. C. Pandeya (Kashi Sanskrit Series, 93, Varanasi: Chowkhamba Sanskrit Series Office, 1969). Tr. in Bühler 1879–82.

Āpastamba Śrautasūtra, ed. R. Garbe (Reprint, 3 vols., Delhi: Munshiram Manoharlal, 1983).

Ārṣeya Brāhmaṇa, ed. with Sāyaṇa's commentary by B. R. Sharma (Tirupati: Kendriya Sanskrit Vidyapeetha, 1967).

Baudhāyana Dharmasūtra, ed. E. Hultzsch (1st edn., Abhandlungen für die Kunde des Morgenlandes, 8, Leipzig, 1884; 2nd edn. Abhandlungen für die Kunde des Morgenlandes, 16, Leipzig, 1922). Ed. with Govinda's commentary by L. Srinivasacharya (Government Oriental Library Series, Bibliotheca Sanskrita, 34, Mysore, 1907). Ed. with Govinda's commentary by U. C. Pandeya (Kashi Sanskrit Series, 104, Varanasi: Chowkhamba Sanskrit Series Office, 1972). Tr. in Bühler 1879–82.

Baudhāyana Gṛhyasūtra, ed. L. Srinivasachar and R. Shama Sastri (3rd edn., Mysore: Oriental Research Institute, 1983).

Baudhāyana Śrautasūtra, ed. W. Caland (3 vols., reprint, Delhi: Munshiram Manoharlal, 1982).

Bṛhaddevatā, ed. and tr. A. A. Macdonell (HOS 5–6, Cambridge, Mass., 1904.)

Caraka Saṃhitā, tr. A. C. Kaviratna and P. Sharma (5 vols., 2nd edn., Delhi: Sri Satguru Publications, 1996–7).

Gautama Dharmasūtra, ed. A. F. Stenzler (London: Trübner, 1876). Ed. with Haradatta's commentary by N. Talekar (AnSS 61, Poona, 1966). Ed. with Maskarin's commentary by L. Srinivasacharya (Government Oriental Library Series, Bibliotheca Sanskrita, 50, Mysore, 1917). Ed. with Maskarin's commentary by Veda Mitra (Delhi: Veda Mitra and Sons, 1969). Tr. in Bühler 1879–82.

Gobhila Gṛhyasūtra, tr. Oldenberg, 1892.

Gopatha Brāhmaṇa, ed. R. Mitra and H. Vidyabhusana (Calcutta: Bibliotheca Indica, 1872).

Jaimini, *Pūrvamīmāṃsāsūtra*, ed. with the commentaries of Śabara and Kumārila (7 vols., AnSS 97, Poona, 1971–81). Tr. G. Jha (3 vols., Gaekwad's Oriental Series, 66, 70, 73, Baroda, 1973–4).

Kātyāyana Śrautasūtra, ed. A. Weber (reprint, Chowkhamba Sanskrit Series, 104, Varanasi, 1972).

Kauṭilya, *Arthaśāstra*, ed. and tr. R. P. Kangle (3 vols., Bombay: University of Bombay, 1965–72).

Mahābhārata, ed. V. S. Sukthankar *et al.* (19 vols., Poona: Bhandarkar Oriental Research Institute, 1927–59).

Manu Smṛti, ed., with the commentaries of Medhātithi, Sarvajñanārāyaṇa, Kullūka, Rāghavānanda, Nandana, Rāmacandra, Maṇirāma, Govindarāja, and Bhāruci, J. H. Dave (6 vols., Bombay: Bharatiya Vidya Bhavan, 1972–84). Tr. Bühler 1886*a*; Doniger and Smith 1991.

Mahānārāyaṇa Upaniṣad, ed. and tr. J. Varenne (2 vols., Série in-8, 11–12, Paris: Institut de Civilisation Indienne, 1960).

Nārada Smṛti, ed. and tr. with Asahāya's commentary by R. W. Lariviere (1989). Tr. Jolly 1889.

Pāṇini, *Aṣṭādhyāyī*, ed. and tr. S. C. Vasu (2 vols., reprint, Delhi: Motilal Banarsidass, 1962).

Patañjali, *Mahābhāṣya*, ed. F. Kielhorn (3rd revised edn. by K. V. Abhyankar. 3 vols., Poona: Bhandarkar Oriental Research Institute, 1962–72).

Ṛgveda Saṃhitā, ed. with Sāyaṇa's commentary by F. Max Müller (6 vols., London: Wm. H. Allen & Co., 1849–74). Tr. K. F. Geldner (HOS 33–6, Cambridge, Mass., 1951–7).

Ṣaḍviṃśa Brāhmaṇa, ed. B. R. Sharma (Tirupati: Kendriya Sanskrit Vidyapeetha, 1967).

Sāmavidhāna Brāhmaṇa, ed. B. R. Sharma (Tirupati: Kendriya Sanskrit Vidyapeetha, 1964).

Śāṅkhāyana Gṛhyasūtra, with extracts from the commentaries of Nārāyaṇa and Rāmacandra (2nd edn., Sri Garib Dass Oriental Series, 42, Delhi: Sri Satguru Publications, 1987). Tr. Oldenberg 1886.

Śāṅkhāyana Śrautasūtra, ed. W. Caland (reprint, Delhi: Motilal Banarsidass, 1980).

Śatapatha Brāhmaṇa, ed. A. Weber (reprint, Chowkhamba Sanskrit Series, 96, Varanasi, 1964). Tr. J. Eggeling (SBE 12, 26, 41, 43, 44, Oxford, 1882–1900).

Śrautakośa, English Section, ed. R. N. Dandekar (2 vols., Poona: Vaidika Saṃśodhana Maṇḍala, 1958–82.)

Taittirīya Āraṇyaka, ed. with Sāyaṇa's commentary by K. V. Abhyankar (2 vols., AnSS 36, reprint, Poona, 1967).

Taittirīya Brāhmaṇa, ed. with Sāyaṇa's commentary by Nārāyaṇa Śāstrī Goḍabole (3 vols., AnSS 37, reprint, Poona, 1979).

Taittirīya Saṃhitā, tr. A. B. Keith (2 vols., HOS 13, 19, Cambridge, Mass., 1914).

Yāska, *Nirukta*, ed. V. K. Rajavade (Poona: Bhandarkar Oriental Research Institute, 1940).

Vaikhānasa Smārtasūtra, ed. W. Caland (Bibliotheca Indica, 242, Calcutta: Asiatic Society of Bengal, 1927). Tr. in Caland 1927.

Varāhamihira, *Bṛhatsaṃhitā*, ed. and tr. M. R. Bhat (2 vols., Delhi: Motilal Banarsidass, 1981–2).

Vasiṣṭha Dharmasūtra, ed. A. A. Führer (2nd edn., Bombay Sanskrit and Prakrit Series, 23, Poona: Bhandarkar Oriental Research Institute, 1930). Ed. with Kṛṣṇapaṇḍita's commentary *Vidvanmodinī* (Benares, 1878). Tr. in Bühler 1879–82.

Viṣṇu Smṛti, ed. with Nandapaṇḍita's commentary by V. Krishnamacharya (2 vols., Adyar Library Series, 93, Madras: Adyar Library and Research Centre, 1964). Tr. in Jolly 1880.

Yājñavalkya Smṛti, ed. with Vijñāneśvara's commentary by U. C. Pandey (Kashi Sanskrit Series, 178, Varanasi: Chowkhamba Sanskrit Series Office, 1967). Ed. with Viśvarūpa's commentary by T. Ganapati Sastri (reprint, Delhi: Munshiram Manoharlal, 1982). Ed. with Śūlapāṇi's commentary by J. R. Gharpure (Bombay, 1939). Ed. with Aparāditya's commentary (2 vols., AnSS 46, 1903–4).

Secondary Sources

Banerjee, S. C. (1962), *Dharma-Sūtras: A Study in Their Origin and Development* (Calcutta: Punthi Pustak).

Bodewitz, H. W. (1973), *Jaiminīya Brāhmaṇa I, 1–65: Translation and Commentary with a Study Agnihotra and Prāṇāgnihotra* (Orientalia Rheno-Traiectina 17; Leiden: E. J. Brill).

—— (1985), 'Yama's Second Boon in the Kaṭha Upaniṣad', *WZKSA* 29: 5–26.

—— (1996), 'Redeath and Its Relation to Rebirth and Release', *Studien zur Indologie und Iranistik*, 20: 27–46.

Böhtlingk, O. (1885*a*), 'Bemerkungen zu Führer's Ausgabe und zu Bühler's Uebersetzung des Vâsiṣṭhadharmaçâstra', *ZDMG* 39: 481–8.

—— (1885*b*), 'Bemerkungen zu Bühler's Ausgabe und Uebersetzung des Âpastambîjadharmasûtra', *ZDMG* 39: 517–27.

—— (1885*c*), 'Einige Bemerkungen zu Baudhâjana's Dharmaçâstra', *ZDMG* 39: 539–42.

—— (1886*a*), 'Bemerkungen zu Bühler's Artikel im 39. Bande dieser Zeitschrift, S. 704 fgg.', *ZDMG* 40: 144–7.

—— (1886*b*), 'Nachtägliches zu Vasishṭha', *ZDMG* 40: 526.

Bühler, G. (1879–82) (tr.), *Sacred Laws of the Āryas* [containing the Dharmasūtras of Āpastamba, Gautama, Vasiṣṭha, and Baudhāyana] (2 vols., SBE 2, 14; Oxford: Oxford University Press).

—— (1885), 'Einige Noten zu Böhtlingk's Bemerkungen über Führer's Ausgabe und meine Uebersetzung des Vasishṭhadharmaśâstra', *ZDMG* 39: 704–9.

—— (1886*a*) (tr.), *The Laws of Manu* (SBE 25; Oxford: Oxford University Press).

—— (1886*b*) 'Einige Bemerkungen zu Böhtlingk's Artikel über Āpastamba', *ZDMG* 40: 527–48.

Caland, W. (1929) (tr.), *Vaikhānasasmārtasūtram* (Calcutta: Asiatic Society of Bengal).

Chatterjee, H. (1971), *The Law of Debt in Ancient India* (Calcutta Sanskrit College Research Series, 75; Calcutta: Calcutta Sanskrit College).

—— (1972–4), *The Social Background of the Forms of Marriage in Ancient India* (Calcutta: Sanskrit Pustak Bhandar).

Dave, K. N. (1985), *Birds in Sanskrit Literature* (Delhi: Motilal Banarsidass). *See* Linke 1997.

Doniger, W., and Smith, B. K. (1991) (tr.), *The Laws of Manu* (London: Penguin).

Dumont, L. (1980), *Homo Hierarchicus: The Caste System and Its Implications* (rev. edn., tr. M. Sainsbury, L. Dumont, and B. Gulati; Chicago: University of Chicago Press; 1st edn. 1966).

Falk, H. (1986), *Bruderschaft und Würfelspiel: Untersuchungen zur Entwicklungsgeschichte des vedischen Opfers* (Freiburg: Hedwig Falk).

Fitzgerald, J. L. (1998), 'Some Storks Eat Carrion; Herons and Ospreys Do Not: Kaṅkas and Kuraras (and Baḍas) in the Mahābhārata', *Journal of the American Oriental Society*, 118: 257–61

Friedrich, E. (1993) (tr.), *Das Āpastamba-Dharmasūtra: Aufbau und Aussage* (Europäische Hochschulschriften, Asiatische und Afrikanische Studien, 31; Frankfurt-on-Main: Peter Lang).

Ghose, B. K. (1927), 'Āpastamba and Gautama', *Indian Historical Quarterly*, 3: 607–11.

Ghosh, A. (1973), *The City in Early Historical India* (Simla: Indian Institute of Advanced Study).

Gonda, J. (1960–1), 'Prayata', *Bhāratīya Vidyā* (*Munshi Indological Felicitation Volume*), 20–1: 45–51.

Halbfass, W. (1988), *India and Europe: An Essay in Understanding* (Albany, NY: State University of New York Press).

Hara, M. (1979), '*Śraddhāviveśa*', *Indologica Taurinensia*, 7: 261–73:

—— (1980), 'Hindu Concepts of Teacher: Sanskrit *guru* and *ācārya*', in M. Nagatomi *et al.* (eds.), *Sanskrit and Indian Studies: Essays in Honor of Daniel H. H. Ingalls* (Dordrecht: Reidel), 93–118.

—— (1992), 'Śraddhā in the Sense of Desire', *Asiatische Studien*, 46: 180–94.

Jamison, S. W. (1991), *The Ravenous Hyenas and the Wounded Sun: Myth and Ritual in Ancient India* (Ithaca, NY: Cornell University Press).

—— (1996), *Sacrificed Wife/Sacrificer's Wife: Women, Ritual, and Hospitality in Ancient India* (New York: Oxford University Press).

—— (1998), 'Rhinoceros Toes: Manu 5.17–18 and the Development of the Dharma System', *Journal of the American Oriental Society*, 118: 249–56.

—— and Witzel, M. (forthcoming), 'Vedic Hinduism'.

Jolly, J. (1880) (tr.), *The Institutes of Vishnu* (SBE 7; Oxford: Oxford University Press).

—— (1889) (tr.), *The Minor Law-Books* [Nārada and Bṛhaspati] (SBE 33; Oxford: Oxford University Press).

Kane, P. V. (1942), 'The Meaning of Ācāryāḥ', *Annals of the Bhandarkar Oriental Research Institute*, 23: 206–13.

—— (1962–75), *History of Dharmaśāstra* (5 vols.; Poona: Bhandarkar Oriental Research Institute).

Kangle, R. P. (1968), 'The Relative Age of the *Gautamadharmasūtra*', in *Mélanges d'Indianisme à la mémoire de Louis Renous* (Paris: Éditions Boccard), 415–25.

Keith, A. B. (1914) (tr.), *The Veda of the Black Yajus School Entitled Taittiriya Sanhita* (2 vols., HOS 18–19; Cambridge, Mass.: Harvard University Press).

Köhler, H. W. (1973), *Śrad-dhā in der vedischen und altbuddhistischen Literature* (thesis, Göttingen, 1948; ed. K. L. Janert, Wiesbaden).

Lariviere, R. (1989) (ed. and tr.), *The Nāradasmṛti* (2 vols.; Philadelphia: South Asia Regional Studies).

Lingat, R. (1973), *The Classical Law of India* (tr. J. D. M. Derrett; Berkeley: University of California Press).

Linke, E. (1997), 'Birds in Sanskrit Literature: Sanskrit-English Index', *Annals of the Bhandarkar Oriental Research Institute*, 78: 121–41. Word Index to Dave 1985.

Lüders, H. (1942), 'Von indischen Tieren', *ZDMG* 96: 23–81.

Malamoud, C. (1972), 'Observations sur la notion de "reste" dans le brāhmanisme', *WZKSA* 16: 5–16. Tr. in Malamoud 1996, 7–22.

—— (1996), *Cooking the World: Ritual and Thought in Ancient India* (tr. D. White; Delhi: Oxford University Press).

Meyer, J. J. (1927), *Über das Wesen der altindischen Rechtsschriften und ihr Verhältnis zu einander und zu Kauṭilya* (Leipzig: Harrassowitz).

Mines, D. P. (1990), 'Hindu Periods of Death "Impurity"', in M. Marriott, *India through Hindu Categories* (New Delhi: Sage Publications), 103–30.

Oldenberg, H. (1886–92) (tr.), *The Gṛihya-Sūtras: Rules of Vedic Domestic Ceremonies* [containing the Sūtras of Śāṅkhāyana, Āśvalāyana, Pāraskara, Khādira, Gobhila, Hiraṇyakeśin, and Āpastamba] (SBE 29–30; Oxford: Oxford University Press).

Olivelle, P. (1981), 'Contributions to the Semantic History of *Saṃnyāsa*', *Journal of the American Oriental Society*, 101: 265–74.

—— (1986), *Renunciation in Hinduism: A Medieval Debate* (2 vols.; Vienna: Institute for Indology, University of Vienna).

—— (1993), *The Āśrama System: The History and Hermeneutics of a Religious Institution* (New York: Oxford University Press).

—— (1996) (tr.), *Upaniṣads* (Oxford: Oxford University Press).

—— (1998), 'Caste and Purity: A Study in the Language of the Dharma Literature', *Contributions to Indian Sociology*, 32/2: 190–216

Pandey, R. B. (1969), *Hindu Saṃskāras: Socio-Religious Study of the Hindu Sacraments* (Delhi: Motilal Banarsidass).

Prater, S. H. (1997), *The Book of Indian Animals* (3rd edn., reprint; Bombay: Natural History Society and Oxford University Press).

Quigley, D. (1993), *The Interpretation of Caste* (Oxford: Clarendon Press).

Renou, L. (1963), 'Sur le genre du sūtra dans la littérature Sanskrite', *Journal Asiatique*, 251: 165–216.

Smith, B. K. (1994), *Classifying the Universe: The Ancient Indian Varṇa System and the Origins of Caste* (New York: Oxford University Press).

Stenzler, A. F. (1849) (tr.), *Yâjnavalkya's Gesetzbuch: Sanskrit und Deutsch* (Berlin: Ferd. Dümmler).

Tambiah, S. J. (1973), 'From Varna to Caste through Mixed Unions', in J. Goody (ed.), *The Character of Kinship* (Cambridge: Cambridge University Press), 191–229.

van Gennep, A. (1960) (1909), *The Rites of Passage* (tr. M. R. Vizedom and G. L. Caffee; Chicago: University of Chicago Press).

Wezler, A. (1998), 'Should the Adopted Son Be a Close Relative? On the Interpretation of VaDhs 15.6 and 7', *Indologica Taurinensia*, 17–18.

Witzel, M. (1989), 'Tracing the Vedic Dialects', in C. Caillat (ed.), *Dialectes dans les littératures Indo-aryennes* (Publications de L'Institut de Civilisation Indienne 55; Paris: Éditions Boccard), 97–265.

—— (1997), 'The Development of the Vedic Canon and its Schools: The Social and Political Milieu', in M. Witzel (ed.), *Inside the Texts, Beyond the Texts: New Approaches to the Study of the Vedas* (Cambridge, Mass.: Department of Sanskrit and Indian Studies, Harvard University), 257–345.

INTRODUCTION

THE texts translated here are the four surviving works of the ancient Indian expert tradition on the subject of *dharma*. Written in a pithy and aphoristic style, these Dharmasūtras represent the culmination of a long tradition of scholarship; they reveal deep learning and document intense disputes and divergent views on a variety of topics as broad as the category of *dharma* itself. *Dharma* includes all aspects of proper individual and social behaviour as demanded by one's role in society and in keeping with one's social identity according to age, gender, caste, marital status, and order of life. The term *dharma* may be translated as 'law' if we do not limit ourselves to its narrow modern definition as civil and criminal statutes but take it to include all the rules of behaviour, including moral and religious behaviour, that a community recognizes as binding on its members. The subject-matter of the Dharmasūtras, therefore, includes education of the young and their rites of passage; ritual procedures and religious ceremonies; marriage and marital rights and obligations; dietary restrictions and food transactions; the right professions for, and the proper interaction between, different social groups; sins and their expiations; institutions for the pursuit of holiness; the king and the administration of justice; crimes and punishments; death and ancestral rites. In short, these unique documents give us a glimpse if not into how people actually lived their lives in ancient India, at least into how people, especially Brahmin males, were ideally expected to live their lives within an ordered and hierarchically arranged society.

Literary History

The Dharmasūtras belong to the same literary tradition that produced the works comprising the scriptural corpus of the Veda. Both in authorship and audience, that literary tradition was by and large limited to the hereditary Brahmin priests.

Although always an élite minority, the Brahmin community at any given time in history was both relatively large in numbers and geographically widespread. The Brahmanical literature, however, was created not by the Brahmins at large but by the few who belonged to expert traditions of knowledge. These traditions were divided along the lines of the 'vedic branches' (*śākhā*) or schools. The vedic branches started as groups of Brahmins affiliated with one of the four Vedas: Ṛg, Yajur, Sāma, and Atharva. But each of them split further into numerous branches due to a variety of factors that are little understood but may have included geographical location, ritual specialization, and doctrinal and ritual disputes. It is within these branches that most of the vedic texts were composed and orally handed down.[1]

Each of these vedic branches has as its foundational text a 'collection' (Saṃhitā) of verses or liturgical formulas[2] and a prose text (Brāhmaṇa) explaining the meaning of the liturgy. The Saṃhitā is by and large common to all the branches of a Veda, even though some may have their own recension of it, while each branch has its own Brāhmaṇa. The Brāhmaṇas were not the work of single authors, and periodic additions were made to them. These additions included esoteric material explaining the hidden meanings of ritual actions and words. Some of these esoteric sections of the Brāhmaṇas came to be called Āraṇyakas (texts that were to be recited in the wilderness outside the village), while others came to be called Upaniṣads. The distinction between these two groups of texts is not altogether clear, since both deal with similar material; some of the Upaniṣads, such as the Aitareya, are embedded within their respective Āraṇyakas, while others, such as the Bṛhadāraṇyaka (lit., 'Great Āraṇyaka'), are viewed as both an Āraṇyaka and an Upaniṣad. Brahmanical theology divides the vedic corpus into

[1] For an accessible account of the vedic literature the reader may consult Olivelle 1996, pp. xxiii–xl. For a more detailed account that, for the first time, attempts to understand the social underpinnings of this literature, see Witzel 1997.

[2] The Saṃhitā of the Ṛgveda is in verse and contains 1028 hymns divided into ten books; the Saṃhitā of the Sāmaveda consists mostly of Ṛgvedic verses set to music; and the Saṃhitā of the Yajurveda is in prose and contains formulas that are recited during a sacrifice.

two categories of texts: *mantra* and *brāhmaṇa*. The former includes the verses and ritual formulas contained in the Saṃhitās, and the latter refers to the Brāhmaṇas, including the Āraṇyaka and Upaniṣad portions. Brāhmaṇa texts, which alone were thought to contain injunctions, constitute the vedic basis of the Dharma literature (see A 2.14.13 n.).

Towards the end of the vedic period, some time after the middle of the first millennium BCE, further expert traditions developed to deal with the ever more complex vedic ritual and to preserve and understand the vedic texts whose language was becoming ever more archaic and abstruse to people many centuries removed from their composition. The expert traditions and the works that grew out of them were classified as the six Vedic Supplements (*vedāṅga*, lit., 'limbs of the Veda'): ritual expositions of the Veda, grammar, astronomy, etymology, phonetics, and metrics (A 2.8.11). Although these expert traditions developed initially within the vedic branches, they became increasingly independent. Especially in the technical areas of grammar and astronomy, it would have been natural for students to gather around renowned teachers and the appeal of their literary works would have transcended the boundaries of the vedic branches. Thus, for example, the great grammatical treatise of Pāṇini, composed probably in the fourth century BCE, became the standard Sanskrit grammar.

Although the earliest texts, such as the hymns of the Ṛgveda, were composed in verse, the liturgical works (*brāhmaṇa*) of the middle vedic period were composed in prose. This practice was continued in the literature of the expert traditions; most ancient works falling within the Vedic Supplements are in prose. Probably because instruction in the expert traditions was carried out orally and the pedagogy of these schools was based on first memorizing the basic texts and then delving into their meaning with the aid of the teacher, the basic texts came to be composed in an aphoristic style known as *sūtra*.[3] A *sūtra* is a sentence from which most non-essential elements have been removed.

[3] For a detailed study of the *sūtra* genre, see Renou 1963.

Individual *sūtras* are often syntactically connected to the preceding, words of earlier *sūtras* being implicit in later ones, a convention technically called *anuvṛtti*. This convention makes the entire composition similar to a chain and each *sūtra* a link in that chain. It is this characteristic that probably gave it the name *sūtra* (lit., 'thread'), the composition being compared to a thread on which each aphorism is strung like a pearl. Given the brevity of each *sūtra*, it is frequently impossible to understand the meaning without the benefit of either an oral explanation or a commentary. The *sūtra* style of composition was perfected and taken to an extreme in the meta-language created in the grammatical tradition and reflected in the work of Pāṇini.

The Dharmasūtras are part of the Vedic Supplements and are written primarily in the *sūtra* style, even though verses are interspersed and the *sūtras* are not as succinct as those of Pāṇini. The Dharmasūtras form part of the 'ritual expositions' known collectively as Kalpasūtras that include three types of expositions: Śrautasūtras dealing with vedic rituals, Gṛhyasūtras dealing with domestic rituals, and Dharmasūtras.

Only two Dharmasūtras, however, those of Āpastamba and Baudhāyana, have come down as part of a larger Kalpasūtra. It appears likely that the subject-matter of Dharma, just as that of grammar, became increasingly divorced from the vedic branches. Unlike Śrautasūtras and Gṛhyasūtras that dealt exclusively with ritual matters and thus could easily be confined to the ritually based vedic branches, Dharma came to include areas of individual and social behaviour and norms, as well as personal, civil, and criminal law. The works on Dharma, just as works on grammar, became universally applicable treatises. The expert tradition of Dharma, which for short I will call the 'legal tradition', continued in later Indian history down to modern times as an independent and free-standing intellectual tradition not specifically tied to the vedic branches.

A large number of works dealing with Dharma appears to have been composed in the centuries immediately prior to the common era; many such works are referred to, or cited in, the four extant Dharmasūtras. But they are now lost; only the four translated here have survived.[4]

What may be called the *sūtra* period of the legal tradition ended around the beginning of the common era. It gave way to the emerging literary genre of the simple verse called *śloka* with four octo-syllabic feet. Most literature of this and succeeding periods, including the epics and the Purāṇas, were composed in this style. The legal texts composed in this style are commonly called Dharmaśāstras or simply Smṛti, the earliest representative of which is the Manu Smṛti (M). The influence of this new genre is already evident in Vasiṣṭha and the later sections (Books 3 and 4) of Baudhāyana, which contain numerous verses. The age of the Smṛtis ended probably in the second half of the first millennium CE, and from about the ninth century the texts produced in the legal tradition consisted of commentaries on earlier Dharmasūtras and Smṛtis and of legal digests (*nibandha*) that deal with topics systematically but consist primarily of quotations from Smṛtis with an added commentary.

Authorship and Dates

Who wrote the Dharmasūtras and when? This is a simple and obvious question without a clear or straightforward answer. Unlike the vedic texts which do not have the names of their authors attached to them, many of the Vedic Supplements are ascribed to historical authors, for example, Pāṇini for the grammatical text bearing his name. The Dharmasūtras also carry the names of their authors: Āpastamba, Baudhāyana, Gautama, and Vasiṣṭha. The first two have entire Kalpasūtras ascribed to them, and ritual traditions bearing their names continued to exist until contemporary times. The two were certainly founders of these ritual and scholastic traditions, but it is

[4] We also possess the Dharmasūtra of Hiraṇyakeśin, but it is merely a different recension of Āpastamba's text. The differences in Hiraṇyakeśin are noted in Bühler's edition of Āpastamba. The Viṣṇu Smṛti (Vi) was probably another such Dharmasūtra containing material from the lost Dharmasūtra of the Kāṭhakas, but it has been radically recast many centuries into the common era by a devotee of Viṣṇu. Another prose work is the Vaikhānasa Dharmasūtra (Vkh), but this too is a work composed several centuries into the common era.

unclear whether they were the historical authors of these texts or whether the texts were ascribed to them because they were composed within the traditions bearing their names.[5] Gautama and Vasiṣṭha, on the other hand, are ancient seers. They could not have been the historical authors of the texts ascribed to them. These texts represent some of the earliest evidence for a phenomenon that became common in the versified Smṛtis, namely the emergence of eponymous literature, that is, the ascription of treatises to eminent persons of the mythical past.

The issue of authorship is further complicated by the fact that, apart from Āpastamba's, these texts contain numerous additions made at later times.[6] If we ignore these, however, it appears very likely that the Dharmasūtras were composed by individual authors, in much the same way as Pāṇini's grammar, even though each author appears to have incorporated a substantial amount of material from other common sources. These were not individual authors writing in isolation; they were part of a tradition of experts whose views and compositions influenced each other.

Regarding the dates of these documents, there is unfortunately little that can be said with any degree of certainty. No evidence external to the texts themselves has survived, the first references to them in other texts coming many centuries after their probable composition. Internal evidence, on the other hand, tends to be quite subjective and, like modern-day statistics, can be and has been used to prove divergent viewpoints. The use of internal evidence is complicated by uncertainty regarding the geographical provenance of these documents; a linguistic feature or a particular custom or rule used to establish

[5] Āpastamba's Kalpasūtra is the best preserved with the least amount of later editorial intervention. Bühler (1879–82, vol. i, pp. xiii–xv) has shown that there are cross-references between the Gṛhyasūtras and Dharmasūtras of Āpastamba pointing to a common author of the two. He also thinks that the entire Kalpasūtra, including the Śrautasūtra, is the work of one author. The grounds for this conclusion rest on thinner evidence and it is rejected by Oldenberg (1878–86, ii, p. xxxii).

[6] I will deal with these probable additions in my preambles to individual Dharmasūtras.

the chronological priority or posteriority of a text may, on the contrary, indicate merely geographical difference.

The geographical provenance of these documents is not very clear. Bühler (1879–82, i, pp. xxxii–xl) has argued that Āpastamba came from South India, probably from Āndhra, and Kane (1962–75, i. 67) accepts this conclusion. In medieval inscriptions Brahmins belonging to the Āpastamba school are located mostly in South India; this is also true in modern times. But does this reflect the situation several centuries before the common era or is it the outcome of later migrations? There is a piece of internal evidence advanced to buttress the argument. Āpastamba once refers to the practice of 'northerners' (*udīcya*, A 2.17.17), but it is unclear what region is meant by 'north'. Even Pāṇini (4.2.109) uses that term, even though he was clearly a northerner, probably from the north-western region.

Bühler (1879–82, ii, pp. xli–xliii) and Kane (1962–75, i. 48) think that Baudhāyana also belonged to the south, even though they admit that the evidence is weaker than for Āpastamba. Here again, I think they have relied too much on evidence coming from much later times that may merely indicate patterns of Brahmanical migrations. Baudhāyana refers to five distinctive practices of the south and the north (B 1.2.1–8). Again, the exact meaning of 'north' and 'south', which are always relative terms, is unclear and cannot be assumed to be the same as the meaning attached to these terms in modern times. My view is that all the Dharmasūtras were probably composed in the area that we today call North India, principally because that appears to have been the region of Brahmanical literary activity during the centuries before the common era. It may well be true that some, such as Āpastamba, belonged to a marginal region rather than the heartland, which may explain some of the linguistic archaism and Prakritic forms present in that text.[7] Gautama's use of the term *yavana* ('Greek') and *bhikṣu* ('mendicant'), terms also used by Pāṇini, and his 'correct' Sanskrit conforming to Paṇinian rules may indicate that he came from the north-western region to which Pāṇini also belonged. There is little

[7] These peculiarities, including Prakritic forms, are also found in the Śrautasūtra of Āpastamba: see Garbe's preface at iii. 5–12.

internal evidence regarding the geographical provenance of Vasiṣṭha.

Turning then to the dates of these documents, it would appear at first sight that it is easier to establish their relative chronology than their dates of composition. But, even here, scholarly opinion is divided, because internal evidence is subject to diverse interpretations. Based on the same evidence, for example, scholars have come to diametrically opposed conclusions regarding the relative age of Āpastamba and Gautama.[8] To offer but one example of the hazards of determining age through internal evidence, Bühler (1879–82, i, pp. xix–xxi; Lingat 1973, 21) thinks that the espousal of 'puritan opinions' with respect to marriage and levirate indicates that Āpastamba is younger than Baudhāyana. Āpastamba vigorously rejects levirate and strongly supports monogamy. But Vasiṣṭha, an undoubtedly late text, not only espouses levirate but even permits a woman whose husband is abroad to go to a male relative of her husband or possibly even a stranger (Va 17.75–80). Evidently, the 'puritanism' is not necessarily a sign of a late text.

A significant point to remember is that these authors were not, as often depicted, simply mouthpieces for an anonymous and static tradition. A close reading of the texts reveals a vibrant intellectual milieu in which authors and their opponents express strongly held and deeply personal views. On the question of levirate, for example, there evidently were strikingly different theological positions espoused by different authors, reminiscent of the current theological debates on abortion and the right to choose.

So how are we to minimize, if not eliminate, subjective bias in evaluating internal evidence? A detailed discussion is not possible within the limits of this introduction, but I propose one criterion. Even though our authors often express personal

[8] The opinion of Bühler (1879–82, i, p. lix) that Gautama 'may be safely declared to be the oldest of the existing works on the sacred law' has been generally accepted: Kane (1962–75, i. 29); Lingat (1973, 19); Banerjee (1962, 46). Āpastamba is placed before Gautama, however, by Ghose (1927), Meyer (1927, 253–326), and Kangle (1968). Kangle's opinion that Gautama is even later than Vasiṣṭha is extreme and can be dismissed, but he has shown that arguments for the priority of Gautama can be used equally well to show that he is later.

opinions, they operated within an expert tradition. When certain features and elements were introduced into this tradition, they were invariably incorporated into later texts. Surveying the Dharma literature, therefore, we can make some predictions. The use of verse, for example, becomes more common and more consistent as time goes on, until Dharma texts come to be composed entirely in verse. Thus the presence of a large number of verses, especially when entire sections are composed in verse, is an indication of lateness. Likewise, we find certain central themes that are introduced at a particular time and then found in all subsequent texts, for example, the discussion of the 'land of Āryas' (*āryāvarta*), the 'legal assembly' (*pariṣad*), and mixed classes. The absence of just one may be accidental or due to other reasons. The absence of a cluster or all of these features, I would argue, shows that a text antedates their introduction into the tradition. There are also structural features discussed below that emerge with time, such as the treatment of inheritance in a special section and placing the section on penance last. The presence of these features indicates lateness.

Verses are interspersed among the prose *sūtras* in all of our texts except Gautama. Usually, they are given as citations with the introductory comment: 'Now, they also quote.' Such verses generally do not introduce new material but simply reinforce injunctions already given in prose passages. In Baudhāyana and Vasiṣṭha, however, there is an increasing use of verse not merely as quotations but as integral parts of the composition, reflecting the genre of the later Smṛtis. Table 1 gives a comparative breakdown of the number of verses in the three texts.

TABLE 1

	Total sūtras	*Total verses*		*Non-quote verses*	
		No.	*%*	*No.*	*%*
Āpastamba	1364	30	2	5	0.4
Baudhāyana	1236	279	22	176	14
Vasiṣṭha	1038	288	28	155	15

According to this indicator, Vasiṣṭha is the youngest with 28 per cent of the text in verse, a large number of which (15 per cent of the text) are non-quote verses. In fact, chapters 26–8 are entirely in verse.[9]

Baudhāyana has undergone numerous emendations and accretions,[10] but even if we limit ourselves to the early section (Book One and sections 1–16 of Book Two), which I have called Proto-Baudhāyana, it is in my estimation later than both Āpastamba and Gautama. Of the 853 *sūtras* in Proto-Baudhāyana, 161, or 19 per cent, are in verse, with 72 (8 per cent) non-quote verses. This argues for Āpastamba predating even Proto-Baudhāyana.

Vasiṣṭha and Proto-Baudhāyana also contain discussions of the 'land of the Āryas', missing in Āpastamba and Gautama, and of the 'legal assembly', missing in Āpastamba but given by Gautama in the last chapter (28.48–9). Another criterion is the treatment of the so-called sacrificial cord. It is clear that in the earliest period the custom was that on certain occasions, such as during rituals, purifications, and eating, a Brahmin should wear an upper garment (*upavīta*), which was a looped shawl, in a special manner over the left shoulder and under the right arm, a manner of wearing called *yajñopavīta* (Kane 1962–75, ii. 287–300). Āpastamba and Gautama use the term with this meaning. Indeed, Āpastamba (2.4.21–2) allows the use of a cord merely as a substitute for the upper garment; there it appears as a ritual abbreviation. Baudhāyana (1.8.5), on the other hand, takes it for granted that it is a cord and describes how it is manufactured. Both Baudhāyana (1.5.5) and Vasiṣṭha (12.14) state that a bath-graduate (*snātaka*) wears a double cord, reflecting the later

[9] This and other arguments presuppose that we have reliably edited texts. We do have critical editions of Āpastamba and Baudhāyana, but the editions of Gautama and Vasiṣṭha are not as reliable (see Note on the Translation). Some of my conclusions may have to be modified when more reliable editions become available.

[10] For a discussion of the composite nature of this text, see the preamble to Baudhāyana. The Baudhāyana school is certainly older than that of Āpastamba, and it is generally true that the literature of the former is probably older than that of the latter. It may well be that the original of the Baudhāyana Dharmasūtra was older than Āpastamba, but the same cannot be said with regard to the extant text. The added sections of Baudhāyana, containing what amounts to a handbook for renouncers (2.17–18) and other ascetic literature, are probably not earlier than the 3rd to 4th centuries CE, possibly contemporaneous with the Vkh.

practice that a student wears a single cord, a graduate and householder a double cord, a hermit a triple cord, and a renouncer four cords (Olivelle 1993, 147). Vasiṣṭha (8.17; 10.31), furthermore, appears to assume that this cord was worn permanently by Brahmins, a later practice unknown to Āpastamba and Gautama. I think we can assert with some certainty that the youngest of these texts is Vasiṣṭha, preceded by Proto-Baudhāyana.

I think that there is sufficient evidence to state that Āpastamba is older than Gautama. The fact that Gautama is composed entirely in prose *sūtras* that are frequently very brief, thus conforming to the aphoristic ideal, has been considered by some as arguing for its antiquity.[11] I think, however, that the omission of all cited verses, a practice common in all other Dharma texts, argues for the author's deliberate attempt to produce an ideal *sūtra* work. If he lived in the north-west, as I believe he did, he may have been influenced to a greater degree by the model offered by Paṇini's grammar. I think Kangle's observation (1968, 424) is accurate: 'Here we have unquestionably the work of a person who was trying to compress in as few words as possible all the teaching of this śāstra [discipline], eschewing all extraneous discussions.' There are, moreover, other indicators that argue for a later date for Gautama. Besides its use of the term *yavana* ('Greek') lacking in other texts, Gautama's frequent use of *āśrama* ('orders of life': 11.29; 19.1; 28.49) points to a time when the *āśrama* system was fully integrated into the exposition of Dharma.[12] Āpastamba's priority is also indicated by the fact that he does not deal with mixed classes at all, a topic found in all other Dharmasūtras and in the later Smṛtis.

The absolute dates of these documents are even harder to establish. Kane (1962–75, i) has given some tentative upper and lower limits: Gautama 600–400, Āpastamba 450–350, Baudhāyana 500–200, and Vasiṣṭha 300–100, all BCE. These

[11] In some ways this argument agrees with what I have said earlier about the increasing frequency of verses in later texts. But in the case of Gautama, however, I think the complete absence of verse appears to be totally artificial and deliberate.

[12] For a more detailed discussion of this, see Olivelle 1993. The early Dharma texts, especially Āpastamba, discuss the *āśramas* only within the context of presenting this theory, often in a hostile manner.

dates are often repeated by scholars, even though they are at best educated guesses. The dates assigned to most ancient Indian documents are generally based on a particular document being before or after some other document, whose date in turn is dependent on a similar estimate, the whole edifice thus constituting 'a chronological house of cards' (Lariviere 1989, ii, p. xx). Kane's estimates are based on assigning rather early dates to the vedic texts, especially the Brāhmaṇas and Upaniṣads.

One piece of internal evidence, I believe, is central to establishing a somewhat reliable chronology of these documents. Gautama (4.21) presents the opinion of some according to which *yavana* is the progeny of a Kṣatriya father and a Śūdra mother. Now, *yavana* is probably the Sanskritized version of the middle-Indic (Prakrit) *yona* derived from the Old Persian *yauna.* This term refers directly to Ionia, an area conquered by the Persian King Darius I (522–486 BCE), but which became a more general term for Greeks. The Archaemenid Empire in the late sixth and early fifth centuries BCE stretched from Greece to the north-western parts of India. The question is, when did the Indians come to designate the Greeks or people of Greek origin by the term *yavana*? It certainly could not have been before Darius I, that is, not earlier than about 500 BCE. The earliest datable record for the term *yona* is in the 5th Rock Edict of Aśoka of 256 BCE, which comes from the north-western region in what is today Pakistan. Pāṇini (4.1.49) uses the term, but his use is merely linguistic and does not necessarily indicate that he knew or was in contact with Greek settlers.[13] The case of Gautama is very different. His reference is to a group of people who, according to some experts on Dharma, originated through the mixed union between Kṣatriyas and Śūdras. Now, it is very unlikely that he is trying to explain the origin of a people he had merely heard about; he must be referring to a people to whom he

[13] Pāṇini is generally placed in the fifth century BCE, although his dating is also an educated guess at best. Bühler (1879–82, i, p. lx) tries to evade the problem created by Gautama's use of *yavana* by taking the passage in question to be a later interpolation. This is too easy a solution and is rightly rejected even by Kane (1962–75, i. 35–6).

and his audience had some connection. It is very unlikely that people of Greek origin in sufficient numbers to attract attention would have lived in north-western India before the invasion of Alexander. The Edict of Aśoka (256 BCE) calls the *yavanas* a border people. I think the use of *yavana* places the upper limit of Gautama in the middle of the third century BCE.

Baudhāyana and Vasiṣṭha are the earliest Dharma writers to include a discussion of the 'land of Āryas'. This is given as the region where proper customs are prevalent. The customs of this land are viewed as normative. A definition of the 'land of Āryas' agreeing almost verbatim with those given by Baudhāyana and Vasiṣṭha is found twice in Patañjali's great commentary, *Mahābhāṣya*, on Pāṇini's grammar. Patañjali can be dated with some precision and certainty to the middle of the second century BCE. So we have a maximum time span of less than one hundred years between Gautama, who is ignorant of the land-of-Āryas theory, and Patañjali, who presents what appears to be a codified definition of that region. I think neither Baudhāyana[14] nor Vasiṣṭha can be placed before the middle of the second century BCE. I am, however, inclined to place Vasiṣṭha closer to the beginning of the common era, or even in the first century CE close to the beginning of the Smr̥ti era. In the later chapters (25.1, 10; 28.10), for example, Vasiṣṭha uses the pronoun 'I', a practice unknown to the earlier writers and common in the later Smr̥tis, which are presented as the personal teaching of a god or sage. In Vasiṣṭha (16.10, 14) we also encounter for the first time the use of written evidence in judicial proceedings.[15]

There is no compelling reason to place Āpastamba at too great a distance in time from Gautama.[16] We would not be far

[14] A possible clue to the lateness of Baudhāyana is a citation (B 2.4.15) that Bühler (1879–82, ii. 235) has correctly identified as coming from a verse Smr̥ti. Although Bühler does not draw this conclusion, it is clear that such a citation places Baudhāyana closer to the beginning of the common era when such versified Dharma texts probably were first composed.

[15] Kane (1962–75, iii. 307) thinks that G 13.4 about listed witnesses is a reference to a written list, which is rather doubtful. But even if we accept Kane's opinion, it is not a reference to documents as evidence in a court of law.

[16] The rather shallow argument based on Āpastamba's mention of Śvetaketu, who also appears in the Upaniṣads, has been properly refuted by Kangle (1968, 422).

wrong in placing his upper limit around the beginning of the third century BCE. We then have a much narrower time span for the composition of the three earlier documents, from the beginning of the third to the middle of the second centuries BCE, and somewhat later for Vasiṣṭha.

Literary Structure

As the Dharmasūtras emerged as a new class of literature, their authors no doubt had to struggle with the task of selecting and organizing their material. Two factors probably played a role in how they structured their texts: the target audience and the subject-matter.

The principal audience of these texts was undoubtedly Brahmin males, who were also the principal creators and consumers of all the literature produced in the vedic branches. The Brahmin is the *implied* subject of most rules in the Dharmasūtras. So, for instance, G 14.1 states that there is a ten-day period of impurity after the death of a relative and goes on to give shorter periods for Kṣatriyas, Vaiśyas, and Śūdras. Although left unstated, the implied subject of the first rule is the Brahmin. Va 18.9 states simply that a child born from a Śūdra woman is a Pāraśava; the implied father is, of course, a Brahmin. When Gautama refers simply to 'the husband of a Śūdra woman' (G 15.18), he is actually referring to a Brahmin husband of such a woman. The principle appears to be that when no class is explicitly mentioned or when the subject is referred to simply by a pronoun, then a rule refers to the Brahmin.[17]

The subject-matter of the Dharmasūtras is *dharma*, a term I will examine in the next section. Although a variety of individual topics are encompassed by that term, including criminal and civil law, the central focus of these texts is on how a Brahmin male should conduct himself during his lifetime. Many other topics, such as marriage, inheritance, and women, are also introduced, but more often than not they are discussed in so far as they are related to the Brahmin male. The text of Āpastamba,

[17] The reader may see examples of this at A 1.2.39; 1.14.23, 26; 1.16.2; 1.31.22; G 7.4; B 1.11.1; Va 2.24; 4.6.

which is the best preserved with the least tampering, has a total of 1,364 *sūtras*. Of these 1,206 (88 per cent) are devoted to the Brahmin, whereas only 158 (12 per cent) deal with topics of a general nature.

Now, the Gṛhyasūtras are also addressed principally to Brahmins and deal with the rites of passage and other rituals that Brahmins are obliged to perform throughout their life. Even though the topics covered by the Dharmasūtras are broader than the merely ritual, nevertheless their authors may have found in the Gṛhyasūtras a ready-made structure for their new compositions, especially because, as in Āpastamba and Baudhāyana, the two classes of texts belonged to a single textual whole called a Kalpasūtra which had the same eponymous author. If we ignore some of the other rites discussed at the beginning and end of the Gṛhayasūtras, the central core of most of these texts is structured in the following manner: marriage, rituals connected with sexual activity, pre-natal rites, birth and infancy rites of passage, childhood rites of passage (including initiation), and finally funeral and ancestral rites. This structure makes perfect sense. The Gṛhyasūtras deal with domestic rites and are therefore addressed to the head of the household. So, it begins with marriage, which establishes a home and a householder, and then tells him the rites he must perform for his children.

The Dharmasūtras, however, changed this structure radically by beginning with the vedic initiation of the young boy and then following him through his growth into adulthood—return home from his teacher's house, marriage, and responsibilities of adult life, including adoption, inheritance, death rituals, and ancestral offerings.[18] The principal reason for this change, I think, is the fact that an individual becomes subject to the prescriptions of *dharma* at his initiation, which is viewed as his second birth making him a 'twice-born' man. It is stated clearly that young children before initiation can act as they please and are not subject to the *dharma* regimen.[19] Significantly, the Dharmasūtras

[18] This new structure, in turn, appears to have influenced later Gṛhyasūtras. Thus, the *sūtras* of Hiraṇyakeśin, Jaimini, Laughākṣi (= Kāṭaka), and Vaikhānasa begin their treatment with vedic initiation.

[19] See A 2.15.19–25; G 2.1–5; B 1.3.6; Va 2.6.

do not deal at all with pre-natal and childhood rites of passage that occupy a central position in the Gṛhyasūtras.[20]

All the Dharmasūtras begin with an examination of the sources of *dharma*, and this practice is followed even in the later Smṛtis. Thereafter, the structure is not uniform. Āpastamba has the most straightforward structure: initiation and the duties of a student; return home and the duties of such a young adult, followed by a parenthetical section on the bath-graduate; marriage and the duties of household life; and finally the king and the administration of justice. He deals with sons, inheritance, adoption, and the like within the context of the householder. Penances, on the other hand, are included within the discussion of the young adult who has completed his studies. This probably reflects the early structure of Dharma texts.

Two noteworthy changes occur in later texts: separate sections outside the discussions of Brahmin students and householders are devoted to inheritance and penance. In Gautama and Baudhāyana penance precedes inheritance. In Gautama these two form the concluding sections of the text, whereas in Baudhāyana they come after the section on marriage but before the section on the householder.[21] Vasiṣṭha shows a further development: he places inheritance immediately after the section on the king and judicial procedure and makes penance the concluding section of the text.

Although some of these differences may be due to the idiosyncrasies of each author, there is, I believe, an underlying chronological development. Evidence for this is found in the later Smṛtis where inheritance is placed in the section on the king and civil law and penance forms the conclusion of the treatise. This sequence fits with the relative chronology given earlier, placing Āpastamba earlier than the other three.

We encounter with some frequency in these documents what appears to be unrelated material introduced in the middle of a discussion having little to do with the topic at hand. At first sight

[20] The only exception is the list of 'sacraments' (*saṃskāra*) in G 8.14–21.

[21] This and other indicators point to later revisions and tampering with the text. I do not think that the somewhat confused sequence of topics in Baudhāyana is evidence for its early date as proposed by Lingat (1973, 21).

it would appear that the authors had little regard for organization. But I think there is a method to the madness. The underlying principle of the *sūtra* genre is to give maximum coverage with the least amount of words. When extraneous material is introduced, it is generally connected to some theme or term in the preceding *sūtra*. Thus at A 1.4.20 a person is prohibited from using water remaining after fire worship for other activities or for sipping. The prohibition of some types of water for sipping permits Āpastamba to mention also other types of water that are unsuitable for sipping in the next *sūtra*. Likewise, the mention of the death of a relative as one of the occasions when vedic recitation is suspended (A 1.10.4) permits him to state some other practices associated with such a death (A 1.10.5–6). Gautama (5.23) states that one should not give anything to a person for an unlawful purpose, even if one had promised to give it. This provides him with the opportunity to give the circumstances when one is permitted to make an untrue statement (G 5.24). An interesting example is found in Baudhāyana. He deals here with the period of impurity following the death of a relative belonging to the same ancestry (1.11.1–2). This prompts him to define the relationship based on ancestry (1.11.9–10), and, because such relations also inherit property, he goes on to deal with inheritance (1.11.11–16), before returning to the original topic of death impurity (1.11.17).

Semantics and Sources of *Dharma*

Dharma is undoubtedly the most central and ubiquitous concept in the whole of Indian civilization. It is central not only in the Brahmanical/Hindu traditions, but also in the Buddhist and Jain. This very centrality, however, also made it possible for the concept to be given new twists and meanings at different times and by different groups, creating a dauntingly broad semantic range. Its very complexity may be the reason for the lack of a single comprehensive study of the term.[22] It is also a challenging term to translate or even to define adequately.

[22] An excellent and accessible discussion of *dharma* in Indian cultural history is given by Wilhelm Halbfass: 'Dharma in Traditional Hinduism' (Halbfass 1988, 310–33).

It first appears in the early vedic literature with reference to the rules and statutes connected with 'the continuous *maintaining* of the social and cosmic order and norm which is achieved by the Aryan [Ārya] through the performance of his Vedic rites and traditional duties' (Halbfass 1988, 315–16). Thus, the term often appears in the plural. Initially, it did not refer to any overarching cosmic order or natural law, which is comprehended by the term *ṛta*.[23] Like the related term *karma* ('action'), *dharma* was at first, and in the Brahmanical tradition continues to be, associated with the ritual. As *karma* is primarily ritual action, so *dharmas* are the rules of correct ritual procedure. As the semantics of *karma* widened to include moral/immoral actions, so *dharma* came to include norms of correct behaviour within both the ritual and the moral/social spheres. These two spheres of activity appear to be poles apart to the modern mind; it was not so to the traditional Indian mind. The ritual, the moral, and the social constituted a continuum. In the Dharmasūtras we see the one overlapping the other and the authors passing from the one to the other imperceptibly. Some actions that may appear to us as sins and others that seem to be merely ritual infractions are often treated together. Ritual expiations, for example, are enjoined for immoral acts. This imperceptible movement from one meaning to another is illustrated by Āpastamba. At A 1.7.18 he uses *dharma* to mean a ritual oblation, whereas in the very next *sūtra* (A 1.7.19) he uses it to mean 'righteous' and/or 'legal'.

In these documents, the term *dharma* is used with this spectrum of meanings: the accepted norms of behaviour, ritual actions and rules of procedure, moral/religious/pious actions and attitudes (righteousness), civil and criminal law, legal procedure and punishment, and penances for infractions of *dharma*. It is *dharma* that provides the guidelines for proper and

[23] Scholars have assigned two somewhat different meanings to this term. It may refer to the cosmic order or harmony, or else to truth. The two aspects can be brought together by seeing 'truth' not in an abstract way but as 'an active realization of the truth'. This active and creative aspect of truth underlies and brings about the cosmic order and harmony. See Jamison and Witzel forthcoming. Some aspects of *ṛta*, especially cosmic order, came to be attached to *dharma* in later times.

productive living and for social organization and interaction. It includes social institutions such as marriage, adoption, inheritance, social contracts, judicial procedure, and punishment of crimes, as well as private activities, such as toilet, bathing, brushing the teeth, food and eating, sexual conduct, and etiquette.

A question that loomed large in the minds of all these authors was an epistemological one: Where can we find these guidelines? What are the sources of *dharma*? This epistemological question is tied to the theological definition of *dharma*. What I have given above is an empirical description of *dharma* gleaned from the way it is used in these documents. The Brahmanical theologians, however, sought to give it a theological definition: *dharma* is the content of vedic injunctions. This definition clearly defines *dharma* as positive, albeit revealed, law, rather than a cosmic or natural law which can be gathered by investigation, introspection, or deductive inference. *Dharma*, according to this definition, can only be gathered by examining the vedic injunctions. Like the Vedas, therefore, *dharma* is not of human origin, and it can have no practical value or visible aim.

This definition is not problematic within the context of the original ritual meaning of *dharma*; rules of the vedic ritual are clearly contained in vedic texts. Beyond that explicit and theological definition, however, in their usage of the term our authors reveal an implied or working definition of *dharma* that greatly expands its semantic range. Some of the elements of such a working definition are contained in the description given above. Our documents also speak of the *dharma* of different regions (*deśadharma*), of different social groups (*jātidharma*), and of different families (*kuladharma*). Our authors even admit that these *dharmas* are gathered from the customs of these groups; by definition, they cannot be found in the Vedas. Even many of the other rules of behaviour contained in these documents cannot be traced to the vedic texts. There is, then, a dissonance between the theologically correct definition and epistemology of *dharma* and the reality of the rules of *dharma* encoded in the Dharmasūtras.

Āpastamba provides an early attempt at resolving this problem (A 1.1.1–3). He calls the *dharmas* (plural) he is going to explain 'accepted customary' (*sāmayācārika*),[24] that is, the *dharmas* that are accepted or agreed upon (*samaya*) by those who know *dharma*. Āpastamba clearly places customary practice at the very heart of *dharma*; not just any custom, however, but only those accepted by an élite group. He then goes on to say that the authority is based also on the Vedas, placing it second after the accepted customs as the source of *dharma*. It is clear that *de facto* Āpastamba had a broad conception of custom, because at the end of his treatise he refers to the knowledge of women and Śūdras as part of the totality of our knowledge of *dharma* and states that one should learn from them the *dharmas* not contained in his treatise (A 2.29.11–12, 15). Elsewhere, he says that after a funeral people should 'do whatever else the women ask them to do' (A 2.15.9). Now, by definition women and Śūdras cannot be counted among those who know the Veda, for they are explicitly forbidden to learn it.

For Āpastamba, I think, vedic prescriptions functioned as a check or a negative criterion: customs of a region or a group are authoritative for those belonging to that region or group provided they are not in conflict with explicit vedic prescriptions (A 1.4.8; 1.30.9; 2.14.10). The empirical nature of *dharma* is brought out clearly in his concluding statement: 'It is difficult to gain mastery of the Law by means of scriptures alone, but by acting according to the markers one can master it. And the markers in this case are as follows: he should model his conduct after that which is unanimously approved in all regions by Āryas who have been properly trained, who are elderly and self-possessed, and who are neither greedy nor deceitful' (A 2.29.13–14). He has a very realistic view of the difficulties inherent in finding the *dharma*: 'The Righteous (*dharma*) and the Unrighteous (*adharma*) do not go around saying, "Here we are!" Nor do gods, Gandharvas, or ancestors declare, "This is righteous and that is unrighteous". An activity that Āryas praise is righteous, and what they deplore is unrighteous' (A 1.20.6–7).

On the flip side, not everything found in the Vedas is *dharma*, at least with regard to contemporary people. Āpastamba notes:

[24] That this definition may have been widespread is indicated by its use also by Gautama 8.11.

'Transgression of the Law and violence are seen among people of ancient times. They incurred no sin on account of their extraordinary power. A man of later times who, observing what they did, does the same, perishes' (A 2.13.7–9; cf. G 1.3–4). Here we have the case of contemporary practice nullifying what is found in the Veda. The theological explanation is that the people of those days had extraordinary power lacking in modern men. This theory developed later into what is known as the *yuga-dharma*, the *dharma* of different world ages; the *dharma* appropriate for ancient ages may be inappropriate for the current depraved age.

Āpastamba proposes a principle that becomes a cornerstone of later thinking on the sources of *dharma*. He says that originally *all rules of dharma* were contained in the Vedas, but now parts of those Vedas are lost. The theory of the 'lost Veda' is used as a hermeneutical strategy to theoretically derive all *dharma* from the Veda, while in practice providing for other sources. The customs from which some elements of *dharma* are derived are actually based on lost vedic texts, which can be 'inferred' from the existence of these customs (A 1.4.8; 1.12.10–11). Thus, we have the distinction between 'explicit vedic texts' (*pratyakṣaśruti*) and 'inferred vedic texts' (*anumitaśruti*). This hermeneutical principle permitted Āpastamba to recognize the customs among good people as a guide to proper living, that is, as *dharma*, while maintaining the theological fiction of the Veda as the sole source of *dharma*.

Gautama (1.1–2) gives the three sources of *dharma* that become standard in later literature: the Veda and the tradition (*smṛti*) and practice (*ācāra*) of those who know the Veda. Baudhāyana (1.1.3–4) explicitly calls *smṛti* the second source, and the practice of cultured people (*śiṣṭa*) the third. Limiting authoritative practice to *śiṣṭas* and the delimitation of the geographical area where such people live (B 1.1.4–6; Va 1.5–16) are introduced by Baudhāyana and Vasiṣṭha and become standard in later literature. Increasingly, *smṛti* comes to refer not to some 'recollection' on the part of *śiṣṭas* but to treatises on *dharma*, such as the Dharmasūtras, which are often referred to simply as *smṛti* (M 2.10). The theological fiction that all *smṛtis* are based on vedic texts, whether explicit or inferred, continues to be maintained in the later Brahmanical tradition.

Gautama (1.4) is the first to enunciate the exegetical principle that when injunctions of equal authority (e.g. two vedic texts) are in conflict a person has the option of following either course. Implied here is the rule that when injunctions are not of equal authority (e.g. a custom or a rule in a Smṛti contradicting a vedic injunction), then the injunction of greater authority prevails (PMS 1.3.3).

Divergent Voices

The Dharmasūtras are normative texts. They contain norms of correct behaviour and action. They tell people what to do; they do not tell us what people actually did. Normative texts have had a bad press lately among scholars. Some argue that these sources are unreliable and worthless for historical purposes, proposing instead the use of archaeological, inscriptional, and art historical materials for historical reconstruction. Clearly, these are invaluable sources for any study of India's past. But I think the dismissal of normative texts is unwise and unwarranted and betrays a singular ignorance of these documents. Many scholars unfortunately derive their knowledge of these texts through secondary sources, which often flatten the intellectual landscape and describe these documents as presenting a uniform code of conduct. The divergent views and dissenting voices are silenced. The reality, as anyone who undertakes a close reading of these documents can see, is very different.

We find, for example, the conservative and adversarial ('That is false!') voice of Hārīta cited repeatedly by Āpastamba.[25] Hārīta is against any form of suicide, including a penance that involves the death of the penitent (A 1.28.16). He has a strict view of what constitutes theft; even coveting someone else's property is a theft. Against the opinion of some that taking small amounts of fodder and the like does not constitute theft,

[25] See A 1.13.11; 1.18.2; 1.19.12; 1.28.1–5, 16; 1.29.12, 16.

Hārīta maintains that one must *always* obtain permission first (A 1.28.1–5).

Scholars have called Āpastamba 'puritanical'. That may be so from one perspective. Within the context of the ideas prevalent in his time, however, I believe Āpastamba's views, especially with regard to sexual morality and women, were innovative and radical. While others permit Brahmins to have up to four wives, Āpastamba encourages monogamy, forbidding the taking of a second wife if the first is able to participate in ritual activities and bear children. After the sacred fires have been established, however, there is a blanket prohibition against taking a second wife (A 2.11.12–14). Āpastamba's view of women, I think, is quite progressive. A man is not allowed to abandon his wife (A 1.28.19). He permits daughters to inherit (A 2.14.4). There can be no division of property between a husband and a wife, because they are linked inextricably together and have joint custody of the property (A 2.29.3). Thus, a wife may make gifts and use the family wealth on her own when her husband is away (A 2.12.16–20). Women are upholders of traditional lore, and Āpastamba tells his audience that they should learn some customs from women (A 2.15.9; 2.29.11). On levirate, that is, the procreation of children by the wife of a deceased husband, Āpastamba is alone in his adamant opposition (A 2.27.2–7), a position in sharp contrast to the lax attitude of Vasiṣṭha, who permits a woman whose husband is missing for five years to have sexual relations with a relative of the husband or even a stranger (Va 17.75–80).

The expert tradition of Dharma during the centuries immediately preceding the common era appears to have been vibrant and dynamic as shown by the numerous contradictory opinions of experts recorded in the extant Dharmasūtras. Such diversity of opinion belies the common assumption that ancient Indian society was uniform and stifling under an orthodoxy imposed by Brahmins. If even the experts recorded in these normative texts disagree so vehemently, the reality on the ground must have been even more chaotic and exhilarating.

NOTE ON THE TRANSLATION

THE translations of Āpastamba and Baudhāyana are based on the critical editions of Bühler and Hultzsch, respectively. We do not have critical editions of Gautama and Vasiṣṭha. I have used the less-than-perfect editions of Stenzler and Führer (see Bibliography: Primary Sources for bibliographic details). I have made full use of the excellent but dated translations of all four Dharmasūtras made by Bühler (1879–82); they have proved to be invaluable, even when I depart from Bühler's interpretations.

The *sūtra* style in which these documents are written is brief and aphoristic. Each aphorism is brief and pithy, sometimes containing only one or two words and frequently without a verb. Texts written in this style were meant to be read with a commentary, written or oral. Translating this type of text presents unusual challenges, because a 'literal' translation will make no sense to an English reader. Bühler uses long parenthetical remarks (often longer than the translated text itself) in an effort to be both literal and comprehensible. The result, however, is less than elegant. He frequently includes commentarial glosses as part of the translation. I have tried to introduce as little non-literal material as possible, but have given up parentheses as an unnecessary crutch. One way I have tried to make the prose readable and brief is to weave several aphorisms into a single English sentence. This is in keeping with the *sūtra* style itself, because, according to the common rule of this style, words of previous *sūtras* are extended to, and implied in, later ones, a literary device technically known as *anuvṛtti*.

I have taken the liberty of introducing titles and subtitles into the translation. Readers should know that they are not found in the original text. I have introduced them only to make it easier for readers to wade through this complex material. The division of the translation into paragraphs, likewise, is mine.

The broadest division of the texts of Āpastamba and Baudhāyana is *praśna* (lit., 'Question', translated here as 'Book'). Each of the two books of Āpastamba and the first two books of

Baudhāyana are divided consecutively into sections called *kaṇḍikā* and *khaṇḍa*, respectively. Their numbers are given in large figures. There is a secondary division called *paṭala* in Āpastamba and *adhyāya* in the first two books of Baudhāyana. I have omitted their numbers so as not to clutter the translation; these divisions are generally omitted in references to these texts. The last two books of Baudhāyana, as well as the texts of Gautama and Vasiṣṭha are divided only into *adhyāyas* (chapters). Their numbers are also given in large figures. The smallest division of all these documents is into *sūtras*. Their numbers are given in small superscript before each *sūtra* so as not to be intrusive, because they frequently appear in the middle of sentences.

As in most Sanskrit texts, pronouns are used frequently here without clear antecedents. When the antecedent is unclear, I have frequently supplied the noun. The general principle, however, is that a 'he' appearing in a section will refer to the person to whom that section is addressed—generally this person is identified in the major title (in upper case, e.g. HOUSEHOLDER). When this is the case, I have left the pronouns in; they are so frequent that substituting the noun every time does not seem practical.

I have tried to identify all quotations, especially vedic ones. Where citations have not been identified, it is to be assumed that they cannot be identified in the extant texts. Vedic citations are usually introduced either with a title (e.g. Aghamarṣaṇa) or with the first few words (*pratīka*). The original readers of these texts knew these citations by heart and it was unnecessary for our authors to cite the entire text. Since I cannot presume that knowledge among readers of this translation, I have given the full texts of the citation in Appendix I.3, except in the case of long texts where it is impractical to reproduce them in full.

Some words pose a special challenge to the translator. The most obvious is *dharma* (see pp. xxxvii–xxxix). Wherever possible I have translated it as Law(s). It is, however, impossible and unwise to be consistent; some nuances and meanings of the term cannot be rendered as Law. I have used other terms, such as righteous(ness) and duty, but to signal to the reader that we are dealing with this central term I have always placed *dharma* within parentheses whenever it is translated with any term other than Law(s). I have left names of social groups (e.g. Kṣatriya) untranslated; they are explained in Appendix II. The term *brāhmaṇa* is rendered 'Brahmin' when it refers to the priestly group so as to distinguish that usage from the *brāhmaṇa* texts of the Veda. Names of common flora and fauna (banyan, rice, dog, crow) have been translated. In the case of less common ones, especially when a specific species may be indicated, I have kept the Sanskrit terms but with an English explanation, e.g. the spotted Ruru antelope. I have dealt with the technical names of rituals in a similar manner; these names are listed in Appendix I.1.

Unless otherwise stated, the terms grandfather, grandson, etc., always mean 'paternal'. Thus, one's great-grandfather is one's father's father's father. Maternal lines are generally ignored. To specify 'paternal' in every case would have been cumbersome.

There appears to be a distinction between two terms often translated with the same word. They are *ṣaṇḍha*, translated as 'eunuch', and *klība*, translated as 'impotent'. I think our texts make a distinction between the two: the first refers to a eunuch, that is, a man whose sexual organs are lacking or have been removed (see Haradatta and Maskarin on G 22.23), whereas the latter refers to an impotent or effeminate man.

DHARMASŪTRAS

The Dharmasūtra of Āpastamba

THE Dharmasūtra forms part of the voluminous Kalpasūtra of Āpastamba containing thirty *praśnas* (lit., 'questions') or books. The first twenty-four comprise the Śrautasūtra. Books 25–6 contain the Mantrapāṭha or the collections of ritual formulas to be used in domestic rites, and book 27 contains the Gṛhyasūtra. The two books of our Dharmasūtra occupy books 28–9, and the final book contains the Śulvasūtra, a treatise on principles of geometry needed for the vedic sacrifice. Āpastamba belongs to the Taittirīya branch of the Black Yajurveda. Opinion is divided as to whether the entire Kalpasūtra was composed by a single individual (Kane 1962–75, i. 54). The Kalpasūtra of Āpastamba has been preserved better than most probably because commentaries were written on it at a relatively early date. Of the several ancient commentaries on the Dharmasūtra, only one survives, that of Haradatta, who wrote commentaries also on Āpastamba's Gṛhyasūtra and Mantrapāṭha and Gautama's Dharmasūtra. Haradatta was probably a South Indian, and Kane dates him to 1100–1300 CE.

This Dharmasūtra is better organized than most. The first book deals with the vedic student and concludes with the bath at the conclusion of studentship and the special observances required of a bath-graduate. Much of Book Two is devoted to the householder, and under this topic Āpastamba deals with matters of civil law such as inheritance. The book concludes with brief sections on the orders of life (*āśramas*) and the king, the latter incorporating civil administration including taxation, criminal law, and judicial procedure.

CONTENTS

Book One

BOOK ONE

SOURCES OF LAW

1 [1] And now we shall explain the accepted customary Laws, [2] the authority for which rests on their acceptance by those who know the Law [3] and on the Vedas.*

SOCIAL CLASSES

[4] There are four classes: Brahmin, Kṣatriya, Vaiśya, and Śūdra. [5] Among these, each preceding class is superior by birth to each subsequent. [6] Those who are not Śūdras and are not guilty of evil deeds may undergo initiation, undertake vedic study, and set up the sacred fires; and their rites bear fruit. [7] Śūdras are to serve the other classes; [8] the higher the class they serve, the greater their prosperity.

THE STUDENT

Initiation

[9] Initiation is the consecration of a person seeking vedic knowledge carried out according to vedic rules, [10] for a Brāhmaṇa declares: 'The Sāvitrī verse is recited for the sake of all the Vedas.'*

Teacher [11] 'From darkness they surely enter into further darkness—an ignorant man who performs an initiation, as also the person whom he initiates', states a Brāhmaṇa. [12] So, to perform the initiation, he should try to get a learned and steadfast man born in a family noted for vedic learning, [13] under whom he should complete his vedic studies unless that man deviates from the Laws.

[14] The teacher (*ācārya*) is the person from whom a man gathers* (*ācinoti*) the Laws. [15] He should never offend the teacher, [16] for he gives birth to him by means of vedic knowledge.

[17]That is his most excellent birth; [18]his parents give birth only to his body.*

Time of Initiation [19]A Brahmin should be initiated in the spring, a Kṣatriya in the summer, and a Vaiśya in the autumn; a Brahmin in the eighth year from conception, a Kṣatriya in the eleventh, and a Vaiśya in the twelfth.

[20]When initiations are performed with an objective in mind, [21]a person seeking eminence in vedic knowledge should be initiated in the seventh year, [22]a person seeking long life in the eighth, [23]a person seeking power in the ninth, [24]a person seeking an abundance of food in the tenth, [25]a person seeking strength in the eleventh, [26]and a person seeking cattle in the twelfth.

[27]In the case of a Brahmin there is no lapse in postponing the initiation until the sixteenth year, in the case of a Kṣatriya until the twenty-second year, and in the case of a Vaiśya until the twenty-fourth year, so as to ensure that the person has the capacity to carry out the observances that we are about to describe.

Failure to be Initiated [28]If his time for initiation has lapsed, a man should live observing the rules of a student of the three Vedas for one season* [29]and then undergo initiation. [30]For a year thereafter he should take a daily bath, [31]after which time he may receive vedic instruction.

[32]When both the father and grandfather of a man have not been initiated, they are all called 'Brahman-killers'.* [33]People should refrain from visiting them and from eating or contracting marriages with them. [34]They may, if they so choose, do a penance—[35]such a person should perform for a year the same penance that was prescribed for a season (A 1.1.28 n.) when the initial time for initiation had lapsed [36]and then undergo initiation.

2 Thereafter, he should take a daily bath [1]for as many years as the number of uninitiated persons in his family. [2]He should take this bath while reciting the seven Pāvamānī verses that begin: 'Whether near or afar', as well as the purificatory formulas called Yajuḥpavitra, Sāmapavitra, and Āṅgirasa; [3]or

else, while reciting just the Calls. [4]Thereafter, he may receive vedic instruction.

[5]When no one can remember that any of a man's ancestors back to his great-grandfather had been initiated, they are all called 'cremation grounds'.* [6]People should refrain from visiting them and from eating or contracting marriages with them. They may, if they so choose, do a penance—such a person should live observing the rules of a student of the three Vedas for twelve years and then undergo initiation. Thereafter, he should take a daily bath while reciting the Pāvamānī verses and the rest (A 1.2.2). [7]He may then be taught the rites to be performed by a householder [8]but not receive vedic instruction. [9]And after he has completed that, his sacramentary rite is performed in the same manner as when the initial time for initiation has lapsed. [10]Afterwards, everything is done as at the regular initiation.

Residency [11]An initiated person should reside as a student in his teacher's house [12]for forty-eight years, [13]or for three-quarters of that time, [14]or for half that time, [15]or for one-quarter of that time; [16]the minimum is twelve years. [17]A student who seeks to acquire vedic knowledge may not reside with anyone else.

A Student's Code of Conduct

General Rules [18]Next, the student's code of conduct. [19]He shall submit to his teacher in all things except those that entail a sin causing loss of caste.* [20]He shall promote his teacher's welfare, never contradict him, [21]and occupy a lower seat and bed.

[22]He shall not eat ritual food,* [23]spices, salt, honey, or meat. [24]He shall not sleep during the day, [25]wear perfume, [26]engage in sexual intercourse, [27]or show himself off. [28]He shall not wash his body.* [29]When anything dirty stains it, however, he may wash it out of his teacher's sight. [30]If he bathes, he should not be boisterous in the water but plunge in like a stick.

Insignia [31]He shall have his hair matted; [32]or, keeping just the topknot matted, let him shave the rest. [33]The girdle of a Brahmin should be a triple string of Muñja grass, twisted clockwise if possible (A 1.7.2 n.); [34] that of a Kṣatriya a bowstring [35] or a string of Muñja grass trimmed with pieces of iron; [36] and that of a Vaiśya a woollen string [37] or, according to some, a plough cord or a string made with Tamāla bark.

[38] A Brahmin's staff should be of Palāśa wood, a Kṣatriya's the prop root of a banyan tree, and a Vaiśya's of Badara or Udumbara wood. Some prescribe just a wooden staff without regard to class.

[39] His garment should be [40] made of hemp, flax, or antelope skin.
3 [41] Some, however, prescribe a garment dyed ochre. [1] It should be dyed madder for a Kṣatriya [2] and yellow for a Vaiśya. [3] The skin of a Hariṇa deer or a black Eṇa doe is prescribed for a Brahmin; [4] if he wears a black skin, he should not use it as a spread to sit or sleep on. [5] The skin of a spotted Ruru antelope is prescribed for a Kṣatriya, [6] and that of a billy goat for a Vaiśya. [7] A sheep skin is suitable for all classes, [8] and so is a shawl of sheep wool. [9] For a Brāhmaṇa declares: 'A person who desires to increase his Brahmanical might should wear only antelope skins, and a person who desires to increase his Kṣatriya might should wear only cloth garments, while a person who desires both should wear both.' [10] Over his upper body, however, he should wear only an antelope skin.

General Rules [11] He shall not watch dancing, [12] nor visit casinos or fairs.* [13] He shall not be given to gossiping [14] but keep things confidential. [15] He shall not engage in recreational activities in places frequented by his teacher. [16] He shall speak with women only as much as is required. [17] He shall be gentle, [18] calm, [19] controlled, [20] modest, [21] firmly resolute, [22] energetic, [23] not given to anger, [24] and free from envy.

Food [25] Morning and evening he shall go out to beg with a bowl, soliciting from those who are not degraded or heinous sinners,* and bringing all he receives to his teacher. [26] For a Brāhmaṇa declares: 'When women (A 1.3.28–30 n.) refuse a steadfast student, he robs them of their sacrifices, gifts, oblations, offspring, cattle, sacred learning, and food supply. One should never refuse a group of students come to beg, therefore, for among them there may be one who is like that and who keeps that vow.'

[27] Almsfood should not be considered leftovers* by inference, but only through perception or testimony. [28] A Brahmin should beg placing 'Madam' at the beginning, [29] a Kṣatriya placing 'Madam' in the middle, [30] and a Vaiśya placing 'Madam' at the end.*

[31] After he has collected the almsfood, he should place it before his teacher and announce it to him. [32] He should eat it when the teacher invites him to do so. [33] If the teacher is not at home, he should announce it to a member of the teacher's family, [34] and, if they also are not at home, to some other vedic scholar. [35] Let him never go out to beg just for his own benefit.

[36] After he has eaten, he should wash his bowl himself. [37] Let him not leave any food uneaten. [38] If he is unable to do so, he should bury the leftovers in the ground, [39] throw them in water, [40] or place them before an Ārya [41] or before a Śūdra who is a family servant.

[42] When he is away from home, he should eat after offering some of the almsfood in the sacred fire. [43] Almsfood is hailed as a sacrificial oblation at which the teacher plays the roles of the deity [44] and the offertorial fire (A 2.16.3 n.). [45] When, after
4 feeding his teacher, [1] he eats what is left over—[2] that is indeed the leftovers from a sacrificial oblation (see A 1.3.27 n.). [3] When he gives to the teacher other things as he obtains them, they are truly the sacrificial fees. [4] This is the sacrifice performed daily by a student.

[5] The teacher should not give him any leftover items of food which are forbidden to him by vedic texts, however, [6] items such as spices, salt, honey, and meat. [7] His other restrictions are also intimated by this rule, [8] for a vedic text has greater force than a practice from which the existence of a corresponding vedic text has to be inferred (cf. PMS 1.3.3). [9] We notice here, moreover, a motive for such a practice, [10] for one derives pleasure from it (cf. PMS 4.1.2).*

[11] It is permissible to eat the leftovers of one's father or an older brother, [12] but not if it would result in breaking the Law (cf. A 1.4.5–6).

Fire Worship [13]At dusk and dawn a student should fetch a pot of water, [14]and every day he should gather firewood from outlying areas and pile it on the ground. [15]After sunset he should not go out to gather firewood. [16]At dusk and dawn, after he has lighted the fire and swept around it, he should put firewood into it according to the instructions. [17]Some say that he needs to perform the fire worship only at dusk. [18]After he has lighted the fire, he should sweep around it with his hand and not with a broom, [19]but before lighting it he may do as he pleases. [20]Let him not use the remainder of the water from the fire worship to carry out mundane activities or for sipping, [21]nor sip water that has been stirred with the hand or poured into one hand.

Conduct towards the Teacher [22]He should forgo sleep* [23]and every day take care of his teacher with activities that procure righteousness (*dharma*) and wealth (A 1.24.23 n.). [24]After taking care of his teacher, he should say when he goes to sleep: 'I have taken care of the man who takes care of the Law.' [25]If the teacher breaks a rule through carelessness or deliberately, the student should point it out to him in private; [26]and if the teacher persists, he should either perform those rites himself [27]or make him desist.* [28]Now, they say that a student who gets up before and goes to bed after his teacher never sleeps. [29]A student who totally dedicates himself in this manner accomplishes in that very state all the rites carrying rewards, as well as those that pertain to a householder.*

5 **General Rules** [1]The term 'austerity' is used with reference to the rules of conduct. [2]When someone breaks these rules, the application to vedic study and the knowledge of the Veda will slip away from him, as well as from his children; [3]he will fall into hell, and his life will be shortened. [4]As a result of breaking these rules, seers are not being born in recent generations. [5]Through a residue of their merits, however, some people are reborn as seers on account of their vedic learning, [6]as, for example, Śvetaketu.

[7]Whatever other science besides the Veda a steadfast man learns from his teacher, it will bear fruit for him just like the

Veda. [8]They point out, moreover, that when such a person thinks of anything, speaks about anything, or looks at anything with a will to accomplishing it, it will happen exactly as he wills.

[9]Activities pleasing to the teacher, those promoting his own well-being, and pursuing his studies: [10]undertakings other than these do not belong to a student. [11]When a student is faithful to his private vedic recitation, takes delight in the Law, and is observant, upright, and gentle, he will attain success.

Conduct towards the Teacher [12]Rising each day during the last watch of the night (B 2.17.22 n.), he should stand before the teacher and extend to him the morning greeting: 'I am so-and-so, sir!', [13]and, before the morning meal, to other very elderly persons living in the same village. [14]He should also greet them when he meets them after he returns from a journey [15]or if he desires heaven or long life.

[16]With joined hands, let a Brahmin greet by stretching his right hand level with his ears, a Kṣatriya level with his chest, a Vaiśya level with his waist, and a Śūdra very low. [17]When returning the greetings of a person belonging to one of the higher classes, the last syllable of his name should be lengthened to three morae (Va 13.46). [18]When he meets the teacher after sunrise, however, he should clasp his feet; [19]at all other times he should exchange greetings, [20]although, according to some, he should embrace the teacher's feet even at other times. [21]After he has pressed his teacher's right foot from the bottom to the top with his right hand, he should clasp it at the ankle. [22]Some say that he should massage both feet with both hands and clasp them both.

[23]He shall remain fully attentive all day long and at the time of vedic study never let anything distract him from his lesson, [24]as also while he is attending to his teacher's work. [25]At times when vedic recitation is forbidden,* he shall recite it mentally. [26]And he should recite the Veda only when he is called upon to do so.

6 [1]Every night he should get his teacher ready for bed by washing and pressing his feet, [2]and, when permitted, lie

down to sleep himself [3]taking care not to stretch his legs towards the teacher. [4]According to some, however, it is not wrong to stretch the legs in that way if the teacher is lying on a bed.*

[5]In the presence of his teacher, moreover, he should not speak while lying down. [6]If the teacher speaks to him, however, he may answer him while remaining seated [7]or, if the teacher is standing, rising to his feet. [8]Let him walk behind the teacher when he is walking [9]and run after him when he is running.

[10]He should not come near the teacher wearing shoes, covering the head, or carrying anything in the hands. [11]He may do so, however, when he is on the road or in the middle of doing something, [12]provided he does not sit too close to the teacher. [13]Let him approach the teacher as he would a god, without idle talk or distracting thoughts and attentive to his words. [14]He shall not sit cross-legged. [15]If the wind is blowing from him towards the teacher, he should change his place. [16]He shall not sit supporting himself with his hand, [17]or leaning against anything. [18]If he is wearing two garments, he should wear one of them over his left shoulder and under his right arm,* [19]but if he is wearing a single garment, he should wrap it around his lower body. [20]Let him face the teacher even when the teacher is not facing him, [21]sitting neither too close nor too far, [22]but at a distance where the teacher, while seated, can reach him with his hands. [23]He shall not sit where the wind blows from the teacher to him. [24]A single student should sit on his teacher's right, [25]while a group may sit as space permits. [26]When the teacher is not provided with a seat and remains standing, he should not sit down. [27]Likewise, while the teacher remains seated, he should not lie down, [28]and when the teacher is doing something, he should, if he is capable, offer to do it himself.

[29]In the presence of the teacher, moreover, he should not clasp the feet of a person of lesser dignity than the teacher, [30]greet such a person using the name of his lineage (A 2.11.15 n.), [31]rise to meet him, or get up after him, [32]even if that person happens to be his teacher's elder.* [33]But he should move away from that place and from his seat. [34]Some say that he may address a pupil of his teacher by name, even if that pupil happens to be an elder

of his (A 1.6.32 n.). [35] Towards a person who is revered for reasons other than being his teacher, however, he should behave as towards his teacher, even if he happens to be a person of lesser dignity than his teacher.

[36–7] After he has eaten in the presence of his teacher, moreover, he should neither give away his leftovers nor sip water without getting up. [38] After asking the teacher 'What shall I do?',

7 [1] he should get up; or he may get up silently. [2] Let him not move counterclockwise but walk around his teacher clockwise* and then leave.

General Rules [3] He should not look at a naked woman [4] or cut anything from plants or trees to smell it. [5] He should refrain from using shoes, umbrellas, and vehicles. [6] 'Let him not smile, [7] or, if he smiles, let him do so covering his mouth'—so states a Brāhmaṇa. [8] He should not kiss a woman with his mouth, [9] covet her in his heart, [10] or touch her without a good reason. [11] A Brāhmaṇa states: 'He shall keep his body dirty, his teeth stained, and his speech true' (A 1.2.28 n.).

[12] He shall regard those who taught his teacher the same subject that he is studying from him as his own teachers. [13] When he sees his teacher clasp the feet of other persons, he should also clasp their feet.

[14] If he has several teachers, the almsfood he gathers comes under the control of the teacher to whom he is currently attached. [15] A student who has returned home should offer the almsfood to his mother; [16] the mother should present it to her husband, [17] and the husband to the teacher. [18] Or else, it may be used for ritual (*dharma*) purposes.

Conclusion of Study

[19] After learning as much as he can, he should present the fee for vedic study, a fee that is procured righteously (*dharma*) and according to his ability. [20] If his teacher has fallen into hardship, however, he may seize it from an Ugra or a Śūdra. [21] Some maintain that it is lawful at all times to seize wealth for the teacher from an Ugra or a Śūdra. [22] Let him not brag about what he has

given [23] or gloat over what he has done. [24] He should refrain from praising himself and disparaging others. [25] When he is ordered to do something, he should go ahead and do just that.

[26] If the teacher is incompetent, however, he may live with another (A 1.2.17). [27] With the exception of clasping the feet and eating the leftovers (see A 1.3.27 n.), he should behave towards his teacher's wife as towards his teacher [28] and conduct himself in the same manner towards a person whom the teacher deputes to teach him [29] and towards older classmates. [30] With the exception of eating the leftovers, he should behave towards his teacher's son as towards his teacher.

A STUDENT WHO HAS RETURNED HOME

Conduct towards the Teacher

[31] Even after he has returned home, the accepted practice is that he should behave towards these individuals exactly the same

8 way [1] as he behaved when he was a student.

[2] He may wear a necklace; apply lotions on his face, oil on his hair and beard, collyrium on his eyes, and oil on his body; and wear a turban, a lungi, a jacket, sandals, and shoes. [3] But let him neither do these nor have them done in places where his teacher may see him, [4] or during private activities [5] such as brushing the teeth, massaging the body, and combing the hair.

[6] The teacher, for his part, should not speak admiringly of his pupil's belongings in the hope of getting them. [7] Some, however, maintain that a bath-graduate who is summoned by or visits his teacher is not expected to take off what he had been wearing, in accordance with the rules, at the time of graduation.

[8] Let him not sit on a seat that is higher, [9] has more legs [10] or is sturdier than his teacher's; [11] nor occupy a seat or bed that is normally used by his teacher. [12] When he is so ordered by the teacher during a journey, he may get on to the same vehicle, but after the teacher. [13] The same rule applies to entering an assembly hall or a harrow, and to occupying a mat or a straw bed.

[14] Except to give good news, he should not speak to the teacher unless the teacher addresses him first. [15] He should

refrain from tapping on, whispering to, laughing in the presence of, calling aloud, using the personal name of, or giving an order to his teacher; [16] although in an emergency he may report something to him.

[17] If they live close by, he should go to see the teacher every morning and evening without being summoned [18] and visit him the very day that he returns from a journey. [19] When his teacher and his teacher's teacher are together, he should first clasp the feet of his teacher's teacher and then try to clasp his own teacher's feet, [20] but the latter should forbid him; [21] in the presence of his teacher's teacher acts of reverence to his own teacher are suspended. [22] He shall go frequently to visit his teacher at his home, bringing with him whatever personal gift he can afford, even if it is only a few tooth cleaners.*

Duties of a Teacher

[23] Next, the teacher's conduct towards his pupil. [24] Loving him like a son and totally devoted to him, the teacher should impart knowledge to him without holding anything back with respect to any of the Laws. [25] Except in an emergency, moreover, he should not employ a pupil for his own purposes to the detriment of the pupil's studies. [26] A pupil ceases to be a pupil when he is inattentive to his teacher and so becomes a dolt.* [27] A teacher, likewise, ceases to be a teacher when he neglects teaching.

[28] When a pupil does something wrong, the teacher should always correct him. [29] Instilling fear, making him fast or bathe, and banishing him from his presence are the punishments, and he should apply them according to the severity of the offence until the student has completed his studies.*

[30] When he has completed his studies and finished his period of studentship, the teacher should dismiss him with the words: 'From now on attend to other duties (*dharma*).'

Vedic Recitation and its Suspension

9 [1] After commencing his annual course of vedic study on the full moon of July–August, he should not recite the Veda

in the evening for a month [2]and should conclude the course of study on the full moon or the lunar mansion Rohiṇī of December–January. [3]According to some, the course of study lasts for four and a half months.*

[4]He should refrain from reciting the Veda in a market town—[5]he may optionally recite it there after smearing an area with the dung of an ox—[6]or in a cremation ground and the surrounding area up to a distance of a rod's throw.* [7]The recitation is not suspended, however, when a cemetery has been overtaken by a village or agricultural land, [8]but he should not recite the Veda at a spot that he knows to have been a cemetery.

[9]The rule pertaining to a cemetery (see A 1.2.5 n.) applies also when Śūdras and outcastes are present, [10]although, according to some, it applies only if they are in the same house. [11]He shall suspend his vedic recitation, however, if he even exchanges glances with a Śūdra woman [12]or any other woman who has violated class boundaries in her sexual relations. [13]If he wants to speak with a menstruating woman when he is about to recite the Veda, he should first speak with a Brahmin and then speak with her. After he has spoken with her, however, he should speak again with a Brahmin and then recite the Veda. In this way the child she bears will prosper (A 2.1.17 n.).

[14]Vedic recitation is suspended in a village in which there is a corpse [15]or a Cāṇḍāla, [16]or when corpses are being carried within its boundaries; [17]in the wilderness when they are within sight; [18]and for the entire day when outsiders visit the village [19]even if they are respectable people.

[20]When it thunders in the evening, vedic recitation is suspended during the night; [21]and when there is lightning, until he has slept. [22]When there is lightning about the time of dawn or at a time when one can distinguish a black cow from a red one at a distance of a rod's throw (A 1.9.6 n.), vedic recitation is suspended for the day until the end of dusk; [23]as also when it thunders at the end of the last watch of the night (B 2.17.22 n.) [24]or, according to some, after midnight; [25]and when cows have to be kept in their pens. [26]When people condemned to death remain in prison, it is suspended until they have been executed.

[27]Let him not recite the Veda while he is mounted on an animal.

[28]Vedic recitation is suspended for two days and nights on

10 new-moon days, [1]as well as on the full-moon days that open a four-month season;* [2]for three days after the conclusion of the annual course of vedic study, the death of an elder (A 1.6.32 n.), an ancestral offering made on the eighth day after the full moon, the commencement of the annual course of vedic study, [3]and the death of a close relative; [4]and for twelve days after the death of one's mother, father, or teacher.

[5]At their death one should also bathe daily for the same period of time; [6]in addition, the mourners should shave themselves completely. [7]Some maintain that students who have returned home should not shave except when they are consecrated for a sacrifice.* [8]A Brāhmaṇa, moreover, declares: 'Empty and uncovered, indeed, is he who is shaven-headed; the topknot is his cover.' [9]At sacrificial sessions, on the other hand, the topknot is shaved because it is explicitly enjoined.

[10]According to some, vedic recitation is suspended for three days and nights after the death of one's teacher. [11]It is suspended for one day upon receiving news of the death of a vedic scholar within one year of his death, [12]but, according to some, only if he was a fellow student.

[13–14]If he wishes to recite or teach or if he is actually engaged in reciting or teaching the Veda during the visit of a vedic scholar, he may do so only after receiving his permission. [15–16]In the presence of his teacher, moreover, he may recite or teach the Veda only after the teacher has said: 'Ho, recite!' [17]Both when he intends to recite and when he has completed his recitation, he should clasp his teacher's feet. [18]Likewise, when someone comes in during vedic recitation, he may continue the recitation only after that person utters the same words.

[19]Vedic recitation is suspended when dogs are barking, donkeys are braying, a wolf or a solitary jackal is howling, or an owl is hooting, and whenever the sound of music, weeping, singing, or Sāman chants is heard (G 16.21 n.). [20]Likewise, when texts of another vedic branch are being recited, the recitation of Sāman chants is suspended. [21]Vedic recitation is suspended also when

there is any other noise that may blend with the recitation; [22] after vomiting until he has slept [23] or consumed some ghee; [24] when there is a foul smell; [25] and when he has indigestion. [26] He should not recite the Veda after the evening meal [27] or when his hands are wet.

[28] After eating food presented during a rite for a newly deceased person,* vedic recitation is suspended for a full day and an evening, [29] or until the food is digested; [30] in addition, however, he should eat some food that has not been so offered.

11 [1] This provision applies also after eating food given by a motherless man on the day that a person starts a fresh vedic book; [2] after eating the food given by a fatherless man on the day that he completes the recitation of a vedic book; [3] and, according to some, after eating at a sacrifice for gods who were originally humans.* [4] Vedic recitation is not suspended, however, after eating the following items given at such occasions: uncooked rice given the previous day and raw meat, [5] as well as roots and fruits of plants and trees.

[6] On the day that he performs the ceremony for commencing the recitation of a vedic book and on the day that he formally commences its recitation, he should not recite that book. [7] On the day he performs the ceremony for commencing or ending the recitation of an entire Veda, moreover, he should not recite that Veda.

[8] Vedic recitation is suspended in a place where the wind howls, swirls up grass on the ground, or drives the rain; [9] at the boundary between a village and the wilderness; [10] and on a highway. [11] When a fellow student is away, collective recitation is suspended for that day. [12] During personal activities [13] such as washing the feet, massaging, and applying oil, [14] he should neither recite nor teach the Veda as long as he is so occupied. [15] Vedic recitation is suspended at dawn and dusk; [16] while sitting on a tree [17] or standing in water; [18] at night when the doors are open; [19] and during the day when the doors are shut. [20] During the spring and summer festivals the recitation of an entire vedic chapter is forbidden, [21] as also the recitation of the daily vedic lesson if it is performed without following the proper procedure.

[22] This is its procedure: [23] he should go near the water before breakfast, purify himself, and, leaving out the chapter he has already finished, do his recitation at a clean spot aloud [24] or, if it is a time for suspending recitation, mentally. [25] They forbid mental recitation when there is unremitting lightning or thunder, when one is impure or has eaten food offered to a newly deceased person, and when there is frost; [26] some forbid it only when one has eaten at an ancestral offering.

[27] When lightning, thunder, and rain occur together out of season, vedic recitation is suspended for three days [28] or, according to some, until the ground becomes dry; [29] if only one or two of these occur, the suspension lasts until the same time the following day. [30] Any time there is a solar or lunar eclipse, an earthquake, or a whirlwind, and any time a meteor falls or a fire erupts, the recitation of all sacred texts is suspended until the same time the following day. [31] When a cloud appears out of season, when a halo appears around the sun or the moon, when a rainbow, a parhelion, or a comet is seen, and when there is a wind, a foul smell, or frost—vedic recitation is suspended for the duration of all these events, [32] and in the case of wind, for an 'hour'* after it has ceased.

[33] Vedic recitation is suspended until after he has slept when he hears a wolf or a solitary jackal howling, [34] and at night in the wilderness if there is no fire or gold. [35] A section of the Veda that has not been previously studied should not be recited outside the proper time* [36] or in the evening. [37] What has already been studied may be recited at any time.

[38] With respect to particulars not given here, one should follow the directives of legal assemblies.*

Private Recitation of the Veda

12 [1] 'Private vedic recitation is austerity'—so states a Brāhmaṇa (TA 2.14). [2] In the same vedic text we hear: 'When a man does his private vedic recitation, whether he does it standing, seated, or lying down, he is in reality performing an act of austerity, for private vedic recitation is austerity' (cf. TA 2.12).

[3]The Brāhmaṇa of the Vājasaneyins (cf. SB 11.5.6.8), moreover, declares: 'Private vedic recitation is indeed a sacrifice offered to the Veda. When thunder rolls, when lightning flashes, when thunderclaps burst, and when the wind howls—they are the Vaṣaṭ calls of that sacrifice. Therefore, when thunder rolls, when lightning flashes, when thunderclaps burst, and when the wind howls, one should recite the Veda without fail so that these Vaṣaṭ calls would not be rendered futile.' [4]This statement is made complete in a passage from a different vedic branch (p. xxii): [5]'If, moreover, the wind howls, thunder rolls, lightning flashes, or thunderclaps burst, he should recite a single Ṛc-verse, a single Yajus-formula, or a single Sāman-chant; or else recite: "Earth! Atmosphere! Sky! I offer truth and austerity into faith!" In this manner, undoubtedly, his private vedic recitation for that day is accomplished.' [6]That being the case, the above provision does not go against the accepted practice of the Āryas, [7]for they teach both the recitation of the Veda and its suspension. That would become meaningless if we listened to the Brāhmaṇa of the Vājasaneyins, [8]for that accepted practice of the Āryas has no tangible motive (A 1.4.8–10 n.). [9]The suspension of vedic recitation laid down in the vedic texts refers to vedic recitation and not to the ritual use of vedic formulas (cf. PMS 12.3.19).

[10]All rites are described in the Brāhmaṇas. The lost Brāhmaṇa passages relating to some of them are inferred from usage. [11]When a practice is undertaken because of the pleasure derived from it, it does not presuppose a vedic text (cf. PMS 4.1.2).* [12]A man who follows such a practice prepares himself for hell.

Great Sacrifices

[13]Next, we present some rites given in the Brāhmaṇas, [14]rites that are eulogized as 'great sacrifices' and 'great sacrificial sessions' (SB 11.5.6.1): [15]every day making a Bali offering to beings,
13 giving food to men according to one's ability, [1]offering at least a piece of wood in the fire as an oblation to the gods while saying Svāhā, making an offering of at least a pot of

water to the ancestors while saying Svadhā, and doing one's private vedic recitation.

Salutation

[2]One should pay homage to people of higher classes [3]and to those who are older. [4]When a man is elated, he becomes proud; when he is proud, he violates the Law; and when the Law is violated, of course, he goes to hell once again.

Study and Conduct towards the Teacher

[5]A teacher cannot give orders to a pupil of his who has returned home.

[6]The syllable OṂ is the gate to heaven. Therefore, when he is about to recite the Veda, he should pronounce that syllable at the beginning, [7]as also after saying something during the recitation that is not part of the recitation. In this way the Veda is kept separate from ordinary speech. [8]During sacrifices, moreover, commands begin with this syllable.* [9]In ordinary life also during rites to secure prosperity, it is this syllable that precedes statements such as, 'May the day be auspicious!', 'May there be well-being!', and 'May there be prosperity!'

[10]Without a mutual agreement,* one should not take up a difficult text, with the exception of the *Triḥśrāvaṇa* and the *Triḥsahavacana*,* [11]but according to Hārīta the Veda should be studied until all doubts are cleared.

[12]In the case of non-vedic texts, subservience does not come into play.*

[13]The pupil should clasp the feet of the person who instructs him on the orders of his teacher for the duration of the instruction. [14]According to some, the pupil should do so always if the instructor is a worthy person. [15]With respect to such a person, however, subservience does not come into play,* [16]as also with respect to older fellow students.* [17]When two people rehearse the Veda with each other, subservience does not come into play.*

Return to Studentship

[18] 'The Veda waxes strong,' they teach.[19] Śvetaketu says: 'If a man, after he has married and settled down, wishes to study the Veda further, he should live at the house of his teacher with a collected mind for two months every year, [20] for by these means I managed to study more of the Veda than during the time I was a student.' [21] But that is forbidden by authoritative texts, [22] for after a man has married and settled down, he is enjoined by vedic

14 texts to perform daily rites,[1] namely, the daily fire sacrifice, hospitality towards guests, [2] and others of this sort.

Duty to Teach

[3] When someone asks him for instruction, he should not spurn him, [4] provided he does not see any fault in him. [5] If by chance he is unable to complete his studies, subservience (A 1.13.12, 15 n.) does indeed continue with respect to that teacher.

Salutation

[6] To his mother and father he should show the same obedience as to his teacher. [7] A student who has returned home should clasp the feet of all his elders (A 1.6.32 n.); [8] he should do so when he returns from a journey as well. [9] He should also clasp the feet of his brothers and sisters according to seniority.

[10] He should pay them homage, moreover, in the prescribed manner. [11] He should rise up and greet an officiating priest, a father-in-law, or a paternal or maternal uncle who is younger than himself, [12] or he may silently clasp his feet.

> [13] A fellow citizen who has been a friend for ten
> years, a fellow student who has been a friend
> for five years, and a vedic scholar known for
> three years deserve to be greeted.

[14] If the relative ages of the persons are known, he should greet the older ones first.

[15] When a person other than an elder (A 1.6.32 n.) is standing at a different level than himself, it is not necessary to greet him,

[16]or he may greet him after climbing up or down to the same level as that person. [17]In every case, however, he should rise up before offering his greetings. [18]He should not offer greetings when he is impure [19]or to a person who is impure; [20]neither should he return a greeting when he is impure.

[21]Wives should be greeted according to the age of their husbands. [22]He should never greet anyone with his shoes on, or with his head covered, or carrying anything in the hand. [23]In greeting women, Kṣatriyas, or Vaiśyas, he should use a pronoun* and not his personal name. [24]Some maintain that he should do so also when he greets his mother or his teacher's wife.

> [25]A 10-year-old Brahmin and a 100-year-old Kṣatriya, you should know, stand with respect to each other as a father to a son. But of the two, the Brahmin is the father!

[26]He should ask a person who is younger or of the same age whether he is doing well, [27]a Kṣatriya whether he is in good shape, [28]a Vaiśya whether his property is unharmed, [29]and a Śūdra whether he is in good health.* [30]Let him not pass by a vedic scholar without talking to him, [31]and likewise a woman in the wilderness.

15 [1]When he is paying his respects to elders (A 1.6.32 n.), the aged, and guests; when he is offering sacrifices and softly reciting prayers;* and when he is eating, sipping water, and doing his private vedic recitation, he should wear his upper garment over his left shoulder and under his right arm (see A 1.6.18 n.).

Purification

[2]He becomes pure by sipping water collected on the ground,* [3]or when a pure person gives him water to sip. [4]He should not sip rain water [5]or water in a crevice, [6]as also warm water without a good reason.

[7]If he lifts up his empty hands against birds, he should touch water. [8]If he is capable, he should not, even for a moment (A

1.11.32 n.), remain impure [9] or naked. [10] He should not perform his purification while he is standing in water; [11] only after coming out should he sip water.

[12] He shall not put firewood in the sacred fire without first sprinkling the wood with water. [13] When he is seated alongside unclean people on a seat made with grass strewn haphazardly, he is considered pure if he does not touch them; [14] the same is true when he is seated on a bed of grass or a wooden seat fixed to the ground.* [15] He should wear a garment only after sprinkling it with water. [16] If a dog touches him, he should plunge into water with his clothes on; [17] or he becomes pure after he has washed that spot, touched it with fire, washed that spot again, as well as his feet, and sipped water. [18] When he is impure he should not go near the fire—[19] according to some, not nearer than the length of an arrow—[20] nor should he blow on it [21] or place it under his bed.

[22] The proper place for a Brahmin to live is a village where there is a lot of firewood and water and where he is able to perform his purifications on his own. [23] When he has washed away the stains of urine or excrement after going to the toilet, the stains of food, the stains from eating, and the stains of semen, and then washed his feet and sipped water, he becomes pure.

16 [1] He should not sip water standing or stooping. [2] Let him sip thrice seated on his haunches and with water sufficient to reach his heart,* [3] wipe his lips three times [4] or, according to some, twice, [5] and touch them with water once [6] or, according to some, twice. [7] With his right hand he should sprinkle water on his left hand and on his feet and head, and then touch the organs,* namely, the eyes, the nostrils, and the ears, with water. [8] He should then wash his hands with water.

[9] Even though he is already pure, however, when he is preparing to take his meal, he should sip water twice, wipe his lips twice, touch his lips with water once, [10] rub the inside of his lips, and then sip water.

[11] He does not become sullied by the hair of his moustache getting into his mouth, so long as he does not touch it with his hand. [12] Sipping water is prescribed when one sees drops of

saliva falling from one's mouth. [13] According to some, sipping is unnecessary if they fall on the ground.

[14] After he has come into contact with nasal mucus or tears while he is sleeping or sneezing, or with blood, hair, fire, cattle, a Brahmin, or a woman; after he has travelled on a highway; after he has touched a filthy substance or an impure man; and after wearing his lower garment, he should touch water,* [15] wet cowdung, plants, or the earth.

Food

Unfit Food [16] Meat that has been cut with a knife used for slaughtering is not fit to be eaten.* [17] He should not break off a piece of cake with his teeth.

[18] When a death has occurred in a house, he should not eat there for ten days, [19] as also after a birth before the mother comes out of the birthing room, [20] and when there is a corpse in a house.

[21] Food that has been touched by an impure person becomes impure but is not rendered unfit to be eaten.* [22] Food that an impure Śūdra brings, on the other hand, is not fit to be eaten, [23] as also food in which there is a hair [24] or some other filth;* [25] food that has come into contact with filthy substances; [26] food in which there is an insect that lives on filth [27] or in which there are mouse droppings or mouse parts;* [28] food that has been touched with the feet [29] or with the hem of a garment; [30] food that has been seen by a dog or a degraded individual; [31] food that has been carried in the hem of a garment; [32] and food that has been brought at night by a slave woman.

17 **Rules of Eating** [33] If, while he is eating, [1] he is touched by a Śūdra, he should stop eating. [2] He shall not eat seated alongside ignoble people; [3] or in a place where, while the group is eating, one of them may get up and give away his left-overs or sip water (A 1.3.27 n.); [4] or where people insult him when they give food; [5] or food that men or other filthy creatures have smelt.

[6] He should not eat on a boat [7] or a terrace.* [8] Let him eat sitting on a specially prepared area of the floor.

Eating Utensils [9]He should eat out of a clay vessel that has not been used before, [10]or, if it has been used, only after scorching it with fire. [11]A vessel made of metal is purified by scrubbing, [12]and one made of wood by scraping. [13]During a sacrifice, vessels are purified in the manner prescribed by the vedic texts.

Forbidden Food [14]He should not eat food obtained from the market, [15]even seasonings, with the exception of raw meat, honey, and salt; [16]oil and ghee, on the other hand, may be used after sprinkling them with water.

[17]He should not eat, drink, or consume cooked food that has been left overnight [18]or turned sour, [19]with the exception of sugar-cane juice, rolled rice, gruel, roasted barley, barley meal, vegetables, meat, flour, milk, milk products, and roots and fruits of plants and trees. [20]He should not consume anything that has turned sour without mixing it with some other food.

[21]It is forbidden to drink any type of liquor; [22]as also the milk of sheep, [23]camels, and deer; the milk of animals in heat or bearing twins; [24]and the milk of a cow during the first ten days after giving birth. [25]Herbs used in the manufacture of liquor are likewise forbidden; [26]as also Karañja garlic, onion, leeks, [27]and any other food that is forbidden. [28]For a Brāhmaṇa states: 'Mushrooms should not be eaten.'

[29]The meat of one-hoofed animals, camels, Gayal oxen, village pigs, and Śarabha cattle are forbidden. [30]It is permitted to eat the meat of milch cows and oxen. [31]A text of the Vājasaneyins states: 'The meat of oxen is fit for sacrifice.'* [32]Among birds that feed by scratching with their feet, the cock is forbidden, [33]and among birds that feed by thrusting their beaks, the Plava heron. [34]Carnivorous birds are forbidden; [35]as also the Haṃsa goose, the Bhāsa vulture, the Cakra bird, and the Suparṇa falcon. [36]The Kruñca curlew and the Krauñca crane are forbidden, with the exception of the Vārdhrāṇasa cranes and Lakṣmaṇa cranes.* [37]Animals with five claws* are forbidden, with the exception of the Godhā monitor lizard, tortoise, porcupine, hedgehog, rhinoceros, hare, and Pūtikhaṣa. [38]Among fish, the Ceṭa is forbidden, [39]as also the snake-head fish,

the Mr̥dura crocodile, carnivorous fish, and others that are grotesque, such as the mermen.

18 **People from Whom Food May Be Accepted** [1]Honey, uncooked food, venison, land, roots, fruits, protection, pasture for cattle, house, and fodder for a draught ox may be accepted from an Ugra. [2]According to Hārīta, even these may be accepted only when they are brought by a pupil (A 1.7.20–1). [3]Alternatively, uncooked food may be accepted, [4]or even cooked food if it does not contain any seasoning, [5]but not a lot.

[6]If he has lost his livelihood, he may eat food obtained on his own from anyone after paying for it with gold or an animal. [7]He should not be overly attracted to this way of life [8]and give it up when he finds his legitimate livelihood (A 2.10.4; cf. A 1.18.15; 1.21.3–4).

[9]A student who has returned home may not eat any food given by people belonging to the three classes beginning with Kṣatriya. [10]As a rule, he may eat the food of a Brahmin, although it may become unfit to be eaten for a particular reason, [11]as during a time when a person required to do a penance is performing the penitential act.* [12]After the man has concluded his penance, he may eat his food. [13]According to some, he is permitted to eat the food of people belonging to any class who adhere to their respective Laws, with the exception of Śūdras, [14]and even of a Śūdra whom he has obtained according to the Law. [15]He may eat it after paying for it with gold or an animal, but let him not be overly attracted to this way of life and give it up when he finds his legitimate livelihood.

[16]He shall not eat the food given by a corporate body [17]or announced through a public invitation; [18]the food of anyone who lives by practising a craft [19]or using weapons; [20]the food of a pawnbroker, [21]a physician, [22]or an usurer; [23]and, prior to the purchase of the Soma, the food of a man who has been consecrated for a sacrifice.* [24]Only after the animal dedicated to Agni and Soma has been killed [25]or after its omentum has been offered, may one eat the food of a man consecrated for a sacrifice, [26]for a Brāhmaṇa states: 'Alternatively, after setting aside the portion to be offered in sacrifice, they may eat the

remainder.'* [27]He shall not eat the food of the following: an impotent man; [28]a royal messenger; [29]a man who makes oblations with substances unfit for offering; [30]a spy; [31]a man who has become a wandering ascetic without following the proper procedure; [32]a man who has relinquished his sacred fires; [33]a vedic scholar who stays away from everybody, eats anybody's food, neglects his vedic recitation, or is married to a Śūdra
19 woman; [1]a drunkard; a mad man; a prisoner; a debtor;* and a moneylender who hounds a man who owes him, as well as the man who makes the lender hound him, so long as they are thus engaged.

[2]Who, then, is the man whose food he may eat? [3]'Anyone who gives willingly,' says Kaṇva. [4]'A pious man,' says Kautsa. [5]'Anyone who gives,' says Vārṣyāyaṇi, [6]for if impurities remain immobile in a person, then there is nothing wrong in eating his food, and if impurities are mobile, then the person will become pure by means of the gift. [7]'Almsfood is pure and may be eaten', according to Eka, Kuṇika, Kāṇva, and Kutsa, as well as Puṣkarasādi; [8]and, according to Vārṣyāyaṇi, food that one receives unasked from anybody. [9]He may eat the food given willingly by a pious person, [10]but even when given by a pious person, he may not eat it if it is given unwillingly. [11]He may eat food that he receives unasked from anyone at all, [12]but, says Hārīta, not if it is received subsequent to an invitation. [13]Now, they quote two verses from a Purāṇa:

> Almsfood brought and handed over even by an evildoer, in the opinion of Prajāpati, is suitable for eating, so long as it has not been previously announced.
>
> If a man spurns such food, his forefathers will not eat from him for fifteen years and the sacred fire will not convey his oblations.

[14]And further:

> It is forbidden to eat the food of physicians, hunters, surgeons, fowlers, unchaste wives, or eunuchs.

[15] Now, they also quote:

> An abortionist* rubs his sin off on the man who eats his food, an innocent person on the man who slanders him, a thief on the king who releases him, and a supplicant on the man who makes false promises.

Path of the Law

20 [1] Let him not follow the Laws for the sake of worldly benefits, [2] for then the Laws produce no fruit at harvest time. [3] It is like this. A man plants a mango tree to get fruits, but in addition he obtains also shade and fragrance. In like manner, when a man follows the Law, he obtains, in addition, other benefits. [4] Even if he does not obtain them, at least no harm is done to the Law.

[5] Let him not become vexed or easily deceived by the pronouncements of hypocrites, crooks, infidels, and fools. [6] The Righteous (*dharma*) and the Unrighteous (*adharma*) do not go around saying, 'Here we are!' Nor do gods, Gandharvas, or ancestors declare, 'This is righteous and that is unrighteous.' [7] An activity that Āryas praise is righteous, and what they deplore is unrighteous. [8] He should model his conduct after that which is unanimously approved in all regions by Āryas who have been properly trained, who are elderly and self-possessed, and who are neither greedy nor deceitful (= A 2.29.14; cf. TU 1.11.4). [9] In this way he will win both worlds.*

Trade as an Occupation

[10] Trade is not sanctioned for Brahmins. [11] In times of adversity, he may trade in permitted goods, eschewing these forbidden ones: [12] human beings, seasonings, dyes, perfumes, foods, skins, barren cows, glue, water, tender grain stalks, wine making ingredients, red and black pepper, grain, meat, weapons, and merits. [13] Among grains, however, the sale of sesame seeds and rice is strictly forbidden. [14] It is also forbidden to barter one of

the above items for another. [15] He may, however, barter food for food, human beings for human beings, seasonings for seasonings, perfumes for perfumes, and knowledge for knowledge. [16] He may trade in permitted goods that have not been bought,

21 [1] as also in Muñja grass, Balbaja grass, roots, and fruits, [2] and in grasses and wood that have not been handcrafted. [3] He should not be overly attracted to this way of life [4] and give it up when he finds his legitimate livelihood.

Acts Making a Man an Outcaste or Sordid

[5] Social interaction with outcastes is not permitted, [6] as also with degraded people. [7] These are the actions causing loss of caste: [8] theft; acts causing infamy; homicide; neglect of the Vedas; abortion; sex with the siblings of one's mother or father or with their children; drinking liquor; sex with those with whom sex is forbidden; [9] sex with a friend of one's female or male elders (A 1.6.32 n.) or with the wife of another man—[10] some maintain that there is no loss of caste when one has sex with a woman other than the wife of an elder—; [11] and the persistent commission of unrighteous (*adharma*) acts.

[12] And these are the actions that make people sordid:* [13] sex with Śūdras on the part of Ārya women; [14] eating the meat of forbidden animals, [15] to wit, dogs, humans, village cocks, village pigs, and carnivorous animals; [16] consuming human urine and excrement; [17] eating a Śūdra's leftovers (A 1.3.27 n.); and sex with a degraded woman on the part of Āryas. [18] According to some, even these cause loss of caste. [19] Sinful actions other than these also make people sordid.

[20] When he comes to know about a sin that would make a man an outcaste, let him not be the first to tell others about it. He should, however, avoid such a person while he is performing religious activities.

Knowledge of the Self

22 [1] He should practise the disciplines pertaining to the inner self, disciplines that have definite consequences and

prevent mental digression. [2]There is nothing higher than the realization of the self. [3]In this regard, we will cite verses that speak to the realization of the self:

> [4]All living beings are the residence of the one who dwells within the cave,* who cannot be slain, and who is free from stain. The one who is immovable but resides within the movable—those who worship him become immortal.

> [5]Whatever there is here, whatever is called a sensory object in this world—casting away all that, a wise man should worship the one who dwells within the cave.

> [6]Follow what is wholesome, not what is unwholesome. Not finding it in my own self, I then seek in others, without attachment, the abode of the good, the one who is the great body of lustre and the lord abiding in everything.

> [7]The one who is the eternal among all creatures; who is wise, immortal, and unchanging; who has no limbs, voice, body, or touch; who is immense and resplendent—he is the whole world, he is the highest goal, he is the centre, he is the fort without compare.*

> [8]When a man worships him everywhere, follows his path always, and, self-possessed, sees that profound one who is difficult to see, he will rejoice in heaven.

23 [1]Seeing all beings in himself, a wise man thinks about it and is not perplexed. A Brahmin who sees himself in all beings, likewise, shines forth in the vault of heaven.

> [2]The one who is profound, finer than a lotus strand, and stands encompassing the universe, who is wider than the earth, unchangeable, and stands containing the universe—he is different

> from the knowledge of this world obtained through the senses; he is not different from the objects of knowledge; he is the highest lord; from him, as he divides himself, all bodies come into being; he is the root; he is everlasting; he is eternal.
>
> [3] In this life, however, the eradication of faults depends on Yoga. The learned man who uproots these faults that torment creatures attains bliss.

[4] We will now enumerate the faults that torment creatures. [5] They are: anger, excitement, rage, greed, perplexity, hypocrisy, malice, lying, overeating, calumny, envy, lust, ire, lack of self-control, and absence of Yoga. Their eradication depends on Yoga.

[6] Refraining from anger, excitement, rage, greed, perplexity, hypocrisy, and malice; speaking the truth; refraining from overeating, calumny, and envy; sharing, liberality, rectitude, gentleness, tranquillity, self-control, amity with all creatures, Yoga, Ārya-like conduct, benevolence, and contentment—there is agreement that these apply to all orders of life. By practising them according to the rules, a man attains the All.

Penances

24 [1] If someone kills a Kṣatriya, he should give a thousand cows to erase the enmity,* [2] a hundred if he kills a Vaiśya, [3] and ten if he kills a Śūdra. [4] In addition a bull is to be given in each case as an expiation. [5] The same applies for killing women of these classes.

[6] If someone kills a man of the first two classes who has studied the Veda or who has been consecrated to perform a Soma sacrifice, he becomes a heinous sinner (A 1.3.25 n.); [7] so too someone who kills an ordinary Brahmin, [8] a Brahmin's foetus whose gender cannot be determined, [9] or a Brahmin woman soon after her menstrual period.*

[10] This is the atonement for such a man. [11] He should build a

hut in the wilderness, curb his speech, carry a skull as a banner, and cover himself from the navel to the knees with a scrap of hempen cloth. [12] His path is the gap between the tracks of cart-wheels, [13] and if he happens to see another person he should step aside. [14] He should set out to the village carrying a broken metal bowl [15] and visit seven houses, saying: 'Who will give almsfood to a heinous sinner?' [16] That is how he maintains himself. [17] If he does not receive anything, he should fast. [18] He should also look after the cows; [19] indeed, when the cows go out and return, he has a second reason for going to the village. [20] After he has lived like this for twelve years and become cleansed, he may associate with good people. [21] Alternatively, he may build a hut on a track usually taken by robbers and live there seeking to recover the cows of Brahmins. He is absolved after he has fought with them three times or after he has recovered the cows. [22] Or else, he is absolved after taking part in the ritual bath that concludes a horse sacrifice.

[23] The same penance applies to a man who, when Law and profit* are in conflict, chooses profit. [24] If someone has killed one of his elders (A 1.6.32 n.) or a vedic scholar who has completed a sacrifice, he should live in the same manner until his last breath. [25] No rehabilitation is possible for such a man in this life; his sin, however, is removed (cf. A 1.28.18; 1.29.1).

25 [1] A man who has had sex with the wife of an elder should cut off his penis together with the testicles and, holding them in his cupped hands, walk towards the south without turning back; [2] or else he should end his life by embracing a red-hot metal column.*

[3] A man who has drunk liquor should drink burning hot liquor.

[4] A thief, his hair dishevelled and carrying a pestle on his shoulder, should go to the king and confess his deed. The king should slay him with that pestle, and, when he is killed, he is absolved. [5] If he is pardoned, the sin falls on the one who pardons him. [6] Alternatively, he may throw himself into a fire, perform severe mortifications, [7] end his life by reducing the amount

he eats, [8] or perform the arduous penance (see A 1.27.7) for a year. [9] Now, they also quote:

> [10] People who have committed a theft, drunk liquor, had sex with the wife of an elder (A 1.6.32 n.)—so long as they have not killed a Brahmin—should eat a little at every fourth mealtime,* dip into water at dawn, noon, and dusk, and remain standing during the day and seated at night. Such people get rid of their sin in three years.

[11] When someone not belonging to the first social class kills a man belonging to the first class, he should go and stand in a battlefield, where they would kill him. [12] Or else, he may have his body hair, skin, and flesh offered as a sacrifice in a fire and then throw himself into that fire.

[13] Crow, chameleon, peacock, Cakravāka goose, Haṃsa goose, Bhāsa vulture, frog, common mongoose, Ḍerikā rat, and dog—the penance for killing any of these is the same as for kill-

26 ing a Śūdra. [1] The penance is the same also for killing a milch cow or an ox without cause [2] and for killing a cart-load of other animals.

[3] If someone uses harsh words against a person against whom one is not permitted to use such words, or if he tells a lie, he should eat food without milk, spices, or salt for three days; [4] if he is a Śūdra, he should not eat for seven days.

[5] These provisions apply also to women.

[6] When, without endangering the man's life, someone cuts off one limb of a man for whose murder he would become a heinous sinner; [7] when someone behaves in a manner unbecoming of an Ārya, engages in slander, and does forbidden things; when someone partakes of food or drink that is forbidden or unfit (A 1.16.16 n.); when someone ejaculates his semen in a Śūdra woman or in any place other than the vagina (B 3.7.2 n.); and when someone performs a nefarious rite intentionally or unintentionally—he should bathe reciting the Abliṅga or Vāruṇī formulas, or other purificatory texts in proportion to the frequency with which he has committed these offences.

[8]Employing the ritual procedure of the cooked oblation,* a student who has broken his vow of chastity should offer an ass, [9]and a Śūdra should eat of that offering.

[10]Next, the penances for studying in contravention of the rules. [11]Engaged in activities beneficial to his teacher, he should keep silence for a year, speaking only during his daily vedic recitation, when addressing his teacher or the teacher's wife, and while he is begging. [12]The same applies also to other sinful acts that do not cause loss of caste, as do the penances that we will enumerate below. [13]Alternatively, he should make an offering to Lust and Anger or recite softly: 'Lust did it!', 'Anger did it!' (cf. G 25.1–6). [14]Or else, on a day of the moon's change* he should either eat some sesame seeds or fast, and on the following day he should bathe and recite the Sāvitrī verse one thousand times either controlling his breath or without controlling his breath.

27 [1]On the full-moon day of July–August he should eat some sesame seeds or fast, and on the following day bathe in a great river* and offer one thousand kindling sticks in the sacred fires while reciting the Sāvitrī verse or simply recite the Sāvitrī verse one thousand times. [2]Or else, he should offer Iṣṭi-offerings and Yajñakratu-sacrifices in order to purify himself.

[3]After eating something unfit to be eaten, he should fast until all the excrement is gone, [4]which happens after seven days. [5]Alternatively, he should bathe each morning and evening during the winter and spring,* [6]or perform the twelve-day arduous penance. [7]This is the procedure for the twelve-day arduous penance: for three days the person does not eat during the night, and for the next three days during the day; for three days he eats what he receives unasked, and for three days he does not eat at all (cf. B 2.2.38). [8]If he repeats this for a year, it is called the year-long arduous penance.

[9]Now, another penance—by reciting the Veda completely three times while abstaining from food, one discharges the penance for committing even a great many sins that do not cause loss of caste.

[10] When someone takes a non-Ārya woman to bed, lends money on interest, drinks a decoction,* or pays obeisance in a manner unworthy of a Brahmin, he should sit on a spread of grass letting the sun scorch his back.

[11] The sin a Brahmin commits by serving a person of the black class* for one day he removes in three years by bathing daily and eating at every fourth mealtime (see A 1.25.10 n.).

28 [1] 'A man who, under any circumstance, covets what belongs to another man is undoubtedly a thief'—that is the view of Kautsa and Hārīta, as also of Kaṇva and Puṣkarasādi. [2] 'There are exceptions in the case of certain belongings,' says Vārṣyāyaṇi—[3] such as legume pods or fodder for a draught ox. Owners normally do not forbid someone from taking these. [4] To take too much of these, however, is a crime.* [5] 'One must always obtain permission first,' says Hārīta.

[6] Let him not visit a teacher or relative who has fallen from his caste with the intention of seeing him [7] or accept anything of value from him. [8] If he meets such a person accidentally, he should clasp his feet and go away silently.

[9] A mother does countless things to bring about male progeny.* So, even if she has fallen from her caste, he must always serve her, [10] but not let her participate in any of his religious activities.

[11] He should separate himself from anything of value that he has obtained unrighteously (*adharma*), proclaiming 'We and unrighteousness don't go together!'; wear a piece of cloth from his navel to his knees; bathe three times a day at dawn, noon, and dusk; eat food without milk, spices, or salt; and not enter a house for twelve years. [12] After that he becomes cleansed, [13] and thereafter he may associate with Āryas.

[14] This same penance applies also to other sins causing loss of caste.

[15] A man who has had sex with the wife of an elder (A 1.6.32 n.), however, should enter a hollow metal column (see A

1.25.2 n.), have fires lit on both sides, and burn himself up. [16]'That is wrong,' says Hārīta; [17]for anyone who kills himself or another man becomes a heinous sinner without a doubt (A 1.3.25 n.). [18]What such a man should do is to live in the above manner* until his last breath. No rehabilitation is possible for such a man in this life; his sin, however, is removed.

[19]A man who has unjustly abandoned his wife should wear a donkey's skin with its hairy side out and beg from seven houses, saying, 'Almsfood for a man who has unjustly abandoned his wife!' That should be his livelihood for six months.

[20]Women who abandon their husbands unjustly, on the other hand, should perform the twelve-day arduous penance (see A 1.27.7) for the same length of time.

[21]Now, a man who has performed an abortion (A 1.19.15 n.) should wear the skin of a dog or a donkey with its hairy side
29 out, carry a human skull as his drinking cup [1]and a post from a bed-frame as his staff, and go around proclaiming the name of his crime and saying, 'Who will give almsfood to an abortionist?' Obtaining his sustenance from a village, he should seek shelter in an abandoned house or at the foot of a tree, with the thought, 'I am not allowed to associate with Āryas.' He should live in this manner until his last breath. No rehabilitation is possible for such a man in this life; his sin, however, is removed.

[2]A man who kills unintentionally reaps the fruit of his sin, [3]but it is greater if he does so with forethought. [4]This principle applies also to other sinful acts [5]and also to meritorious deeds.

[6]A Brahmin should not take a weapon into his hands even to examine it. [7]'When someone kills an assailant who is trying to kill him, he commits no sin; for then wrath alone confronts wrath'—so states a Purāṇa (cf. B 1.18.13).

[8]Now, heinous sinners (A 1.3.25 n.) should live in a common settlement and, convinced that this is in keeping with the Law, they should officiate at each other's sacrifices, teach each other, and marry each other. [9]When they father sons, they should tell them: 'Go away from us, for then you will be accepted from amongst us as Āryas.' [10]When a man falls from his caste, moreover, his virile power does not fall with him, [11]the truth of which

can be gathered from the fact that a man lacking a limb fathers a child possessing all the limbs.

[12] 'That is false,' says Hārīta. [13] A wife is comparable to a curd-pot, [14] for if someone were to put impure milk into a curd-pot and mix in the curdling substance, that curd cannot be used for ritual purposes. In like manner, there can be no association with what is produced by the semen of a sordid man* (cf. B 2.2.18–24).

[15] Sorcery and cursing make a man sordid but do not cause loss of caste. [16] 'They do cause loss of caste,' says Hārīta.

[17] People guilty of sins that make them sordid should follow the life prescribed for sins causing loss of caste for twelve months, for twelve fortnights, for twelve times twelve days, for twelve times seven days, for twelve times three days, for twelve days, for seven days, for three days, or for one day. [18] In this manner sins that make a man sordid should be expiated in accordance with the way the deed was committed* (cf. B 2.2.17).

THE BATH AT THE END OF STUDENTSHIP

30 [1] 'He should bathe after learning the Veda'—that is the view of some; [2] likewise after completing the forty-eight-year vow. [3] 'He should bathe after learning the Veda and completing the vow,' contend others. [4] One should behave towards all of these as towards a bath-graduate;* [5] the specific reward of honouring such a person depends on the degree of his diligence and learning.

Observances of a Bath-Graduate

[6] Next, the observances of a bath-graduate. [7] He should cultivate the practice of leaving and entering a village from the east or the north. [8] At the time of the morning and evening twilights he should sit silently outside the village. [9] When there is a conflict between rules, what is enjoined by a vedic text prevails.*

[10] With respect to clothes, he should avoid all that are dyed, [11] as well as those that are naturally black. [12] He should wear clothes that are neither shiny [13] nor, if at all possible, squalid.

[14]During the day he should refrain from covering his head, except when he voids urine or excrement.

[15]He should void urine and excrement, however, after covering his head and spreading something on the ground.* [16]He should avoid voiding urine or excrement in the shade; [17]but he may discharge urine in his own shadow. [18]He should not void urine or excrement wearing footgear, or on ploughed land, on a road, or in water. [19]Likewise, he should refrain from spitting and having sexual intercourse in water [20]and from voiding urine or excrement in front of a fire, the sun, water, a Brahmin, a cow, or a divine image. [21]In cleaning himself after voiding urine or excrement, he should avoid using stones, clods, or green branches that he has broken off from plants or trees.

[22]If at all possible, he should not stretch his feet toward a fire, water, a Brahmin, a cow, a divine image, or a door, or in the direction from which the wind is blowing.

[23]Now, they also quote:

31 [1]He should eat his food facing the east, void excrement facing the south, discharge urine facing the north, and wash his feet facing the west.

[2]He should, moreover, void urine and excrement moving far away from his house in the direction of the south or the south-west, [3]but after sunset he should refrain from voiding urine or excrement outside the village or far from his house.

[4]Let him refrain from pronouncing the name of a god while he is impure; [5]from speaking harshly about either the gods or the king; [6]from touching Brahmins or cows with his feet [7]or even with his hand without good cause; [8]and from speaking ill of cows, sacrificial fees, or nubile girls. [9]He should not disclose it when a cow is causing damage [10]or when she is with her calf, unless there is a reason.

[11]When speaking of a cow that does not yield milk, he should not say, 'She is not a milch-cow', but simply say, 'She is going to be a milch-cow.' [12]Nor should he call a lucky thing 'lucky', but just call it 'holy' or 'auspicious'. [13]He should not step over a rope to which a calf is tied [14]or pass between the posts to which

a swing is attached. [15]He should not announce, 'That man is my adversary.' If he announces 'That man is my adversary', he will create for himself a rival who hates him. [16]He should not point out a rainbow to someone by saying 'Look, the Indra's bow!' [17]or count flying birds (cf. G 9.19–24; B 2.6.11–19; Va 12.32–3).

[18]He should avoid looking at the sun as it rises or sets. [19]During the day the sun protects creatures, and during the night, the moon. Therefore, on the night of the new moon he should try his very best to guard himself by keeping himself pure and chaste and by performing rites appropriate for the occasion, [20]for on this night the sun and the moon dwell together.

[21]He should not enter a village along a hazardous path. If he does so, he should softly recite this verse: 'Homage to Rudra, the lord of the dwelling! . . .' or another verse addressed to Rudra.

[22]He should not give his leftovers (A 1.3.27 n.) to someone who is not a Brahmin. If he does so, he should pick his teeth, place what he has picked from his teeth on the leftovers, and then give it.

[23]He should avoid giving in to anger and other such faults that bring suffering to creatures.

32 [1]A man who is engaged in teaching the Vedas should refrain from sex during the rainy season and autumn, [2]and if he has sexual intercourse, let him not sleep with her the entire night. [3]While he is lying down, moreover, he should refrain from teaching, [4]nor should he teach sitting on the bed in which he sleeps.

[5]Let him not appear in public wearing a garland or anointed with oil. [6]At night he should always adorn himself for his wife. [7]He should refrain from submerging his head in water; [8]from bathing after sunset; [9]from using seats, footwear, and tooth cleaners made with Palāśa wood;* [10]and from boasting in the presence of the teacher by saying, for instance, 'I have taken a fine bath.'

[11]He should keep awake until nightfall.* [12]Vedic recitation is forbidden at night, with the exception of teaching the Law to pupils [13]and reciting the Veda mentally by himself. [14]Teaching

the Veda is permitted after midnight. [15] If he gets up in the last watch of the night, he should not go back to sleep thinking that vedic recitation is forbidden.* [16] He may, if he so wishes, rest leaning against something* [17] or recite the Veda mentally.

[18] Let him never visit vile men or regions inhabited by such men, [19] as also casinos and fairs (A 1.3.12 n.). [20] If he has to go to a fair, he should leave after walking around it clockwise (A 1.7.2 n.). [21] He should also avoid visiting cities.

[22] Neither should he elucidate a question. [23] Now, they also quote:

> [24] When a man explains something wrongly, it tears up his root and sprout, his children, cattle, and house. This is how Death, weeping, explained the question put to him: 'O Dharmaprahrāda, not on Kumālana.'*

[25] He should avoid climbing on to a donkey-cart or climbing on to or descending into precarious places; [26] as also crossing a river by swimming;* [27] using unsafe boats; [28] cutting grass, crushing clods of earth, and spitting, without a good reason; [29] and anything else that is forbidden.

BOOK TWO

THE HOUSEHOLDER

1 [1] After marriage, the special observances of the couple living the household life come into force.

Eating

[2] The man should eat at the two appointed times (A 1.25.10 n.), [3] but not so much that he is overly sated. [4] On new- and full-moon days,* moreover, both should fast. [5] Eating at every other mealtime (A 1.25.10 n.) is a genuine fast, [6] and then they may eat until they are quite sated.

Wedding Anniversary

[7] On the anniversary day let the couple eat whatever they like, [8] sleep on the floor, [9] and abstain from sexual intercourse. [10] On the following day the man should offer an oblation of cooked food. [11] The procedure for this offering is explained in the section on the new- and full-moon offerings. [12] In the world people require the couple to perform the above rites on every anniversary day.*

Rites

[13] On whatever occasion he is required to place the sacred fire on the altar, he should draw three lines from west to east and three lines from south to north, sprinkle water on them, and kindle the fire. [14] He should pour out the water used for that towards the north or the east and draw fresh water.

[15] Their water vessels should never be empty—this is an observance incumbent on a couple living the household life.

Rules of Sexual Intercourse

[16] He shall not engage in sex during the daytime. [17] When his wife is in season,* he must have sexual intercourse with her as required by his vow. [18–19] And if his wife wants it, he may have sex with her between the seasons as well, in accordance with the Brāhmaṇa passage.* [20] He should only engage in sexual intercourse wearing the garment reserved for approaching his wife. [21] Let him, moreover, lie with his wife only for the duration of sexual intercourse; [22] after that they should lie separately [23] and afterwards take a bath.

2 [1] Or else, they may cleanse the stains, sip some water, and sprinkle their bodies with water.

Rebirth as Reward and Punishment

[2] People of all classes enjoy supreme and boundless happiness when they follow the Laws specific to them. [3] Then, upon a man's return to earth, by virtue of the residue of his merits he obtains a

high birth, a beautiful body, a fine complexion, strength, intelligence, wisdom, wealth, and an inclination to follow the Law. So, going around like a wheel, he remains happy in both worlds. [4]This is similar to the way the seeds of plants and trees, when they are sown on a well-ploughed field, increase their fruit.

[5]This example explains also the way the fruits of sins increase. [6]When a thief or a heinous sinner (A 1.3.25 n.), whether he is a Brahmin, a Kṣatriya, or a Vaiśya, completes his sojourn in the next world living in an interminable hell, he is born here again—a Brahmin as a Cāṇḍāla, a Kṣatriya as a Paulkasa, and a Vaiśya as a Vaiṇa. [7]In like manner, others, when they fall from their castes as a result of their sinful acts, are born as outcastes in wombs that are the aftermath of their sins.

Penances for Contact with Outcastes

[8]As it is a sin to touch a Cāṇḍāla, so is it to speak to or to look at one. These are the expiations for such offences: [9]for touching, submerging completely in water; for speaking, speaking to a Brahmin; for looking, looking at the heavenly lights.

Food

3 **Preparation of Food** [1]Ārya men who are pure should cook the food intended for the offering to All-gods. [2]The cook should refrain from speaking, coughing, or sneezing while facing the food. [3]Should he touch his hair, body, or garment, he should wash himself with water.

[4]Alternatively, Śūdra men under the supervision of an Ārya may do the cooking. [5]They are to follow the identical procedure of sipping (A 1.16.1–10), [6]with the additional requirement that every day they should shave the hair of their heads, bodies, and beards; clip their nails; [7]and bathe with their clothes on. [8]Alternatively, they may shave only on the eighth day of each fortnight or on new- and full-moon days.

[9]If the food has been prepared by them out of his sight, the householder should place it over the fire and sprinkle it with water. Such food, they say, is pure enough even for gods.

[10]When the food has been prepared, the cook should stand and announce it to his master saying, 'It is done.' [11]The latter responds: 'It is well done, this splendid food! May it never fail!'

Food Offerings [12]The burnt oblations and Bali offerings made with the food of the couple living a household life lead to heaven and prosperity. [13]While the householder is learning the ritual formulas to be used in them, he should sleep on the floor, abstain from sex, and avoid spices and salt for twelve days. [14]While he is learning the ritual formula to be used in the final offering, he should fast for one day.*

[15]The ground where each Bali offering is made should be consecrated. He should sweep the area with his hand, sprinkling water on it, put down the offering, and then sprinkle water all around.

[16]Using the first six ritual formulas, he should offer at each formula an oblation with his hand into the domestic or the cooking fire, [17]and as before sprinkle water all around at the beginning and the end. [18]In like manner, when Bali offerings are made together in a particular place, the sprinkling is done only once at the very end. [19]If there is a sauce, the offerings should be mixed with it.

[20]With the seventh and eighth formulas the offerings should be made behind the fire—the one to the north of the other—; [21]with the ninth formula, near the water-pot; [22]with the tenth and eleventh formulas, in the middle of the house—the one to the east of the other—; [23]and with the last four formulas,* in

4 the north-eastern part of the house. [1]With the ritual formula addressed to Love he makes a Bali offering near the bed; [2]with the formula addressed to mid-space, at the threshold; [3]with the next formula, at the door; [4]and with the formulas that follow, at the seat of Brahman.* [5]With the formula addressed to ancestors he should make an offering towards the south with his upper garment slung over his right shoulder and under his left arm (A 1.6.18 n.) and his hand turned towards the right. [6]The offering to Rudra is to be made towards the north in the same manner as to the gods. [7]In the

case of the last two, the sprinkling around with water is done separately because they follow different rules (*dharma*). [8] The offering thrown in the air is made reciting the last formula, and it is done only at night* (A 2.3.14 n.).

[9] If a man makes these offerings steadfastly in the prescribed manner, he obtains heaven forever, as well as prosperity.

Distribution of Food and Reception of Guests [10] Let him also give a portion of the food as alms. [11] He should always feed his guests first, [12] and then the children, the aged, the sick, and pregnant women. [13] The master and mistress should never rebuff anyone who comes asking for food at the proper time.

> [14] If there is no food, then a place on the floor, some water and straw, and a pleasant welcome—these are never wanting in the house of a good man.

[15] A couple who acts this way wins a world without end.

[16] Let him give water and a seat to a Brahmin who has not studied the Veda but not rise up to greet him. [17] If the man deserves to be greeted, he may rise up to greet him. [18] Neither should he rise to greet a Kṣatriya or a Vaiśya. [19] When a Śūdra comes as a guest, he should get him to do some work and then give him food. [20] Or else, his servants should bring provisions from the royal store and honour the Śūdra as a guest.

Rules of Eating [21] He should always wear an upper garment [22] or, in place of that garment, wear just a cord slung over his left shoulder and under his right arm (A 1.6.18 n.). [23] He should sweep the place where the meal is taken, remove what has fallen down, sprinkle the place with water, scrape the remnants from the cooking pots, mix those remnants with water, and put them down in a clean spot towards the north as an offering for Rudra. In this way the house becomes auspicious.

The Teacher and the Annual Course of Study

[24] Tradition says that only a Brahmin can be a teacher. [25] In times of adversity a Brahmin may study under a Kṣatriya or a Vaiśya

[26] and walk behind him. [27] But after that time the Brahmin shall walk ahead.

5 [1] After commencing the annual study of all the Vedas and the Upaniṣads, vedic recitation is suspended for that day. [2] After completing the vedic study he should not go away immediately. [3] If he is in a hurry to leave, he should do his private vedic recitation in the presence of the teacher and then go as he pleases. In this manner good fortune comes to both.

Conduct towards the Teacher [4] If a teacher comes to visit a pupil of his who has returned home, the pupil should go out to meet him, clasp his feet—and he should not wash afterwards, showing abhorrence for it—make the teacher go ahead, fetch the necessary articles, and pay homage to him in the prescribed manner. [5] When his teacher is present, he should use a seat, bed, food, refreshments, and clothes of lower quality than his teacher's. [6] Standing up and supporting the water pot with his left hand, he should pour water for his teacher to sip; [7] he should do the same for other distinguished guests. [8] He should seek to follow his teacher in rising, sitting, strolling, and smiling. [9] In the presence of his teacher, he should refrain from voiding urine or excrement, breaking wind, speaking in a loud voice, laughing, spitting, cleaning his teeth, blowing his nose, frowning, clapping, and cracking his finger joints, [10] as well as from embracing or speaking to his wife or children tenderly.

[11] He should refrain from interrupting* his teacher [12] or his superiors, [13] and from calumniating and reviling any creature [14] or some Vedas by comparing them unfavourably with another.

[15] If he fails to excel in a particular Veda, let him return to his teacher and, observing the vows, master it.

Rules for a Teacher [16] These are the restrictions that a teacher should observe from the commencement of the annual course of vedic study until its completion. He should abstain from shaving the hair on his body, eating meat, partaking of an ancestral offering, and sexual intercourse. [17] He may optionally have sex with his wife during her season (A 2.1.17 n.). [18] In accordance with the vedic precepts, he should be intent on imparting vedic knowledge to his pupils and on observing the restrictions. If he acts in this manner, he will bring bliss to his ancestors, to his descendants, and to himself. [19] When a man shuns sensual objects with his mind, speech, breath, sight, and hearing, objects to which the skin, the penis, and the stomach cling, he becomes fit for immortality.

6 [1] If he has any doubt about the caste or conduct of someone who has come to him for the sake of the Law, he should kindle the sacred fire and ask him about his caste and conduct. [2] Should the man vouch for his uprightness, the teacher should declare: 'Fire, who sees, Wind, who listens, and Sun, who reveals—they vouch for his uprightness. May he be upright and free from sin', and then set about teaching him.

Reception of Guests

[3] A guest comes blazing like a fire. [4] When someone has studied one branch from each of the Vedas* in accordance with the Law, he is called a 'vedic scholar'. [5] When such a man comes to the home of a householder devoted to the Law proper to him—and he comes for no other purpose than to discharge the Law—then he is called a 'guest'. [6] By paying him homage, the householder obtains peace and heaven.

[7] He should go out to meet the guest, receive him according to his age, and have a seat brought for him—[8] if possible, some say, a seat that has many legs. [9] He should wash the guest's feet. Some say that this should be done by a pair of Śūdras, [10] one of them being employed in pouring the water. [11] He should have water brought for the guest; according to some, in a clay pot. [12] If the guest is a student who has not yet returned home, there is no need to have water brought for him; [13] in his case, however, there is the additional requirement to perform the vedic recitation along with him. [14] After addressing the guest with kind words, the host should refresh him with drinks and food, or at a minimum with some water, [15] and offer him a room, a bed, a mattress, a pillow with a cover, and lotion.

[16] He should summon his cook and give him rice or barley to

be prepared for the guest. [17] When the food has been dished out, he should look at it, thinking: 'Is this portion larger or this?' [18] and make sure to tell the guest: 'Take the larger portion.'

[19] A man should not eat the food of someone whom he hates or who hates him, or of someone who suspects him of a sin or who is suspected of a sin; [20] 'for that man', it is stated, 'eats the other's evil.'

7 [1] This is the sacrifice to Prajāpati that a householder offers incessantly—[2] the fire within the guests* is the offertorial fire, the fire within his house is the householder's fire, the fire used for cooking is the southern fire. [3] A man who eats before his guest eats up the vigour, prosperity, progeny, livestock, sacrifices, and good works of his family. [4] When milk is poured over it, that food is equal to an Agniṣṭoma sacrifice; when ghee is poured over it, it is equal to an Ukthya sacrifice; when honey is poured over it, it is equal to an Atirātra sacrifice; when meat is poured over it, it is equal to a Dvādaśāha sacrifice; and when water is poured over it, it procures the increase of progeny and a long life. [5] 'Whether you hold them dear or not,' it is stated, 'guests lead you to heaven.' [6] When a man gives food in the morning, at noon, and in the evening, they constitute the three pressings of Soma; [7] when he rises as his guest gets up to leave, it constitutes the final rite of the Soma sacrifice; [8] when he addresses the guest with kind words, it constitutes the praise of the priestly fee; [9] when he follows the guest as he leaves, it constitutes the Viṣṇu steps; [10] and when he returns, it constitutes the final bath.*

[11] That is the procedure when a guest comes to a Brahmin.

[12] If a guest comes to a king, he should have the guest treated with greater honour than himself.

[13] If a guest comes to a man who has set up the three ritual fires, he himself should go out to meet the guest and tell him: 'Vrātya, where did you stay? Vrātya, here is water. Vrātya, let this refresh you.' [14] Before offering his daily fire oblation, he should say softly in a hushed voice, 'Vrātya, may you obtain whatever you have set your mind on. Vrātya, may you obtain whatever you wish. Vrātya, may you obtain whatever you like.

Vrātya, may you obtain whatever you desire.' [15] If a guest comes after he has arranged the fires but before he has made the offerings, he himself should go out to meet the guest and tell him: 'Vrātya, give me leave so I may make the offerings.' After he is given leave, he should make the offerings. If he makes the offerings without being given leave, a Brāhmaṇa text states, he commits a sin.

[16] 'By giving shelter to guests for one night,' it is stated, 'a man wins earthly worlds; with a second night he wins intermediate worlds; with a third night heavenly worlds; with a fourth night farthermost worlds; and by giving shelter for an unlimited number of nights, he wins unlimited worlds.'

[17] If an unaccomplished man arrives saying that he is a guest, the householder should give him a seat, water, and food, saying: 'I give this to a vedic scholar.' In this way he will gain prosperity.

8 [1] If a person has already paid his respects to a guest whom he has provided with accommodation, thereafter he does not have to rise up or get off his couch to greet him.

[2] Let him eat what is left over after he has fed his guests. [3] He should not consume all the savoury dishes* in his house so that there is nothing left for his guests [4] or have exquisite dishes prepared for his own use.

[5] A man who is capable of reciting the Veda is worthy of receiving a cow and the honey mixture, [6] as also a teacher, an officiating priest, a bath-graduate, and a king who follows the Law. [7] A cow and the honey mixture are to be given to a teacher, an officiating priest, a father-in-law, and a king, when they visit after the lapse of one year. [8] The honey mixture is made by mixing honey into curd or milk, [9] or, when they are unavailable, into water.

[10] The Veda has six supplements: [11] ritual expositions of the Veda, grammar, astronomy, etymology, phonetics, and metrics. [12] [OBJECTION] The term 'Veda', however, extends to the entire body of traditional texts dealing with rites undertaken on the authority of explicit vedic injunctions or meanings implicit in vedic statements, contradicting thereby the number given above. [13] [ANSWER] Experts in exegesis, on the contrary, are in

agreement that supplementary texts should not be called by the name of the principal texts.*

[14] While he is taking his meal, if at some point he remembers that he has spurned a guest, he should stop eating and fast

9 that day. [1] On the next day he should satisfy that guest to his heart's content and follow him as he leaves.

[2] If a guest has come in a carriage, he should follow him as far as the carriage; [3] others he should follow until they give him leave to return. [4] If a guest forgets to do so, he may turn back at the village boundary.

Distribution of Food [5] He should make all creatures, down to dogs and Cāṇḍālas, partake of the offering to All-gods. [6] Some, however, maintain that he should not give food to unworthy people.

[7] An initiated man should avoid eating the leftover food (A 1.3.27 n.) of women or uninitiated men.

[8] He should pour water before giving any gift; [9] within the sacrificial enclosure, however, he should follow the vedic prescriptions. [10] The rule is that the distribution of food should be carried out in a way that does not cause inconvenience to those who receive food every day. [11] If he wants, he may deprive himself, his wife, or his son, but never his slaves or workers; [12] but he should not deprive himself to such a degree that he is unable to carry out his ritual duties. [13] Now, they also quote:

> A sage's meal is eight mouthfuls, a forest dweller's sixteen, a householder's twenty-two, and a student's an unlimited quantity.
>
> A man who has set up the three ritual fires, a draught ox, and a student—these three are able to do their tasks only if they eat. They cannot do them if they do not eat. (B 2.13.7–8; Va 6.20–1)

10 **Rules about Begging** [1] The appropriate reasons for begging are the following: to pay the teacher, to celebrate a marriage, to perform a sacrifice, trying to support one's parents,

and when a worthy person would have to suspend an obligatory act. [2]In such a case, the householder should investigate the supplicant's qualities and give according to his ability. [3]The gratification of the senses, however, is not an appropriate reason for begging, and he should pay no heed to such requests.

Law with respect to Classes

Lawful Occupations [4]The occupations specific to a Brahmin are studying, teaching, sacrificing, officiating at sacrifices, giving gifts, receiving gifts, inheriting, and gleaning, [5]as well as appropriating things that do not belong to anybody.

[6]The occupations specific to a Kṣatriya are the same, with the exception of teaching, officiating at sacrifices, and receiving gifts, and the addition of meting out punishment and warfare.

[7]The occupations specific to a Vaiśya are the same as those of a Kṣatriya, with the exception of meting out punishment and warfare, and the addition of agriculture, cattle herding, and trade.

[8]A man should neither choose as his officiating priest a man who is not deeply versed in the Veda or haggles over his fees, [9]nor officiate at the sacrifice of a man who does not engage in vedic recitation.

[10]In war, people should conduct themselves according to the strategies taught by those proficient in such matters. [11]Āryas condemn the killing of those who have thrown down their weapons, who have dishevelled hair, who fold their hands in supplication, or who are fleeing.

[12]When those who have been instructed in the precepts go astray because of the weakness of their senses, the preceptor should impose an expiation proportionate to the gravity of the infraction and in accordance with the rules. [13]If a guilty person refuses to follow his orders, he should send him to the king, [14]and the king should send him to his personal priest well versed in Law and Government (A 1.24.23 n.). [15]The latter should compel those who are Brahmins [16]by some forcible means, except corporal punishment and slavery, and reduce them into subjection with penitential acts.

11 [1] With respect to persons belonging to other classes, the king, after he has carefully examined their actions, may impose on them even the capital punishment. [2] If there is a doubt, however, he should not impose a punishment. [3] Only after conducting a careful inquiry, including even the use of ordeals and interrogations, should a king proceed with punishment. [4] A king who behaves in this manner wins both worlds.

Rules of Precedence [5] The road belongs to the king, except when he meets a Brahmin; [6] and when he does, it is to the Brahmin that the road belongs. [7] All must yield to vehicles, people carrying heavy loads, the sick, and women; [8] so also must people of lower classes yield to people of higher classes. [9] For their own well-being, moreover, all must yield to fools, outcastes, drunkards, and madmen.

Rebirth [10] By following the righteous (*dharma*) path people belonging to a lower class advance in their subsequent birth to the next higher class, [11] whereas by following an unrighteous (*adharma*) path people belonging to a higher class descend in their subsequent birth to the next lower class.

Marriage

Marrying a Second Wife [12] So long as his wife participates in religious rites and bears children, a man may not take another wife. [13] If she is wanting in either of these, he may take another prior to establishing his sacred fires, [14] for a wife who participates in the ritual establishment of his sacred fires becomes associated with the rites to which the establishment of the sacred fires is only supplementary.*

Marriage of Daughters [15] He shall not give his daughter in marriage to a man belonging to the same lineage* as he, [16] or to a blood relation of her mother.

Types of Marriage [17] At a 'Brahma' marriage, he should enquire about the groom's family, virtue, learning, and health; adorn the girl with jewellery to the best of his ability; and give her for bearing children, for companionship, and for carrying out rituals. [18] At a 'Seer's' marriage, the bridegroom should give a bull and a cow to the bride's father. [19] At a 'Divine' marriage, the father should give the girl in marriage to the officiating priest during the course of a sacrifice. [20] When a couple in love engages in sexual intercourse, it is a 'Gandharva' marriage.

12 [1] When the groom gives a bride-price to the best of his ability and then marries the girl, it is a 'Demonic' marriage. [2] When a group of men violently overcomes the girl's guardians and carries her away, it is a 'Fiendish' marriage.

[3] Among these, the three enumerated first are the most excellent, and each preceding one is better than the one that follows. [4] The excellence of the marriage determines the excellence of the children that issue from it.

Miscellaneous Rules and Penances

[5] When a Brahmin has touched some place with his hand, no one should step on that spot without first sprinkling it with water. [6] Let him not pass between a fire and a Brahmin, [7] or between Brahmins; [8] he may optionally do so, but only after obtaining their permission.

[9] He should not carry fire and water at the same time [10] and should refrain from mixing together different sorts of fires.* [11] When a fire is being carried towards a person, he should not circumambulate (A 1.7.2 n.) it before it has been placed on the ground. [12] Let him not clasp his hand behind his back.

[13] If the sun sets while a person is asleep, he should remain seated that night, without eating and observing silence. The next morning he should bathe and then break his silence. [14] If the sun rises while a person is asleep, he should remain standing that day, without eating and observing silence. [15] According to some, he should control his breath until he becomes exhausted; [16] he should do so also when he has seen a bad dream, [17] desires to accomplish some objective, [18] or has transgressed some other rule.

[19] When he has a doubt whether the result of an action is evil

or not, he should not do it; [20] the same is true when he has a doubt as to whether it is permitted or not to engage in vedic recitation. [21] Let him not speak about doubtful matters as if they were clear (A 1.32.22–4).

[22] A man who is asleep when the sun sets or rises, or has bad nails or black teeth; a man who marries a younger sister while her older sister remains unmarried or an older sister whose younger sister is already married; a man whose younger brother has set up the ritual fires or performed the Soma sacrifice before him; a man whose younger brother gets married before him; and a man whose younger brother receives his portion of the estate before him or who receives his portion of the estate before his older brother—all these must perform the penances for sins that make a man sordid (A 1.29.17–18), each succeeding offender performing a more severe penance than the preceding. [23] According to some, after performing the required penance, he should get rid of the condition that necessitated it.

Sons

13 [1] When a man has sexual intercourse with his wife during her season (A 2.1.17 n.), a wife who belongs to the same class as he and has not been married before, and whom he has married in the manner prescribed in the scriptures—sons born to him have a claim to follow the occupations of his class, [2] and neither parent may deprive such a son of his share in the estate.

[3] It is a sin to engage in sexual intercourse with a woman who has been married before, or whom he has not married with the proper rites, or who belongs to a different class than he; [4] and a son born from their union undoubtedly participates in their sin.

To Whom Belongs a Son [5] 'A son belongs to the man who fathers him'*—so states a Brāhmaṇa. [6] Now, they also quote:

> Only now, Janaka, have I become jealous about my wives; I was not so formerly. When we are in the abode of Death, they say, a son belongs to the man who fathered him. After he dies, the

> man who deposited the seed takes the son to himself in the abode of Death. People guard their wives, therefore, fearful of the seed of strangers.
>
> Diligently guard this progeny of yours, lest strangers sow their seeds in your field; in the transit to the next world, a son belongs to the man who fathered him. Otherwise a husband makes this progeny of his worthless for himself. (cf. B 2.3.34; Va 17.9)

Law in Previous Times [7] Transgression of the Law and violence are seen among people of ancient times. [8] They incurred no sin on account of their extraordinary power. [9] A man of later times who, observing what they did, does the same, perishes (cf. G 1.3–4).

[10] The custom of donating or selling one's children is not recognized as legitimate. [11] It is said in the Veda that at the time of marriage the groom should voluntarily give a gift to the bride's father in order to fulfil the Law: 'Therefore, the groom should give one hundred cows together with a chariot to the bride's father. The latter should repudiate that gift.' The term 'sale' used in connection with this rite is only a figure of speech, for their union is brought about through the Law (cf. PMS 6.1.15).

Inheritance [12] After gratifying the eldest with a choice portion

14 of wealth, [1] he should, while he is still alive, divide his estate equally among his sons, excluding those who are impotent, mad, or fallen from their caste. [2] If there are no sons, the closest relative belonging to the same ancestry* as the deceased takes his inheritance. [3] If there are no relatives belonging to the same ancestry, his teacher or, if there is no teacher, his student should take the inheritance and use it to perform rituals for the benefit of the deceased. [4] Alternatively, the daughter [5] or, if none of these is available, the king should take the inheritance.

[6] According to some, the eldest son inherits the entire estate. [7] In some regions gold, black cattle, and black produce of the earth* belong to the eldest son. [8] The chariot and the household

furniture belong to the father,* [9] while the jewellery and the money given by her relatives belong to the mother, maintain others. [10] That* is forbidden by the scriptures, [11] for in the Veda we find this statement, which makes no special allowance, 'Manu divided his estate among his sons' (TS 3.1.9.4). [12] [OBJECTION] But we also find in the Veda the statement that posits a single heir, 'Therefore, they invest the eldest son with wealth' (TS 2.5.2.7). [13] [ANSWER] Experts in exegesis, however, maintain that such statements are not injunctions but only reiterate common facts, as in the examples: 'Among domestic animals, therefore, goats and sheep range together'; 'Therefore, the face of a bath-graduate appears to sparkle'; and 'Therefore, a billy goat and a vedic scholar display the greatest desire for a mate.'* [14] The reason is that all sons who live righteously are entitled to inherit. [15] He should, on the contrary, disinherit a son who uses the wealth in unrighteous ways, even if he is the eldest.

[16] There is no division of property between a husband and a wife, [17] because from the time of their marriage they are linked together in performing religious rites, [18] as also in receiving the rewards of their meritorious deeds [19] and in acquiring wealth; [20] for while the husband is away people do not consider it a theft for the wife to make a gift when the occasion demands.

Family and Regional Customs

15 [1] The above principle resolves issues relating to customs of regions and families.*

Observances at the Death of a Relative

[2] Blood relations of the mother and relations of the father up to the sixth degree (A 2.14.2 n.), or as far back as the relationship is known—when any of these dies, one should bathe, unless the deceased is a child less than one year old, [3] in which case only its parents [4] and those who carry the corpse need to bathe.

[5] At the death of a wife or a principal elder,* people should fast from the time of death until the same time the next day [6] and display the signs of mourning: [7] the mourners should dishevel

and throw dust on their hair, wear a single garment, face the south, submerge themselves once in the water, come out of the water, and sit down. [8] They should repeat this three times. [9] They should pour out water in such a way that the deceased recognizes it, then return to the village without looking back, and do whatever else the women ask them to do.* [10] Some prescribe these same observances also at the death of other relatives.

Ritual Food Offerings [11] At all rituals one should feed individuals who are upright and learned in the Vedas. [12] He should offer gifts in proper places, at appropriate times, on the occasion of purificatory rites, and to proper recipients.

[13] He should not eat food from which a portion has not been first offered in the fire or given to a guest. [14] Food containing spices or salt cannot be used for a burnt offering, [15] as also when it is mixed with some other inferior food. [16] When he offers a burnt offering of food unfit to be offered, he should take out some hot ashes from the northern side of the fire and offer it in those ashes. In this way the offering takes place, but it is not offered in the fire.

[17] A woman should not make an offering in the fire, [18] nor should a man who has not been initiated.

Impurity of Children [19] Children do not become impure until the first feeding with solid food has taken place; [20] according to some, until they have completed one year; [21] or until they are able to distinguish the cardinal points; [22] or until they have undergone initiation, which is the superior position, [23] for it is through this that they come under the jurisdiction of the scriptures. [24] This last view is the authoritative one, [25] and it is the traditional teaching.*

Ancestral Offerings

16 [1] In ancient times gods and men used to live together in this world. Then the gods went to heaven by performing rites, while men were left behind.* Those among them who perform rites in the same manner get to dwell in that world together with the gods and Brahman. For this purpose Manu proclaimed

this rite bearing the name 'Ancestral Offering'; [2]he did that also for the prosperity of the people. [3]In this rite the ancestors are the deity to whom the offering is made, while the Brahmins stand in the place of the offertorial fire.*

Time [4]It is to be offered every month. [5]An afternoon in the fortnight of the waning moon is preferable, [6]as also the last days of the fortnight of the waning moon.

[7]No matter what day of the fortnight of the waning moon it is offered, it gives delight to the ancestors. The specific reward earned by the performer, however, depends on the time that he offers it. [8]If he offers it on the first day, his children will turn out to be mostly girls; [9]on the second day, his children will not turn out to be thieves; [10]on the third day, his children will be eminent in vedic knowledge; [11]on the fourth day, he will become rich in small animals; [12]on the fifth day, his children will turn out to be boys, and he will have a lot of offspring and not die childless; [13]on the sixth day, he will be adept at travelling and gambling; [14]on the seventh day, he will be successful in agriculture; [15]on the eighth day, he will become prosperous; [16]on the ninth day, he will acquire one-hoofed animals; [17]on the tenth day, he will be successful in business; [18]on the eleventh day, he will acquire iron, tin, and lead; [19]on the twelfth day, he will become rich in cattle; [20]on the thirteenth day, he will have many sons and friends, and his children will be beautiful but die young; [21]on the fourteenth day, he will be successful in battle; [22]and on the fifteenth day, he will become prosperous.

Types of Food [23]The materials used in this rite are sesame and beans, rice and barley, water, roots, and fruits. [24]When the food is made greasy (cf. A 2.19.17–20), however, the gratification it gives the ancestors is more ample and lasts longer, [25]as also when one gives righteously (*dharma*) acquired wealth to a worthy person. [26]With cow's meat their gratification lasts for a year, [27]and even longer than that with buffalo meat. [28]This rule makes clear that the meat of domestic and wild animals
17 is fit to be offered. [1]With the meat of a rhinoceros offered on a rhinoceros skin, their gratification lasts an

unlimited time, [2] as also with the flesh of the Śatabali fish [3] and the Vārdhrāṇasa crane.

Quality of Invitees [4] Pure and with a composed mind and firm resolve, he should feed Brahmins well versed in the Vedas, Brahmins who are not related to him by blood or lineage, or by a relationship established by sacrifice or pupillage.* [5] But if outsiders lack the required qualities, he should feed a man who possesses them, be it his own full brother. [6] This rule clarifies the issue also with respect to pupils.

[7] Now, they also quote:

> [8] Feeding-one-another is the name of almsfood given to ghouls. It reaches neither ancestors nor gods. Bereft of merit, it wanders in this very world, like a cow, her calf dead, wandering among the corrals.

[9] The meaning is: gifts of food that are eaten by one another, going from one house to the other, perish in this very world. [10] Among those possessing equal qualities, an older person is better, as also a poor person who desires to attend.

Procedure [11] On the day before the rite he issues the invitations to the Brahmins, [12] and the next day he issues a second invitation. [13] The third invitation consists of summoning them. [14] Some assert that everything at an ancestral offering is repeated three times: [15] everything is repeated a second and a third time exactly as it was done the first time.

[16] After all the offerings have been made, he should cut off portions from all and eat a tiny lump of the remainder in the prescribed manner. [17] It is the custom of northerners, however, to pour water taken from the water pot into the hands of the seated Brahmins (see p. xxvii).

[18] He addresses them: 'Let me take out some food. Let me offer it in the fire.' [19] 'Take it out as you wish. Offer it in the fire as you wish.' After he has been given leave in this manner, he should take it out and offer it in the fire.

[20] Letting dogs or degraded people (A 1.3.25 n.) look at an ancestral offering is condemned. [21] A leper, a bald man, an

adulterer, and a son of a Brahmin soldier or of a Śūdra by a Brahmin woman—these, when they eat at an ancestral offering, defile those alongside whom they eat.* [22] A man who knows the three 'Honey' verses, a man who knows the Trisuparṇa, an expert in the three Nāciketa fire altars, an expert in the four types of sacrifices, a man who maintains the five sacred fires,* a man who sings the Jyeṣṭha Sāmans, a man who recites the Veda, a son of a vedic savant, and a vedic scholar—these, when they eat at an ancestral offering, purify those alongside whom they eat.

[23] An ancestral offering should not be performed after nightfall, [24] and once it is started the performer should not eat until it is completed; [25] the only exception being when there is a lunar eclipse.*

18 **Prohibitions** [1] He should abstain from the following: butter, butter-milk, oil-cake, honey, meat, [2] black grain, food given by Śūdras or by others whose food one is forbidden to eat, [3] food unfit for sacrifice, lying, anger, and whatever would provoke someone to anger. From these twelve a man should abstain, if he desires a good memory, fame, intelligence, heaven, and prosperity.

[4] Wrapping a cloth around himself from navel to knees, he should bathe at dawn, noon, and dusk; live on uncooked food; never seek a shady spot; and remain standing during the day and seated at night. He should keep this vow for a year. This is said to be equal to the forty-eight-year vow.*

Daily Ancestral Offering [5] Next, the daily ancestral offering. [6] Men who are upright should cook the food at a clean spot outside the village. [7] New vessels are used for this purpose, [8] both the vessels in which the food is cooked and those out of which it is eaten. [9] And he should give them away to those who have partaken of the meal. [10] He should feed only individuals who possess the required qualities [11] and not give any leftover food to anyone who does not possess the same qualities. [12] He should do this for a year. [13] The last of these offerings should be made with the meat of a red goat. [14] He should have a screened altar constructed [15]and feed the Brahmins on its northern side. [16]They point out that in this way he sees both the Brahmins eating and his ancestors gathered at the altar.* [17]Thereafter, he may either continue to do it or stop, [18]for the ancestors let him know that the ancestral offering has satisfied them.

Rite for Prosperity [19]A man who wants to be prosperous should,
19 on the day of the constellation Tiṣya,* [1]get some white mustard seeds made into powder, rub it on his hands, feet, face, and ears, and eat it. Then, if there is no strong wind, he should sit on a seat—the first preference is that it be the skin of a billy goat—and eat in silence facing the south. [2]They point out, however, that when a man eats facing in that direction his mother's life is shortened. [3]The vessel for eating is made of copper, with its centre gilded with gold, [4]and no one else should eat from it. [5]He should make a lump small enough to be swallowed [6]without dropping any fragments on the ground. [7]Then, without keeping the bowl down [8]or after putting it down, [9]he should swallow the whole lump by pushing it into the mouth with his thumb, [10]not making any sound with his mouth [11]or shaking his hand. [12]After he has sipped water, he should keep his hands raised so long as they are dripping [13]and then hold them over the fire. [14]During the day, moreover, he should not eat anything besides roots and fruits [15]and avoid sacrificial milk-rice or food offered to gods or ancestors. [16]He should eat wearing his upper garment over his left shoulder and under his right arm (A 1.6.18 n.).

Monthly Ancestral Offering [17]The obligatory ancestral offering, however, should be made only with greasy food. [18]The first alternative is to use ghee and meat, [19]but when these are unavailable sesame oil and vegetables may be used. [20]During the constellation Maghā (A 2.18.19 n.), moreover, he should use a greater amount of ghee when feeding Brahmins according to the rules of ancestral offerings.

20 [1]At a monthly ancestral offering he should use one measure each* of sesame seeds in whatever manner he is

able. [2]He should feed only individuals who possess the required qualities, and not give any leftover food to anyone who does not possess the same qualities.

Rite for Prosperity [3]A man who wants to be prosperous should fast for at least one night during a fortnight of the waxing moon falling within the half-year when the sun moves north; on a day of the constellation Tiṣya (A 2.18.19 n.) prepare a milk-rice oblation; make an offering of that in the fire to the Great King;* feed a Brahmin with that milk-rice mixed with ghee; and get him to proclaim success with a formula signifying prosperity.

[4]He should repeat this every day until the next Tiṣya day. [5]During the second Tiṣya cycle he should feed two Brahmins, [6]and during the third, three Brahmins. [7]By increasing the number in this manner for a whole year, [8]he will attain great prosperity. [9]The fast takes place only at the very beginning.

Miscellaneous Rules [10]He should refrain from eating foods whose essence has been extracted (G 9.58); [11]standing on ashes or grain husks; [12]washing the feet by rubbing one foot with the other; placing one foot on the other; [13]swinging the feet; [14]placing one foot over the other knee; [15]making noises by striking the nails against each other; [16]cracking the finger joints without a good reason; [17]and other acts that are forbidden.

[18]He should be a man who applies himself to acquiring wealth in righteous (*dharma*) ways, [19]distributes it to worthy people, [20]gives not to unworthy people if they pose no threat to him, [21]conciliates people, [22]and enjoys pleasures that are not forbidden by the Law. [23]In this manner he wins both worlds.

ORDERS OF LIFE

21 [1]There are four orders of life:* the householder's life, living at the teacher's house, the life of a sage, and that of a forest hermit. [2]If a man remains steadfast in any of these, he attains bliss. [3]A common prerequisite for all is to live at the teacher's house following one's initiation, [4]and all are required not to abandon vedic learning. [5]After he has learnt the rites, he may undertake the order that he prefers.

Student

[6] Following the rules of a novice student,* a student should serve his teacher until death, leaving his body in his teacher's house.

Wandering Ascetic

[7] Next, the wandering ascetic. [8] From that very state,* remaining chaste, he goes forth. [9] With regard to him they admonish:

> [10] He should live as a silent sage, without fire or house, without shelter or protection.

Speaking only when he is engaged in private vedic recitation and obtaining food from a village to sustain himself, he should live without any concern for this world or the next. [11] Discarded clothes are prescribed for him. [12] Some say that he should go completely naked. [13] Abandoning truth and falsehood, pleasure and pain, the Vedas, this world and the next, he should seek the Self. [14] When he gains insight, he attains bliss.

[15] But that is contradicted by the scriptures. [16] If a man attains bliss when he gains insight, moreover, he should not feel pain in this very world. [17] This clarifies what will be said later on.*

Forest Hermit

[18] Next, the forest hermit. [19] From that very state (A 2.21.8 n.), remaining chaste, he goes forth. [20] With regard to him they admonish:

> [21] He should live as a silent sage with a single fire, but without house, shelter, or protection.

Let him speak only when he is engaged in private vedic recitation.

22 [1] Clothes made of materials from the wild are prescribed for him.

[2] Thereafter, he should roam about, living on roots, fruits, leaves, and grasses, [3] and finally on what he happens to find lying about. [4] After that he should sustain himself on water, air,

and space. [5]Among these, each subsequent pursuit is more exceptional in terms of its reward.

[6]Now, some teach an orderly sequence limited to the forest hermit. [7]After completing his vedic studies, a man should marry a wife, set up the sacred fires, and begin to perform the rites taught in the Vedas, at a minimum the Soma sacrifice. [8]Then he should build a dwelling outside the village and live there either with his wife, children, and sacred fires, [9]or alone. [10]He should live by gleaning [11]and from that time onwards never accept gifts. [12]Only after he has bathed should he offer oblations in the fire. [13]He should enter the water slowly and bathe facing the sun, without splashing. [14]This procedure of bathing is applicable to all.

[15]Some say that he should prepare two sets of utensils for cooking and eating, as well as two sets of knives, axes, sickles, and mallets. [16]He should give one* of the two sets, take the other, and set out to the wilderness. [17]From then on he should use only wild produce to offer fire sacrifices, to sustain himself, to attend to guests, and to clothe himself. [18]He should use rice porridge in rites that call for cakes. [19]And he should recite everything, including his private vedic recitation, in an inaudible voice, [20]never permitting wild animals to hear him. [21]He should have a shelter only for his sacred fires, [22]while he himself lives in the open [23]sitting and sleeping on the bare ground.* [24]When he has obtained a new stock of grain, he should get rid of the old.

23 [1]Alternatively, if he desires greater severity, he should gather food with his bowl each and every day both in the morning and in the evening. [2] Thereafter, he should roam about, living on roots, fruits, leaves, and grasses, and finally on what he happens to find lying about. After that he should sustain himself on water, air, and space. Among these, each subsequent pursuit is more exceptional in terms of its reward.

Superiority among Orders

[3][VIEW OF OPPONENTS] Now, they quote a couple of verses from a Purāṇa:

> [4]The eighty thousand seers who desired offspring went along the sun's southern course. They obtained cremation grounds.
>
> [5]The eighty thousand seers who did not desire offspring went along the sun's northern course. They, indeed, attained immortality.

[6]Such is the praise of those who live celibate lives. [7]And further, these are men who make whatever they want happen by their mere thought, [8]for example, producing rain, bestowing children, seeing what is far away, moving as quickly as thought, and others of this sort. [9]Therefore, on the basis of vedic testimony and visible results, some claim that these orders of life are superior.

[10][AUTHOR'S VIEW] It is the firm view of the most eminent scholars of the triple Veda, however, that the Vedas are the ultimate authority. The rites using rice, barley, animals, ghee, milk, and potsherds and involving the participation of the wife that are prescribed in the Vedas must be performed with the loud and soft recitation of ritual formulas, they hold, and any practice opposed to those rites is devoid of authority. [11]With regard to the statement about 'cremation grounds', on the other hand, that passage enjoins the funerary rites at the death of those who have performed many sacrifices. [12]Thereafter, the Vedas declare, they obtain an eternal reward designated by the term 'heaven'.

24 [1]The scriptures declare, moreover, that immortality consists of offspring: 'In your offspring you are born again. That, O mortal, is your immortality' (TB 1.5.5.6). [2]Furthermore, we can see with our very eyes that the son is a distinct clone of the father himself. One can even see that they are identical, only the bodies are distinct. [3]And the sons, as they continue to perform the prescribed rites, increase the fame and heavenly life of their departed ancestors. [4]Each subsequent generation does the same for those that preceded it. [5]They dwell in heaven until the dissolution of creation. [6]'At the new creation, they serve as the seed', says the Bhaviṣyat Purāṇa. [7]And there is also the declaration of Prajāpati:

> [8] Study of the triple Veda, studentship, procreation, faith, austerity, sacrifice, giving gifts—those who perform these dwell with us. Anyone who praises other things becomes dust and perishes.

[9] If any of the children commit sins, they alone perish, like the leaf of a tree. They do not harm their ancestors. [10] As in this world a parent is not tied to the actions of his children, so in the next world he is not tied to the results of their actions. [11] This principle is illustrated by the following fact. [12] This creation is the work of Prajāpati and the seers. [13] We see the bodies of those seers who have done meritorious deeds shining brilliantly far above.*

[14] It may well be that someone, through a portion of his accumulated merits or by means of austerity, attains a limited world together with his body and even makes what he wants happen by his mere thought. But that is no reason to make one order of life superior to another.

KING

25 [1] We have explained the general and specific Laws of all the classes. We will now present specifically the Laws pertaining to a king.

Royal Fort

[2] He should have a residence and a fort constructed, with their gates facing the south. [3] The residence is within the fort, [4] and in front of the residence is the lodge, which is known as the Audience Hall. [5] To the south of the fort is the assembly hall with doors on both the south and the north sides so that one can see what goes on within and without.

Duties [6] In every one of these buildings fires should be kept burning continuously, [7] and every day offerings should be made in these fires in the same manner as at the domestic ritual.

[8] The king should put up in the lodge at least those guests who are vedic scholars. [9] They should be given accommodation, as well as beds, food, and drink, in accordance with their distinction.

[10] The king should not live more opulently than his elders (A 1.6.32 n.) and ministers. [11] And in his realm no one should suffer from hunger, illness, cold, or heat, either through want or by design.

Gambling [12] In the middle of the assembly hall he should erect a gaming table, sprinkle it with water, and place there dice—they should be in pairs, of Vibhītaka seeds,* and in adequate numbers. [13] Āryas who are upright and honest may gamble there.

[14] Weapons contests, dancing, singing, and concerts should not be held without the presence of royal officials.

Protection of Subjects

[15] A king provides protection only when there is no fear of

26 thieves in the villages or wild tracts of his realm. [1] If he gives land and wealth to Brahmins according to their worth without depriving his own dependants, he will win eternal worlds. [2] When a king is killed attempting to recover property stolen from Brahmins, they call it a sacrifice at which his own body serves as the sacrificial post and an unlimited amount is given as the sacrificial fee. [3] This explanation covers also other heroes who sacrifice their lives fighting for a just cause.

Appointment of Security Officers [4] To protect his subjects he should appoint over villages and towns Āryas who are upright and honest. [5] Their subordinates should also be men possessing the very same qualities. [6] They must protect a town from thieves up to nine miles* on all sides, [7] and a village up to a couple of miles.* [8] They must be forced to make good anything that is stolen within those limits.

Collection of Taxes

[9]The king should get them to collect lawful taxes. [10]The following persons are exempt from taxes: vedic scholars, [11]women of all classes, [12]pre-pubescent boys, [13]those who are living in someone's house for the purpose of study, [14]ascetics devoted to the Law, [15]Śūdras who are personal servants, [16]people who are blind, dumb, deaf, and sick, [17]and those who are excluded from acquiring property.

Sexual Misconduct

Rape [18]If a young man all primped up barges accidentally into the presence of another man's wife or a young woman, he should be verbally reprimanded; [19]but if he does so deliberately and with a malicious intent, he should be punished. [20]If intercourse took place, his penis should be cut off along with the testicles. [21]If it was with a young woman, he should be banished and his property confiscated. [22]Thereafter, the king should support those women [23]and from then onwards guard them from sexual congress. [24]If they agree to perform the expiation, however, he should hand them over to their respective guard-
27 ians. [1]Once the expiation has been performed, the guardians should treat them as before, for their relationship is based on the Law.

Levirate [2]'A man should not introduce to an outsider the woman who has assumed his lineage (A 2.11.15 n.), [3]for a wife is given to the family'—so they admonish. [4]That is now forbidden because of the weakness of the flesh, [5]for with respect to the husband all are equally outsiders. [6]When this is violated, both husband and wife will undoubtedly end up in hell, [7]for the happiness resulting from following this restriction is far greater than that resulting from children obtained by following that custom.

Adultery [8]An Ārya who has sex with a Śūdra woman should be banished, [9]while a Śūdra who has sex with an Ārya woman should be executed, [10]and that wife of his should be emaciated.

[11]If a man has sex once with a married woman of his own class, they say, the punishment is one-quarter of what is prescribed for one fallen from his caste. [12]Each time he repeats it, likewise, one-quarter is added, [13]and the fourth time he gets the full punishment.

Crime and Punishment

[14]If a Śūdra hurls abusive words at a virtuous Ārya, his tongue shall be cut out. [15]If, while he is speaking, walking on the road, lying in bed, or occupying a seat, a Śūdra pretends to be equal to Āryas, he should be flogged. [16]If a Śūdra kills a man, steals, or appropriates land, he should be executed and his property confiscated.

[17]If a Brahmin is guilty of these crimes, however, he should be blindfolded.* [18]Alternatively, those who transgress their specific duties should be kept in secret confinement [19]until they relent. [20]If they do not relent, they should be banished. [21]A teacher, an officiating priest, a bath-graduate, and the king may save him from punishment, except in the case of a capital crime.

28 [1]If someone takes a piece of land on lease and it produces no harvest because he puts no effort into it, then, if he has the means, he should be made to pay the landowner what would have been his due. [2]An indentured farmhand who quits working should be flogged; [3]so also a herdsman, [4]and his flock should be impounded. [5]If cattle escape from the corral and begin to eat the crops, one may emaciate them but not abuse them. [6]If someone takes charge of cattle and lets them die or become lost, he should pay restitution to the owners.

[7]If someone sees cattle that have been carelessly allowed to wander into the wilderness, he should bring them to the village and return them to their owners. [8]If such negligence happens again, he should return them after first impounding them, [9]and thereafter he should ignore them.

[10]If someone unknowingly takes the property of another, such as fuel, water, roots, flowers, fruits, perfume, fodder, or vegetables, he should be verbally reprimanded. [11]If he does so

knowingly, his clothes should be taken away. [12] Even if it is done intentionally, no one should be punished for taking food to save his life.

[13] If the king fails to inflict punishment when it is called for, the sin recoils upon him.

29 [1] Those who direct, those who consent, and those who carry out an act share in its fruit, whether it is heaven or hell, [2] but those who are more closely involved with the act receive a larger share of the fruit.

Marital Property

[3] The husband and wife have joint control over their property. [4] With their consent and for their benefit, others also may tend to it.

Judicial Process

[5] Men who are learned, of good family, elderly, wise, and unwavering in their duties shall adjudicate lawsuits, [6] in doubtful cases investigating the matter by examining the evidence and using ordeals.

Witnesses [7] In the morning of an auspicious day and in the presence of a blazing fire, water, and the king, both sides should be asked to present their case and, with everyone's approval, the chief witness should answer the questions truthfully. [8] Should he answer untruthfully, the king should punish him; [9] and in addition hell awaits him after death. [10] Should he answer truthfully, he will go to heaven and all beings will sing his praises.

CONCLUSION OF THE STUDY OF LAW

[11] The knowledge found among women and Śūdras forms the conclusion, [12] and they point out that it is a subsidiary component of the Atharva Veda.

[13] It is difficult to gain mastery of the Law by means of scriptures alone, but by acting according to the markers one can master it. [14] And the markers in this case are as follows: he

should model his conduct after that which is unanimously approved in all regions by Āryas who have been properly trained, who are elderly and self-possessed, and who are neither greedy nor deceitful. In this way he will win both worlds (= A 1.20.8–9; cf. TU 1.11.4).

15 According to some, one should learn the remaining Laws from women and people of all classes.

That concludes the Āpastamba Dharmasūtra.

The Dharmasūtra of Gautama

THE Dharmasūtra of Gautama has come down as a separate treatise without any connection to a larger Kalpasūtra. Traditionally, Gautama has been associated with the Sāmaveda. This connection is supported, among other factors, by the fact that the twenty-sixth chapter on penance is taken from the Sāmavidhāna Brāhmaṇa belonging to the Sāmaveda. The Dharmasūtra does not contain the *praśna* (Book) division found in the texts forming part of the Kalpasūtras. Its division into chapters resembles the internal division of the later Smṛtis. There are two extant commentaries on Gautama by Maskarin and Haradatta. Maskarin can be assigned to 900–1000 CE and is therefore older than Haradatta, who also commented on Āpastamba. It appears that Haradatta has made extensive use of Maskarin's commentary, a usage that would amount to plagiarism if it was done today.

CONTENTS

SOURCES OF LAW

1 [1]The source of Law is the Veda, [2]as well as the tradition (A 2.15.25 n.) and practice of those who know the Veda.

[3]Transgression of the Law and violence are seen in great men. They do not constitute precedents, however, on account of the weakness of the men of later times (cf. A 2.13.7–9).

[4]When injunctions of equal force are in conflict with each other, there is an option.*

THE STUDENT

Time of Initiation

[5]A Brahmin's initiation shall be performed in his eighth year, [6]or, if performed with an objective in mind, in his ninth or fifth year. [7]The years are counted from conception.

[8]The initiation is a second birth (A 1.1.16–18 n.). [9]The teacher is the man from whom one receives initiation [10]or instruction in the Veda.

[11]A Kṣatriya's initiation shall be performed in his eleventh year, and a Vaiśya's in his twelfth.

[12]In the case of a Brahmin, the time for the Sāvitrī does not elapse until the sixteenth year, [13]in the case of a Kṣatriya until the twenty-second year, [14]and in the case of a Vaiśya until two years after that (see A 1.1.28 f).

A Student's Code of Conduct

Insignia [15]Their girdles are a cord of Muñja grass, a bowstring of Mūrvā, or a cord of thread, respectively; [16]and their skins are that of a black antelope, a spotted Ruru antelope, and a billy goat, respectively. [17]The garments of all students, irrespective of class, are made of hemp, flax, tree bark, or a woollen blanket, [18]or else of raw cotton; [19]some even allow dyed cotton—[20]dyed with tree resin for a Brahmin, [21] and with madder and turmeric for the other two, respectively.

[22] A Brahmin's staff is made of wood-apple or Palāśa wood, [23] and those of the other two of banyan and Pīlu wood, respectively. [24] Alternatively, for all students, irrespective of class, the staff may be made of any wood suitable for use in a sacrifice. [25] Staffs should be undamaged, bent in the manner of a sacrificial post,* and have their barks intact. [26] They should reach the crown of the head, the forehead, and the tip of the nose, respectively, for each class.

[27] Students may shave their heads completely, wear their hair matted, or keep just the topknot matted.

Purification [28] If, while holding something in his hand, he happens to become impure, he should sip water without laying it down.*

[29] The cleansing of things—articles made of metal, clay, wood, and cloth are cleaned by scrubbing, scorching, scraping, and washing, respectively. [30] Stone, gem, shell, and mother-of-pearl are cleaned in the same way as metal; [31] bone and mud, in the same way as wood—[32] mud also by plastering; [33] and ropes, wicker, and skin, in the same way as cloth. [34] Articles that have become extremely unclean, on the other hand, should be thrown away.

[35] He should commence his personal purification facing either the east or the north. [36] Seated on a clean spot, placing his right arm between his knees, and wearing his upper garment over his left shoulder and under his right arm (A 1.6.18 n.), he should wash both his hands up to the wrists. Then, he should silently sip three or four times an amount of water sufficient to reach his heart (A 1.16.2 n.), wipe his lips twice, sprinkle water on his feet, rub water on the cavities of his head,* and place his hand on the crown of his head. [37] After sleeping, eating, and sneezing, he should sip water over again.

[38] Bits of food sticking between the teeth are like the teeth themselves, unless they are touched with the tongue [39] or, according to some, until they get detached.

[40] When they get detached, a person should

know that he is cleansed of them by simply swallowing, just like saliva.

[41] Saliva spattering from the mouth does not make a man impure unless it falls on his body.

[42] In the case of filthy substances, purification consists in removing their stains and smell [43] by washing first with water and then with earth and water,* [44] which is done also when urine, excrement, or semen falls on a person, or when one is stained with the remnants of food.

[45] In cases covered by vedic rules, purification is carried out in the manner prescribed in the Veda.*

Rules of Study [46] Clasping the teacher's left hand—excluding the thumb—with his right, the pupil should address the teacher: 'Teach, Sir!' [47] Focusing his eyes and mind on the teacher, [48] the pupil should touch his vital organs* with Darbha grass, [49] control his breath three times for fifteen morae each, [50] and sit on a bed of grass with the tips of their blades pointing east. [51] The five Calls should begin with OṂ and end with 'Truth'.*

[52] The pupil shall clasp the teacher's feet each morning [53] and also when he begins and ends his vedic recitation. [54] When he is given permission, he should sit at the teacher's right facing the east or the north. [55] And he should repeat after the teacher the Sāvitrī verse [56] when he first begins to receive instruction in the Veda, [57] while the syllable OṂ should be recited also at other times.

[58] If someone passes between the teacher and the pupil, this preparatory ceremony should be repeated. [59] If a dog, a mongoose, a snake, a frog, or a cat passes between them, he should observe a fast for three days and spend some time away from the teacher's house, [60] whereas if it is some other animal, he should control his breath and consume some ghee. [61] He shall do the same if he happens to recite the Veda in a cemetery.

2 **Uninitiated Children** [1] Before his initiation, a child may behave, speak, and eat as he pleases. He may not partake of ritual offerings and should observe chastity. He may void urine and excrement whenever he has the urge. [2] The set of rules

regarding sipping water and other rituals of purification do not apply to him, other than wiping, washing, and sprinkling with water, [3] and no one is made impure by his touch. [4] No one should ever employ him to make fire oblations or Bali offerings, [5] and he should not be made to recite the Veda, except for uttering 'Svadhā'.

General Rules [6] Restrictive rules come into force from the time a person is initiated. [7] The rule of chastity has already been given. [8] He shall put wood into the sacred fire, beg his food, speak the truth, bathe—[9] only after the beard-shaving rite, according to some—,* [10] and perform the twilight worship outside the village.

[11] Controlling his speech, he should remain standing during the morning twilight worship from the time the stars are still visible until the sun comes into view, and remain seated during the evening from the time the sun is still visible until the stars come into view, [12] without ever gazing directly at the sun.

[13] He should abstain from the following: eating honey and meat; wearing perfumes and necklaces; sleeping during the day; applying oil and collyrium; travelling in carriages; using shoes and umbrellas; lust, anger, greed, perplexity, and squabbling; playing musical instruments; bathing and cleaning the teeth (A 1.2.28 n.); excitement, dancing, singing, calumny, and dangers; [14] wrapping his neck; sitting cross-legged, leaning against something, or stretching out his feet within sight of his elders; [15] spitting, laughing, yawning, and cracking his fingers; [16] looking at or touching a woman if there is a hint of sexual intimacy; [17] gambling, degrading services, taking what is not given, and causing injury to living beings; [18] uttering the names of his teacher, the teacher's sons and wives, and of persons consecrated for a sacrifice; [19] and speaking harsh words. [20] If he is a Brahmin, he should always abstain from liquor.

[21] He shall occupy a bed and seat lower than his teacher's, get up before and go to bed after him, [22] and keep his tongue, arms, and stomach under strict control.

Conduct towards the Teacher [23] He should utter the personal and lineage names (A 2.11.15 n.) of his teacher with respect [24] and behave in the same manner towards revered people and his superiors. [25] He should answer his teacher after getting up from his bed or seat [26] and go to him when he calls, even if he is out of sight. [27] If he sees his teacher standing or sitting on a lower place or answering the call of nature, he should get up. [28] If the teacher is walking, he should walk behind him, apprising him of the things to be done and reporting to him what has been done. [29] Let him recite the Veda only when he is called upon to do so [30] and apply himself to doing what is pleasing and beneficial to his teacher.

[31] He shall behave in the same manner towards his teacher's wife and sons, [32] with the exception of eating their leftovers (A 1.3.27 n.), assisting them with their bath or dressing, and washing, rubbing, or clasping their feet. [33] When he returns from a journey, he should clasp the feet of his teacher's wives; [34] some maintain that a pupil who has reached the legal age* should not do so in the case of young wives.

Food [35] Almsfood may be obtained from people of all classes, excepting heinous sinners (A 1.3.25 n.) and outcastes. [36] The word 'Madam' should be placed at the beginning, middle, or end of the request, respectively, according to the class (A 1.3.28–30 n.). [37] If he does not receive any elsewhere, he may beg from the house of his teacher, a relative, or an elder (A 1.6.32 n.), or from his own house; [38] let him, however, avoid having to beg from ones given earlier in the list.

[39] He should eat the almsfood after announcing it to his teacher and with his permission, [40] and, in the absence of the teacher, to his wife or son, or to a fellow student or a virtuous person. [41] Placing some water at his side, let him eat silently and contentedly, but without craving.

Punishment [42] A pupil shall be disciplined without resorting to corporal punishment, [43] or, if that is not viable, with a slender rope or cane. [44] If the teacher strikes with anything else, the king should punish him.

Conclusion of Study [45] To study a single Veda, he should live as a student for twelve years, [46] and to study all the Vedas, twelve years each [47] or until he has grasped them.

[48] After completing his studies, he should present the teacher with a gift. [49] After he has done that or after obtaining the teacher's permission, he may take the concluding bath.

[50] The teacher is the foremost of his elders (A 1.6.32 n.); [51] according to some, the mother.

ORDERS OF LIFE

Argument of Opponents

3 [1] He* has a choice, some assert, among the orders of life: [2] student, householder, mendicant, or anchorite (A 2.21.1 n.). [3] The householder is their source, because the others do not produce offspring.

Student [4] Among these, the rules of a student have already been given (A 2.21.6 n.). [5] He shall remain subject to his teacher until death [6] and pray softly (A 1.15.1 n.) during any time that remains after attending to his teacher's business. [7] When his teacher is no more, he should serve his son; [8] and if there is no son, an older fellow student or the sacred fire. [9] A man who conducts himself in this manner attains the world of Brahman and becomes a man who has mastered his senses.

[10] All these rules of a student apply to people in subsequent orders as well, so long as they are not inconsistent with the provisions specific to each.

Mendicant [11] A mendicant shall live without any possessions, [12] be chaste, [13] and remain in one place during the rainy season.* [14] Let him enter a village only to obtain almsfood [15] and go on his begging round late in the evening, without visiting the same house twice [16] and without pronouncing blessings. [17] He shall control his speech, sight, and actions; [18] and wear a garment to cover his private parts, [19] using, according to some, a discarded piece of cloth after washing it. [20] He should not pick any part of a plant or a tree unless it has fallen of itself. [21] Outside the rainy season, he should not spend two nights in the same village. [22] He shall be shaven-headed or wear a topknot; [23] refrain from injuring seeds; [24] treat all creatures alike, whether they cause him harm or treat him with kindness; [25] and not undertake ritual activities.

Anchorite [26] An anchorite shall live in the forest, living on roots and fruits and given to austerities. [27] He kindles the sacred fire according to the procedure for recluses* [28] and refrains from eating what is grown in a village. [29] He shall pay homage to gods, ancestors, humans, spirits, and seers [30] and entertain guests from all classes, except those who are proscribed. [31] He may also avail himself of the flesh of animals killed by predators. [32] He should not step on ploughed land [33] or enter a village. [34] He shall wear matted hair and clothes of bark or skin [35] and never eat anything that has been stored for more than a year.

Author's Judgement

[36] There is, however, only a single order of life,* the Teachers maintain, because the householder's state alone is prescribed in express vedic texts.*

THE HOUSEHOLDER

Marriage

4 [1] A householder should marry a wife who comes from the same class as he, who has not been married before, and who is younger than he. [2] A marriage can be contracted only between persons not belonging to a family with the same ancestral seer (A 2.11.15 n.) [3] and not related within six degrees on the side of the legal [4] or the biological father (cf. G 28.32–3), [5] or within four degrees on the mother's side.

Types of Marriage [6] When one dresses up a girl, adorns her with jewellery, and gives her to a man of learning, character, and virtue who has relatives, it is a 'Brahma' marriage. [7] At a 'Prajāpati' marriage, the nuptial formula is 'May you jointly fulfil the Law'. [8] At a 'Seer's' marriage, the bridegroom should give a bull and a cow to the father of the girl. [9] When one adorns a girl with jewellery and gives her to the officiating priest within the sacrificial arena, it is a 'Divine' marriage. [10] When a man on his own has intercourse with a willing woman, it is a 'Gandharva' marriage. [11] When a man courts the guardians of the girl with money, it is a 'Demonic' marriage. [12] When a man abducts her by force, it is a 'Fiendish' marriage. [13] When a man has intercourse with an unconscious girl, it is a 'Ghoulish' marriage.

[14] The first four types are in accordance with the Law; [15] the first six, according to some.

Mixed Classes [16] Children born in keeping with the natural order of classes from women of the class immediately below the man's are Savarṇas, Ambaṣṭhas, and Ugras; from women two classes below the man's, Niṣādas and Dauṣyantas; and from women three classes below the man's, Pāraśavas. [17] Children born in the reverse order of classes from women of the class immediately above the man's are Sūtas, Māgadhas, and Āyogavas; from women two classes above the man's, Kṣattṛs and Vaidehas; and from women three classes above the man's, Cāṇḍālas.

[18] From men of the four classes, a Brahmin woman gives birth respectively to Brahmins, Sūtas, Māgadhas, and Cāṇḍālas; [19] from the same men, a Kṣatriya woman gives birth respectively to Mūrdhāvasiktas, Kṣatriyas, Dhīvaras, and Pulkasas; [20] from the same men, a Vaiśya woman gives birth respectively to Bhṛjyakaṇṭhas, Māhiṣyas, Vaiśyas, and Vaidehas; [21] and from the same men, a Śūdra woman gives birth respectively to Pāraśavas, Yavanas, Karaṇas, and Śūdras. That is the opinion of some.

[22] By successively marrying persons of the higher or the lower class, in the seventh generation the offspring moves to the one or the other class; [23] in the fifth, according to the Teachers. [24] This is true also in the case of those born to parents belonging to different mixed classes.

[25] Children born to parents in the reverse order of classes, on the other hand, are outside the Law, [26] as also those born to a Śūdra woman.* [27] A child of a Śūdra man from a woman of a different class shall be treated like an outcaste, [28] the one listed last being the vilest.

Sons [29] Virtuous sons purify—[30] a son born from a 'Seer's' marriage purifies three ancestors; [31] a son born from a 'Divine' marriage, ten; [32] a son born from a 'Prajāpati' marriage, also ten; [33] while a son born from a 'Brahma' marriage purifies the ten ancestors before him and the ten descendants after him.

5 **Rules of Sexual Intercourse** [1] A man should have sexual intercourse with his wife when she is in her season (A 2.1.17 n.), [2] or at any time, except on days when it is forbidden.

Ritual Duties

[3] He shall pay homage to gods, ancestors, humans, spirits, and seers. [4] Every day he shall perform his private vedic recitation, [5] the offering of water to his ancestors, [6] and other rites, according to his ability. [7] Let him set up his sacred fire either on the day of his marriage or upon the division of the paternal estate [8] and perform in it his domestic rites, [9] as well as sacrifices to gods, ancestors, and humans, private vedic recitation, and Bali offerings.

[10] Fire oblations are offered to Fire, Dhanvantari, All-Gods, Prajāpati, and Fire who makes the offering flawless.

[11] Oblations are offered also to the guardian deities of the directions, each in his respective place—[12] to the Maruts at the doors to the house, [13] to the guardian deities of the house after entering the house, [14] to Brahman at the centre of the house, [15] to the waters by the water pot, [16] to space in the intermediate region, [17] and to night-stalkers in the evening.

Gifts

[18] He shall give almsfood after getting the recipient to wish him well and pouring water. [19] The same applies to other righteous (*dharma*) gifts. [20] A gift bears an equal reward when it is given to a non-Brahmin, twice as much when it is given to a Brahmin, a thousand times as much when it is given to a vedic scholar, and an infinite reward when it is given to one who has mastered the entire Veda. [21] Goods should be distributed outside the sacrificial arena to those begging in order to pay the teacher's fee, to

perform a wedding, or to procure medicine, as also to the indigent, to those preparing to perform a sacrifice, to students, to travellers, and to those who have offered the Viśvajit sacrifice. [22] When others come to beg, let him give them cooked food.

[23] When a request is made for an unlawful (*adharma*) purpose, he should not give, even if he has already promised to do so. [24] Untrue statements made by people who are angry, jubilant, afraid, in pain, greedy, young, old, feeble-minded, drunk, or mad are not sins causing loss of caste.

Guests

[25] He should give food first to guests, children, the sick, pregnant women, females in his household, and the old, as well as the menials. [26] When his teacher, father, or friend is visiting, however, he should check with them before cooking the meal.

[27] When his officiating priest, teacher, father-in-law, or paternal or maternal uncle visits him, he shall offer them the honey mixture (A 2.8.8). [28] It needs to be repeated only after the interval of a year; [29] but on the occasion of a sacrifice or a wedding, it should be repeated even if a year has not elapsed. [30] It should also be offered to a king and to a vedic scholar.* [31] To a Brahmin who is not a vedic scholar, he should offer a seat and water; [32] but to one who is a vedic scholar he should have water for washing the feet and the welcome water* prepared, as also lavish food [33] or the normal food prepared in a special way. [34] To a Brahmin without vedic learning but of good conduct, he should give average food; [35] but to one with the opposite qualities, just some straw and water, and a place on the floor, [36] or at the very least, a word of welcome.

[37] He should show respect to the guest and not eat before him. [38] To those who are his equals or superiors, he should offer a room, bed, and seat as good as his; treat them hospitably; and follow them as they leave; [39] somewhat less than that if it is a man inferior to him.

[40] A guest is defined as a man from a different village who comes when the sun is setting behind the trees to spend just one night. [41] He should ask him whether he is doing well; or whether

he is in good shape; or whether he is in good health, in accordance with his class (A 1.14.26–9 n.), [42] the last being used in the case of a Śūdra. [43] A non-Brahmin is never a guest of a Brahmin, unless he has come on the occasion of a sacrifice. [44] A Kṣatriya, however, should be fed after the Brahmins, [45] and the others should be fed together with his servants to show compassion.

Salutation

6 [1–3] His mother and father, their relations, his older brothers, his teachers, and their teachers—each day when he meets them he should clasp their feet, as also when he returns from a journey. [4] When he meets several of them together, he should first clap the feet of the one who is most superior. [5] When he meets a knowledgeable person, he should greet him by stating his own name and saying, 'I am so-and-so'. [6] Some say that there is no restrictive rule about salutation between husband and wife. [7] Except upon returning from a journey, there is no need to greet women other than his mother, paternal uncle's wife, and his sisters; [8] nor should he clasp the feet of his brothers' wives or his mother-in-law. [9] In the case of an officiating priest, a father-in-law, or a paternal or maternal uncle who is younger than himself, on the other hand, he should rise up to receive him but there is no need to offer a formal greeting. [10] An aged fellow townsman or even an 80-year-old Śūdra should be treated in the same way by a man young enough to be his son, [11] as also an Ārya even younger than himself, by a Śūdra.

[12] Such a person, moreover, should refrain from saying the other's name, [13] as also a royal officer who has not studied the Veda, the name of the king. [14] A friend born on the same day as oneself should be addressed 'Mister!' or 'Sir!', [15] as also a fellow townsman ten years older than oneself; [16] an artist five years older; [17] a vedic scholar of one's own vedic branch (p. xxii) who is three years older; [18] an ignorant Brahmin following the occupations of a Kṣatriya or a Vaiśya; [19] and a man consecrated for a sacrifice before the purchase of Soma (A 1.18.23 n.).

Rules of Precedence [20] People should be honoured on account of wealth, relatives, occupation, birth, learning, and age, but each succeeding one is more important than each preceding, [21] but vedic learning is the most important of all, [22] because it is the source of Law [23] and because it is so stated in the vedic texts.

[24] One must yield the way to people in vehicles, extremely old people, the sick,* women, bath-graduates (A 1.30.9 n.) and kings; [25] and a king to a vedic scholar.

Times of Adversity

7 [1] These are the rules for times of adversity. A Brahmin may receive vedic instruction from a non-Brahmin, [2] walk behind him, and obey him. [3] Once the study is completed, however, the Brahmin becomes the more honourable of the two.

[4] One may teach, officiate at the sacrifices of, and receive gifts from people of all classes, [5] each preceding occupation being more honourable. [6] When these occupations are unavailable, one may live by the occupations of a Kṣatriya, [7] and when even these are unavailable, by the occupations of a Vaiśya.

[8] One may not trade in the following goods: [9] perfumes, condiments, prepared foods, sesame seeds, hemp or linen cloth, skins, [10] garments that are dyed red or washed, [11] milk and milk products, [12] roots, fruits, flowers, medicines, honey, meat, grass, water, poisons, [13] and animals for slaughter; [14] and, under any circumstance, human beings, barren cows, heifers, and pregnant cows. [15] According to some, one may also not trade in land, rice, barley, goats, sheep, horses, bulls, milch-cows, and oxen. [16] One is restricted to bartering [17] condiments for condiments [18] and animals for animals; [19] but not salt, prepared food, or [20] sesame seeds. [21] One may, however, exchange uncooked food for an equal amount of cooked food for immediate use.

[22] When none of this is possible, however, one may sustain oneself by any occupation except that of a Śūdra; [23] some permit even that when one's life is at stake. [24] Even then, however, one is not allowed to mix with that class or to eat forbidden food. [25] When his life is at stake, even a Brahmin may live by the use of arms, [26] and a Kṣatriya may resort to the occupations of a Vaiśya.

The Brahmin and the King

8 [1]There are in the world two who uphold the proper way of life—the king and the Brahmin deeply learned in the Vedas. [2]And on them depend the life of the fourfold human race and of internally conscious creatures that move about, fly, and crawl; [3]as well as their increase, protection, non-intermixture, and adherence to the Law.

[4]He alone is deeply learned in the Vedas [5]who knows the secular sciences, the Vedas, and the Vedic Supplements; [6]who is well read in the dialogues, epics, and Purāṇas; [7]who relies on them and patterns his conduct after them; [8]who has been sanctified by the forty sacramentary rites (G 8.14–21); [9]who is devoted to the three occupations [10]or to the six (G 10.1–2); [11]and who has been trained in the accepted customary Laws (A 1.1.1 n.).

[12]The king should exempt such a man from six things: [13]he should not be subjected to corporal punishment, imprisonment, fines, banishment, upbraiding, and abandonment.

Sacramentary Rites [14]Impregnation rite, quickening a male foetus, parting the wife's hair, birth rite, naming, first feeding with solid food, tonsure, and initiation;* [15]the four vows* associated with vedic study; [16]bath at the conclusion of study, marrying a helpmate in fulfilling the Law, and performing the five sacrifices to gods, ancestors, humans, spirits, and Veda (A 1.12.13 f.); [17]as well as of the following: [18]the seven kinds of sacrifices using cooked food, viz., ancestral offerings on the eighth day after the full moon, offerings on full-moon and new-moon days, ancestral offerings, and offerings on the full-moon days that open a four-month season (A 1.10.1 n.); [19]the seven kinds of sacrifices with burnt offerings, viz., setting up the vedic fires, daily fire offering, new- and full-moon sacrifices, sacrifice of first fruits, seasonal sacrifices, Nirūḍhapaśubandha, and Sautrāmaṇī; [20]the seven kinds of Soma sacrifices, viz., Agniṣṭoma, Atyagniṣṭoma, Ukthya, Ṣoḍaśin, Vājapeya, Atirātra, and Aptoryāma—[21]these are the forty sacramentary rites.

Virtues [22]Next, the eight virtues of the self: [23]compassion towards all creatures, patience, lack of envy, purification, tranquillity, having an auspicious disposition, generosity, and lack of greed.

[24] A man who has performed the forty sacramentary rites but lacks these eight virtues does not obtain union with or residence in the same world as Brahman. [25] A man who may have performed only some of the forty sacramentary rites but possesses these eight virtues, on the other hand, is sure to obtain union with and residence in the same world as Brahman.

THE BATH-GRADUATE

9 [1] Such a man (A 1.30.9 n.), after he has completed his studies, should bathe according to the rules (A 1.30.4 n.), marry a wife, and, as he continues to observe the Laws proper to a householder described above, subject himself to the following vows.

[2] He shall always keep himself clean and smelling good and cultivate the habit of bathing. [3] If he has the means, he should not wear old or dirty clothes, [4] nor ones that are dyed red or costly, or that have been worn by others—[5] not even garlands or shoes; [6] if he does not have the means, he should wash the garment before wearing it. [7] Let him not grow his beard without a good reason.*

[8] He should not carry fire and water at the same time; [9] drink water from his cupped hands; [10] stand while he sips water that has been drawn out;* [11] or sip water given by a Śūdra or an impure person, or taken with one hand. [12] He should not discharge urine, excrement, or bodily filth facing or looking at the wind, a fire, a Brahmin, the sun, water, a divine image, or a cow; [13] nor should he stretch his feet towards any of these divinities.

[14] He should not use leaves, clods, or stones to clean himself of urine or excrement; [15] stand on ashes, hair, potsherds, or filth; [16] or converse with barbarians or with sordid (A 1.21.12–19) or unrighteous people. [17] If he happens to converse with them, he should mentally reflect on virtuous men [18] or speak with a Brahmin.

[19] When speaking of a cow that does not yield milk, he should

say 'She is going to be a milch-cow'; [20] and when speaking of something unlucky, he should say 'It's a lucky thing'. [21] In referring to a skull, he should use the word *bhagāla* in place of *kapāla*;* [22] and in referring to a rainbow, the word *maṇidhanus* ('jewelled bow') in place of *indradhanus* ('Indra's bow': see A 1.31.17). [23] He should neither inform anyone that a cow is suckling her calf [24] nor prevent her from doing so.

[25] After engaging in sexual intercourse, he should not be tardy in purifying himself. [26] And he should not do his private vedic recitation sitting on the same bed. [27] After reciting the Veda in the last watch of the night (B 2.17.22 n.), moreover, he should not go back to bed. [28] He should not have intercourse with his wife when she is indisposed [29] or having her period, [30] or embrace her when she is in that state. [31] Neither should he embrace an unmarried girl.

[32] He should refrain from the following: blowing on a fire with his mouth; engaging in polemics; wearing perfume and necklaces outdoors; scratching himself with disgusting things; eating with his wife; looking at a woman applying oil on herself; entering by a back door; washing the feet by rubbing one foot with the other; eating food placed on a chair; crossing a river by swimming (A 1.32.26 n.); climbing trees; climbing on to or descending into dangerous places; and putting his life in danger. [33] He should not get into an unsafe boat. [34] Let him take care of himself in every possible way.

[35] He should go about with his head uncovered during the day [36] and covered at night. [37] He should cover his head also when he is voiding urine or excrement, [38] which he should never do without spreading something on the ground (A 1.30.15 n.), [39] or close to his house, [40] or upon ashes or cow-dung, on a ploughed field, in a shadow, on a road, or in a beautiful spot. [41] He should void both urine and excrement facing the north during the day [42] and at dawn and dusk, [43] but facing the south at night.

[44] He should avoid seats, footwear, and tooth cleaners made with Palāśa wood (A 1.8.22 n.; 1.32.9 n.) [45] and refrain from eating, sitting, greeting, or paying homage with his shoes on.

[46] He should not spend the morning, midday, or afternoon fruitlessly, but pursue righteousness, wealth, and pleasure to the

best of his ability, [47] but among them he should attend chiefly to righteousness (A 1.24.23 n.).

[48] He should not look at someone else's wife when she is naked, [49] or draw a seat to himself with his foot. [50] He should not let his penis, stomach, hands, feet, speech, or sight get out of control; [51] engage in cutting, breaking, gashing, or crushing anything or in cracking the finger joints without a good reason; [52] or step over a rope to which a calf is tied. [53] Let him not carry tales from one family to another.* [54] He should not go to a sacrifice unless he has been chosen to officiate, [55] but he may go there freely to witness it.

[56] He should not eat food placed in his lap [57] or brought at night by a servant; [58] and foods whose nutrients have been extracted, such as de-creamed milk products, whey, oil-press residue, and buttermilk. [59] Morning and evening, however, he should take his meal, revering the food and never disparaging it.

[60] He should never sleep naked at night, [61] or bathe naked. [62] And whatever people who are self-possessed, elderly, properly trained, and free from hypocrisy, greed, and perplexity, and who know the Vedas instruct him to do, he should carry it out. [63] He may approach the king for the sake of a livelihood, [64] but not anyone else except gods,* elders, and righteous people. [65] He should try to live in a place well supplied with firewood, water, fodder, Kuśa grass, and garland material; served by many roads; inhabited mainly by Āryas; full of energetic people; and ruled by a righteous man (B 2.6.31). [66] When he passes people or things that are distinguished or auspicious, as also temples, intersections of two roads, and the like, he should keep his right side towards them (A 1.7.2 n.).

[67] The rule for times of adversity is that he should observe all the rules of conduct mentally. [68] He shall speak the truth; [69] behave like an Ārya; [70] teach only cultured men; [71] be cultured by adhering to ritual purifications; [72] take delight in the vedic texts; [73] never hurt any creature; be gentle and steadfast; and be devoted to self-control and gift giving.

[74] A bath-graduate who lives in this manner will liberate his parents and his relatives of past and future generations from sins, and he will never fall from the world of Brahman.

OCCUPATIONS OF THE FOUR CLASSES

10 [1] Study, sacrifice, and giving gifts pertain to all twice-born classes.

Brahmin

[2] In addition to these, teaching, officiating at sacrifices, and receiving gifts pertain to Brahmins, [3] but only the former are obligatory. [4] Vedic instruction may be imparted outside the above mentioned rules to a teacher, relative, friend, or elder (A 1.6.32 n.), or when it is imparted in exchange for knowledge or money. [5] A Brahmin may also engage in agriculture and trade if he does not do the work himself, [6] and in lending money on interest.

King and Kṣatriya

[7] To a king pertains, in addition, the protection of all creatures, [8] as also meting out just punishment. [9] He should support Brahmins who are vedic scholars, [10] non-Brahmins who are unable to work, [11] those who are exempt from taxes, [12] and novice students (A 2.21.6 n.).

War [13] He should also take measures to ensure victory, [14] especially when danger threatens; [15] travel about in a chariot armed with a bow; [16] and stand firm in battle without fleeing. [17] He commits no sin if he kills someone in battle, [18] except the following: those who have lost their horses, charioteers, or arms; those who join their hand in supplication or have dishevelled hair; those who are fleeing or hunkering down; those who have climbed on to a ledge or a tree; messengers; and those who say they are cows or Brahmins.* [19] If another Kṣatriya depends on the king for his livelihood, he too must participate in the king's undertakings. [20] The victor should take the booty of battle, [21] but the mounts* go to the king, [22] as well as a choice portion of the booty unless it has been won in single combat. [23] Everything else, however, the king should distribute equitably among his men.

Taxes [24]Farmers shall pay one-tenth, or one-eighth, or one-sixth of their produce to the king as taxes. [25]According to some, there is a tax of one-fiftieth on cattle and gold. [26]There is a duty of one-twentieth on merchandise, [27]and one-sixtieth on roots, fruits, flowers, medicine, honey, meat, grass, and firewood. [28]The grounds for taxation is the king's duty to protect the people; [29]he should always be attentive to them.* [30]The king shall obtain his livelihood by means of this additional duty of his.

[31]Every month each artisan shall work one day for the king. [32]This applies also to people who live by manual labour [33]and to those who operate boats and carriages. [34]The king should give them food when they work for him. [35]Every month traders should give the king a piece of merchandise below its market value.

Ownership [36]If someone finds lost property whose owner is unknown, he should disclose it to the king. [37]The king should have it publicized and keep it safely for a year, [38]after which time a quarter goes to the finder and the rest to the king.

[39]Ownership is established by inheritance, purchase, partition, possession, and discovery; [40]additionally, acceptance for Brahmins, [41]conquest for Kṣatriyas, [42]and wages for Vaiśyas and Śūdras. [43]A treasure-trove is the property of the king, [44]except when it is found by an upright Brahmin. [45]According to some, even a non-Brahmin who discloses a find should receive one-sixth.

[46]When property is stolen by thieves, the king should recover it and return it to its rightful owner [47]or pay compensation from his treasury. [48]He should keep the property of children safely until they reach the legal age (G 2.23 n.) or have completed their studies.

Vaiśya and Śūdra

[49]To a Vaiśya pertain in addition agriculture, trade, animal husbandry, and lending money on interest.

[50]The Śūdra is the fourth class with a single birth (A 1.1.16–18 n.). [51]Speaking the truth, refraining from anger, and

purification apply to him also. [52] According to some, he should simply wash his hands and feet in place of sipping water. [53] He should make ancestral offerings; [54] support his dependants; [55] be faithful to his wife; [56] serve the upper classes; [57] seek his livelihood from them; [58] use their discarded shoes, umbrellas, clothes, and mats and the like; [59] and eat their leftovers (A 1.3.27 n.). [60] He may also support himself by working as an artisan. [61] The Ārya whom he serves must support him even when he is unable to work, [62] and under similar circumstances he should support the upper-class man [63] using his savings for that purpose. [64] When he is given leave, he may use the word 'Homage!' as his mantra. [65] According to some, he may offer sacrifices on his own using cooked food.

[66] All should serve the people belonging to classes higher than themselves. [67] If Āryas do the jobs of non-Āryas and vice versa, they become equal.

THE KING

11 [1] The king rules over all except Brahmins. [2] He should be correct in his actions and speech [3] and trained in the triple Veda and logic. [4] Let him be upright, keep his senses under control, surround himself with men of quality, and adopt sound policies. [5] He should be impartial towards his subjects [6] and work for their welfare.

[7] As he sits on a high seat, all except Brahmins should pay him homage seated at a lower level, [8] and even Brahmins should honour him. [9] He should watch over the social classes and the orders of life in conformity with their rules, [10] and those who stray he should guide back to their respective duties (*dharma*), [11] 'for the king,' it is stated, 'takes a share of their merits (*dharma*).'

[12] He should appoint as his personal priest a Brahmin who is learned, born in a good family, eloquent, handsome, mature, and virtuous; who lives according to the rules; and who is austere. [13] He should undertake rites only with his support, [14] 'for a Kṣatriya, when he is supported by a Brahmin,' it is said, 'prospers and never falters.' [15] He should also pay heed to what his astrologers and augurs tell him, [16] for, according to some, his

welfare* depends also on that. [17] In the fire within the assembly hall, he should perform rites to secure prosperity in connection with a propitiation, festive day, military expedition, long life, or auspiciousness, as well as rites to stir enmity, to subdue or slay his enemies, or to bring them to their knees. [18] His officiating priests shall carry out the other rites as prescribed.

The Judicial Process

[19] His administration of justice shall be based on the Veda, the Legal Treatises, the Vedic Supplements (A 2.8.10–11), and the Purāṇa. [20] The Laws of regions, castes, and families are also authoritative if they are not in conflict with the sacred scriptures. [21] Farmers, merchants, herdsmen, moneylenders, and artisans exercise authority over their respective groups. [22] He should dispense the Law after he has ascertained the facts from authoritative persons of each group.

[23] Reasoning is the means of reaching a correct judgment. [24] Having reached a conclusion in this manner, he should decide the case equitably. [25] If there is conflicting evidence, he should consult those who are deeply learned in the triple Veda and reach a decision, [26] for, it is said, acting in that way, he will attain prosperity.

Punishment

[27] 'Brahmins united with Kṣatriyas', it is stated, 'uphold the gods, ancestors, and human beings.' [28] The word 'punishment' (*daṇḍa*), they say, is derived from 'restraint' (*damana*); therefore, he should restrain those who are unrestrained.

[29] People belonging to the different classes and orders of life who are steadfastly devoted to the Laws proper to them enjoy the fruits of their deeds after death; and then, with the residue of those fruits, take birth again in a prosperous region, a high caste, and a distinguished family, with a handsome body, long life, deep vedic learning, and virtuous conduct, and with great wealth, happiness, and intelligence. [30] Those who act to the contrary disperse in every direction and perish. [31] The teacher's

advice and the king's punishment protect them; [32] therefore, one should never belittle the king or the teacher.

Criminal and Civil Law

12 **Abuse and Assault** [1] If a Śūdra uses abusive language or physical violence against twice-born people (A 1.1.16–18 n.), the part of his body used for the crime should be chopped off. [2] If he has sex with an Ārya woman, his penis should be cut off and all his property confiscated; [3] if the woman had a guardian, then, in addition to the above, he shall be executed. [4] And if he listens in on a vedic recitation, his ears shall be filled with molten tin or lac; [5] if he repeats it, his tongue shall be cut off; [6] if he commits it to memory, his body shall be split asunder. [7] If, while he is occupying a seat, lying on a bed, speaking, or walking on the road, he seeks to be their equal, he should be beaten.

[8] If a Kṣatriya hurls abusive words at a Brahmin, he shall be fined a hundred;* [9] if there is physical violence, the fine is doubled. [10] A Vaiśya guilty of the same crime shall be fined one and a half times as much as a Kṣatriya. [11] A Brahmin guilty of the same crime against a Kṣatriya, on the other hand, shall be fined fifty, [12] half that amount if it is against a Vaiśya, [13] and none at all if it is against a Śūdra. [14] If a Kṣatriya is guilty of the same crime against a Vaiśya, or a Vaiśya against a Kṣatriya, the fine shall be the same as that levied on a Brahmin *vis-à-vis* a Kṣatriya, and on a Kṣatriya *vis-à-vis* a Brahmin, respectively.

Theft [15] When a Śūdra steals, he must be made to repay the loss eightfold, [16] and the fine is progressively doubled for thieves belonging to each of the prior classes. [17] If the felon is a learned man, he should be punished more severely. [18] For stealing small amounts of fruits, vegetables, or grain, the fine is five Kṛṣṇalas (G 12.8 n.).

Property Damage [19] The owner is at fault when his animals cause damage; [20] but if a herdsman was looking after them at the time, then it is the herdsman's fault. [21] If the damage is done to an unfenced field by the side of a road, then the fault lies with both the herdsman and the owner of the field. [22] For damage done by a cow, the fine is five Māṣas (G 12.8 n.); [23] by a camel or a donkey, six; [24] by a horse or a buffalo, ten; [25] by sheep or goats, two for each. [26] If the whole field is destroyed, the fine is the value of the crop.

[27] If a man consistently neglects what is prescribed and does what is forbidden, his property, beyond what is necessary to clothe and feed himself, shall be confiscated. [28] One may gather grass for a cow, wood for the fire, and flowers from vines and trees as if they were his own, and, if they are not fenced in, also fruits.

Rates of Interest [29] The legal (*dharmya*) rate of interest is five Māṣas a month for twenty.* [30] According to some, this rate does not apply for longer than a year. [31] If the loan remains outstanding for a longer period of time, the principal is doubled.* [32] No interest accrues if the lender makes use of the borrower's collateral, [33] or when the borrower is eager to settle the debt but is prevented from doing so. [34] The types of interest are: cyclical rate, periodic rate, [35] contractual rate, manual labour, daily rate, and use of the collateral.* [36] In the case of animal products, wool, farm produce, and beasts of burden, the interest shall not exceed five times the loan.

Ownership [37] When others make use of the property of a person who is neither mentally incapacitated nor a minor before his very eyes for ten years, it belongs to the user, [38] unless the user is a vedic scholar, a wandering ascetic, or a royal officer. [39] There is no such limit on the period of use in the case of cattle, land, and women.*

Debts [40] Those who inherit the property of someone have to pay his debts. [41] Sons are not accountable for a surety's bond, a business debt, a bride price, debts relating to liquor or gambling, or fines. [42] So long as a person has a blameless reputation, he is not accountable for an open or sealed deposit, something borrowed or purchased, or a collateral for a loan that is lost without his fault.

Punishment [43] A thief, his hair dishevelled and carrying a pestle, should go to the king proclaiming his deed. [44] He is cleansed by being killed or released, [45]but by not killing him the king assumes the sin.

[46]There shall be no corporal punishment of Brahmins; [47]they are punished by extricating them from such deeds, publishing their crimes, sending them into exile, and branding them. [48]If a king fails to punish, he should perform a penance.

[49]A man who knowingly becomes an associate of a thief shall be treated like a thief, [50]as also a man who illicitly (*adharma*) receives goods from him.

[51]Punishment should be meted out after taking into account the type of a man he is, his strength, the gravity of the crime, and how often he has committed it. [52]Alternatively, the man may be pardoned according to the verdict of an assembly of men learned in the Vedas.

13 **Witnesses** [1]If there is conflicting evidence, the truth shall be ascertained by means of witnesses. [2]They should be numerous, of blameless reputation with respect to their duties, worthy of the king's trust, and neither friendly nor hostile towards either party. [3]They may even be Śūdras. [4]Unless a Brahmin is listed in the plaint, however, he should not be forced to testify at the behest of a non-Brahmin.

[5]Witnesses should not speak until they are convened and questioned; [6]but if they then refuse to speak, they commit an offence. [7]If they speak the truth, they will go to heaven; if they do the contrary, hell awaits them. [8]Even those not listed in the plaint may be obliged to give evidence. [9]No objection can be raised against a witness in cases involving violence [10]or for things he may have said inadvertently. [11]If the execution of the Law* is thwarted, the guilt falls on the witnesses, the assessors, the king, and the transgressor. [12]According to some, the witnesses are to be placed under oath to speak the truth; [13]if they are not Brahmins, the oath should be administered in the presence of divine images, the king, and Brahmins.

[14]If a witness gives false testimony with regard to small farm animals, he slays* ten; [15]with regard to cattle, ten times as many; with regard to horses, ten times as many as for cattle; with regard to human beings, ten times as many as for horses. [16]If he

gives false testimony with regard to land, he slays all; [17] and if he steals land, he goes to hell. [18] The penalty for false testimony with regard to land applies also to water [19] and sexual intercourse; [20] the penalty in the case of farm animals applies also to honey and ghee; [21] the penalty in the case of cattle applies also to clothes, gold, grain, and the Veda; [22] and the penalty in the case of horses applies also to carriages. [23] When a witness gives false testimony, he should be reprimanded and punished. [24] It is not an offence to give false testimony if a man's life depends on it, [25] but not if it is the life of an evil man.

[26] The king shall be the judge, or else a learned Brahmin. [27] Witnesses should appear before the judge. [28] If they are unable to appear, the judge may wait for one year. [29] But in cases affecting cows, draught oxen, women, and begetting children, he should summon them immediately, [30] as also when the matter is urgent.

[31] Of all the Laws, speaking the truth before the judge is the most important.

IMPURITY

Death Impurity

14 [1] A ten-day period of death impurity affects people belonging to the same ancestry (A 2.14.2 n.) as the deceased, unless they are officiating as priests in, or are consecrated for, a sacrifice, or are vedic students. [2] In the case of Kṣatriyas, the period of impurity lasts for eleven days; [3] in the case of Vaiśyas for twelve days—[4] or, according to some, for a fortnight—; [5] and in the case of Śūdras for a month. [6] If during that period another period of impurity arises, they become pure at the end of the time remaining from the first period of impurity; [7] but if only one day remains, then at the end of two days; [8] and if it happens on the morning after the conclusion of the first period, then at the end of three days.

[9] When people are killed while defending cows or Brahmins,* their relatives become pure immediately; [10] as also when they are killed due to the king's anger [11] or in a battle; [12] and when they

die voluntarily by walking without food or drink, by fasting, by a sword, in a fire, by poison, by drowning, by hanging, and by jumping from a precipice.

[13] Relationship caused by ancestry (A 2.14.2 n.) ceases with the fifth or seventh generation.

[14] These same rules of impurity come into effect also at the birth of a child; [15] they apply to the parents [16] or just to the mother.

[17] When there is a miscarriage, the period of impurity lasts for as many days as the months since conception, [18] or else for three days.

[19] If someone hears of a relative's death after ten or more days, the period of impurity lasts two days plus the intervening night, [20] as also at the death of a maternal relative not belonging to his ancestry or of a fellow reciter of the Veda. [21] For a fellow student,* the period of impurity lasts for a day, [22] as also for a vedic scholar who lives close by.

Contact with a Corpse

[23] When someone comes into contact with a corpse, the period of impurity lasts for ten days if it is done for a consideration. [24] The period of impurity for such contact in the case of Vaiśyas and Śūdras is the same as that given above, [25] or for as many days as there are seasons* in a year. [26] The latter rule is applicable also to the two higher classes; [27] or else their impurity lasts for three days, [28] as also when someone comes in contact with the corpse of his teacher, the teacher's son or wife, a man for whom he performs priestly functions, or his pupil.

[29] If a person of a lower class comes in contact with the corpse of a higher class person, or a person of a higher class with the corpse of a lower class person, then the period of impurity is what is prescribed for the class to which the dead man belonged (G 14.1–5).

Contact with Impure Persons

[30] When a man touches an outcaste, a Cāṇḍāla, a woman who

has just given birth or is menstruating, a corpse, or someone who has touched any of these, he becomes purified by bathing with his clothes on; [31] as also when he has gone behind a corpse [32] or touched a dog. [33] According to some, the spot touched by the dog should be washed.

Libations to the Deceased

[34] Those who belong to the same ancestry should offer water to a deceased person whose tonsure ceremony (G 8.14 n.) has been performed [35] and for the wives of such a person; [36] according to some, also for their married relatives.

[37] All should sleep and sit on the floor; remain chaste; [38] not wash themselves; [39] not eat meat until the funeral oblation has been offered; [40] offer libations of water on the first, third, fifth, seventh, and ninth day after the death; [41] discard the garments worn during these rites; [42] but on the last day give them to people of the lowest class. [43] Parents must offer these libations to a child who has teethed.

Immediate Purification

[44] When infants, people who have gone to a distant region, wandering ascetics, and people who do not belong to the same ancestry die, a person is purified immediately; [45] as also kings, lest their duties be impeded; [46] and a Brahmin, so as not to interrupt his daily vedic recitation.

ANCESTRAL OFFERINGS

15 [1] Next, the ancestral offerings. [2] One should offer them to one's ancestors on the new-moon day, [3] or else after the fourth day of the fortnight of the waning moon [4] or on any day of that fortnight according to one's faith. [5] If materials, location, or Brahmins of special significance are at hand, however, one does not have to observe any restriction with regard to time.

Quality of Invitees

[6] One should obtain the best possible food, get it prepared to the best of one's ability, [7] and feed an uneven number of Brahmins—but at least nine [8] or as many as he can afford—[9] Brahmins who are vedic scholars, gifted with eloquence and beauty, mature in years, and virtuous. [10] It is best to feed people who are young; [11] according to some, they should be of the same age as the deceased ancestor. [12] One should not use this rite to strike a friendship.

[13] In the absence of a son, those belonging to the same ancestry, those belonging to the same ancestry as his mother, or his pupils should make the ancestral offering; [14] and if even these are unavailable, his officiating priest or teacher.

Types of Food

[15] By offering sesame, beans, rice, barley, and water, the ancestors are satisfied for a month; by offering fish or the meat of antelope, Ruru antelope, rabbit, turtle, boar, or sheep, for several years; by offering cow's milk or milk pudding, for twelve years; by offering the meat of a Vārdhrīṇasa crane, sacred basil, or the meat of a goat, a red goat, or a rhinoceros, mixed with honey, for an unlimited time.*

Unfit Invitees

[16] He should not feed the following: a thief; a man who is impotent; an outcaste; an infidel or a man who lives like an infidel; someone who has relinquished his sacred fires; someone who has married a younger sister with an unmarried older sister or an older sister whose younger sister is already married; someone who officiates at the sacrifices of women or a group of men; a goat herder; someone who has given up fire sacrifices, drinks liquor, or behaves improperly; a false witness; a door-keeper; [17] the lover of a married woman and that woman's husband; [18] someone who eats the food of a man born from an adulterous union or sells Soma; an arsonist; a poisoner; a man who has

broken his vow of chastity as a student; someone who is in the service of a guild; someone who has sex with a forbidden woman; a sadist; a man whose younger brother gets married before him or who gets married before his older brother; someone whose younger brother has set up the ritual fires before him or who has set up the ritual fires before his older brother; someone who is suicidal; a man who is bald-headed or has bad nails, black teeth, or white leprosy; the son of a remarried woman; a gambler; someone who does not engage in the soft recitation of prayers (A 1.15.1 n); a servant of the king; someone who cheats by using false weights and measures; the husband of a Śūdra woman;* someone who neglects his private vedic recitation; a man with spotted leprosy; a usurer; someone who lives as a merchant or artisan; someone who is fond of archery, playing music, keeping the beat at performances, dancing, and singing; [19] and those who have divided the paternal estate against their father's wishes.

[20] According to some, he may invite his pupils and people belonging to his ancestry. [21] He should feed more than three persons, or a single distinguished person.

Sexual Abstinence

[22] If someone has sex with a Śūdra woman soon after eating at an ancestral offering, he will plunge his ancestors in her excrement for a whole month. [23] That whole day, therefore, he should remain chaste.

Pollution and Remedies

[24] An ancestral offering is ruined if it is seen by a dog, a Cāṇḍāla, or an outcaste. [25] Therefore, he should offer it in an enclosed place; [26] alternatively he should scatter sesame seeds over the offering, [27] or a man who purifies those alongside whom he eats (A 2.17.21 n.) may remove the defilement. [28] These are the persons who purify those alongside whom they eat: a man who knows the six Vedic Supplements (A 2.8.10–11); a man who sings the Jyeṣṭha Sāmans; an expert in the three Nāciketa fire

altars; a man who knows the three 'Honey' verses; a man who knows the Trisuparṇa; a man who maintains the five sacred fires (A 2.17.22 n.); a bath-graduate; a man who knows the vedic Hymns and Brāhmaṇa texts; a man who knows the Law; and a descendant from a line of vedic scholars.

[29] The above rules apply also to sacrificial offerings. [30] According to some, however, the prohibition of a bald man and those listed after him applies only to ancestral offerings.

ANNUAL COURSE OF STUDY

16 [1] After commencing the annual course of study on the full-moon day of July–August or August–September, he should study the Vedas [2] for four and a half months, or five months, or else during the time the sun moves south.

[3] During this period he should remain chaste, refrain from shaving, and abstain from meat. [4] Optionally, these rules may be observed for just two months.

Suspension of Vedic Recitation

[5] He should suspend vedic recitation during daytime when the wind whirls up the dust; [6] at night when he can hear the wind blow; [7] when the sound of a lute, drum, side drum, chariot, or wailing is heard; [8] when dogs are barking, jackals are howling, and donkeys are braying; [9] when the sky turns crimson; when a rainbow appears; when there is frost on the ground; [10] when clouds appear out of season; [11] when he has the urge to void urine or excrement; [12] in the middle of the night, at the time of twilight, and while standing in water; [13] when it is raining—[14] but, according to some, only when the water is running down the eaves—; [15] when Venus and Jupiter are surrounded by halos, [16] as also the sun and the moon; [17] when he is frightened, travelling in a vehicle, lying down, or has lifted his feet; [18] when he is in a cremation ground, at the village boundary, on a highway, or in an impure state; [19] when there is a foul smell; when there is a corpse or a Cāṇḍāla in the village; when a Śūdra is near by; [20] and when he experiences an acrid belching.

[21]The recitation of the Ṛgveda and the Yajurveda, moreover, is suspended as long as the recitation of the Sāmaveda is heard.* [22]When there is a lightning strike, an earthquake, an eclipse, or the fall of a meteor, vedic recitation is suspended until the same time the next day; [23]as also when there is thunder, rain, or lightning during twilight when the fires are visible. [24]When these happen during the rainy season, however, the suspension lasts only that day. [25]When there is lightning during the night, moreover, the suspension lasts until the last watch of the night (B 2.17.22 n.); [26]but if it occurs during or after the third part of the day, the suspension lasts the whole night. [27]According to some, a meteor has the same effect as lightning with respect to the suspension of vedic recitation, [28]as does thunder when it occurs in the afternoon [29]or even at dusk. [30]If there is thunder before midnight, the suspension lasts for the whole night; [31]if it happens during the day, the suspension lasts throughout the daylight hours, [32]as also when the king of that realm dies, [33]and when one student goes on a journey and another stays behind with the teacher (cf. A 1.11.11).

[34]The suspension lasts for a day and a night when there has been a social disturbance or a fire; when he has finished reciting one Veda; when he has vomited; when he has eaten at an ancestral offering or at a sacrifice to humans (A 1.11.3 n.); [35]on the new-moon day—[36]alternatively, the suspension here may last for two days—; [37]and on the full-moon days of the lunar months October–November, February–March, and June–July.

[38]At the three eighth-day offerings during the three fortnights of the waning moon following the full moon of November–December, the suspension lasts for three days; [39]according to some, the suspension takes place only at the last of these eighth-day offerings. [40]When the annual course of study is commenced and concluded, the suspension is in effect on that day, as well as on the preceding and following days. [41]In the opinion of all authorities, when rain, lightning, and thunder occur together, the suspension lasts for three days, [42]as also when there is heavy rain.

[43]On a festive day vedic recitation is suspended after the meal. [44]Immediately after commencing the annual course of study,

recitation is suspended during the first four 'hours' (A 1.11.32 n.) of the night. [45] According to some, vedic recitation is always suspended in a town. [46] Even mental recitation is suspended when a person is impure. [47] After making an ancestral offering, the suspension lasts until the same time the next day, [48] as also when uncooked food is distributed at an ancestral offering.

[49] Vedic recitation is also suspended for reasons given in each vedic branch (p. xxii).

FOOD

Food Transactions

17 [1] A Brahmin may eat food given by twice-born men renowned for their devotion to their respective duties. [2] He may also accept gifts from them.

[3] Firewood, water, fodder, roots, fruits, honey, a promise of safety, what is given unasked, beds, seats, shelter, carriages, milk, curd, roasted grain, Śapharī fish, millet, garlands, venison, and vegetables should not be refused from anyone, [4] as also other things needed to take care of the ancestors, gods, teacher, and dependants. [5] If he is unable to sustain himself by other means, he may accept food from a Śūdra. [6] A man who looks after his animals or ploughs his fields, a friend of the family, his barber, and his personal servant—these are people whose food he may eat, [7] as also a merchant who is not an artisan.

[8] This type of food is not fit to be eaten every day.

Unfit Food

[9] The following are unfit to be eaten: food into which hair or an insect has fallen; [10] what has been touched by a menstruating woman, a black bird, or someone's foot; [11] what has been looked at by an abortionist (A 1.19.15 n.) [12] or smelt by a cow; [13] food that looks revolting;* [14] food that has turned sour, except curd; [15] re-cooked food; [16] food that has become stale, except vegetables, chewy or greasy foods, meat, and honey; [17] food given by

someone who has been disowned by his parents, a harlot, a heinous sinner (A 1.3.25 n.), a hermaphrodite, a law enforcement agent, a carpenter, a miser, a jailer, a physician, a man who hunts without using the bow or eats the leftovers of others, a group of people, or an enemy, [18] as also by those listed before a bald man as people who defile those alongside whom they eat (G 15.16–18; A 2.17.21 n.); [19] food prepared for no avail; a meal during which people sip water or get up against the rules, [20] or at which different sorts of homage are paid to people of equal stature and the same homage is paid to people of different stature; [21] and food that is given disrespectfully.

Forbidden Food

[22–3] It is forbidden to drink the milk of a cow, a goat, or a buffalo, during the first ten days after it gives birth; [24] the milk of sheep, camels, and one-hoofed animals under any circumstances; [25] the milk of an animal from whose udders milk flows spontaneously or of an animal that has borne twins, gives milk while pregnant, [26] or has lost her calf.

[27] The following are forbidden foods: animals with five claws (A 1.17.37 n.), with the exception of the hedgehog, hare, porcupine, Godhā monitor lizard, rhinoceros, and tortoise; [28] animals with teeth in both jaws,* with a lot of hair, or without any hair; one-hoofed animals; Kalaviṅka sparrows; Plava herons; Cakravāka geese; Haṃsa geese; [29] crows; Kaṅka herons; vultures; falcons; water birds; red-footed and red-beaked birds; village cocks and pigs; [30] milch-cows and oxen; [31] meat of animals whose milk-teeth have not fallen and of animals that are sick or wantonly killed; [32] young shoots; mushrooms; garlic; resins; [33] red juices* flowing from incisions on trees; [34] woodpeckers; Baka egrets; Balāka ibis; parrots; Madgu cormorants; Ṭiṭṭibha sandpipers; Māndhāla flying foxes; and night birds.

[35] Birds that feed by thrusting their beaks or scratching with their feet and that do not have webbed feet may be eaten, [36] as also fish that are not grotesque, [37] and animals that have to be killed for the sake of the Law.* [38] He may avail himself of animals killed by predators after washing them, so long as he does

not detect any flaw in them and after getting them verbally declared as suitable.

WOMEN AND MARRIAGE

Duties of a Wife

18 [1] A wife cannot act independently in matters relating to the Law. [2] She should never go against her husband [3] and keep her speech, eyes, and actions under strict control.

Levirate [4] When her husband is dead, she may seek to obtain offspring through her husband's brother [5] after she has been appointed to the task by the elders (A 1.6.32 n.). She should not have sex with him outside her season (A 2.1.17 n.). [6] Alternatively, she may obtain offspring through a relative* belonging to the same ancestry, lineage, or line of seers (A 2.14.2 n.; A 2.11.15 n.), or just a relative; [7] according to some, however, through no one other than her husband's brother. [8] She shall bear no more than two children.

To Whom Belongs a Son [9] The offspring belongs to the man who fathers it, [10] unless there has been a compact (G 18.5) [11] or it has been fathered on a wife whose husband is still alive. [12] If it is fathered by an outsider, however, the offspring belongs to that outsider, [13] or to both; [14] but if the husband cares for that offspring, then it belongs to him alone (A 2.13.5 n.).

Remarriage of a Wife [15] If her husband is missing, she shall wait for six years. If he is heard from, she shall go to him. [16] If her husband has become an ascetic, on the other hand, she shall give up all attachments. [17] When a Brahmin has gone away to study the Veda, his wife should wait for twelve years.

Marriage of a Younger Brother [18] Likewise, when an older brother is missing, a younger brother of his should wait for the same length of time before getting married or establishing the sacred fires; [19] for six years, according to some.

Time of Marriage for Girls [20] When three menstrual periods have passed, a girl may discard the jewellery her father has given her and join herself on her own to a man of blameless reputation. [21] A girl shall be given in marriage before she reaches puberty, [22] and a man who fails to give her incurs a sin. [23] According to some, she should be given in marriage before she begins to wear clothes.*

LEGITIMATE SEIZURE OF PROPERTY

[24] To perform a marriage or in connection with the course of the Law (G 13.11 n.), a person may take money from a Śūdra, [25] or even from a non-Śūdra who has plenty of livestock but neglects his rituals, [26] who owns a hundred cows but has not set up the sacred fires, [27] or who owns a thousand cows but has not offered a Soma sacrifice.

[28] A man may do so also when he has had nothing to eat until the seventh mealtime (A 1.25.10 n.), but not to hoard, [29] taking even from people who do not neglect their rituals. [30] If the king interrogates him, he should confess, [31] for if he is learned and virtuous, the king is required to support him. [32] If the king does not act when the course of the Law (G 13.11 n.) is in jeopardy, he is at fault.

PENANCES

19 [1] We* have explained the Law pertaining to the social classes and the Law pertaining to the orders of life.

Justification of Penance

[2] Now, a man here is tainted by foul actions, as, for example, by officiating at sacrifices of people for whom it is forbidden to officiate, by eating what is forbidden to eat, by saying what is forbidden to say, by failing to do what is enjoined, and by indulging what is forbidden. [3] There is a debate as to whether such a man is required to perform a penance or not.

[4] Some say that he is not required to do so, [5] arguing that an act can never be wiped out. [6] The other, and correct, view is that he is required to do so, [7] as it is stated, 'After offering the

Punaḥstoma sacrifice, he gets to participate again in the Soma sacrifice', [8] or after offering the Vrātyastoma. [9] Likewise, 'A man who offers a horse sacrifice overcomes all sins, he overcomes even the murder of a Brahmin' (SB 13.3.1.1); [10] and, 'A heinous sinner (A 1.3.25 n.) should be made to offer the Agniṣṭut sacrifice.'

General Penances

[11] The expiations for such a man are softly reciting prayers (A 1.15.1 n.), austerity, ritual offering, fasting, and giving gifts. [12] Upaniṣads; the conclusions of the Vedas (*vedānta*); the Hymn-Collections of all the Vedas; the 'Honey' verses; Aghamarṣaṇa hymn; Atharvaśiras; Rudra hymn; Puruṣa hymn; the Sāmans called Rājana, Rauhiṇi, Bṛhat, Rathantara, Puruṣagati, Mahānāmnī, Mahāvairāja, and Mahādivākīrtya; any of the Jyeṣṭha Sāmans; Bahiṣpavamāna Sāman; Kūṣmāṇḍa verses; Pāvamānī verses; and the Sāvitrī verse—these are the purificatory texts. [13] Living on milk alone; eating only vegetables; eating only fruits; living on gruel made with one handful of barley; eating gold; consuming ghee; and drinking Soma juice—these are the cleansing activities. [14] All mountains; all rivers; sacred lakes; sacred fords; dwellings of seers; cow-pens; and temples—these are the appropriate places. [15] Observing chastity; speaking the truth; bathing at dawn, noon, and dusk; remaining in wet clothes after the bath; sleeping on the floor; and fasting—these are the austerities. [16] Gold; cow; garment; horse; land; sesame seeds; ghee; and food—these are the gifts. [17] One year; six months; four months; three months; two months; one month; twenty-four days; twelve days; six days; three days; and a day and night—these are the lengths of time.

[18] When no specific penance has been prescribed, people may perform these optionally, [19] the heavier penances for grave sins and the lighter penances for minor sins. [20] The arduous penance (B 2.2.38), the very arduous penance (B 2.2.40), and the lunar penance (G 27; B 3.8) are expiations for all types of sins.

Excommunication from Caste

20 [1]A man should disown a father who assassinates a king; sacrifices for a Śūdra; uses a Śūdra's money for a sacrifice; divulges the Vedas; is an abortionist (A 1.19.15 n.); lives with very low caste men; or cohabits with a woman of a very low caste. [2]Assembling the father's vedic teachers and blood relations, they should perform on his behalf all the funerary rites, beginning with the offering of water, [3]and overturn his water pot. [4]A slave or a workman should bring a dirty pot from a garbage dump, fill it with water from a slave woman's pot, and, facing the south, overturn it with his foot, pronouncing the man's name and saying, 'I deprive that man of water'. [5]All of them, their upper garments slung over their right shoulders and under their left arms (A 1.6.18 n.) and their topknots untied, should touch that slave, [6]while the vedic teachers and blood relations look on. [7]They should then bathe and enter the village.

Contact with an Outcaste [8]Thereafter, if someone were to speak with that man, he should remain standing reciting the Sāvitrī verse for one night if it was done unintentionally, [9]and for three nights if it was done intentionally.

Readmission into Caste [10]An excommunicated man may be purified by performing a penance, however, and when he has been so purified, they should fill a golden pot with water from a very sacred lake or from a river and make the man take a bath with the water from that pot. [11]They should then give that pot to him. Taking that pot, he should pray silently: 'The sky is appeased, the mid-space is appeased and auspicious, the earth is appeased. I here take hold of the radiant one.' [12]Reciting these Yajus formulas, as well as the Pāvamānī, Taratsamandī, and Kūṣmāṇḍa verses, he should offer ghee in the sacred fire. [13]He should then give gold or a cow to a Brahmin, [14]as well as to his teacher.

[15]A man whose penance lasts until death (cf. G 23.1–11), on the other hand, becomes pure only after he dies. [16]They should perform for him all the funerary rites beginning with the offering of water.

[17] The same rite of bathing with water consecrated by the 'appeasement' formulas given above is to be performed for all secondary sins causing loss of caste.

Sins Causing Loss of Caste

21 **Grievous Sins** [1] People who murder a Brahmin; drink liquor; have sex with the wife of an elder (A 1.6.32 n.) or with a woman who is related through his mother or father, or through marriage; steal gold; become infidels; habitually commit forbidden acts; refuse to disown someone fallen from his caste; or disown someone who has not fallen from his caste—these have fallen from their caste, [2] as also those who instigate sins causing loss of caste, [3] and those who associate with outcastes for a year.

Consequences of Falling from Caste [4] Falling from one's caste entails exclusion from the occupations of twice-born people [5] and going empty-handed into the next world. [6] Some call this condition 'hell'.

Expiations [7] According to Manu, no expiation is possible for the first three sins. [8] Some maintain that a man does not fall from his caste by having sex with women other than the wives of his elders (A 1.6.32 n.).

Fall of Women [9] A woman falls from her caste by carrying out an abortion and by having sex with a low-caste man.

Sins Similar to Grievous Sins [10] Giving false evidence, slanderous statements that will reach the king's ear, and false accusations against an elder (A 1.6.32 n.) are equal to sins causing loss of caste.

Secondary Sins [11] People who defile those alongside whom they eat and listed before a bald man (G 15.16–18; A 2.17.21 n.); people who kill cows, forget the Veda, or recite sacred formulas for such people; students who break their vow of chastity; and those who let the time for their initiation lapse (G 1.12–14)—these are guilty of secondary sins causing loss of caste.

[12] One should disown an officiating priest or a teacher who is ignorant or does not teach, or who commits a sin causing loss of caste. [13] If anyone disowns them for other reasons, he falls from his caste, [14] as also, according to some, all those who receive him.

[15] A man shall never deprive his father or mother of sustenance, [16] but he should not accept any share of their estate.*

Other Sins [17] When someone accuses a Brahmin of a sin, he incurs a sin equal to it; [18] twice as large if the man he accuses is innocent. [19] When someone is hurting a weaker man, if a person, although he is able, does not rescue him, that person incurs a sin equal to that of the man causing the hurt. [20] A man will be excluded from heaven for a hundred years if he threatens a Brahmin in anger; [21] for a thousand years, if he strikes; [22] and, if he draws blood, for as many years as the number of dust particles that the spilled blood lumps together.

Description of Penances

22

[1] Next, the penances.

Killing Humans and Animals [2] A man who has killed a Brahmin shall emaciate his body and throw himself into a fire three times,* [3] or make himself a target during an armed battle. [4] Or else, for twelve years he should live a chaste life and, carrying a skull and the post from a bed-frame, enter a village only to beg for food while proclaiming his crime. [5] When he sees an Ārya, he should get out of the road. [6] In this manner he becomes purified, as he remains standing during the day and seated at night, and bathes at dawn, noon, and dusk. [7] He is purified also if he saves a Brahmin's life; [8] if he is defeated three times while attempting to recover the property stolen from a Brahmin; [9] or if he takes part in the ritual bath at the end of a horse sacrifice [10] or even of another sacrifice as long as it concludes with the Agniṣṭut offering.

[11] The same penance applies to a man who makes an attempt on the life of a Brahmin, even if he does not kill him, [12] as also to one who kills a Brahmin woman soon after her

menstrual period [13] or a Brahmin's foetus whose sex cannot be determined (A 1.24.8–9 n.).

[14] If someone kills a Kṣatriya, he should observe the standard vow of chastity for six years and give a thousand cows together with a bull (A 1.24.1 n.); [15] if he kills a Vaiśya, he should do so for three years and give a hundred cows together with a bull; [16] and if he kills a Śūdra, he should do so for one year and give ten cows together with a bull, [17] as also when he kills a Brahmin woman who is not in her season.

[18] The penance for killing a cow is the same as for killing a Vaiśya; [19] it is the same also for killing a frog, a mongoose, a crow, a chameleon, a rat, a mouse, or a dog, [20] and for killing a thousand animals with bones [21] or a cart-load of animals without bones. [22] Or else, he may give some small amount for each animal with bones that he has killed.

[23] If someone kills a eunuch,* he should give a load of straw and a Māṣa (G 12.8 n.) of lead; [24] if he kills a boar, a pot of ghee; [25] if he kills a snake, an iron bar; [26] if he kills a wanton woman who is a Brahmin only in name, a leather bag; [27] and if he kills a prostitute, nothing at all.

Adultery, Drinking, and Other Sins [28] If someone frustrates the acquisition of a wife, food, or wealth, for each such offence he should observe a life of chastity for one year; [29] if he commits adultery, for two years; [30] and if he does so with the wife of a vedic scholar, for three years. [31] If he has received anything from her, he should throw it away [32] or return it to its owner. [33] If someone employs ritual formulas on behalf of proscribed people, he should observe a life of chastity for one year if the formulas contained a thousand words; [34] as also a man who extinguishes his sacred fires, neglects vedic recitation, or commits a secondary sin causing loss of caste, [35] and a woman who goes against her husband. She should be kept under watch, however, and receive food. [36] If someone has sex with an animal other than a cow,* he should offer ghee in the sacred fire while reciting the Kūṣmāṇḍa verses.

23 [1]They should pour hot liquor into the mouth of a Brahmin who has drunk liquor. He is purified after he dies. [2]If he has drunk it inadvertently, he should subsist on hot milk, hot ghee, hot water, and hot air, for a period of three days each; this is the arduous penance (cf. B 2.2.37–8). After that he should undergo initiation. [3]The same penance should be performed when someone consumes urine, excrement, or semen, [4]as also a part of a predatory animal, a camel, or a donkey, [5]or of a village cock or pig. [6]If someone smells the breath of a man who has drunk liquor, he should control his breath and eat some ghee, [7]as also when he is bitten by an animal mentioned above.

Incestuous Sex [8]A man who has had sex with the wife of an elder (A 1.6.32 n.) should lie on a heated iron bed; [9]embrace a red-hot column (A 1.25.2 n.); [10]or tear out his penis together with the testicles and, holding them in his cupped hands, walk straight toward the south-west until he collapses. [11]He is purified after he dies.

[12]Sex with one's female friend or sister, a woman belonging to one's lineage (A 2.11.15 n.), the wife of one's pupil, one's daughter-in-law, and a cow is equal to sex with the wife of an elder. [13]According to some, it is equal to a student's breaking the vow of chastity.

Illicit Sex [14]If a woman has sex with a low-caste man, the king should have her publicly devoured by dogs [15]and have the man executed, [16]or punish him in the manner stated above (G 12.2).

Breaking the Vow of Chastity [17]A student who has broken his vow of chastity should sacrifice a donkey to Nirṛti at a crossroad. [18]Wearing its skin with the hairy side out and carrying a red bowl, he should beg food from seven houses while proclaiming his deed. [19]He will be purified in a year. [20]If he discharges semen out of fear, because of an illness, or in sleep, or if he neglects to put wood into the sacred fire or to go begging for food, he should offer ghee or two pieces of firewood in the sacred fire reciting the two Retasyā verses.

Miscellaneous Sins [21]Someone who is asleep at sunrise should stand during that day, remaining chaste and without eating any food; while someone who is asleep at sunset should stand during that night reciting the Sāvitrī verse. [22]When someone sees a sordid man (A 1.21.12–19), he should control his breath and look at the sun.

Eating Improper Food [23]If a man eats something unfit to be eaten or consumes an impure substance, he should rid himself of all the excrement [24]by not eating for at least three days; [25]or else he should subsist for seven days on fruits that have fallen on their own without skipping any.* [26]If he eats anything listed before the animals with five claws (G 17.22–7), he should throw up and eat some ghee.

Sins of Speech [27]If someone uses abusive words, tells a lie, or inflicts an injury, he shall practise austerities for a maximum of three days. [28]If his words were true, however, he should offer a sacrifice using the Vāruṇī formulas and the Mānavī hymns. [29]According to some, telling a lie at a marriage, during sex, in jest, or in grief is not a sin, [30]but not if it concerns an elder (A 1.6.32 n.), [31]because when a man tells a lie with regard to an elder even in his mind and even with respect to something trivial, he brings ruin upon himself and upon seven generations before him and after him.

Illicit Sex [32]If someone has sex with a low-caste woman, he should perform an arduous penance (B 2.2.38) for a year; [33]for twelve days, if he does it inadvertently; [34]for three days, if he has sex with a woman during her menstrual period.

Secret Penances

24 [1]For sins unknown to the public, a man may perform a secret penance. [2]A person who yearns to accept or actually accepts something that he is forbidden to accept should stand in water and recite the four Taratsamandī verses, [3]while a person who yearns to eat food that is unfit to be eaten should sprinkle some earth on it.

[4]A man who has sex with a woman during her menstrual period, according to some, is purified by bathing, [5]while,

according to others, this applies only when the woman is his wife.

[6]The penance for performing an abortion (A 1.19.15 n.) is this. He should live on milk for ten days, on ghee for a second ten-day period, and on water for a third ten-day period, partaking of these only once a day in the morning. During this period he should keep his clothes wet and make offerings of his hair, nails, skin, flesh, blood, sinews, bones, and marrow in the sacred fire, saying at the conclusion of each offering: 'I offer in the mouth of the self, in the jaws of death.' [7]And this is another penance for it. [8]The observances are the same as above. [9]He should offer ghee in the sacred fire, while reciting the verse 'You, O Fire, take us across . . . ', the Great Calls, and the Kūṣmāṇḍa verses.

[10]Alternatively, for the murder of a Brahmin, for drinking liquor, for stealing, and for having sex with the wife of an elder (A 1.6.32 n.), a man may perform the same observance, tire himself out by controlling his breath, and silently recite the Aghamarṣaṇa hymn. This is equal to participating in the ritual bath at the end of a horse sacrifice.

[11]Or else, a man may indeed purify himself by reciting the Sāvitrī verse one thousand times. [12]By reciting the Aghamarṣaṇa hymn three times while standing in water a man is freed from all sins.

25

[1]So, they ask: 'Into how many does a student who has broken his vow of chastity enter?'—[2]'Into the Maruts with his breaths; into Indra with his strength; into Bṛhaspati with the splendour of his vedic learning; and into just the Fire with everything else.' [3]Such a student should kindle the sacred fire on the night of the new moon and offer as penance two oblations of ghee, [4]while reciting: 'O Lust, I have spilled semen! I have spilled semen, O Lust! To Lust, Svāhā!' and 'O Lust, I have been squeezed out! I have been squeezed out, O Lust! To Lust, Svāhā!' He should then put a piece of firewood into the fire, sprinkle water around the fire, offer the Yajñavāstu oblation, come near the fire, and worship it three times, reciting the verse 'May the Maruts sprinkle me . . .' [5]There are three

worlds here; he does this to conquer these worlds, to subjugate these worlds. [6] Some take this same rite to be a universally applicable penance, saying with regard to it: 'A man who is in some way impure should make an offering and recite the ritual formulas in the above manner, giving a choice gift as the sacrificial fee.'

[7] When someone cheats, slanders, does forbidden things, eats forbidden foods; when someone ejaculates his semen in a Śūdra woman or in any place other than the vagina (B 3.7.2 n.); or when someone performs witchcraft even intentionally—he should bathe, reciting the Abliṅga or Vāruṇī formulas, or other purificatory texts. [8] If someone commits an offence by speaking or thinking of something forbidden, he should recite the five Calls (cf. G 1.51 n.).

[9] Alternatively, for all sins he may sip water in the morning reciting, 'May the day and the sun purify me', and in the evening reciting, 'May the night and Varuṇa purify me.' [10] Or else, by merely offering eight pieces of firewood into the sacred fire while reciting the formulas 'You are the expiation of sins committed against the gods . . . ', one is freed from all sins (B 4.3.6–7).

Arduous Penances

26 [1] Next we will describe the three types of arduous penances. [2] During three days a man should eat in the morning food fit for sacrifice and not eat anything in the evening; [3] during the next three days he should eat only in the evening; [4] during the following three days he should not request food from anyone; [5] and during the final three days he should fast.

[6] A person who wants the penance to act quickly should remain standing during the day and seated at night; [7] speak the truth; [8] not talk with non-Āryas; [9] sing the Raurava and Yaudhājaya Sāmans every day; [10] bathe at dawn, noon, and dusk while reciting the verses 'Waters, you are refreshing . . . '; and dry himself while reciting the eight purificatory verses 'Golden-coloured, pure, and purifying . . .'

[11] Next, he offers libations of water, saying—

[12]Homage—to the creator of ego-consciousness, to the creator of illusion, to the giver of gifts, to the effacer of sins, to the performer of austerities, to Punarvasu—Homage!

Homage—to the one worthy of Muñja grass offerings, to the one worthy of water offerings, to the one who finds wealth, to the one who finds all—Homage!

Homage—to the one who assures success, to the one who assures total success, to the one who assures great success, to the one who best assures success—Homage!

Homage—to Rudra, to the Lord of cattle, to the Great God, to the Three-eyed God, to the Lone Itinerant, to the Supreme Lord, to Hari, to Śarva, to Īśāna, to the Dread God, to the Wielder of the Thunderbolt, to the Violent God, to the Matted God—Homage!

Homage—to the Sun, to Āditya—Homage!

Homage—to the Blue-necked God, to the Dark-throated God—Homage!

Homage—to the Black God, to the Brown God—Homage!

Homage—to the First-born God, to the Best God, to the Eldest God, to Indra, to the Yellow-haired God, to the Continent God—Homage!

Homage—to the True God, to the Purifying God, to the Fire-coloured God, to Passion, to the God whose form is passion—Homage!

Homage—to the Brilliant God, to the God of brilliant form—Homage!

Homage—to the Fiery God, to the God of fiery form—Homage!

Homage—to Sobhya, to the Fine Man, to the Great Man, to the Middle Man, to the Highest Man, to the Chaste Student—Homage!

Homage—to the God who wears the moon on
his forehead, to the God who wears a skin—
Homage! (cf. SāmB 1.2.7)

[13] The worship of the sun is carried out in the very same manner, [14] as also the offering of ghee in the sacred fire. [15] At the end of the twelve days, he should cook an oblation of milk rice and offer it in the sacred fire to the following deities, saying, [16] 'To Fire Svāhā! To Soma Svāhā! To Fire and Soma Svāhā! To Indra and Fire Svāhā! To Indra Svāhā! To All-gods Svāhā! To Brahman Svāhā! To Prajāpati Svāhā! To Fire who makes the offering flawless Svāhā!' [17] After that he should gratify the Brahmins.

[18] These very rules explain the procedure of the very arduous penance, [19] at which he should eat only as much as he can take in a single mouthful.

[20] Taking only water is the third type of arduous penance, and it is called the 'penance beyond the very arduous penance'.

[21] By performing the first, a man becomes pure, cleansed, and fit to engage in the occupations of his class. [22] By performing the second, he is freed from all except the grievous sins causing loss of caste. [23] By performing the third, all his sins are wiped away.

[24] By performing all three types of arduous penances, he becomes a bath-graduate with respect to all the Vedas, he becomes known to all the gods—[25] so also a man who knows this.

Lunar Penance

27 [1] Next, we will describe the lunar penance. [2] To it also apply the rules given under arduous penance. [3] A person who performs this as a penitential vow should shave his head. [4] On the day before the full moon he should fast. [5] He should offer libations of water, offer ghee in the sacred fire, consecrate the sacrificial oblation, and worship the moon using the following formulas: 'Swell up . . . ', 'May the juices unite in you . . . ', and 'Being born, it becomes ever new . . . '. [6] He should offer ghee in the sacred fire, reciting the four verses 'O gods, whatever

offence we have committed against the gods . . . ', [7] and at the end put pieces of firewood into the fire, reciting the formulas 'You are the expiation for sins committed against the gods . . . '

[8] The mouthfuls of food should be consecrated by mentally reciting these formulas, one for each mouthful: 'OṂ! Earth! Mid Space! Sky! Austerity! Truth! Fame! Prosperity! Vigour! Refreshment! Strength! Lustre! Male! Law! Auspicious!'; [9] or else he may consecrate all of them, saying 'Homage Svāhā!' [10] The mouthfuls shall be of such a size as not to distend the mouth.

[11] The sacrificial oblations are milk rice, almsfood, barley flour, husked grain, barley gruel, vegetables, milk, curd, ghee, roots, fruits, and water, each succeeding being more excellent than each preceding.

[12] On the full-moon day he should eat fifteen mouthfuls, and during the fortnight of the waning moon reduce the amount of food by one mouthful a day. [13] On the new-moon day he should fast, and during the fortnight of the waxing moon increase the amount of food by one mouthful a day. [14] Some invert this procedure (B 3.8.26 n.). [15] This is a month of the lunar fast.

[16] A man who completes one such month becomes free from sin, free from evil; and he wipes out all offences. [17] A man who completes a second such month purifies his ten ancestors and ten descendants, with himself as the twenty-first, and also those alongside whom he eats (A2.17.21 n.). [18] A man who completes one year in this manner will dwell in the same world as the moon.

INHERITANCE

28 [1] After their father's death, the sons may divide the estate, [2] or, if the father so wishes, even during his lifetime but after their mother has reached menopause. [3] Alternatively, the eldest son may inherit the entire estate, and he should maintain the others just as the father. [4] When the estate is partitioned, however, ritual activities increase.

[5] The additional share of the eldest son consists of

one-twentieth of the estate, a pair of livestock, a carriage yoked to animals with teeth in both jaws (G 17.28 n.), and a bull. [6]The additional share of the middle son consists of animals that are one-eyed, old, hornless, and tailless, if there are more than one of these in the herd. [7]The additional share of the youngest son consists of sheep, grain, iron utensils, a house, a cart yoked with oxen, and one of each kind of livestock. [8]All the rest are to be divided equally.

[9]Alternatively, the eldest son may take two shares, [10]and the others one each. [11]Or else, each son may take one kind of property, selecting according to seniority whatever he likes, [12]as also ten heads of livestock, [13]but not of one-hoofed animals or slaves. [14]A bull is the additional share of the eldest, [15]while fifteen cows and a bull are the additional share of the eldest son from the seniormost wife. [16]Alternatively, the eldest son born from a wife who is not the seniormost may receive a share equal to that of his younger brothers born from the seniormost wife. [17]Or else, the special shares are fixed within each group of brothers from the same mother.

Appointed Daughter

[18]A father who has no son should offer an oblation to Fire and Prajāpati, proclaim 'Your son is for my benefit', and appoint his daughter. [19]According to some, he may appoint the daughter by his mere intention. [20]Because of this uncertainty, a man should not marry a girl who has no brother.

Property of a Sonless Man

[21]The estate of a man who dies sonless is shared by those related to him through ancestry (A 2.14.2 n.), lineage, or a common seer (A 2.11.15 n.), and by his wife.

Levirate [22]Alternatively, the widow may seek to procure a son. [23]When her brother-in-law is alive, a son born to such a widow by another person does not share in the inheritance.

Women's Property [24]The wife's property goes to her daughters who are unmarried or indigent. [25] A sister's dowry goes to her uterine brothers after her mother dies, [26] or, according to some, even before.

Inheritance after Partition [27] When a brother who, after partitioning, has not reunited dies, the eldest brother takes his estate. [28] When a brother who, after partitioning, has reunited dies, his coparcener takes his estate. [29] When a son is born after the partition, he alone inherits the paternal estate.

Estates of Coparceners [30] A learned coparcener, if he so wishes, does not have to give what he has earned on his own to his coparceners who are not learned, [31] whereas coparceners who are not learned should share equally what they have earned on their own.

Legal Heirs

[32] A natural son, a son begotten on the wife, a son given in adoption, a contrived son, a son born in secret, and a son adopted after being abandoned by his birth parents—these share in the inheritance. [33] A son of an unmarried woman, a son born to a woman who was pregnant at marriage, a son born to a re-married woman, a son born to an appointed daughter, a son who hands himself over for adoption, and a purchased son—these share in the lineage* (A 2.11.15 n.) [34] and receive one-quarter of the estate in the absence of the sons in the list beginning with the natural son.

[35] A son born to a Brahmin by a Kṣatriya wife, if he happens to be the eldest and possesses good qualities, receives an equal share of the estate, [36] but he is not entitled to the additional share reserved for the eldest son. [37] When a Brahmin has sons by Kṣatriya and Vaiśya wives, the division takes place in the same way as between sons by Brahmin and Kṣatriya wives; [38] so also when a Kṣatriya has such sons. [39] When his father dies without heirs, even a son by a Śūdra wife may receive a share sufficient to maintain himself, if he has been obedient like a pupil (cf. B 2.3.10–13).

[40] According to some, even a son by a wife of the same class as

the husband does not receive a share of the inheritance if he lives an unrighteous life.

[41] When a Brahmin dies childless, Vedic scholars should divide his estate among themselves; [42] or, according to some, the king should take it.

[43] Mentally retarded and impotent brothers should receive maintenance, [44] whereas a son of a mentally retarded brother receives a share of the inheritance. [45] When a man fathers sons through women belonging to a caste higher than his, they are to be treated like the sons by a Śūdra wife.

[46] Sources of water, security measures, and cooked food are not to be divided, [47] as also women belonging to the family.

RESOLVING DOUBTS REGARDING THE LAW

[48] In matters that are unclear, one should follow what is endorsed by a minimum of ten persons who are cultured, skilled in reasoning, and free from greed. [49] A legal assembly is said to consist of a minimum of ten members—four who have mastered the four Vedas; three belonging to the three orders enumerated first; and three who know three different Legal Treatises. [50] When such persons are unavailable, however, one should follow in doubtful cases what is recommended by a learned and cultured Brahmin who knows the Veda, [51] because such a man is incapable of hurting or favouring creatures.

[52] A man who knows the Law, by his knowledge of and adherence to the Law, obtains the heavenly world to a greater degree than those who follow the Law.

[53] That is the Law.

That concludes the Gautama Dharmasūtra

The Dharmasūtra of Baudhāyana

THE Dharmasūtra of Baudhāyana, as that of Āpastamba, forms part of the Kalpasūtra ascribed to this eponymous author and divided into *praśnas* (lit., 'questions') or books. Unlike Āpastamba's, however, the ritual texts of Baudhāyana have been tampered with repeatedly and contain numerous additions and interpolations. The extent and structure of the entire Kalpasūtra are not altogether clear. It appears that the first twenty-nine books contain the Śrautasūtra and other ritual treatises; book 30 contains the Śulvasūtra (vedic geometry); and the next four books comprise the Gṛhyasūtra. The last four books are the Dharmasūtra. The only commentary on the Dharmasūtra is by Govindasvāmin. His commentary is clearly inferior to that of Haradatta on Āpastamba and Gautama, and his date is uncertain but he cannot be very ancient.

There is scholarly agreement that the last two books of the Dharmasūtra are later additions (Bühler 1879–82, ii, pp. xxxiii–xxxv; Kane 1962–75, i. 42–3). Chapters 17 and 18 of Book Two containing the rite of renunciation is also undoubtedly a late addition from a renunciatory handbook. The text appears to have come under the influence of people quite partial to, or interested in, ascetic practice, which would account for the inclusion of several sections on various types of ascetics (B 2.17–18; 3.1–3). The original Dharmasūtra, what I call 'Proto-Baudhāyana', consisted of Book One and the first sixteen chapters of Book Two. Even this section, however, may have undergone tampering and interpolation.

The organization of the treatise leaves a lot to be desired, especially when we compare it with Āpastamba. Identical topics are treated in different places: funerary rites at 1.11.24–6 and 2.14–15; inheritance at 1.11.11–16 and 2.3. Marriage (1.20) is introduced long before the section dealing with the householder (2.4). Baudhāyana contains more detailed descriptions of rituals—sacrifices, twilight worship, bathing, quenching libations (*tarpaṇa*)—than any other Dharmasūtra.

CONTENTS

BOOK ONE

BOOK TWO

BOOK THREE

BOOK FOUR

BOOK ONE

SOURCES OF LAW

Principal Sources

1 [1]The Law is taught in each Veda, [2]in accordance with which we will explain it. [3]What is given in the tradition (A 2.15.25 n.) is the second, [4]and the conventions of cultured people are the third.* [5]Now, cultured people are those who are free from envy and pride, possess just a jarful of grain, and are free from covetousness, hypocrisy, arrogance, greed, folly, and anger. [6]As it is said:

> Cultured people are those who have studied the Veda together with its supplements (A 2.8.10–11) in accordance with the Law, know how to draw inferences from them, and are able to adduce as proofs express vedic texts. (G 3.36 n.)

Legal Assembly

[7]When these fail to address an issue, it falls on a legal assembly with a minimum of ten members. [8]Now, they also quote these verses:

> Four men, each proficient in one of the four Vedas; one exegete; one man who knows the Vedic Supplements; one legal scholar; and three learned Brahmins belonging to three different orders of life—these constitute a legal assembly with a minimum of ten members.
>
> [9]Or they could be five, or three; or even a single man, if he is of unimpeachable conduct, may explain the Law, but not others, be they in their thousands.
>
> [10]An uneducated Brahmin is like an elephant

made of wood or a deer made of leather: all three are so only in name.

[11] When fools, befuddled by darkness, make a pronouncement without knowing the Law, that sin, compounded a hundredfold, engulfs those who proclaim it.

[12] The Law has many gates and its path is narrow and difficult to follow. When there is a doubt, therefore, one man, however learned, should not pronounce on it.

[13] When twice-born men, riding in the chariot of the Legal Treatises and wielding the sword of the Veda, make a pronouncement even in jest, that, the tradition tells us, is the highest Law.

[14] As the wind and the sun make the water collected on a stone disappear, so a sin clinging to a sinner vanishes like that water.

[15] A man who knows the Law should determine the penances after examining a man's build, strength, and age, as well as the time and the deed.

[16] Even if people who have not kept the vows or studied the Veda and who use their caste only to make a living come together in their thousands, they are incapable of constituting a legal assembly.

Regional Differences

2 **The South and the North** [1] There are five areas in which the practices of the south and the north differ from each other (see p. xxvii). [2] We will explain the ones peculiar to the south. [3] They are: eating in the company of an uninitiated person, eating in the company of one's wife, eating stale food, and marrying the daughter of the mother's brother or the father's sister.

[4]The ones peculiar to the north are: selling wool, drinking rum, trafficking in animals with teeth in both jaws, making a living as a soldier, and travelling by sea.

[5]If a man follows the practices of the former in the latter, and those of the latter in the former, he becomes defiled. [6]Each practice is based solely on the authority of the customs of that region.

[7]That is untrue, say Gautama (cf. G 11.20). [8]A man should pay heed to neither set of practices, because they are shown to be opposed to the tradition of cultured people.

Land of the Āryas [9]The region to the east of where the Sarasvatī disappears, west of Kālaka forest, south of the Himalayas, and north of Pāriyātra mountains is the land of the Āryas.* The practices of that land alone are authoritative.

[10]According to some, the land of the Āryas is the region between the rivers Ganges and Yamunā. [11]In this connection, moreover, the Bhāllavins cite this verse (Va 1.14):

> [12]The boundary river in the west and land of the rising sun in the east—between these as far as the black antelope roams, so far does vedic splendour extend.

Border Regions

> [13]The inhabitants of Avanti, Aṅga, Magadha, Surāṣṭra, the Deccan, Upāvṛt, and Sindh, as well as the Sauvīras, are of mixed blood.

[14]If someone visits the lands of the Āraṭṭas, Kāraskaras, Puṇḍras, Sauvīras, Vaṅgas, Kaliṅgas, or Prānūnas, he should offer a Punastoma or a Sarvapṛṣṭhā sacrifice. [15]Now, they also quote:

> When someone travels to the land of the Kaliṅgas he commits a sin through his feet. The seers have prescribed the Vaiśvānarī sacrifice as an expiation for him.

> [16] When someone has committed even a multitude of sins, they commend the Pavitreṣṭi for their removal; for it is the highest means of purification.

[17] Now, they also quote:

> When someone performs every season the Vaiśvānarī, the Vrātapatī, and the Pavitreṣṭi, he is completely released from all sins.

THE STUDENT

Initiation

3 **Length of Time** [1] Forty-eight years, according to ancient practice, is the period of studentship for studying the Veda; [2] alternatively, twenty-four years, or twelve years per Veda, [3] or at least one year for each book, [4] or, given the uncertainty of life, until he has learned it. [5] A vedic text states: 'A man should establish his sacred fires while his hair is still black.'

Uninitiated Children

> [6] Before the cord of Muñja grass is tied, they do not impose any ritual observances on a child, for until he is born through the Veda, he is equal to a Śūdra in conduct.

Time of Initiation [7] The years are counted from conception. A Brahmin should be initiated in the eighth year after conception, [8] a Kṣatriya three years later than a Brahmin, [9] and a Vaiśya one year later than a Kṣatriya.

[10] According to the order of the classes, spring, summer, and autumn are the seasons in which they are initiated; [11] the Gāyatrī, the Triṣṭubh, and the Jagatī are the metres used in their initiation;* [12] and the time for their initiation does not lapse until the sixteenth, the twenty-second, and the twenty-fourth year, respectively.

A Student's Code of Conduct

Insignia [13] Their girdles are made of Muñja grass, a bowstring, and hemp; [14] their skins are those of a black antelope, a spotted Ruru antelope, and a billy goat; [15] and their staffs should be cut from a tree suitable for use in a sacrifice and reach the crown of the head, the forehead, and the tip of the nose, respectively for each class.*

Begging [16] He should go around begging for almsfood using the seven-syllabic formula, with 'Madam' (*bhavati*) at the beginning, 'almsfood' (*bhikṣām*) in the middle, and 'give' (*dehi*) at the end, without pronouncing the syllables *kṣā* (of *bhikṣām*) and *hi* (of *dehi*) too loudly. [17] He should request almsfood from people of all classes, a Brahmin placing 'Madam' at the beginning, a Kṣatriya placing 'Madam' in the middle, and a Vaiśya placing 'Madam' at the end (A 1.3.28–30 n.). [18] The people from whom the request is made should be Brahmins and so forth who are devoted to the occupations proper to their class.

General Rules [19] Every day he should fetch firewood from a wild tract and offer it in the sacred fire. [20] He shall speak the truth and remain modest and free from pride. [21] He should get up before his teacher, go to sleep after him, [22] and never disobey his teacher's commands in any matter, except when it entails a sin causing loss of caste. [23] Let him speak with women only as much as is required, [24] and refrain from dancing, singing, playing musical instruments, wearing perfumes or necklaces, using shoes or umbrellas, and applying oil or collyrium.

Etiquette of Greeting [25] He should clasp the teacher's right leg with his right hand and the teacher's left leg with his left hand. [26] If he desires long life and heaven, he may, if he so wishes, act in the same manner towards other virtuous people with his teacher's permission. [27] After saying 'I am so-and-so, sir!' while he touches his ears so as to concentrate his mind, [28] let him clasp the legs below the knees and above the feet.

[29] He should not do so while he or the person greeted is seated, lying down, or impure. [30] If he is able, he should not remain impure even for a moment (A 1.11.32 n.). [31] He should not greet

anyone while he is carrying firewood, holding a water pot, flowers, or food in his hand, or engaged in other similar activities. [32] When he meets someone, he should not greet him in an exaggerated way.* [33] If he has reached the age of puberty, he shall not greet his brother's wives and the young wives of his teacher, [34] but it is not an offence to sit with them in a boat, on a rock, plank, elephant, terrace, or mat, or in a carriage.

Conduct towards the Teacher [35] Assisting in getting dressed, rubbing the body, attending during the bath, and eating the leftovers (A 1.3.27 n.)—he should perform these for this teacher, [36] as also for the teacher's son, with exception of eating his leftovers even if he is very learned, [37] and for the teacher's wife, with the exception of assisting in getting dressed, rubbing the body, attending during the bath, and eating the leftovers.

[38] He should run after his teacher when he is running, walk behind him when he is walking, and stand by him when he is standing.

General Rules and Final Bath [39] When he bathes, he should not be boisterous in the water [40] but plunge in like a stick.

[41] During a time of adversity, he may study under a teacher who is not a Brahmin; [42] and, while he is studying, he shall obey him and walk behind him. [43] This very activity purifies both of them. [44] The same applies to the brothers, sons, and other pupils of the teacher; [45] whereas he should only rise up and greet an officiating priest, a father-in-law, or a paternal or a maternal uncle who is younger than he. [46] Kātya states that these persons should return the greeting, [47] because this rule is illustrated in the story of the young Āṅgirasa.*

4 [1] If he gets no merit or money, or even the customary obedience, then he should go to the grave with his knowledge. Let him not sow it on barren soil.

[2] As a fire burns up dry grass, so the Veda burns a man who requests it without showing any respect. Let him, therefore, never disclose the Veda to those who fail to honour him according to their ability.

[3]They proclaim this teaching with regard to him:

> [4]Now, Brahman handed over the creatures to Death. The only creature he did not hand over to him was the student. Death said to Brahman: 'Let me have a share of him also.' Brahman replied: 'Only on the night that he fails to bring a piece of firewood.'
>
> [5]The night, therefore, on which a student fails to bring a piece of firewood, he spends by subtracting it from his life span. A student should bring a piece of firewood, therefore, lest he spend that night by subtracting it from his life span.
>
> [6]It is a long sacrificial session that a man undertakes here, when he undertakes the life of a student. The piece of firewood that he offers in the sacred fire when he is about to be initiated as a student constitutes its introductory rite; the piece of firewood he offers when he is about to take the concluding bath constitutes its final rite; and the pieces of firewood he offers in between those two constitute the offerings of the sacrificial session.
>
> [7]Now, a Brahmin, when he is about to undertake the life of a student, enters the creatures in four parts. With one-quarter he enters the fire, with one-quarter death, and with one-quarter the teacher; while one-quarter remains within himself. When he offers a piece of firewood in the fire, he buys back that quarter of himself that is in the fire. He consecrates and places it within himself, and it enters him.
>
> And when, making himself poor and feeling no shame, he begs for almsfood and observes chastity, he buys back that quarter of himself that is in death. He consecrates and places it within himself, and it enters him.
>
> And when he does what his teacher tells him to do, he buys back that quarter of himself that is in the teacher. He consecrates and places it within himself, and it enters him.
>
> And when he performs his private vedic recitation, he buys back that quarter of himself that is in himself. He consecrates and places it within himself, and it enters him.*
>
> After he has taken the bath that concludes his student life, he should never beg for almsfood. He may beg almsfood even

after the final bath to assuage the hunger of his relatives and ancestors, and for the sake of other rites.*

If he cannot find another woman (A 3.28–30 n.) from whom he could beg for almsfood, he may even beg from the wife of his own teacher or from his mother. He should not let the seventh night pass without begging for almsfood.

> He commits a sin by failing to beg for almsfood and to feed the sacred fire with firewood. If he fails to do that for seven nights, he should undergo the penance prescribed for a student who has broken his vow of chastity.* (B 2.1.30–5)
>
> All the Vedas enter a man who knows this and who acts in this way. [8] As a fire glows when it is set ablaze, so does a man here who knows this and lives the life of a student glow when he has taken his final bath.(SB 11.3.3; GoB 1.2.6)

So states a Brāhmaṇa.

THE BATH-GRADUATE

General Rules

5 [1] Next, the rules of a bath-graduate (A 1.30.4 n.). [2] He shall wear a lower and an upper garment; [3] carry a bamboo staff [4] and a pot filled with water; [5] wear a double sacrificial cord (A 1.6.18 n.), [6] a turban, a skin as an upper garment, and shoes; carry an umbrella; maintain the sacred domestic fire; and offer the new-moon and full-moon sacrifices. [7] On the days of the moon's change (A 1.26.14 n.), moreover, he should get the hair of his head, beard, and body shaved and his nails clipped.

[8] This is how he should maintain himself. [9] He should ask for uncooked food from Brahmins, Kṣatriyas, Vaiśyas, and Rathakāras, [10] or even for almsfood.* [11] When he does so, he should stand in silence. [12] And with that food he should perform all the cooked oblations offered to gods and ancestors, as well as rites for securing prosperity. [13] By following this procedure, says

Baudhāyana, the supreme seers attain the highest abode of Prajāpati, the supreme lord.

Water Pot

6 [1]Now, they prescribed for him the use of a water pot.

> [2]Fire is said to reside in the right ear of a billy goat and in the right hand of a Brahmin, as well as in water and in a clump of Kuśa grass.*

After performing his purification, therefore, he should rub the water pot all around with his hand, while reciting 'Blaze up, O Fire . . .' This, indeed, amounts to surrounding it with fire and is better than firing the pot again.*

[3–4]Nevertheless, they point out the following: 'If in his mind he has an inkling that the pot has been slightly sullied, he should set fire to some Kuśa or ordinary grass and burn the pot all around in a clockwise pattern (A 1.7.2 n.). When pots have been touched by dogs, crows, and the like, he should burn them even more until they become fiery red.' [5]When they have come into contact with urine, faeces, blood, semen, and the like, they should be thrown away.

[6]If his water pot breaks, he should offer a hundred oblations of ghee reciting the Calls or simply recite them softly a hundred times. [7]While reciting

> Earth has gone to earth, the mother has joined the mother. May we become rich in sons and cattle, and may he who hates us shatter apart (ṢaḍB 1.6; KS 25.5.29)

he should collect the broken pieces, throw them into water, recite the Sāvitrī verse ten times, and once again take another pot. [8]Taking refuge in Varuṇa by reciting 'That is yours, Varuṇa. Once again it has come to me. OṂ', let him meditate on this syllable.

> [9]If he accepts the pot from a Śūdra, he should recite the Sāvitrī verse one hundred times; from

a Vaiśya, tradition says, fifty times; from a Kṣatriya, twenty-five times; and from a Brahmin, they say, ten times.

[10] Vedic savants ponder the question: 'After the sun has set, is it or is it not permissible for a man to take water?' [11] The superior view is that it is permissible for him to do so; [12] he should control his breath while he is taking water, [13] for fire undoubtedly takes up water.*

[14] 'When someone has washed his hands and feet with water from his pot,' it is stated, 'he remains impure *vis-à-vis* others as long as he remains wet. He uses that water only to purify himself; he should not use it for other rites.' [15] 'Or else,' says Baudhāyana, 'he becomes pure at each purification by washing his hands up to the wrists.'

[16] Now they also quote:

7 [1] The water pot was ordained in ancient times by Brahman and the foremost of sages for the purification of twice-born people. One should, therefore, carry it at all times.

If a man cares for his own well-being, he should use it without hesitation to purify himself, to drink, and to perform his twilight devotions.

[2] Let him perform them with a clear mind. A wise man should not sully his mind. The Self-existent One came into being carrying a water pot. Therefore, he should go about carrying a water pot.

[3] While he is voiding urine or excrement, he should hold the water pot in his right hand; and while he is sipping water, he should hold it in his left hand.* That is the settled practice among good people.

[4] As the sacrificial cup is said to be pure because it comes into contact with Soma, so the water pot remains always pure because it comes into contact with water.

> [5] Let him, therefore, avoid using it in rites for ancestors and gods, and in fire rituals.

[6] He should, therefore, never go on the road without his water pot, not even to the village boundary or from one house to another, [7] or, according to some, even a step beyond the length of an arrow. [8] 'He needs to do so only if he wants to perform his rites without interruption,' says Baudhāyana. [9] And scripture states that there is a Ṛgvedic verse to this effect.*

Purification

8 **Internal and External Purification** [1] Next, the method of purification.

> [2] Water cleanses the body, and knowledge the understanding. Abstaining from hurting others cleanses one's inner being, and truth cleanses the mind.

[3] Internal purification is the cleansing of the mind. [4] We will explain external purification.

The Sacrificial Cord [5] A sacrificial cord is made using three triple strings of Kuśa grass or cotton [6] and reaches up to the navel. [7] It is put on by raising the right arm and lowering the left arm and the head. [8] The opposite procedure is used in rites for the ancestors. [9] When it is worn around the neck, it is called 'pendent'; [10] and when it is worn below, it is called 'low-hung' (A 1.6.18 n.).

Washing and Sipping [11] He should perform his purification seated on his haunches in a clean spot and facing the east or the north. Placing his right arm between his knees, he should wash his feet and then his hands up to the wrists. [12] He should not use the water left over from washing his feet for sipping; [13] or, if he uses it, he should pour some on the ground before sipping.

[14] He should sip using the part of the hand sacred to Brahman. [15] The base of the thumb is the part of the hand sacred to Brahman; [16] the top of the thumb is the part sacred to ancestors; the

tips of the fingers is the part sacred to gods; and the base of the fingers is the part sacred to seers.*

[17] He shall not use for sipping water that drips from the fingers; water with bubbles or froth; water that is warm, pungent, salty, muddy, or discoloured; or water that has a bad odour or taste. [18–19] Three times he should sip water sufficient to reach his heart (A 1.16.2 n.)—without laughing, talking, standing, or looking around; without bowing his head or stooping; never with his topknot untied, his neck wrapped, or his head covered; never hurriedly or without wearing his sacrificial cord over his left shoulder and under his right arm; never with his feet spread apart or his loins wrapped, or without holding his right arm between his knees; and without making a noise. [20] He should wipe his lips three times; [21] twice, according to some. [22] Śūdras and women do both the sipping and the wiping just once. [23] Now, they also quote:

> A Brahmin is purified by water reaching the heart, a Kṣatriya by water reaching the throat, and a Vaiśya by water taken into the mouth; whereas a woman and a Śūdra are purified by wetting the lips. (A 1.16.2 n.)
>
> [24] Drops clinging to the teeth are to be treated like the teeth themselves, because a man bears them like the teeth themselves; he does not have to sip water when they drop. A man is purified from them just as he would be from his own saliva.

[25] Now they also quote:

> Bits of food sticking to the teeth are to be treated like the teeth themselves. A man is purified by just swallowing whatever is in the mouth or what remains in the mouth after sipping.

[26] Then he should apply water to the cavities of his head (G 1.36 n.); to his feet, navel, and head; and finally to his left hand.

[27] If he is sullied while he is holding a metal utensil, he should

set it down, sip some water, and sprinkle water on it as he picks it up again. [28] And if he is sullied while he is holding a dish of food, he should set it down, sip some water, and sprinkle water on it as he picks it up again. [29] And if he is sullied while he is holding a pot of water, he should set it down, sip some water, and sprinkle water on it as he picks it up again. [30] The same should be done, but in the opposite way,* in the case of earthenware, [31] while there is an option in the case of wooden utensils.

Purification of Things [32] When articles become sullied, they are purified in the following ways—if they are metal, by scrubbing them with cowdung, earth, and water, or with just one of them; [33] if they are copper, silver, or gold, by using an acidic cleanser; [34] if they are earthenware, by firing them; [35] if they are wooden, by scraping them; [36] if they are wicker, by using cowdung (G 1.42 n.); [37] if they are made of dried fruits, by using a cow's hair scourer; [38] if they are skins of the black antelope, by using wood-apple and rice; [39] if they are goat's wool blankets, by using areca nuts; [40] if they are woollen, by putting them in the sun; [41] if they are linen, by using a paste of yellow mustard; [42] and if they are cotton, by using earth (G 1.42 n.). [43] Skins are purified like cotton; [44] stones and gems like metal; [45] bones like wood; [46] conch-shells, horn, mother of pearls, and ivory like linen, [47] or by using milk.

[48] Alternatively, when articles come into contact with urine, faeces, blood, semen, or a corpse, they are to be scrubbed twenty-one times using one of the scrubbing agents listed above, depending on how they strike one's eyes and nose.* [49] Non-metal articles that come into contact with them, however, should be discarded.

[50] Ritual vessels used in sacrifices are cleansed in the manner prescribed in the Veda. [51] A vedic text states: 'They are not sullied by coming into contact with Soma juice.'

> [52] Time, fire, cleansing the mind, water and the like, applying cowdung, and ignorance—these, they say, are the six ways of purification for creatures.

[53] Now, they also quote:

> The time, the place, himself, the article, the purpose of the article, the cause, and the condition—after examining these, a smart man who knows the methods of purification and wants to adhere to the Law should perform the purification.

Purity of Persons and Things

9

[1] The hand of an artisan is always clean, as also goods displayed for sale. Almsfood received by a student is always pure. So states a vedic text.

[2] A calf is pure when it makes the milk to flow, a bird when it makes a fruit to fall, women when one is making love, and a dog when it catches a deer.

[3] All factories are pure, except liquor breweries. Streams with constantly flowing water do not become polluted, as also dust blown up by the wind.

[4] Flowers and fruits of flowering and fruit-bearing trees, likewise, do not become polluted even if they are growing in unclean places.

[5] If a Brahmin touches a sanctuary tree,* a funeral pyre, a sacrificial post, a Cāṇḍāla, or a man who sells the Veda, he should bathe with his clothes on.

[6] One's own bed, seat, clothes, wife, children, and water pot are pure with respect to oneself; but they are impure *vis-à-vis* others.

[7] When seats, beds, vehicles, boats, roads, and grass come into contact with Cāṇḍālas or outcastes, they are purified by just the wind.

[8] Grain from a threshing floor and water from a well or reservoir, as also milk from a dairy

farm—these may be consumed even if they are given by someone whose food one is not allowed to eat.

[9] Gods invented three means of purification for Brahmins: being unaware that something is impure, sprinkling it with water, and getting it verbally declared as suitable.

[10] Water collected on the ground sufficient for cows to slake their thirst may be used for purification, as long as it is not saturated with foul substances or has a bad odour, colour, or taste.

[11] A piece of ground, on the other hand, is made pure by sweeping, sprinkling with water, smearing with cowdung, scattering clean soil, or scraping, depending on the degree of the defilement. [12] Now, they also quote:

10 [1] Each drop of water when sprinkled purifies an area as large as a cow's hide* irrespective of whether the ground has been swept or not, so long as one does not notice anything filthy on it.

Purity of Food [2] Food that has been prepared out of one's sight should be heated and sprinkled with water, [3] as also viands bought at the market. [4] And it is said:

For the gods, being apprehensive and desirous of pure things, do not relish the oblations offered by people without a spirit of generosity.*

[5] And also:

The food of a man who is pure but not generous and the food of a man who is generous but impure—having pondered over this, the gods pronounced them to be equal.

But Prajāpati told them: 'They are not equal; they are clearly unequal. The food of the man who is not generous is totally useless, and the food cleansed by generosity excels it by far.'

[6] Now, they also quote:

> Lack of generosity is the highest sin; generosity is clearly the highest austerity. The gods, therefore, do not eat an oblation offered without a spirit of generosity. [7] Such a fool will never go to heaven, though he may have offered sacrifices or distributed gifts.
>
> [8] A man whose conduct is plagued by vacillation, who pursues his own objectives, and who violates the scriptural provisions—such a man, tradition says, is a fool, because he thwarts the course of the Law. (G 13.11 n.)

[9] Vegetables, flowers, fruits, roots, and herbs bought at the market, however, should be washed.

Excretions [10] After spreading some dry grass, pieces of wood unfit for ritual use, or some clods of earth on the ground and covering his head, he should void urine and excrement facing the north during the day and the south during the night.

[11] After voiding urine, he should first wash the organ with earth and water (G 1.42 n.), [12] and then the left hand three times. [13] He should do the same after voiding excrement, [14] but three times in turn for the anus and the left hand. [15] After a seminal discharge, he should do the same as after voiding urine.

The Lower Body [16] After tying or untying the lower garment, he should wash himself [17] or else touch wet grass, cowdung, or the earth. [18] When he is engaged in ritual activity, he should avoid touching below the navel, [19] for a vedic text states: 'A man's body is clean above the navel and unclean below the navel' (TS 6.1.3.4).

Purity and Occupations

[20] Śūdras employed by Āryas should shave their hair and cut their nails every fortnight or every month and follow the Ārya mode of sipping water.

[21] A Vaiśya may live by lending money on interest, [22] but only at a rate of five Māṣas for twenty-five (G 12.29 n.). [23] Now, they also quote:

> When a man takes a loan at the going rate of interest and then lends it at a higher rate, he is an usurer and is denounced in all the codes of Law.
>
> Usury and abortion were once weighted in a balance. The abortionist rose to the top, while the usurer trembled.
>
> [24] Brahmins who are cattle herders, traders, artisans, bards, servants, and usurers should be treated like Śūdras.

[25] Men of the first two classes, nevertheless, may freely lend money on interest to people who neglect their ritual duties, to misers, to infidels, and to wicked people.

> [26] By not offering sacrifices, by not getting married, by spurning vedic study, and by neglecting Brahmins, respectable families fall into disrepute.
>
> [27] One does not incur the sin of neglecting a Brahmin when the man is a fool and bereft of vedic knowledge, for one does not offer an oblation in the ash ignoring a blazing fire.
>
> [28] When they are bereft of vedic knowledge, respectable families fall into disrepute by dealing in cattle, horses, and vehicles, by engaging in agriculture, and by entering the royal service.
>
> [29] When they are rich in vedic knowledge, even poor families are counted among the respectable and attain great fame.
>
> [30] Vedic study impedes agriculture, and agriculture impedes vedic study. A man who is able may pursue both, but if he is unable, he should give up agriculture.

[31] Surely, a fat, unruly, fierce, and bellowing bull, attacking creatures and saying what he pleases, does not reach the gods. It is the tiny ones with emaciated bodies who reach there.

[32] At various times in his youth a man may have foolishly done all sorts of good or evil deeds. If, however, in his later years he leads a virtuous life, only that will follow him, not the acts of his youth.

[33] Leading an austere and vigilant life, let him always grieve in his heart when he recalls his misdeeds. He will thus be freed from those sins.

[34] When a man pours water for others to sip and drops of that water fall on his feet, they do not make him impure. They are just like water that collects on the ground.

Death of a Relative

11 **Period of Impurity** [1] With reference to births and deaths, they say that the period of impurity of people belonging to the same ancestry (A 2.14.2 n.) lasts for ten days, except for officiating priests, those consecrated for a sacrifice, and students. [2] Among people belonging to the same ancestry, the relationship based on common ancestry extends to the seventh generation. [3] Only a bath is prescribed when a child dies before it is seven months old or before teething.

[4] When a child dies before it is 3 years old or before teething, no offerings of food or water are prescribed, and it should not be cremated.

[5] The same is true when unmarried girls die. [6] Some do perform these rites for married women, [7] but they do it just to curry favour with people; ritual formulas are thought not to apply to women.

> [8] When unmarried women die, their relatives become pure in three days, but their uterine brothers are purified by following the procedure given above.

[9] Furthermore, one's great-grandfather, grandfather, father, oneself, one's uterine brothers, son by a wife of the same class, grandson, and great-grandson—but not the great-grandson's son—they say, belong to the same ancestry; among these, one's son and grandson share an undivided oblation. [10] Those who share in separate oblations, they say, belong to the same family line.*

Inheritance [11] In the absence of other heirs, the estate goes to the relatives belonging to the same ancestry (A 2.14.2 n.); [12] in their absence, to the relatives belonging to the same family line (B 1.11.9–10 n.); [13] in their absence, the teacher who had been like a father to the deceased, or a student or officiating priest of the deceased may take it; [14] and in their absence, the king—but let him donate that property to persons deeply versed in the three Vedas. [15] The king himself, however, should never appropriate the property of Brahmins. [16] Now, they also quote:

> Poison kills just one man, but a Brahmin's property destroys even his sons and grandsons. Poison is not truly poison, they say; the true poison is the property of a Brahmin.

'Therefore, a king should never appropriate the property of Brahmins, for it is said that the property of Brahmins is the deadliest poison.'

Death and Birth Impurity [17] If a birth and a death occur at the same time, the ten-day period of impurity is observed in common for both. [18] If, moreover, before the completion of the ninth day of one ten-day period of impurity other periods of ten-day impurity arise, then the impurity ends after the first ten-day period. [19] At a birth, meanwhile, the ten-day period of impurity affects only the mother and the father. [20] According to some, it affects only the mother, because it is she that people avoid;

[21] while according to others, it affects only the father, because of the predominance of the semen, [22] for the scriptures record sons who took birth outside the womb. [23] Without a doubt, however, both the mother and the father become impure, because they participate equally.

Funerary Rites [24] When a death has occurred, however, the relatives should wear their sacrificial cords over their right shoulders and under their left arms (A 1.6.18 n.) and, placing the younger ones first, go down to a bathing place. They should submerge in the water, rise up, climb up to the bank, sip some water, and offer a libation of water to the deceased person—repeating this sequence of acts three times. They should finally climb up to the bank, sip some water, touch a piece of coal and water at the door to the house, and remain seated there on mats for ten days eating food without spices or salt.

[25] The ancestral offering is performed either on the eleventh or the twelfth day. [26] With respect to other rites, one should follow the local customs.

Death Impurity for Distant Relatives [27] Even when a person unrelated by common ancestry dies (A 2.14.2 n.), one should observe a period of impurity for three days, for a day and a night, or for a single day, depending on how closely one is related to the deceased. [28] At the death of one's teacher, tutor, or a son of theirs, the period of impurity lasts for three days,* [29] as also at the death of an officiating priest. [30] At the death of a pupil, a person studying under the same teacher, or a classmate during one's vedic studentship, one should observe a period of impurity for three days, for a day and a night, and for a single day, respectively.

[31] After miscarriages women remain impure for the same number of days as the months of pregnancy.

Impurity from Touch

[32] When someone accidentally touches the corpse of an outsider, he becomes pure immediately after taking a bath with his clothes on; [33] whereas if someone does so deliberately, he

remains impure for three days. [34]The same is true in the case of a menstruating woman; [35]the observances for her are explained in the passage: 'A son born from such a woman is a heinous sinner'* (TS 2.5.1.6).

> [36]If someone touches a man who sells the Veda,
> a sacrificial post, an outcaste, a funeral pyre, a
> dog, or a Cāṇḍāla, he should take a bath.
>
> [37]If a Brahmin has an open wound filled with
> pus and bloody discharge and a worm appears
> in it, what penance should he observe?
>
> [38]A man who has been bitten by a worm is
> purified after he has bathed in and drunk a
> mixture of cow's urine, cowdung, milk, curd,
> ghee, and a decoction of Kuśa grass.

[39]If someone is touched by a dog, he should bathe with his clothes on. [40]Alternatively, he becomes pure by washing that spot, touching it with fire, washing it again, washing his feet, and sipping some water. [41]Now, they also quote:

> If a Brahmin is bitten by a dog, he is purified
> by going into a river that flows into the sea,
> controlling his breath one hundred times, and
> consuming some ghee.
>
> Alternatively, he becomes pure at once by bath-
> ing with water from a golden or silver pot, from
> a cow's horn, or from new earthen pots.

Forbidden Food

12 [1]It is forbidden to eat village animals*—[2]the carnivorous and birds, [3]as well as cocks and pigs, [4]with the exception of goats and sheep.

[5]It is permissible to eat the following: porcupine, Godhā monitor lizard, hare, hedgehog, tortoise, and the rhinoceros—these, excluding the rhinoceros, are the five five-clawed animals (A 1.17.37 n.); [6]Ṛśya antelope, Hariṇa deer, Pṛṣata deer, the

buffalo, the wild boar, and Kuluṅga antelope—these, excluding the Kuluṅga antelope, are the five animals with cloven feet; [7]the following birds: partridge, pigeon, Kapiñjala partridge, Vārdhrānasa crane, peacock, and Vāraṇa bird—these, excluding the Vāraṇa bird, are the five birds that feed scratching with their feet; [8]and the following fish: Sahasradaṃṣṭra, Cilicima, Varmi, Bṛhacchiras, Mahāśakari,* Rohita, and Rājīva.

[9]It is forbidden to drink the milk of an animal during the first ten days after it has given birth or of an animal that is pregnant, [10]whose calf has died, or that is suckling a calf that is not hers. [11]It is forbidden to drink the milk of sheep, camels, and one-hoofed animals. [12]If someone drinks milk that is forbidden, with the exception of cow's milk, he should perform an arduous penance; [13]in the case of cow's milk, on the other hand, he should fast for three days.

[14]One should not eat stale food—except vegetables, soup, meat, ghee, cooked grains, molasses, curd, honey, and barley meal—; [15]as also foods that have turned sour, including molasses.

Annual Course of Study

[16]People should commence the annual course of study on the full-moon day of July–August or August–September and conclude it on the full-moon day of December–January or January–February.

Sacrifices

13 **Sacrificial Garments** [1]The gods take delight in a pure sacrifice; [2]for the gods are pure and love pure things, [3]a point affirmed by this vedic verse:

> Pure oblations to you, O Maruts, who are pure. A pure sacrifice I offer to the pure ones. By ritual ordinance the lovers of rites have reached the truth, they who are pure, of pure birth, and purifying. (RV 7.56.12; TB 2.8.5.5)

[4] Among clothes, new ones are pure. Therefore, he should perform everything connected with the sacrifice wearing new clothes. [5] The patron of the sacrifice, his wife, and the officiating priests should wear clothes that have been washed and dried in the wind and are not worn out—[6] this provision applies after the measuring out of the altar, [7] during long Soma sacrifices, and at sacrificial sessions. [8] On other occasions, one should follow the specific prescriptions. [9] So, when fire offerings, animal sacrifices, and Soma sacrifices are performed for the purpose of sorcery, the officiating priests should wear red turbans and clothes; while reciting the Vṛṣākapi hymn, they should wear multi-coloured clothes and shawls; [10] and at the establishment of the sacred fires, linen clothes are used, and if they are not available, cotton or woollen clothes.

[11] Clothes that are tainted by urine, excrement, blood, semen, and the like should be washed with earth and water (G 1.42 n.). [12] Silk* and bark garments are cleaned like ordinary clothes; [13] and black antelope skin, like bark garments. [14] He shall not wear a cloth that has been wrapped around his loins or on which he has slept without first washing it. [15] He should not use in a rite for the gods a cloth that has been used by humans without first laundering it.

Sacrificial Ground [16] When polluted, compact earth is purified by smearing with cowdung; [17] loose soil, by tilling; [18] and wet soil, by covering it with clean soil. [19] The ground is purified in four ways: by cows trampling it underfoot, by tilling it, by burning it, and by rain falling on it; [20] the fifth way is to smear it with cowdung, and the sixth is through the lapse of time.

Sacrificial Utensils [21] Grass placed on unconsecrated ground must be washed. [22] Grass that may have become polluted out of sight must be sprinkled with water. [23] Small pieces of wood shall be cleaned in the same way, [24] while large pieces of wood must be washed and dried when they become polluted. [25] If the quantity is large, however, it may be sprinkled with water. [26] Wooden vessels touched by a person sullied with remnants (A 1.3.27 n.) must be scrubbed; [27] whereas those that are tainted by the stain of remnants must be scraped; [28] and those that are tainted with urine, faeces, blood, semen, and the like must be thrown away.

[29]These provisions apply unless there is a special rule, [30]as, for example, washing with Darbha grass and water at all these rituals: daily fire sacrifice, Gharmocchiṣṭa, Dadhigharma, Kuṇḍapāyinām Ayana, Utsargiṇām Ayana, Dākṣāyaṇa Sacrifice, Iḍādadha, Catuścakra, and Brahmaudana. [31]At all Soma sacrifices the utensils are washed only with water at the washing mound Mārjālīya. [32]Those that are tainted with urine, faeces, blood, semen, and the like must be thrown away.

14 [1]Earthen vessels touched by a person sullied with remnants (A 1.3.27 n.) must be heated over a fire; [2]whereas those that are tainted by the stain of remnants must be fired anew; [3]and those that are tainted with urine, faeces, blood, semen, and the like must be thrown away.

[4]Metal vessels must be scrubbed as before and then washed. [5]Materials used for scrubbing are cowdung, earth, and ash. [6]When metal vessels have been tainted with urine, faeces, blood, semen, and the like, they must be recast [7]or completely immersed in cow's urine or in a great river (A 1.27.1) for seven days. [8]Vessels made of stone are to be treated the same way.

[9]Vessels made of gourd, wood-apple, or skin* should be scrubbed with cow's hair; [10]whereas those woven out of Naḷa reeds, bamboo, Śara reeds, or Kuśa grass should be washed with cowdung and water.

Sacrificial Offerings [11]When unhusked rice becomes tainted, it must be washed and dried. [12]If the quantity is large, however, it may be sprinkled with water. [13]Husked rice, on the other hand, shall be thrown away, [14]as also cooked sacrificial oblations. [15]If a large quantity has been polluted by a dog, a crow, and the like, however, after taking out a portion from that place as food for humans, one may sprinkle water reciting the passage 'The purifier, the heavenly one . . . .' [16]Honey water and milk preparations are purified by pouring them from one vessel into another. [17]Likewise, one may use oil or ghee that has been touched by a person sullied with remnants after pouring it into water. [18]If an impure substance has been put into the sacred fire, he shall make the fires ascend the fire-drills, produce a new fire by churning the fire-drills,* and offer the Pāvamāneṣṭi sacrifice.

[19]Purification, proper place, ritual formulas, ritual sequence, purpose, materials and their consecration, and proper time—when there is a conflict between these, each preceding item is more important than each succeeding one.

15 **Sacrificial Actions** [1]One should enter the sacrificial arena from the north [2]and leave it in the same direction. [3]In rites for ancestors, however, one should do the opposite. [4]One should wash anything that one has touched with the feet. [5]After touching one's body or the hem of the garment, one should touch water; [6]as also after cutting or breaking something; after digging; after removing something; after a rite to the ancestors, fiends, Nirṛti, or Rudra; and after a rite of sorcery.

[7]When a sacrificial tool is used while reciting a ritual formula, a man should not move it around his body; [8]sacrificial tools are more closely connected with the sacrifice, [9]whereas the officiating priests are more distant. [10]The patron of the sacrifice and his wife are closer to the sacrifice than the officiating priests; [11]the ghee is closer than the sacrificial tools; the sacrificial oblations are closer than the ghee; the sacrificial animal is closer than the sacrificial oblations; the Soma is closer than the sacrificial animal; and the sacred fires are closer than the Soma.

[12]In accordance with the ritual acts they are performing, the officiating priests should not turn away from the sacrificial arena—[13]if he is facing the east, he should turn towards his right shoulder, [14]and if he is facing the west, towards his left shoulder.

[15]The passageway to and from the sacrificial area lies between the Cātvāla pit and the Utkara mound. [16]In the absence of a Cātvāla pit, it lies between the offertorial fire and the Utkara mound. [17]Those who carry out the ritual acts, as well as the patron of the sacrifice and his wife, should walk through that passageway [18]as long as the sacrifice is not completed. [19]After it has been completed, however, the passageway lies on the side that does not contain the Utkara mound.*

[20]One should not put into the sacred fire logs or kindling wood that have not been sprinkled with water, or that have not been dedicated,* or that are wet. [21]The Brahman priest and the patron of the sacrifice should walk in front of [22]or, according to

some, behind the offertorial fire. [23]The seat of the Brahman priest is located to the south of the offertorial fire; the seat of the patron of the sacrifice, to the west of the Brahman priest's seat; [24]the seat of the Hotṛ priest, to the north of the northern corner of the sacrificial arena; [25]the seat of the Āgnīdhra priest, at the Utkara mound; [26]and the seat of the patron's wife, behind the householder's fire. [27]Each and every time any of these seats is used, one should spread Darbha grass on it. [28]Each person should be provided with a pot of water to be used for sipping.

Observances [29]A man who has been consecrated for a sacrifice shall observe the following vows. [30]He should not disclose a sin committed by someone else; become angry; weep; or look at urine or faeces. [31]If he sees any filth, let him recite softly: 'Mind, uncontrolled; eyesight, feeble; sun, the greatest of lights. O Consecration, do not forsake me.' [32]And if it rains on him, let him recite softly: 'Place strength in me, O Flowing Waters; place vigour in me; place strength in me. Do not destroy my consecration or my austerity.'*

SOCIAL CLASSES

16 [1]There are four classes: Brahmin, Kṣatriya, Vaiśya, and Śūdra. [2]Of these, according to the order of the classes, a Brahmin may have four wives, [3]a Kṣatriya three, [4]a Vaiśya two, [5]and a Śūdra one.

Mixed Classes

[6]Sons born from wives of the same class as the husband's or the class immediately below his are Savarṇas; [7]sons born from wives two or three classes below the husband are Ambaṣṭhas, Ugras, and Niṣādas; [8]and sons born from wives in the reverse order of class are Āyogavas, Māgadhas, Vaiṇas, Kṣattṛs, Pulkasas, Kukkuṭas, Vaidehakas, and Cāṇḍālas (cf. G 4.16–21; Va 18.1–6).

[9]From a wife belonging to the first class an Ambaṣṭha fathers a Śvapāka. [10]From a wife belonging to the second class an Ugra

fathers a Vaiṇa. [11]From a wife belonging to the third class a Niṣāda fathers a Pulkasa, [12]while the inverse produces a Kukkuṭa.

[13]A fifth-generation son fathered by a Niṣāda from a Niṣāda woman rids himself of the Śūdra status, [14]and one may perform his initiation. One may officiate at a sacrifice of a sixth-generation son. [15]Together with the seventh-generation son, these are given respectively the following appellations: a man of unmodified seed, a man of equal seed, and an equal.

> [16]Sons fathered by an uninitiated man are
> Vrātyas, excluded from initiation—so state the
> wise with equal reference to the three classes.

17 [1]Rathakāra, Ambaṣṭha, Sūta, Ugra, Māgadha, Āyogava, Vaiṇa, Kṣattr̥, Pulkasa, Kukkuṭa, Vaidehaka, Cāṇḍāla, Śvapāka, and so forth—[2]among these, sons of equal class are born from wives of the same class as their husbands; [3]whereas a Brahmin fathers a Brahmin from a Kṣatriya wife, an Ambaṣṭha from a Vaiśya wife, and a Niṣāda from a Śūdra wife, [4]or, according to some, a Pāraśava; [5]a Kṣatriya fathers a Kṣatriya from a Vaiśya wife, and an Ugra from a Śūdra wife; [6]and a Vaiśya fathers a Rathakāra from a Śūdra wife.

[7]A Śūdra fathers a Māgadha from a Vaiśya wife, a Kṣattr̥ from a Kṣatriya wife, and a Cāṇḍāla from a Brahmin wife; [8]a Vaiśya fathers an Āyogava from a Kṣatriya wife, and a Vaidehaka from a Brahmin wife; and a Kṣatriya fathers a Sūta from a Brahmin wife.

[9]Among these, the union of an Ambaṣṭha man with an Ugra woman produces a son in the proper order of class; [10]whereas the union of a Kṣattr̥ man and a Vaidehaka woman produces a son in the reverse order of class.

[11]From an Ugra father and a Kṣattr̥ mother is born a Śvapāka; [12]from a Vaidehaka father and a Ambaṣṭha mother, a Vaiṇa; [13]from a Niṣāda father and a Śūdra wife, a Pulkasa; [14]and from a Śūdra father and a Niṣāda wife, a Kukkuṭa.

> [15]The wise say that sons born from a union
> between people of different classes are Vrātyas.

KING

18 [1]Receiving one sixth as taxes, a king should protect his subjects.

[2]Brahman, clearly, placed his grandeur in Brahmins along with the duties of studying and teaching, offering and officiating at sacrifices, and giving and receiving gifts, for the preservation of the Vedas. [3]In Kṣatriyas he placed his strength along with the duties of studying, offering sacrifices, giving gifts, using weapons, and protecting the treasury and creatures, for the enhancement of government. [4]In Vaiśyas he placed the duties of studying, offering sacrifices, giving gifts, agriculture, trade, and animal husbandry, for the enhancement of economic activity. [5]In Śūdras he placed the service of the higher classes, [6]for it is said, 'they were created from his feet.'

[7]The king should select as his personal priest a man pre-eminent in all matters [8]and follow his instructions.

War

[9]The king should not turn back in battle [10]or strike with barbed or poisoned weapons. [11]He should not engage in battle people who are afraid, intoxicated, mad, or delirious, or who have lost their armour; as also women, children, old people, and Brahmins, [12]unless they are trying to kill him. [13]Now they also quote:

> When someone kills even a teacher born in an illustrious family who is trying to kill him, it does not make him a murderer of a learned Brahmin; there wrath recoils on wrath. (cf. A.1.29.7)

Duties and Taxes

[14]The duty on goods imported by sea is 10 per cent plus a choice piece of merchandise. [15]He should assess an equitable tax also on other types of merchandise corresponding to their value, a tax that would not be oppressive.

[16]When the owner has disappeared, the king should look after

his estate for one year, after which he may appropriate it, so long as it does not belong to a Brahmin.

Punishment

[17] A Brahmin, clearly, is not subject to capital punishment for any crime. [18] When a Brahmin kills a Brahmin, has sex with the wife of an elder, steals gold, or drinks liquor, the king should brand the man's forehead with the mark of a headless corpse, a vagina, a jackal, or a tavern banner, respectively, using a heated iron and banish him from his kingdom.

[19] When a man belonging to the Kṣatriya or lower class kills a Brahmin, he should be executed and all his property confiscated. [20] When such people kill a man of equal or lower class, the king should impose a suitable punishment in accordance with their ability.

19 [1] If someone kills a Kṣatriya, to erase the enmity he should hand over to the king a thousand cows and in addition a bull (A 1.24.1 n.); [2] a hundred if he kills a Vaiśya, and ten if he kills a Śūdra—here too, in addition a bull. [3] The provision for killing a Śūdra applies also to the killing of a woman or a cow, except when it is a Brahmin woman soon after her menstrual period (A 1.24.8–9 n.), or it is a milch cow or a draught ox. [4] If someone kills a milch cow or a draught ox, after paying the penalty he should perform a lunar penance (B 3.8). [5] The provision for killing a Kṣatriya applies to the killing of a Brahmin woman soon after her menstrual period. [6] Haṃsa goose, Bhāsa vulture, peacock, Cakravāka goose, chameleon, crow, owl, frog, Ḍiḍḍika rat, Ḍerikā rat, dog, Babhru mongoose, common mongoose, and the like—the punishment for killing any of these is the same as for killing a Śūdra.

Witnesses

[7] To gain the respect of the world, a witness should give testimony consistent with what he saw or heard.

> [8] One-quarter of a crime* falls on the offender, one-quarter on the witness, one-quarter on all the officials of court, and one-quarter on the king.
> When a man who should be condemned is, in fact, condemned, then the king is released from guilt and the court officials are set free; upon the offender falls the guilt.
>
> [9] Sharp-witted, he should interrogate a designated* witness in the following manner:
>
> [10] 'Whatever good you may have done from the day you were born until the day you die, all that will go to the king, if you tell a lie.
>
> [11] 'He slays for sure three fathers and three grandfathers, as also seven generations of his descendants born or yet to be born—when a witness gives false testimony.
>
> [12] 'He slays three grandfathers with false testimony concerning gold (G 13.14 n.); five with false testimony concerning farm animals; ten with false testimony concerning cows; a hundred with false testimony concerning horses; a thousand with false testimony concerning men; and all with false testimony concerning land—when a witness gives false testimony.'

[13] People of all four classes who have sons can be witnesses, except vedic scholars, the royalty, wandering ascetics, and those who lack humanity.* [14] If a witness abides by his recollection, he will receive praise from those in authority; [15] whereas if he acts to the contrary, he will fall into hell. [16] Such a man should live on hot milk for twelve days (B 2.2.37) or offer ghee in the sacred fire while reciting the Kūṣmāṇḍa verses.

MARRIAGE

20 [1] There are eight types of marriages. [2] When a girl is given to a vedic student who requests her, after enquiring into

his learning and character, it is a 'Brahma' marriage. [3]After dressing her up and adorning her with jewellery, when a girl is given with the formula, 'Here she is! May you jointly fulfil the Law', it is a 'Prajāpati' marriage. [4]When the groom first offers parched grain in the sacred fire and gives a cow and a bull to the girl's father, it is a 'Seer's' marriage. [5]When a girl is given to the officiating priest within the sacrificial arena while the sacrificial gifts are being taken away, it is a 'Divine' marriage. [6]When the groom takes the girl after gratifying her parents with money, it is a 'Demonic' marriage. [7]When a lover has sex with his beloved through mutual consent, it is a 'Gandharva' marriage. [8]When a man takes away a girl by force, it is a 'Fiendish' marriage. [9]When a man has intercourse with a girl who is asleep, intoxicated, or insane, it is a 'Ghoulish' marriage.

[10]Of these, only the first four are suitable for Brahmins, and even among these each preceding type is better than each following. [11]Of the last four, each subsequent type is worse than each preceding. [12]Among the latter, moreover, the sixth and seventh flow from the Kṣatriya nature, because that is the dominant feature of Kṣatriyas; [13]while the fifth and the eighth are suitable for Vaiśyas and Śūdras, [14]for Vaiśyas and Śūdras are lax about their wives [15]because they are occupied with agricultural and servile work. [16]Some commend the 'Gandharva' form of marriage for all, because it flows from love.

21 [1]'The excellence of the marriage', it is stated, 'determines the excellence of the children that issue from it.' [2]Now they also quote:

> It is laid down that a woman who is purchased for money is not a wife. She cannot take part in rites for gods or ancestors, and Kaśyapa has declared her to be a slave.
>
> [3]When people, bewitched by greed, deliver a daughter of theirs for a payment, these wicked men, selling their own selves and guilty of a heinous crime, fall into a gruesome hell, slay their families up to the seventh generation (G

> 13.14 n.), and repeatedly die and are reborn—
> all this is decreed when a payment takes place.

SUSPENSION OF VEDIC RECITATION

[4] Vedic recitation is suspended for a day and a night on the following occasions: full-moon day; eighth day of each fortnight; new-moon day; fall of a meteor; earthquake; visiting a cemetery; and the death of the king, a vedic scholar, or someone who has studied under the same teacher. [5] When there is wind, a foul smell, or frost, and at the sound of dancing, music, weeping, or the singing of Sāmans (G 16.21 n.), vedic recitation is suspended for their duration. [6] When thunder, rain, and lightning occur together outside the rainy season, vedic recitation is suspended for three days; [7] and even during the rainy season when they occur without rain, it is suspended until the same time the next day.

[8] When someone has received a gift or eaten food at an ancestral offering, the suspension lasts for the remainder of that day—[9] after eating, however, until the food has been digested—[10] for a Brahmin's hand is his mouth.* [11] Now, they also quote:

> There is no difference between what is eaten
> and what is received, states a vedic text.

[12] At the death of one's father, the suspension lasts for three days. [13] A Brahmin* who is a renowned vedic savant has clearly two kinds of semen, the one located above the navel and the other below. By means of the semen above the navel he begets offspring when he initiates Brahmins, when he teaches them, when he makes them offer sacrifices, and when he makes them good people. All these become his children. By means of the semen going downward from the navel, on the other hand, he obtains the children of his loins. About a vedic scholar and savant, therefore, they never say, 'You have no children' (Va 2.5). [14] 'Therefore,' it is said, 'a learned Brahmin has two names, two mouths, two kinds of semen, and two births.'

[15] Within sight or hearing of a Śūdra or a degraded person, furthermore, vedic recitation is suspended for the duration.

[16]When someone hears the howling of a jackal at night, he should not recite the Veda until he has slept.

[17]During the morning and evening twilights and on the days of the moon's change (A 1.26.14 n.), one should not recite the Veda, [18]eat meat, or have sex with one's wife; [19]'for on the days of the moon's change,' it is stated, 'fiends and ghouls undertake their nefarious wanderings'.

[20]Also when other omens or portents occur, vedic recitation is suspended for a day and a night, with the exception of mental recitation; [21]and even mental recitation is suspended when there is a birth or a death.

[22]Now, they also quote:

> The eighth day slays the teacher, the fourteenth day slays the pupil, and the fifteenth day slays the knowledge; therefore, he should refrain from recitation during the days of the moon's change. (A 1.26.14 n.)

BOOK TWO

PENANCES

1 [1]Next, the penances.

Penances for Killing

[2]A man who has killed a learned Brahmin should do the following for twelve years. [3]He should carry a skull and a post from a bed-frame; wear the skin of an ass; reside in the wilderness; and, using the head of a corpse as his flag, get a hut built in a cemetery and live in it. He should maintain himself by begging almsfood from seven houses while proclaiming his crime. When he does not receive any almsfood, he should fast. [4]Alternatively, he may offer a horse sacrifice, a Gosava sacrifice, or an Agniṣṭut sacrifice; [5]or cleanse himself by participating at the bath that concludes a horse sacrifice. [6]Now, they also quote:

> When someone kills a Brahmin unintentionally, according to the Law he becomes guilty of a sin. Seers prescribe an expiation for such a man, so long as it is done unintentionally. No expiation is possible for anyone who kills intentionally.

> [7] A man who raises his hand should perform an arduous penance; if he strikes, he should perform the very arduous penance; and if he draws blood, he should perform both an arduous and a lunar penance (B 2.2.38, 40; 3.8). Therefore, a man should neither raise his hand nor draw blood.

[8] This penance should be observed for nine years when one kills a Kṣatriya, [9] for three years when one kills a Vaiśya, [10] and for one year when one kills a Śūdra [11] or a woman. [12] The penance for killing a Brahmin woman soon after her menstrual period (A 1.24.8–9 n.) is the same as for killing a Brahmin.

Incestuous Sex

[13] A man who has had sex with the wife of an elder (A 1.6.32 n.) should lie on a heated iron bed; [14] embrace a red-hot column (A 1.25.2 n.); [15] or cut off his penis together with the testicles, hold them in his cupped hands, and walk in a south-westerly direction until he collapses.

Theft

[16] Making his hair dishevelled and carrying a pestle of Sidhraka wood, a thief should go to the king and say 'Bludgeon me with this.' The king should bludgeon him with it. [17] Now, they also quote:

> A thief should go to the king carrying a pestle on his shoulder: 'Punish me with this, O King, calling to mind the duty of a Kṣatriya.'

Whether he is punished or released, the thief is
absolved of his sin. By not punishing him, the
king assumes the sin of the thief.

Drinking Liquor

[18] If a man drinks liquor, he should scald his body by drinking hot liquor. [19] If he drinks inadvertently, he should perform the arduous penance (B 2.2.38) for three months and undergo initiation over again, [20] at which the cutting of hair and nails, the observances, and the restrictive rules are omitted, because they have already been performed. [21] Now, they also quote:

> If a Brahmin, a Kṣatriya, or a Vaiśya unintentionally drinks liquor or consumes urine or excrement, he should undergo initiation over again.
>
> [22] If someone drinks water left overnight in a vessel for keeping liquor, on the other hand, he should live for six days on milk boiled with Śaṅkhapuṣpī grass.

Penances Relating to Students

[23] If a student dies while carrying out his teacher's orders, the teacher should perform three arduous penances (B 2.2.38). [24] He should do the same penance if he fails to complete his pupil's instruction.*

[25] A student should begin his vow over again if he participates at a funeral of anyone except his father, mother, or teacher. [26] If he is sick, he may freely eat all the leftovers* of his teacher as medicine (A 1.3.27 n.), [27] and he may treat himself with anything he wants. [28] When he recovers, he should get up and worship the sun, reciting the verse 'The goose seated in the light . . .'

[29] If he ejaculates semen during the day, he should drink three times water sufficient to reach the heart (A 1.16.2 n.) while reciting the Retasyā verses. [30] A student who has sex with a woman has broken his vow of chastity. [31] He should offer a sacrifice

using an ass as the sacrificial animal. [32]The animal and the sacrificial cake are offered to Nirṛti, Rākṣasa, or Yama. [33]'The portion to be eaten by the sacrificer', it is stated, 'should be cut from the animal's penis, while the other portions are offered in water.' [34]Alternatively, he should put firewood into the sacred fire on the night of the new moon; perform the preliminary rites of a Dārvīhoma; and make two offerings of ghee, saying: 'O Lust, I have broken the vow of chastity! I have broken the vow of chastity, O Lust! To Lust, Svāhā! O Lust, I have done wrong! I have done wrong, O Lust! To Lust, Svāhā!' (cf. G 25.1–6). [35]After making these offerings, he should stretch his cupped hands, turn slightly away, and address the fire:

> May the Maruts pour upon me, may Indra and Bṛhaspati; and may this fire pour upon me long life and strength. May they make me live long. (TA 2.18)

Excommunication from and Readmission to Caste

[36]Now, his relatives should turn over his water pot at a formal assembly, while he says: 'I, so-and-so, am guilty of this.' After he has undergone the penance and touched water, milk, ghee, honey, and salt, Brahmins should ask him: 'Have you undergone the penance?' He should reply, 'Yes.' After he has undergone the penance, they should let him participate in sacrifices.

Improper Marriage

[37]If someone has sexual relations with a woman unaware that she belongs to the same lineage as he (A 2.11.15 n.), he should support her like his mother. [38]If she bears his child, he should perform the arduous penance (B 2.2.38) for three months and make an offering of ghee reciting these two verses: 'Whatever blemish there is in me . . .', and 'Fire has put back the sight . . .'

> [39]Someone whose younger brother gets married before him or who gets married before his

older brother; the woman who gets married to such a man; the man who gives her away; and the fifth, the man who officiates at the wedding—all these go to hell.

[40] Someone whose younger brother gets married before him or who gets married before his older brother, the man who gives the woman away, and the man who officiates at the wedding are purified by performing the arduous penance (B 2.2.38) for twelve days, whereas the woman is purified by performing it for three days.

Sins Causing Loss of Caste

2 [1] Next, the sins causing loss of caste: [2] undertaking a sea voyage; [3] stealing a Brahmin's property or a deposit; [4] bearing false witness with regard to land; [5] trading in all sorts of merchandise; [6] serving Śūdras; [7] fathering children by a Śūdra woman; [8] and becoming a child of a Śūdra.* [9] When people have done any one of these,

[10] they should eat a little at every fourth mealtime (A 1.25.10 n.); bathe at dawn, noon, and dusk; and remain standing during the day and seated at night. In three years they wipe off their sin.

[11] It takes three years of bathing at every fourth meal-time to remove the sin a Brahmin commits by serving the black class (A 1.27.11 n.) for one day.

Secondary Sins Causing Loss of Caste

[12] Next, the secondary sins causing loss of caste: [13] sexual intercourse with a woman with whom sex is forbidden; sexual intercourse with a woman friend of a female or male elder (A 1.6.32 n.), with a degraded woman (A 1.3.25 n.), or with an out-

caste woman; practising medicine; officiating at a sacrifice offered by several individuals; obtaining one's livelihood by staging theatrical performances; teaching dance; looking after cattle and buffaloes; and other similar professions, as well as violating virgins.

[14] The expiation for these is to live as an outcaste for two years.

Sins Making a Man Sordid

[15] Next, sins that make people sordid: [16] gambling; sorcery; living by gleaning on the part of a man who has not established the sacred fires; begging almsfood by a man who has returned home from his teacher's, as well as his residing at his teacher's house for more than four months; teaching a man who has returned home from his teacher's; and practising astrology.

[17] The expiation for these lasts twelve months, twelve fortnights, twelve times twelve days, twelve times six days, twelve times three days, twelve days, six days, three days, a day and a night, and one day, in accordance with the way the deed was committed (A 1.29.18 n.).

Outcastes

[18] Living in a common settlement, outcastes should carry out their duties (*dharma*), officiating at each other's sacrifices, teaching each other, and getting married to each other. If they father sons, they should tell them: 'Go away from us, for then you will attach yourself to the Āryas'. [19] A man does not, moreover, fall from his caste together with his virility, [20] the truth of which one can gather from the fact that a man lacking a limb fathers a child possessing all the limbs.

[21] 'That is false,' says Hārīta. [22] Wives are comparable to curd-pots, for if someone were to put impure milk into a curd-pot and mix in the curdling substance, cultured people do not use it for ritual purposes. [23] In like manner, there can be no association with what is produced by the semen of a sordid man (A 1.29.14 n.).

[24] If they so wish, people born from the semen of sordid men

may perform a penance, [25] males one-third of the penance prescribed for those fallen from their caste, and females one-ninth.

Sale of Forbidden Goods

[26] Now, they also quote:

> If a man uses sesame for any purpose other than eating, anointing, and giving as a gift, reborn as a worm, he will plunge into a pile of dog shit together with his ancestors.

[27] A man who sells sesame sells his own ancestors. A man who sells rice sells his own life. A man who haggles when he gives his daughter in marriage sells shares of his merits. [28] He may sell grasses and wood that have not been handcrafted. [29] Now, they also quote:

> Domestic animals with teeth in one jaw (G 17.28 n.), stones with the exception of salt, and undyed thread—these are the goods, O Brahmin, that you may sell.

Types of Penances

[30] For a sin that does not entail loss of caste, a man may give a vedic savant a brown or red cow with a lot of hair after anointing it with ghee and sprinkling black sesame seeds over it; [31] or else he may make offerings while reciting the Kūṣmāṇḍa verses during twelve days, [32] for it is said, 'a man is thus freed from any sin short of murdering a Brahmin' (A 1.19.15 n.).

[33] When a man is accused of a sin causing loss of caste, he should perform an arduous penance, [34] while the accuser should perform it for one year.

> [35] When someone associates with an outcaste—not, however, by officiating at his sacrifices, by teaching him, or by contracting a marriage with him—but by travelling in the same vehicle or sitting on the same seat as he, or by eating

together with him, he himself becomes an outcaste within a year.*

[36]The penance for eating an impure substance is to fast until all the excrement is gone, which happens after seven days.

[37]The hot-arduous penance consists of consuming hot water, hot milk, and hot ghee for three days each, and fasting for three days. [38]The arduous penance consists of eating only in the morning for three days, eating only in the evening for three days, eating what is received unasked for three days, and fasting for three days. [39]Eating only in the morning one day, eating only in the evening the next day, eating what is received unasked the following day, and fasting on the last day—to do this for three successive four-day periods constitutes the arduous penance for women, children, and the elderly. [40]When a man performs the same penance as above but eats only a single mouthful at each meal, it is the very arduous penance. [41]The third type* is subsisting on water alone, and it is the penance beyond the very arduous penance.

[42]During an arduous penance, one should bathe at dawn, noon, and dusk; [43]sleep on the floor; [44]wear a single garment; and have the hair of the head, beard, and body shaved and the nails clipped. [45]Women must do the same, with the exception of shaving the head.

3 [1]When a Brahmin always carries his water with him (B 1.7.6), wears his sacrificial cord constantly (A 1.6.18 n.), does his private vedic recitation every day, refrains from eating the food of Śūdras, has sex with his wife during her season (A 2.1.17 n.), and makes offerings in the sacred fire according to the rules, he will not fall from the world of Brahman.

INHERITANCE

Partitioning of the Paternal Estate

[2]'Manu divided his estate among his sons' (TS 3.1.9.4), states a

vedic text. [3]Because it makes no special allowance, a man should divide his estate equally among all his sons. [4]Alternatively, the eldest son may take for himself a choice piece of property (cf. B 1.18.14), [5]for a vedic text states: 'Therefore, they invest the eldest son with wealth' (TS 2.5.2.7). [6]Or else, the eldest son may take an additional one-tenth of the estate, [7]while the others take equal shares. (cf. A 2.14.6–15)

[8]While the father is alive, the partitioning of the estate takes place only with his consent.

[9]Among the four social classes, the special share of the eldest is a cow, a horse, a goat, and a sheep, respectively.

[10]When there are sons from mothers of different classes, they should divide the estate into ten equal portions and take four, three, two, and one portion according to the class. [11]When a natural son (B 2.3.14) is born, however, other sons belonging to the same class take one-third of the estate as their share. [12]Among two sons, the one born from a mother of the same class as the father and the other born from a mother of the class immediately below the father's, the latter, if he is endowed with good qualities, may take the share reserved for the eldest, [13]for the one who is endowed with good qualities becomes the supporter of the others. (cf. G 28.35–9)

Types of Sons

[14]A son whom a man fathers by himself* through a wife who belongs to the same class as he and whom he has married according to the proper rites should be recognized as his *natural son*. Now, they also quote:

> From my body you spring—from every inch!
> From my heart you are born! You are my self,
> bearing the name 'son'. May you live a hundred
> years. (BU 6.4.9)

[15]A male child born to a man's daughter following an agreement (G 28.18) should be recognized as his *son by an appointed daughter*; any other child is his grandson by his daughter. [16]Now, they also quote:

> At the ancestral offering, the son of an appointed daughter should offer the first ancestral oblation to his mother and the second and third to his mother's father and paternal grandfather, respectively.

[17] When someone else fathers a son on the wife of a person who is dead, impotent, or sick, after she has received permission (Va 17.55–66), he is a *son begotten on his wife.* [18] He has two fathers, belongs to two lineages (A 2.11.15 n.), and makes ancestral offerings to and inherits the property of two different fathers. [19] Now, they also quote:

> When a man with two fathers offers an ancestral offering, he invokes two names at each offering and offers three offerings to six ancestors. Acting in this manner, he will not stumble.*

[20] When a boy is given for adoption by his parents or by one of them and is accepted as one's own child, he is a *son given in adoption.* [21] When a man accepts as his own a boy who is willing and is akin to him, he is a *contrived son.* [22] When a boy is born secretly in the house and is found out afterwards, he is a *son born in secret.* [23] When a boy is abandoned by his parents or by one of them and is accepted by someone as his own child, he is a *son adopted after being abandoned.* [24] When someone has sex with an unmarried woman without permission, the child she bears is a *son of an unmarried woman.* [25] When someone marries a pregnant woman, whether he is aware of her pregnancy or not, the child she bears is a *son received with the marriage.* [26] When a boy is sold by his parents or by one of them and is accepted as one's own child, he is a *purchased son.* [27] When a woman leaves a husband who is impotent or has become an outcaste and marries another husband, a boy born to such a remarried woman is a *son of a remarried woman.* [28] When a boy without mother or father gives himself over to someone, he is a *son given in adoption by himself.* [29] When a man belonging to the highest of the twice-born classes fathers a son by a Śūdra woman, that son is a

Niṣāda; [30] whereas if they cohabit through lust, the son is a *Pāraśava*. These are the various types of sons.

Inheritance of Different Sons

[31] Now, they also quote:

> A natural son, a son by an appointed daughter, a son begotten on the wife, a son given in adoption, a contrived son, a son born in secret, and a son adopted after being abandoned—these, they declare, share in the inheritance.
>
> [32] A son of an unmarried woman, a son born to a woman who was pregnant at marriage, a purchased son, a son of a remarried woman, a son given in adoption by himself, and a Niṣāda—these, they declare, share in the lineage (A 2.11.15 n.). (cf. G 28.32–4)

[33] 'Only the first of these receives a share', says Aupajaṅghani.

> [34] Only now, Janaka, have I become jealous of my wives; I was not so formerly. For when we are in the abode of Death, they say, a son belongs to the man who fathered him. After he dies, the man who deposited the seed takes the son to himself in the abode of Death. People should, therefore, guard their wives, fearful of the seed of strangers.
>
> [35] Diligently guard this progeny of yours, lest strangers sow their seeds in your field; in the transit to the next world, a son belongs to the man who fathered him. Otherwise a husband makes this progeny of his worthless for himself. (cf. A 2.13.6; Va 17.9)

[36] They should closely guard the shares of minors together with the accrued interest until they reach the legal age (G 2.34 n.) [37] and maintain those who are legally incompetent with

food and clothing, [38] namely, those who are blind, mentally retarded, impotent, addicted to vice, and sick, [39] as well as those who neglect their duties, [40] but not those who have fallen from their caste or the offspring of such persons.

[41] No association is permitted with outcastes. [42] Even if she has become an outcaste, however, a man should support his own mother, but without speaking with her (A 1.28.9–10).

Inheritance of Women

[43] Daughters should take their mother's jewellery and anything else customarily given to her. [44] It is not possible for women to act independently. [45] Now, they also quote:

> Her father takes care of her in her childhood; her husband takes care of her in her youth; and her son takes care of her in her old age. A woman is not fit to act independently.
>
> [46] Women are considered to be devoid of strength and not to inherit property (TS 6.5.8.2), says a vedic text.

WOMEN

Adultery

[47] If women strive to do what is beneficial to their husbands, they will win the heavenly world. [48] When she is unfaithful, she should perform an arduous penance (B 2.2.38). [49] If it is with a Śūdra man, she should perform a lunar penance (B 3.8). [50] If it is with a Vaiśya and so forth in the reverse order of classes, she should perform the penance beyond the very arduous penance (B 2.2.40), and so forth.* [51] Brahmin and other male offenders should observe chastity for one year, [52] whereas a guilty Śūdra man should be burnt with a straw-fire (see Va 21.1–3).

[53] Now, they also quote:

4 [1] Everybody except a Brahmin is subject to corporal punishment for adultery. [2] People of

all four classes should guard their wives more closely than their wealth.

[3]There is no corporal punishment, however, when the adultery involves actresses or the wives of minstrels, for such women lure these men and stir even people with great self-control.

[4]Women have an unparalleled means of purification and they never become sullied, for month after month their menstrual flow washes away their sins.

[5]The Moon granted them purification; Gandharva, a sweet voice; and Fire, the capacity to eat anything. Women, therefore, are free from taint.*

Divorce and Widowhood

[6]In the tenth year a man may dismiss a wife who bears no children, in the twelfth year a wife who bears only daughters, and in the fifteenth year a wife all of whose children die; a wife who is sharp-tongued, however, he should dismiss immediately.

[7]When her husband dies, a wife should abstain from honey, meat, liquor, and salt, and sleep on the floor for one year; [8]for six months, according to Maudgalya. [9]After that time, if she has no son, she may bear one through a brother-in-law with the consent of her elders. [10]Now, they also quote:

One should not enjoin a leviratic union on a woman who is barren, who has borne a son or reached menopause, whose children have died, or who is unwilling—that is, a woman from whom a fruitful outcome cannot be expected.

Women with Whom Sex Is Forbidden

[11] Father's sister, maternal uncle's sister, sister, sister's daughter, daughter-in-law, maternal uncle's wife, friend's wife—these are women with whom sex is forbidden. [12] Penances for having sex with forbidden women are the arduous penance, the very arduous penance, and the lunar penance (B 2.2.38; 3.8). [13] The same applies to sex with a Cāṇḍāla woman. [14] Now, they also quote:

> When a Brahmin has sex with a Cāṇḍāla woman, eats her food, or accepts gifts from her without knowing that she is a Cāṇḍāla, he falls from his caste; whereas if he does so knowingly, he sinks to the same level as she.
>
> [15] When someone heedlessly has sex with the wife of his father, an elder (A 1.6.32 n.), or the king, he becomes guilty of sex with an elder's wife. The atonement for such a man has been given above.*

HOUSEHOLDER

Lawful Occupations

[16] If a man is unable to maintain himself by teaching, officiating at sacrifices, and receiving gifts, he may live according to the Kṣatriya Law, because it comes next. [17] Gautama says no, because the Kṣatriya Law is too brutal for Brahmins. [18] Now, they also quote:

> To protect cows and Brahmins, and when the social classes are in danger of intermixing, Brahmins and Vaiśyas may take up arms out of concern for the Law.

[19] Or he may follow the livelihood of a Vaiśya, because it comes next. [20] He should plough the land before breakfast, [21] using a pair of uncastrated bulls whose noses have not been pierced, without beating them with a prod but urging them on repeatedly.

Duties of a Householder

[22] The ritual fire* is established at marriage. A man should perform his rites in it until he has established his vedic fires. [23] From the time he establishes his vedic fires, he should offer the following rites without fail: establishing the vedic fires, daily fire offering, new- and full-moon sacrifices, sacrifice of first fruits at winter and summer solstices, animal sacrifices, seasonal sacrifices, Ṣaḍḍhotṛ offering at the beginning of a season, and the Jyotiṣṭoma sacrifice in the spring. In this way he obtains bliss. [24] Now, they also quote:

> Surely, a man who is accustomed to sleeping during the day, eats food given by anybody, or has lapsed from the vow he has undertaken cannot attain heaven.

[25] He should refrain from miserliness, guile, and crookedness. [26] Now, they also quote this verse recorded in the dialogue between the daughters of Uśanas and Vṛṣaparvan:

> You, undoubtedly, are the daughter of a man who flatters, who supplicates, and who accepts gifts, while I am the daughter of a man who is being flattered, who gives, and who accepts no gifts.*

Bathing and Libations

5 [1] Bathing by immersing oneself in water promotes austerity. [2] After he has offered water to quench the gods, let him offer water to quench his ancestors, [3] pouring water from the appropriate part of the hand (B 1.8.14–16 n.), saying, 'Bearing vigour . . .' (see B 2.10.4). [4] Now, they also quote:

> Men belonging to the three twice-born classes should get up in the morning and offer water to quench the gods, seers, and ancestors, water that is unconfined and flows freely.
>
> [5] Let them not use water that is confined, for

then the builder of the dam will obtain a share of that offering. [6] Therefore, let him avoid dams and wells built by others.

[7] Now, they also quote:

> Or else, after taking out three lumps of mud, he may use confined water in a time of adversity but not regularly; from a well he should take out three lumps of mud, as well as three potfuls of water.

[8] If a man accepts a lot of gifts from someone from whom he is permitted to accept or anything from someone from whom he is forbidden to accept; or if he officiates at a sacrifice of someone at whose sacrifices he is forbidden to officiate; or if he eats the food of someone whose food he is forbidden to eat—he should silently recite the Taratsamandī verses. [9] Now, they also quote:

> People who associate with an outcaste teacher or pupil, or who associate with outcastes by eating their food or performing religious services for them sink into deep darkness.

Duties of a Bath-Graduate

[10] Next, the observances of a bath-graduate.

Feeding Guests [11] Using a portion of whatever food he may have, every morning and evening he should make an offering to the All-gods and a Bali offering, and according to his ability offer hospitality to Brahmins, Kṣatriyas, Vaiśyas, and Śūdras who have arrived as guests (G 5.40–3 n.). [12] If he is unable to give food to many, he should give to a single person endowed with the proper qualities [13] or to the person who arrives first. [14] If a Śūdra comes as a guest, he should employ him in some work. [15] Alternatively, he may give a goodly portion* to a vedic scholar.

[16] The distribution of food should be carried out in a way that does not cause inconvenience to those who receive food every day, [17] but he should never eat without giving food to someone.

[18] Now, on this matter they also quote a couple of verses sung by Food:

> Without giving me to ancestors, gods, dependants, guests, and friends, when a man in his folly eats what has been cooked, he eats poison—I eat him and I am his death.
>
> After performing the daily fire sacrifice and the oblation to All-gods and offering hospitality to guests, when a man who is content and purified eats me—the food left over after feeding his dependants—with a spirit of generosity, he relishes me and I am his ambrosia.

[19] Provisions should be distributed according to one's ability outside the sacrificial arena to virtuous Brahmins, vedic scholars, and masters of the Veda when they come begging in order to give the teacher's gift, to perform a wedding, or to procure medicine; when they are indigent or preparing to perform a sacrifice; or when they are students, travellers, or people who have offered the Viśvajit sacrifice (G 5.21). [20] When others come to beg, he shall give them cooked food.

Rules of Eating [21] Having washed his hands and feet thoroughly and sipped some water, he should sit in a clean and enclosed place; receive respectfully the food presented to him; get rid of lust, anger, hatred, greed, and folly; and eat the food using all his fingers and without making any noise.

6 [1] Let him not put back on to his plate a ball of rice from which he has taken a bite. [2] If he eats food mixed with meat, fish, or sesame, he should wash with water, warm himself over a fire, [3] and bathe after sunset. [4] He should refrain from using a seat, clogs, or tooth cleaners made of Palāśa wood (A 1.32.9 n.). [5] He should not eat food placed on his lap [6] or on a stool.

General Rules [7] He should carry a bamboo staff; wear a pair of gold earrings; [8] and refrain from washing the feet by rubbing one foot with the other and from placing one foot on the other. [9] He should not wear a necklace outdoors [10] or look at the sun at sunrise or sunset. [11] He should not point out a rainbow to someone by saying 'Look, the Indra's bow!'; [12] if he does so, let him say 'Look, a jewelled bow!' (cf. A 1.31.16; G 9.19–24; Va 12.32–3) [13] He should not pass between the cross-beam and bolt of a city gate [14] or the posts to which a swing is tied; [15] step over a rope to which a calf is tied; [16] or step on ashes, bones, hair, grain husks, potsherds, or bath water.

[17] He should not tell anyone when a cow is suckling her calf. [18] When he speaks of a cow that does not yield milk, he should not say, 'She is not a milch-cow'; [19] if he speaks of her, he should simply say, 'She is going to be a milch-cow.' [20] He should not use harsh, cruel, or rude words.

[21] He should not go on a journey alone, [22] with outcastes, or with a woman or a Śūdra. [23] He should not venture out when evening is approaching.

[24] He should not bathe naked [25] or at night; [26] cross a river by swimming (A 1.32.26 n.); [27] look down into a well [28] or a pit; [29] or sit down in a place from where someone may eject him.

> [30] A man should give way to a Brahmin, a cow, a king, a blind man, an old man, someone weighed down by a heavy load, a pregnant woman, and a feeble person.

[31] A righteous man should try to live in a village well supplied with firewood, water, fodder, kindling wood, Kuśa grass, and garland material; served by many roads; full of wealthy and energetic people; inhabited mainly by Āryas; and not easily accessible to robbers (G 9.65).

> [32] If a Brahmin married to a Śūdra woman lives for twelve years in a village which obtains its water from wells, he becomes equal to a Śūdra.
>
> [33] 'A man who keeps himself well under control will attain final bliss even if he lives in a city with his body covered with the city dust and his eyes and face coated with it'—now that is something impossible.

[34]The dust coming from carriages, horses, elephants, grain, and cows is auspicious, whereas the dust of brooms, dogs, goats, sheep, donkeys, and garments is dirty.

[35]He should honour those deserving of honour.

[36]A seer, a learned man, a king, a bridegroom, a maternal uncle, a father-in-law, and an officiating priest—these, according to tradition, are the people that the authoritative texts decree as entitled to the welcome water (G 5.32 n.) at specific times.

[37]A seer, a learned man, and a king should be honoured whenever they come; a bridegroom and an officiating priest, at the beginning of the rite; and a maternal uncle and a father-in-law, when they visit after a lapse of one year.

[38]He should raise the right hand in the fire stall, in the midst of cows, in the presence of Brahmins, at the private vedic recitation, and at a meal.

[39]He should wear an upper garment during these five activities: private vedic recitation, voiding urine and excrement, giving a gift, eating, and sipping water.

[40]He should never offer an oblation in the fire, eat food, give a gift, make an offering, or accept a gift without keeping his right hand between his knees; the same, according to tradition, applies to sipping water.

[41]'Creatures depend on food and food is life'—so states a vedic text (cf. TU 2.2). Therefore, people should give food, for food is the highest sacrificial offering.

[42]Sin is allayed by a burnt offering; a burnt offering is allayed by giving food; and the giving

of food is allayed by the concluding gift—so have we heard in a vedic text.

Twilight Worship

7 [1]Next, we will explain the procedure of the twilight worship. [2]After going to the bathing place, he should bathe if he is ritually impure—or, if he is already ritually pure, omit the bath—; wash his feet and hands; sip some water; and sprinkle his body with water while reciting the following: the Surabhimatī verse, the Ablinga verses, the Vāruṇī verses, the Hiraṇyavarṇa verses, the Pāvamāṇī verses, the Calls, and other purificatory formulas. In this way he becomes ritually pure. [3]Now, they also quote:

> Bathing by immersion in water is prescribed for all classes, whereas sprinkling oneself with water while reciting ritual formulas is characteristic of twice-born people.

[4]At the beginning of any ritual activity and prior to the time for twilight worship, a man becomes ritually pure by sprinkling himself with water while reciting this same set of purificatory formulas.

[5]Now, they also quote: 'Seated facing the east on a spread of Darbha grass and holding some blades of Darbha grass in his right hand filled with water, he should recite the Sāvitrī verse one thousand times.' [6]Alternatively, he may recite it one hundred times while controlling his breath; [7]or recite it mentally ten times together with the seven Calls, placing the syllable OṂ at the beginning and the end. [8]Let him tire himself by controlling his breath three times while reciting the 'Brahman's Heart' text.*

[9]In the evening one performs the worship using the two verses addressed to Varuṇa: 'Hear this cry of mine, O Varuṇa . . .' and 'To you, therefore, I go . . .' [10]In the morning one performs the worship in the same way, but standing and facing the east. [11]During daytime one performs the worship using the two

verses addressed to Mitra: 'The fame of Mitra, supporter of the people . . .' and 'Mitra draws people together . . .'

[12]The morning twilight worship should be started long before sunrise and concluded after the sun has risen, [13]while the evening twilight worship should be started before sunset and concluded long after the sun has set.

[14]The full performance of the twilight worship leads to the uninterrupted sequence of days and nights.* [15]In this connection, moreover, there are a couple of verses sung by Prajāpati:

> When Brahmins do not worship the morning twilight before the sun rises and the evening twilight before the sun sets, how can they be considered Brahmins?
>
> When Brahmins never worship the morning or the evening twilight, a righteous king may freely employ them to do the work of Śūdras.

[16]In that event, a man should fast during the night if he neglects the evening twilight worship and during the day if he neglects the morning twilight worship. [17]He obtains thereby the reward of standing during the morning and sitting during the evening twilight worship. [18]Now, they also quote:

> Whatever sin a man may have committed through his sexual organ, feet, arms, mind, or speech, he frees himself from it by worshipping the evening twilight.

[19]He also unites himself with the night, and Varuṇa does not seize him. [20]Likewise, by worshipping the morning twilight he frees himself from sins committed during the night. [21]He also unites himself with the day; Mitra, moreover, protects him, and Sun leads him up to heaven. [22]'When in this manner a Brahmin worships during the twilights between the day and the night,' it is stated, 'he becomes purified by Brahman; he becomes Brahman; and, abiding by the dictates of scripture, he wins the world of Brahman.'

Bath

8 [1]Then, he should wash his hands, take the water pot and a lump of earth, go to a bathing place, and wash his feet and his body three times. [2]Now, some indeed declare: 'A cemetery, water, a temple, a cowpen, and a place where there are Brahmins—one should not enter them without washing the feet.' [3]He enters the water then, while reciting:

> To the golden-horned Varuṇa I go for refuge. I beg of you; grant me a place to bathe. Whatever sin I may have committed—eating the food of bad men, accepting gifts from evil men, sins committed in thought, word, or deed—may Indra, Varuṇa, Bṛhaspati, and Savitṛ purify me from all that over and over again. (MNU 130–3)

[4]Then he takes water in his cupped hands, saying: 'May the waters and plants be amiable towards us' (MNU 122); [5]and pours that water in the direction in which lives an enemy of his, saying: 'May the waters be inimical to the man who hates us and whom we hate' (MNU 123).

[6]He then washes himself and whirls the water around three times with his hand in a clockwise motion (A 1.7.2 n.), saying: 'Whatever hazard, whatever filth, whatever sinister there is in the water—may all that be banished' (MNU 135). [7]After he has submerged himself in the water and emerged, [8]let him not, while he is still in the water, perform personal purification, wash his clothes by beating them on a rock, or sip water. [9]If he uses water drawn from a confined source (B 2.5.4–7), he should pay homage to it, saying: 'Homage to Fire, lord of the waters! Homage to Indra! Homage to Varuṇa! Homage to Vāruṇī! Homage to the waters!' (MNU 134).

[10]After he has climbed back on to the bank and sipped water, he should sip again, saying:

> May the waters cleanse the earth! May the earth, so cleansed, cleanse me! May Brahmaṇaspati and Brahman cleanse the earth! May the earth, so cleansed, cleanse me!

> If I have eaten leftovers (A 1.3.27 n.) or unfit food, if I have committed an improper act, if I have accepted gifts from evil men—may the waters cleanse me of all that, Svāhā! (MNU 317–20).

[11] He then prepares two purificatory blades of grass and rubs his body with water. After he has rubbed his body with water while reciting the three verses: 'Waters, you are refreshing . . .'; the four verses: 'Golden coloured, pure, and purifying . . .'; and the passage, 'The purifier, the heavenly one . . .'; he goes into the water and controls his breath three times while reciting the Aghamarṣaṇa hymn. Then he climbs back on to the bank, squeezes the water from his clothes, puts on fresh clothes that are not worn-out and that have been washed and dried in the air, and sips some water. Seated facing the north on a bed of Darbha grass and holding blades of Darbha grass in his hand, he should recite the Sāvitrī verse one thousand times, one hundred times, or an unlimited number of times—ten times at the minimum.

[12] Next, he worships the sun, reciting these formulas: 'Gazing, beyond the darkness, upon the highest light . . .'; 'The rays carry you up . . .'; 'The resplendent face of the gods . . .'; 'That bright eye rising in the east . . .'; and 'He who has arisen . . .'

[13] Now, they also quote: 'The syllable OṂ, the three Calls, and the Sāvitrī verse—these five veda-sacrifices (cf. B 2.11.1) purify a Brahmin from sin every day.'

Quenching Libations

[14] Purified by the five veda-sacrifices, he then quenches the deities with libations:

9

> [1] OṂ Fire, Prajāpati, Soma, Rudra, Aditi, Bṛhaspati, and Serpents—I quench these deities of the eastern gate, together with the constellations, the stars, the days and nights, and the 'hours' (A 1.11.32 n.). OṂ I quench also the Vasus.

[2]OṂ Ancestors, Aryaman, Bhaga, Savitṛ, Tvaṣṭṛ, Wind, Indra, and Fire—I quench these deities of the southern gate, together with the constellations, the stars, the days and nights, and the 'hours'. OṂ I quench also the Rudras.

[3]OṂ Mitra, Indra, Great Ancestors, Waters, All-Gods, Brahmā, and Viṣṇu—I quench these deities of the western gate, together with the constellations, the stars, the days and nights, and the 'hours'. OṂ I quench also the Ādityas.

[4]OṂ Vasus, Varuṇa, Aja Ekapād, Ahirbudhnya, Pūṣan, Aśvins, and Yama—I quench these deities of the northern gate, together with the constellations, the stars, the days and nights, and the 'hours'. OṂ I quench the All-Gods. OṂ I quench also the Sādhyas.

[5]OṂ I quench Brahmā. OṂ I quench Prajāpati. OṂ I quench the Four-faced God. OṂ I quench Parameṣṭhin. OṂ I quench Hiraṇyagarbha. OṂ I quench Svayaṃbhū. OṂ I quench Brahmā's male attendants. OṂ I quench Brahmā's female attendants. OṂ I quench Fire. OṂ I quench Wind. OṂ I quench Varuṇa. OṂ I quench Sun. OṂ I quench Moon. OṂ I quench the constellations. OṂ I quench Sadyojāta. OṂ Earth, I quench the Person. OṂ Atmosphere, I quench the Person. OṂ Sky, I quench the Person. OṂ Earth Atmosphere Sky, I quench the Person. OṂ I quench the Earth. OṂ I quench the Atmosphere. OṂ I quench the Sky. OṂ I quench Mahar. OṂ I quench Janas. OṂ I quench Tapas. OṂ I quench Satya. (see App. I.1 Calls)

[6]OṂ I quench the god Bhava. OṂ I quench the god Śarva. OṂ I quench the god Īśāna. OṂ I quench the god Paśupati. OṂ I quench

the god Rudra. OṂ I quench the god Ugra. OṂ I quench the god Bhīma. OṂ I quench the Great God.*
OṂ I quench the wife of the god Bhava. OṂ I quench the wife of the god Śarva. OṂ I quench the wife of the god Īśāna. OṂ I quench the wife of the god Paśupati. OṂ I quench the wife of the god Rudra. OṂ I quench the wife of the god Ugra. OṂ I quench the wife of the god Bhīma. OṂ I quench the wife of the Great God.

OṂ I quench the son of the god Bhava. OṂ I quench the son of the god Śarva. OṂ I quench the son of the god Īśāna. OṂ I quench the son of the god Paśupati. OṂ I quench the son of the god Rudra. OṂ I quench the son of the god Ugra. OṂ I quench the son of the god Bhīma. OṂ I quench the son of the Great God.

OṂ I quench the Rudras. OṂ I quench Rudra's male attendants. OṂ I quench Rudra's female attendants.

[7]OṂ I quench Vighna. OṂ I quench Vināyaka. OṂ I quench Vīra. OṂ I quench Sthūla. OṂ I quench Varada. OṂ I quench Hastimukha. OṂ I quench Vakratuṇḍa. OṂ I quench Ekadanta. OṂ I quench Lambodara.* OṂ I quench Vighna's male attendants. OṂ I quench Vighna's female attendants.

[8]OṂ I quench Sanatkumāra. OṂ I quench Skanda. OṂ I quench Indra. OṂ I quench Ṣaṣṭī. OṂ I quench Ṣaṇmukha. OṂ I quench Jayanta. OṂ I quench Viśākha. OṂ I quench Mahāsena. OṂ I quench Subrahmaṇya. OṂ I quench Skanda's male attendants. OṂ I quench Skanda's female attendants.

[9]OṂ I quench Āditya. OṂ I quench Soma. OṂ I quench Aṅgāraka. OṂ I quench Budha.

OṂ I quench Bṛhaspati. OṂ I quench Śukra. OṂ I quench Śanaiścara. OṂ I quench Rāhu. OṂ I quench Ketu.

10 OṂ I quench Keśava. OṂ I quench Nārāyaṇa. OṂ I quench Mādhava. OṂ I quench Govinda. OṂ I quench Viṣṇu. OṂ I quench Madhusūdana. OṂ I quench Trivikrama. OṂ I quench Vāmana. OṂ I quench Śrīdhara. OṂ I quench Hṛṣīkeśa. OṂ I quench Padmanābha. OṂ I quench Dāmodara. OṂ I quench the goddess Śrī. OṂ I quench the goddess Sarasvatī. OṂ I quench Puṣṭi. OṂ I quench Tuṣṭi. OṂ I quench Garutmat.* OṂ I quench Viṣṇu's male attendants. OṂ I quench Viṣṇu's female attendants.

11 OṂ I quench Yama. OṂ I quench King Yama. OṂ I quench Dharma. OṂ I quench King Dharma. OṂ I quench Kāla. OṂ I quench Nīla. OṂ I quench Mṛtyu. OṂ I quench Vaivasvata. OṂ I quench Citra. OṂ I quench Citragupta. OṂ I quench Audumbara.* OṂ I quench Vaivasvata's male attendants. OṂ I quench Vaivasvata's female attendants.

12 OṂ I quench the deities of the earth. OṂ I quench Kāśyapa. OṂ I quench mid-space. OṂ I quench Knowledge. OṂ I quench Dhanvantari. OṂ I quench Dhanvantari's male attendants. OṂ I quench Dhanvantari's female attendants.

13 Next, wearing the sacrificial cord over his neck (A 1.6.18 n.)—

14 OṂ I quench the Seers. OṂ I quench the Great Seers. OṂ I quench the Supreme Seers. OṂ I quench the Brahman Seers. OṂ I quench the Divine Seers. OṂ I quench the Royal Seers. OṂ I quench the Seers by learning. OṂ I

quench the Seers of Janas. OṂ I quench the Seers of Tapas. OṂ I quench the Seers of Satya. OṂ I quench the Seven Seers. OṂ I quench the Seers of the Kāṇḍas.* OṂ I quench the Subordinate Seers. OṂ I quench the wives of the Seers. OṂ I quench the sons of the Seers. OṂ I quench the grandsons of the Seers.

OṂ I quench Kāṇva Baudhāyana. OṂ I quench Āpastamba, the composer of the Sūtra. OṂ I quench Satyāṣāḍha Hiraṇyakeśin. OṂ I quench Vājasaneyin Yājñavalkya. OṂ I quench Āśvalāyana Śaunaka. OṂ I quench Vyāsa. OṂ I quench Vasiṣṭha.*

OṂ I quench the syllable OṂ. OṂ I quench the Calls. OṂ I quench the Sāvitrī. OṂ I quench the Gāyatrī. OṂ I quench the Metres. OṂ I quench the Ṛg Veda. OṂ I quench the Yajur Veda. OṂ I quench the Sāma Veda. OṂ I quench the Atharva Veda. OṂ I quench the Atharva-Āṅgirasas. OṂ I quench the Itihāsa-Purāṇas. OṂ I quench all the Vedas. OṂ I quench all the servants of gods. OṂ I quench all beings.

10 [1] Next, wearing the sacrificial cord over his right shoulder and under his left arm (A 1.16.18 n.)—

OṂ I quench the fathers—Svadhā! Homage! OṂ I quench the grandfathers—Svadhā! Homage! OṂ I quench the great-grandfathers—Svadhā! Homage! OṂ I quench the mothers—Svadhā! Homage! OṂ I quench the paternal grandmothers—Svadhā! Homage! OṂ I quench the paternal great-grandmothers—Svadhā! Homage! OṂ I quench the maternal grandfathers—Svadhā! Homage! OṂ I quench the mother's paternal grandfathers—Svadhā! Homage! OṂ I quench the mother's paternal great-grandfathers—Svadhā! Homage! OṂ I quench the maternal grandmothers—Svadhā! Homage! OṂ I quench the mother's paternal grandmothers—Svadhā! Homage! OṂ I quench the mother's paternal great-grandmothers—Svadhā! Homage!

[2] OṂ I quench the teacher—Svadhā! Homage! OṂ I quench the teacher's wives—Svadhā! Homage! OṂ I quench the elders (A 1.6.32 n.)—Svadhā! Homage! OṂ I quench the wives of the elders—Svadhā! Homage! OṂ I quench the friends—Svadhā! Homage! OṂ I quench the wives of friends—Svadhā! Homage! OṂ I quench the relatives—Svadhā! Homage! OṂ I quench the wives of the relatives—Svadhā! Homage! OṂ I quench the residents of the house—Svadhā! Homage! OṂ I quench the wives of the residents of the house—Svadhā! Homage! OṂ I quench all men—Svadhā! Homage! OṂ I quench all women—Svadhā! Homage!

[3] He pours water from the parts of the hand sacred to the appropriate deities (B 1.8.14–16 n.). [4] He recites: 'Bearing vigour, immortality, ghee, milk, nectar, and brew, you are the refreshing drink. Quench my fathers! May you be quenched! May you be quenched! May you be quenched!' (VS 2.34).

[5] He should never participate in divine rites wearing a single garment or wet clothes, [6] nor, according to some, even in ancestral rites.

Great Sacrifices

11 [1] Now, these are the five great sacrifices, which are the same as those called great sacrificial sessions, namely, sacrifice to gods, sacrifice to ancestors, Bali sacrifice to beings, sacrifice to humans, and sacrifice to the Veda.

[2] Every day he should make an offering to the gods with the

ritual exclamation 'Svāhā', even if it is just a piece of firewood. In this way he fulfils that sacrifice to gods.

[3] Every day he should make an offering to the ancestors with the ritual exclamation 'Svadhā', even if it is just a cup of water. In this way he fulfils that sacrifice to ancestors.

[4] Every day he should pay homage, even if it is with just some flowers. In this way he fulfils that Bali sacrifice to beings.

[5] Every day he should give food to Brahmins, even if it is just some roots, fruits, or vegetables. In this way he fulfils that sacrifice to humans.

[6] Every day he should perform his private vedic recitation, even if it is just the syllable OṂ. In this way he fulfils that sacrifice to the Veda. [7] Clearly, the sacrifice to the Veda is private vedic recitation. Now, at this sacrifice to the Veda, the Juhū spoon is indeed speech; the Upabhṛt spoon is the mind; the Dhruvā spoon is sight; the Sruva spoon is intelligence; the concluding bath is truth; and the conclusion of the rite is the heavenly world. When a man performs his private vedic recitation with this knowledge, he wins as great a heavenly residence as a man who gives as a gift this world filled with wealth—indeed, he wins a heavenly residence even greater than that, a residence that is unending; and he overcomes repeated death.* 'Therefore,' a Brāhmaṇa text declares, 'one should perform one's private vedic recitation' (SB 11.5.7.2).

[8] Now, they also quote: 'When someone recites a text pertaining to a particular rite, even if he does so while lying on a couch, well-anointed and fully satisfied, he has thereby actually performed that rite' (SB 11.5.7.3–4).

ORDERS OF LIFE

Argument of Opponents

[9] Now, some do indeed posit a fourfold division of this Law

—In the absence of a vedic text to support their position,

however, the text 'Four paths . . .' must refer to rites, [10] namely, Iṣṭi sacrifices, animal sacrifices, Soma sacrifices, and ghee offering—*

[11] a division enunciated in this verse:

> Four paths leading to the gods traverse between heaven and earth. Among these, all you gods, place us on that which brings unfailing prosperity. (TS 5.7.2.3)

[12] That division consists of the student, the householder, the forest hermit, and the wandering ascetic.

Student [13] A student shall serve his teacher until death.

Forest Hermit [14] A forest hermit lives in conformity to the treatise on anchorites. [15] An anchorite shall live in the forest, subsisting on roots and fruits, given to austerities, and bathing at dawn, noon, and dusk. Having kindled the hermit fire (G 3.27 n.), he shall refrain from eating what is grown in a village; pay homage to gods, ancestors, spirits, humans, and seers; and entertain guests from all classes, except those who are proscribed. He may also avail himself of the flesh of animals killed by predators. He should not step on plowed land or enter a village. He shall wear matted hair and clothes of bark or skin, and never eat anything that has been stored for more than a year.

Wandering Ascetic [16] A wandering ascetic should wander forth according to the rule, abandoning his relatives and free of possessions. [17] Going into the wilderness, [18] he has his head shaven except for the topknot; [19] wears a loin cloth; [20] resides in one place during the rainy season (G 3.13 n.); [21] and wears ochre clothes.

[22] He should go out to beg when the pestle has been laid aside, the coals have gone cold, and the plates have been put away;* [23] without hostility to any creature by violent word, thought, or deed; [24] carrying a cloth to strain water for use in purification [25] and using water that has been drawn out (G 9.10 n.) and properly strained for ablutions; [26] and claiming, 'Rejecting vedic

rites and cutting ourselves off from both sides, we embrace the middle course.'

Author's Judgement

27 There is, however, only a single order of life (G 3.36 n.), the teachers maintain, because no offspring is produced in the others.*

28 With respect to the above position they cite this: 'There was once a demon named Kapila, the son of Prahlāda.* It was he who created these divisions in his campaign against the gods. No wise man should pay any heed to them.'

29 In the absence of a vedic text to support their position, the text 'Four paths . . .' must refer to rites, namely, Iṣṭi sacrifices, animal sacrifices, Soma sacrifices, and ghee offering.

30 Now, this verse is cited in support of their position:

> This is the eternal greatness of a Brahmin—he is not made greater or smaller by actions. It is his trail that the self knows; and knowing him, he is no longer stained by sinful actions. (TB 3.12.7–8; cf. B 2.17.7–8)

31 One should respond:

> A man who knows not the Veda does not at the moment of his death think of that great all-perceiving self, by whose power the sun, ablaze with splendour, gives warmth and a father comes to have a father through his son in birth after birth. (TB 3.12.7)
>
> 32 These men who rove neither near nor afar, who are neither Brahmins nor pressers of Soma—they master speech and with evil speech spin their thread without understanding, like a spinster. (RV 10.71.9)

33 There are innumerable texts that refer to the debts that people incur, such as: 'Through offspring, O Fire, may we obtain

immortality' (RV 5.4.10; TS 1.4.46.1); and 'At his very birth, a Brahmin is born with a triple debt—of studentship to the seers, of sacrifice to the gods, and of offspring to the ancestors' (TS 6.3.10.5).

> [34] Study of the triple Veda, studentship, procreation, faith, austerity, sacrifice, giving gifts—those who perform these dwell with us. Anyone who praises other things becomes dust and perishes.

HOUSEHOLDER (continued)

Offerings to Vital Breaths

12 [1] Next, we will describe the fire offerings to the vital breaths* performed by men who offer sacrifices in their selves, the Śālīnas and the Yāyāvaras (B 3.1).

[2] When he has finished all his daily obligations, he should sit facing the east on a place that has been swept and smeared with cowdung; worship the food as it is being brought, saying: 'Earth, Atmosphere, Sky, OṂ!'; and thereafter remain silent. [3] When the food is placed before him, he should sprinkle water over it clockwise (A 1.7.2 n.), reciting the Great Calls. While continuing to hold the vessel in his left hand, he drinks some water prior to the meal, saying: 'You are an underlayer for the Immortal!' (MNU 479); and makes five offerings of food to the vital breaths, saying:

> Established in the out-breath, I offer the Immortal. Enter me kindly, so as not to burn me. To the out-breath, Svāhā!
> Established in the in-breath, I offer the Immortal. Enter me kindly, so as not to burn me. To the in-breath, Svāhā!
> Established in the inter-breath, I offer the Immortal. Enter me kindly, so as not to burn me. To the inter-breath, Svāhā!

> Established in the up-breath, I offer the Immortal. Enter me kindly, so as not to burn me. To the up-breath, Svāhā!
> Established in the link-breath, I offer the Immortal. Enter me kindly, so as not to burn me. To the link-breath, Svāhā! (MNU 480–4)

[4] After making the five offerings of food to the vital breaths, he should complete the rest of his meal silently, reflecting in his mind on Prajāpati. He should not speak during the meal. [5] If he happens to speak during the meal, he should say softly 'Earth, Atmosphere, Sky, OṂ', and begin eating once again.

[6] If he sees a piece of skin, hair, or nail, an insect, or mouse droppings, he should take out a lump from that place; sprinkle the food with water; scatter some ash over it; sprinkle it with water again; have it declared suitable; and then avail himself of it. [7] Now, they also quote:

> Seated facing the east, he should eat the food in silence without disparaging it or scattering it on the ground and with his mind on the food. After eating, he should warm his hands over the fire.

[8] He should not bite off with his teeth pieces from cakes, bulbs, roots, fruit, and meat, which are to be eaten whole. [9] He shall not eat until he is completely full.

[10] After the meal he drinks some water, saying: 'You are the overlayer of the Immortal' (MNU 486); sips some water; and rubs some water over his heart, saying: 'You are the bond of the vital breaths. You are Rudra. You are Death. Enter me. May you wax strong through this food' (MNU 498).

[11] He then sips water again and lets drops of water from both his hands fall on the big toe of his right foot, as he recites:

> The Man the size of a thumb dwells in the thumb as the lord of all, the sovereign of the world, and the enjoyer of the universe—may he be pleased. (MNU 492–3; cf. B 2.15.2)

[12] He should perform the consecration of the food that has been offered with his arms raised, reciting these five formulas:

> Having established myself in the out-breath, in faith I have offered the Immortal. May my out-breath wax strong through this food (B 1.10.4 n.).
> Having established myself in the in-breath, in faith I have offered the Immortal. May my in-breath wax strong through this food.
> Having established myself in the inter-breath, in faith I have offered the Immortal. May my inter-breath wax strong through this food.
> Having established myself in the up-breath, in faith I have offered the Immortal. May my up-breath wax strong through this food.
> Having established myself in the link-breath, in faith I have offered the Immortal. May my link-breath wax strong through this food. (MNU 487–91)

[13] Let him then recite, 'May my self become fit for immortality in Brahman' (MNU 485), [14] and focus his mind on his self while reciting the syllable OṂ.

[15] A man who offers sacrifices to his self far surpasses people who perform all the various kinds of sacrifices. [16] Now, they also quote:

13 [1] As the tip of a reed stuck in a fire goes up in flames, so indeed do all his sins burn up when a man offers sacrifices to his self. (cf. CU 5.24.3)

> [2] A man who eats alone reaps evil alone; in vain does the foolish man procure his food. (RV 10.117.6; TB 2.8.8.3)

[3] In this manner let him offer every day morning and evening, [4] or he may offer just water in the evening.

Eating

[5] Now, they also quote:

> He should first feed the guests, next the pregnant women, then the children, the elderly, the indigent, and especially the sick.
>
> But a man who eats before giving food to these people according to rule does not realize that he is being eaten—he does not eat but is being eaten.
>
> [6] After giving to ancestors, gods, and servants, as well as to his parents and teacher, he should eat what remains in silence—that is the fixed rule.

[7] Now, they also quote:

> A sage's meal is eight mouthfuls, a forest dweller's sixteen, a householder's twenty-two, and a student's an unlimited quantity.
>
> [8] A man who has set up the three vedic fires, a draught ox, and a student—these three are able to accomplish their tasks only if they eat. They cannot accomplish them if they do not eat. (A 2.9.13; Va 6.20–1)

[9] And:

> When a householder or a student practises austerity by not eating, however, by his failure to perform the offering to the vital breaths he becomes equal to a student who has broken his vow of chastity.

[10] That is true outside a penance; such fasting is indeed prescribed during a penance. [11] Now, they also quote:

> When a man never eats between his morning and evening meal, he observes a continuous fast.

> [12] As one must recite softly (A 1.15.1 n.) the ritual formulas used at the daily offering in the three vedic fires (A 2.17.22 n.) when the material for that offering is unavailable, so one must recite softly the ritual formulas used at the offering to the vital breaths when one is prevented from eating.

[13] Acting in this manner, a man becomes fit for becoming Brahman.

ANCESTRAL OFFERINGS

14 [1] An offering to ancestors is a rite that is praiseworthy and secures long life, heaven, and prosperity.

[2] A man who knows the three 'Honey' verses; an expert in the three Nāciketa fire altars; a man who knows the Trisuparṇa; a man who maintains the five sacred fires (A 2.17.22 n.); a man who knows the six Vedic Supplements (A 2.8.10–11); a man who performs the 'Head' vow; a man who sings the Jyeṣṭha Sāmans; and a bath-graduate—these purify the people alongside whom they eat (A 2.17.21 n.). [3] When such individuals are not available, [he may invite] a man who knows the secret texts.* [4] Ṛg verses, Yajus formulas, and Sāman chants are the glory of an ancestral offering. He should, therefore, feed a man who knows them, even if he happens to belong to his own ancestry (A 2.14.2 n.).

> [5] As he feeds them, he should get them to listen successively to the 'Fiend-killing' Sāmans, the 'Svadhā-containing' Yajus formulas, and 'Honey' Ṛg verses.

[6] On the day before or on that very morning, he should invite an uneven number of persons, at least three, who are of good conduct and vedic savants, who are not related by marriage or ancestry (A 2.14.2 n.), or by a relationship established by sacrifice (A 2.17.4 n.), and who are upright and learned in the Vedas. He gets them to sit facing the east or the north on seats covered with Darbha grass.

[7] Then he presents them with water mixed with sesame seeds,

adorns them with perfumes and necklaces, and says, 'I will make a fire offering.' After they have given him permission, he puts wood into the sacred fire, spreads sacred grass around it, completes the rites up to the Agnimukha, and offers three oblations of that very food in the fire, saying:

> To Soma, who has absorbed the ancestors, svadhā! Homage! Svāhā!
> To Yama, accompanied by Aṅgirases and ancestors, svadhā! Homage! Svāhā!
> To Fire, who conveys the offering, who makes the offering flawless, svadhā! Homage! Svāhā!

[8] The above three offerings should be made only with food that has been sprinkled with the remaining ghee.

[9] He should give a lump of rice to crows, [10] for it is stated: 'Ancestors roam about in the guise of crows.'

[11] Then he touches the remaining food with his hand and thumb, reciting these formulas:

> [12] You are as vast as the earth—the fire sees you, and the Ṛg-verses are your glory to forestall any error in giving you. The earth is your bowl, and the sky is your lid. I offer you in the mouth of Brahman. I offer you in the out-breath and in-breath of learned Brahmins. You are inexhaustible. May you never be exhausted for my fathers over there in that world.
>
> You are as vast as mid-space—the wind hears you, and the Yajus formulas are your glory to forestall any error in giving you. The earth is your bowl, and the sky is your lid. I offer you in the mouth of Brahman. I offer you in the out-breath and in-breath of learned Brahmins. You are inexhaustible. May you never be exhausted for my grandfathers over there in that world.
>
> You are as vast as the sky—the sun discloses you, and the Sāman chants are your glory to forestall any error in giving you. The earth is

your bowl, and the sky is your lid. I offer you in the mouth of Brahman. I offer you in the out-breath and in-breath of learned Brahmins. You are inexhaustible. May you never be exhausted for my great-grandfathers over there in that world.

15 [1] Now, these do indeed happen—

[2] He should sprinkle that food with the ghee remaining after the fire oblations. When food is given without touching it with the thumb, it does not gladden the ancestors at all.

[3] With perverse minds the demons surely wait for their chance nearby when someone offers food to the ancestors without using both hands.

[4] Goblins and ghouls snatch that offering—but they do not get a share when sesame seeds are scattered; and demons snatch it when he is overcome by anger.

[5] When someone engages in the soft recitation of prayers (A 1.15.1 n.), performs a sacrifice, or accepts a gift dressed in ochre clothes—an oblation made in this way at a rite to gods or ancestors does not reach its deity. (A 2.16.3 n.)

[6] When someone gives or receives food without touching it with the thumb or sips water standing, he does not reap its benefits.

[7] At the beginning and the end, water should be given to each guest. [8] Rites beginning with the Jaya offering are to be performed following the procedure laid down, [9] whereas the rules for the other rites are given under the Aṣṭakā offering on the eighth-day after the full moon.*

[10] He should feed two at an offering to the gods and three at an offering to ancestors, or one at either offering. Even a rich man should not indulge in feeding a larger number.

[11] A large number is detrimental to five things: offering proper hospitality, doing things at the right place and the right time, carrying out purifications, and finding Brahmins of quality. Therefore, he should refrain from feeding a large number.

[12] In front of him he feeds his fathers, to his left his grandfathers, to his right his great-grandfathers, and behind him the supplicants for morsels.*

THE IMPORTANCE OF CHILDREN

16 [1] Next, some instructions for a person desirous of offspring. [2] The pair of Aśvins have proclaimed that fame rests on fathering offspring:

> [3] Endowed with longevity, given to austerity, devoted to private vedic recitation and sacrifice, and controlling his senses, a man should diligently beget offspring, each within his own class.
>
> [4] A Brahmin from his very birth becomes saddled with three debts. After he has paid them, free from doubts regarding the Law, he becomes autonomous.
>
> [5] After a man has worshipped the seers by his private vedic recitation, Indra with Soma sacrifices, and his ancestors with offspring, he will rejoice in heaven free from debt.
>
> [6] He wins the worlds through a son, attains eternal life through a grandson, and climbs to the very summit of heaven through his son's grandson.

[7] It is, moreover, stated: 'At his very birth a Brahmin is born with three debts—of studentship to the seers, of sacrifice to the

gods, and of offspring to the ancestors' (TS 6.3.10.5). In this manner, the Veda points out that people are saddled with debts. [8] By fathering a virtuous son a man rescues himself.

> [9] A man who obtains a virtuous son rescues seven generations after him and seven generations before him—that is, six others with himself as the seventh—from sin and danger.

[10] By fathering offspring and thus continuing the line, therefore, he reaps the reward. [11] So a man should work hard at fathering offspring [12] through the use of medicines and incantations. [13] This instruction for him is here presented in conformity with the Veda, [14] because it produces rewards for people of all classes.

PROCEDURE OF RENUNCIATION

17 [1] Next, we will explain the procedure of renunciation.*

Time for Renunciation

[2] Some say: 'From that very state, remaining chaste, he goes forth' (A 2.21.8 n.). [3] Alternatively, it is meant for Śālīnas and Yāyāvaras (B 3.1) who are childless. [4] Or else, a widower may undertake it, or someone who has settled his children in their respective duties. [5] Some prescribe renunciation for people over 70 [6] or for a forest hermit who has retired from ritual activities.

Praise of Renunciation

> [7] This is the eternal greatness of a Brahmin—he is not made greater or smaller by actions. It is his trail that the self knows; and knowing him, he is no longer stained by sinful actions. (TB 3.12.7–8; cf. B 2.11.30)

[8] 'Eternal' because he leads to the cessation of rebirth; [9] and 'greatness' because he makes him attain the Immense.

Rite of Renunciation

Preliminary Rites [10] After getting the hair of his head, beard, and body shaved and his nails clipped, he gets these things ready: [11] staffs, sling,* water strainer, water pot, and bowl. [12–13] Taking these, he goes to the outskirts of the village, or to the village boundary, or to a fire stall; eats the triple mixture of ghee, milk, and curd, or drinks some water; and then fasts.

> [14] OṂ Earth! I enter Sāvitrī. That excellent [glory] of Savitṛ.
> OṂ Atmosphere! I enter Sāvitrī. The glory of god we meditate.
> OṂ Sky! I enter Sāvitrī. That he may stimulate our prayers.

He recites this first foot by foot, then half-verse by half-verse, and finally the whole verse and each section of the verse.

[15] It is stated: 'Taking himself from one order of life to the other, he becomes purified by the Veda.' [16] Now, they also quote:

> When he has offered fire sacrifices and gained control of his senses by going from one order to the other and finally becomes wearied of giving alms and making offerings, he then becomes a mendicant.

[17] And such a mendicant is fit for the eternal state.

[18] Before sunset he puts firewood into the householder's fire, brings the southern fire to that spot, draws the blazing offertorial fire out of the householder's fire, melts the ghee over the householder's fire, and strains that ghee. He then puts firewood into the offertorial fire and, taking four spoonfuls of ghee in the Sruc spoon, offers a full oblation, saying, 'OṂ Svāhā!' [19] 'This', it is stated, 'is the placing of firewood in the fire for the sake of Brahman.'*

[20] Then, in the evening after he has performed his daily fire sacrifice, he spreads some grass to the north of the householder's fire; places the sacrificial vessels upside down in pairs on that grass; spreads some Darbha grass to the south of the offertorial

fire at the location of the Brahman priest's seat (A 2.4.4 n.); covers that grass with a black antelope skin; and spends the night there keeping awake.

[21] When a Brahmin who knows this dies after fasting during that night of Brahman and after depositing the sacred fires (B 2.17.27 n.), he rises above all sins, even the sin of killing a Brahmin.

Last Sacrifice [22] Then, at the time sacred to Brahman,* he gets up and performs his daily fire sacrifice at the proper time. [23] Next, he spreads grass along the spine of the sacrificial arena,* fetches water, and makes an offering to the Fire common to all men with an oblation prepared in twelve potsherds. This well-known sacrifice is the last he will offer.

[24] The vessels used in the daily fire sacrifice that are not made of clay or stone he throws into the offertorial fire. [25] The two fire-drills (B 1.14.18 n.) he throws into the householder's fire, saying, 'May you two be of one mind with us.' [26] He deposits the sacred fires in himself,* breathing in the smell of each fire three times, saying: 'With that body of yours worthy of sacrifice, O Fire . . .'

Formula of Renunciation [27] Then, standing within the sacrificial arena he recites, 'OṂ Earth, Atmosphere, Sky! I have renounced! I have renounced! I have renounced!'—three times softly and three times aloud; [28] 'for the gods', it is stated, 'are triply true' (TS 3.4.10.5). [29] Filling his cupped hands with water, he pours it out, saying, 'I give safety to all creatures!' [30] Now, they also quote:

> When a sage goes about after giving safety to all creatures, no creature in this world will pose any threat to him as well.

[31] He curbs his speech.

Taking the Insignia [32] He takes the staff, saying: 'Friend, protect me'; [33] the sling, saying: 'Born beyond this firmament . . .'; [34] the water strainer, saying: 'With that purifier of a thousand streams . . .'; [35] the water pot, saying: 'The light by which the gods went up on high . . .'; [36] and the bowl, reciting the seven Calls.

Concluding Rites [37]Taking with him the staffs, the sling, the water strainer, the water pot, and the bowl, he goes near a place of water; bathes; sips water; and washes himself, reciting the Surabhimatī verses, the Abliṅga verses, the Vāruṇī verses, the Hiraṇyavarṇa verses, and the Pāvamānī verses. Entering the water, he controls his breath sixteen times while reciting the Aghamarṣaṇa hymn; comes out of the water; squeezes the water from his clothes; wears another clean garment; and sips water.

He then takes the water strainer, saying: 'OṂ Earth, Atmosphere, Sky!', and offers quenching water: 'OṂ Earth, I quench. OṂ Atmosphere, I quench. OṂ Sky, I quench. OṂ Mahar, I quench. OṂ Janas, I quench. OṂ Tapas, I quench. OṂ Satyam, I quench.'

[38]Taking water in his cupped hands, he offers it to the ancestors in the same manner as to the gods, saying: 'OṂ Earth Svadhā! OṂ Atmosphere Svadhā! OṂ Sky Svadhā! OṂ Earth, Atmosphere, Sky, Mahar, Homage!'

[39]Then he worships the sun, reciting the two formulas: 'The rays carry you up . . .', and 'The resplendent face of the gods . . .'

[40]'Brahman is OṂ. Clearly, that light, the one that shines there, is Brahman. The one that shines there is the Veda. The one that shines there is that which should be known'—in this manner, indeed, he offers quenching water to his self, he pays homage to his self. Brahman is the self. The light is the self. [41]He should repeat the Sāvitrī verse one thousand times or one hundred times or an unlimited number of times.

Rules of Conduct

[42]He fetches water, taking with him the water strainer, saying: 'Earth, Atmosphere, Sky!' [43]From now on he should not sip water that has not been drawn up (G 9.10 n.), strained, and completely purified.

18 [44]From now on he should not wear white clothes. [1]Let him carry a single or a triple staff (B 2.17.11 n.). [2]And he has these vows: abstaining from injuring living beings, speaking the truth, not stealing, abstaining from sex, and renunci-

ation. [3] He also has five secondary vows: not giving way to anger, obedience to the teacher, not giving in to carelessness, purification, and purity with respect to food.

Rules about Food

Begging [4] Next, begging for almsfood. He should seek to obtain almsfood from Śālīnas and Yāyāvaras (B 3.1) after they have completed their offerings to the All-gods. [5] He should make the request placing the word 'Lady' at the beginning (A 1.3.28–30) [6] and wait there no longer than the time it takes to milk a cow.

Eating [7] Then, returning from his begging, he places the bowl on a clean spot; washes his hands and feet; and announces the almsfood to the sun with the formulas: 'The rays carry you up . . .', and 'The resplendent face of the gods . . .', and to Brahman with the formula, 'Brahman was first born in the east . . .'

[8] It is stated: 'From the time that he has placed the firewood in the fire, the sacred fires remain within the patron of the sacrifice himself. The householder's fire is his out-breath; the south-fire is his in-breath; the offertorial fire is his inter-breath; the hall fire is his up-breath; and the hearth fire is his link-breath. These five fires (A 2.17.22 n.) remain within his self. So he offers oblations only in his self.'

[9] 'This is a man who offers sacrifices in his self,' it is said, 'a man who is firmly rooted in the self, firmly established in the self, a man who guides his self to final bliss.'

[10] After distributing portions of his food to living creatures out of compassion, he should sprinkle water over the remainder and eat it as if it were medicine. [11] After he has eaten and sipped some water, he recites softly the formula, 'May my speech be in my mouth . . .'; and worships the sun reciting the Jyotiṣmatī verse: 'Gazing, beyond the darkness, upon the highest light . . .'

> [12] Merely to sustain his life, let him eat a simple
> meal that he receives without solicitation or
> obtains from houses not previously selected, or
> that he comes by accidentally.

[13] Now, they also quote:

> A sage's meal is eight mouthfuls, a forest dweller's sixteen, a householder's twenty-two, and a student's an unlimited quantity.
>
> [14] He may obtain almsfood from all classes, or food given by a single individual from twice-born people. Or else, he may obtain almsfood from all classes, but never food given by a single individual from even twice-born people.

Special Vows

[15] Now, with reference to those times when teachers explain an Upaniṣad, they cite these rules: 'Intent on standing during the day; keeping silence; sitting on the haunches during the night; bathing at dawn, noon, and dusk; and keeping the vow of eating at every fourth, sixth, or eighth mealtime (A 1.25.10 n.)—he observes the vow of living on grain, oil-cake, barley, curd, and milk.'

[16] It is stated: 'While observing silence on that occasion, he may speak when necessary with those deeply versed in the triple Veda, with his teachers, with sages, or with learned people belonging to other orders of life, pressing his teeth together and without opening his mouth—but never with women or when he is liable to break his vow.' [17] Standing, keeping silence, and sitting on the haunches—let him observe only one of these, not all three at once. [18] 'During a time of distress, however,' it is said, 'a man who is taking part in it should observe at least as much as required for him not to break his vow.'

[19] 'For a man intent on standing during the day; keeping silence; sitting on the haunches during the night; bathing at dawn, noon, and dusk; and keeping the vow of eating at every fourth, sixth, or eighth mealtime—

> eight things do not undo his vow: consuming water, roots, ghee, milk, or sacrificial food; eating at the request of a Brahmin or at the command of the teacher; and taking medicine.'*

Daily Rites

[20] Morning and evening, he should recite softly the ritual formulas used in the daily fire sacrifice; [21] he should do so after he has performed the evening twilight worship, reciting the verses addressed to Varuṇa, and the morning twilight worship, reciting the verses addressed to Mitra (cf. B 2.7.9–11).

> [22] He should live as a silent sage, without fire or
> house, without shelter or protection. He should
> enter a village only to seek almsfood and speak
> only during his private vedic recitation.

[23] 'Limited indeed are the Ṛg verses,' it is stated, 'limited the Sāman chants, and limited the Yajus formulas. But this alone is without end—*brahman*. He should announce this to the one who makes the response. This is the response.'* (TS 7.3.1.4) [24] He remains in this manner until he is freed from his body. A renouncer of Veda is a man who abides at the root of the tree. [25] The tree is the Veda, and its root is the syllable OṂ. The syllable OṂ is the quintessence of the Veda. [26] Prajāpati has declared: 'Meditating on OṂ, containing OṂ within himself, he becomes fit for becoming Brahman.'

Conclusion

[27] He should wash the Brahman-bowl* reciting the seven Calls.

BOOK THREE

HOLY HOUSEHOLDERS

Śālīnas, Yāyāvaras, and Cakracaras

1 [1] Next, we describe those who desire to follow the Law of Śālīnas, Yāyāvaras, and Cakracaras. These sustain themselves by nine means of livelihood. [2] We will show below that

these means derive their names from the activities by which people procure their livelihood (B 3.2).

[3]The name 'Śālīna' is derived from their living in houses (*śālā*). [4]'Yāyāvara' is derived from the fact that they follow (*yā*) an excellent (*vara*) means of livelihood, [5]and 'Cakracara' from their going (*caraṇa*) in sequence (*anukrama*).

[6]We will explain these means of livelihood. [7]They are nine: Ṣaṇṇivartinī, Kauddālī, Dhruvā, Saṃprakṣālanī, Samūhā, Pālanī, Śiloñchā, Kāpotā, and Siddhecchā. [8]Among these means is counted also a tenth means of livelihood, living on forest produce (Vanyā: B 3.3).

Rite of Initiation

[9]This is the procedure for adopting any of the above means of livelihood up to the ninth. [10]After getting the hair of his head, beard, and body shaved and his nails clipped, he gets ready [11]a black antelope skin, a water pot, a staff, a shoulder pole, and a sickle. [12]He begins the process of going away by offering the Traidhātavīya sacrifice or the Vaiśvānarī sacrifice.

[13]Then, after sunrise the next morning, he should get his fires to blaze up following the procedure laid down in his particular ritual text; melt the ghee over the householder's fire; strain that ghee; heat and clean the Sruc and Sruva spoons; and, taking four spoonfuls of ghee in the Sruc spoon, offer an oblation to the guardian deity of the house in the offertorial fire. [14]After reciting the invitatory verse: 'Accept us, O guardian of the house . . .', he makes the offering while reciting the offertory verse: 'May we, O guardian of the house, obtain your fellowship . . .'

[15]This should be done, some say, by everyone who has set up the three sacred fires, [16]while according to others, only by Yāyāvaras.

[17]After leaving his home, he stops at the outskirts of the village or the village boundary. There he builds a hut or cabin, or occupies one that has already been built.

Rules of Conduct

[18] He should use the black antelope skin and the other articles that he had prepared for those purposes for which they are intended.

[19] Attending to the sacred fires, offering the new- and full-moon sacrifices, and carrying out in sequence the five great sacrifices (B 2.11.1)—these are well known. Offering oblations with vegetables that he has grown is sanctioned. [20] Saying, 'I offer what is pleasing to all the gods', or silently, he consecrates and cooks them.

[21] He stops teaching, officiating at sacrifices, and accepting gifts, as well as other sacrificial activities.

[22] Sacrificial food fit to be used during the performance of a vow is sanctioned. [23] It is as follows—food that is mixed with ghee or curd, without spices, salt, or meat, and not stale.

[24] Let him either remain chaste or engage in sexual intercourse with his wife only during her season (A 2.1.17 n.). [25] On each day of the moon's change (A 1.26.14 n.) he should get the hair of his head, beard, and body shaved and his nails clipped, and carry out purificatory rites. [26] Now, they also quote:

> The Veda points out two types of purification which are practised by cultured people: external purification is the elimination of stains and smell, whereas internal purification is the abstention from injuring living beings.
>
> [27] The body is purified by water, and the intellect by knowledge; the inner self is purified by abstaining from injuring living beings, and the mind by truth.

Nine Means of Livelihood

2 [1] Now, with respect to *Ṣaṇṇivartinī*—[2] he cultivates six Nivartaṇas* of fallow land and gives to the owner his share of the crop or, if permitted, keeps it to himself. [3] Let him plough

the land before breakfast, using a pair of uncastrated bulls whose noses have not been pierced, without beating them with a prod but urging them on repeatedly. [4] In this manner he cultivates six (*ṣaṇ*) Nivartaṇas, from which is derived the name 'Ṣaṇṇivartinī'.

[5] With respect to *Kauddālī*—he tills an area close to water with a spade, a ploughshare, or a sharp stick; sows seeds there; and grows bulbs, roots, fruits, and cereals. [6] He cultivates with a spade (*kuddāla*), from which is derived the name 'Kauddālī'.

[7] A man who lives by the *Dhruvā* mode wraps his head with a white cloth, saying, 'I wrap you up, O head, for prosperity.' He takes the black antelope skin, saying, 'You are the lustre of sacred knowledge. I take you for the lustre of sacred knowledge'; the water strainer, reciting the Abliṅga verses; the water pot, saying, 'You are strength. I take you for strength'; the shoulder pole, saying, 'You are grain. I take you for bounty'; and the staff, saying, 'Friend, protect me.'

[8] Then, upon leaving his residence, he recites softly the Calls and the formulas for consecrating the quarters:

> Earth, atmosphere, sky, constellations, the quarters, fire, wind, and sun—may these deities protect me along the road.

[9] After reciting softly the formula 'Do not hurt us in our children . . .', he enters the village and shows himself at the door of one house after another with his shoulder pole; and because of this they call it 'showing oneself' (*saṃdarśanī*). [10] When every other means of livelihood fails, he sustains himself steadfastly (*dhruvam*) by just this means; and because of this it is known as 'Dhruvā'.

[11] With respect to *Saṃprakṣālanī*—he throws away the cereals he obtains—does not save or hoard them—and washes (*saṃprakṣāl*) the dishes and keeps them upside down (*ni-ubj*); from which is derived the name 'Saṃprakṣālanī'.*

[12] With respect to *Samūhā*—in whatever unfenced area he finds cereal plants, either along roads or in fields, he sweeps

(*samūh*) them up with a broom and sustains himself with those cereals; from which is derived the name 'Samūhā'.

[13]With respect to *Pālanī,** which is described as simply *Ahiṃsikā*—he asks for husked rice grains from virtuous people and thus protects (*pāla*) live seeds; from which is derived the name 'Pālanī'.

[14]With respect to *Śiloñchā*—in whatever unfenced area he finds cereal plants, either along roads or in fields, he gleans (*uñch*) ears of grain one by one from time to time and sustains himself with those gleaning (*śila*); from which is derived the name 'Śiloñchā'.

[15]With respect to *Kāpotā*—in whatever unfenced area he finds cereal plants, either along roads or in fields or in other places with unrestricted access, he gleans with just two fingers those cereals one by one and eats like a pigeon (*kapota*); from which is derived the name 'Kāpotā'.

[16]With respect to *Siddhecchā*—exhausted by these means of livelihood because of either old age or sickness, he asks (*iccha*) for cooked (*siddha*) food from virtuous people; from which is derived the name 'Siddhecchā'. [17]Such a person should deposit the sacred fires in his self (B 2.17.26 n.) and conduct himself like a renouncer, with the exception of the water strainer and ochre clothes.

[18]There is also the living on forest produce obtained from fruit-bearing trees, vines, and creepers, and from cereal plants such as wild millet and sesame. This means of livelihood is called *Vanyā* because one lives on forest produce (*vanyā*). [19]Now, they also quote:

> To move around with animals, to dwell with them alone, and to sustain oneself just like them—that is the visible token of heaven.

FOREST HERMIT

3 [1]Next, the two types of forest hermits: [2]those who cook and those who do not cook.

Hermits Who Cook

[3]Of these, the hermits who cook are of five types: *Sarvāraṇyaka*—eating all forest produce; *Vaituṣika*—eating only husked grain; *Kandamūlabhakṣa*—eating only bulbs and roots; *Phalabhakṣa*—eating only fruits; and *Śākabhakṣa*—eating only leafy vegetables.

[4]Of these, the Sarvāraṇyakas are of two types, using two kinds of forest produce. They are the *Indrāvasiktas*—those who use plants produced by rain; and the *Retovasiktas*—those who use animals produced from semen. [5]Of these, the Indrāvasiktas collect the produce of vines, shrubs, creepers, and trees; cook it; offer the daily fire sacrifice with it morning and evening; give portions of it to ascetics, guests, and students; and eat what remains. [6]The Retovasiktas collect the flesh of animals killed by tigers, wolves, hawks, or other predators; cook it; offer the daily fire sacrifice with it morning and evening; give portions of it to ascetics, guests, and students; and eat what remains.

[7]Vaituṣikas, avoiding grains with husks (B 2.2.13), collect husked rice kernels; cook it; offer the daily fire sacrifice with it morning and evening; give portions of it to ascetics, guests, and students; and eat what remains.

[8]Those who eat only bulbs and roots, or only fruits, or only leafy vegetables, also do likewise.

Hermits Who Do Not Cook

[9]There are, likewise, five types of hermits who do not cook: *Unmajjakas**—the submerged; *Pravṛttāśins*—eating what is found; *Mukhenādāyins*—taking with the mouth; *Toyāhāras*—subsisting on water; and *Vāyubhakṣas*—subsisting on air.

[10]Of these, Unmajjakas avoid using iron and stone implements. [11]Pravṛttāśins take food in their hands. [12]Mukhenādāyins take food with their mouths. [13]Toyāhāras subsist only on water. [14]Vāyubhakṣas do not eat at all.

[15]Accordingly, ten observances are prescribed for anchorites (Vaikhānasas). [16]After subscribing to the treatise meant for him, he shall carry a staff, keep silence, and be vigilant. [17]Anchorites

abstain from food and become purified. [18] Here is the gist of what the treatise prescribes for all Brahma-anchorites:*

> [19] Let him not hurt even gnats or mosquitoes. Let him suffer cold and undertake ascetic practices. Residing in the forest, let him be content and find delight in bark garments, skins, and water.
>
> [20] When guests arrive during a meal time, he should first* receive them hospitably. Let him be intent on honouring gods and Brahmins, offering daily fire sacrifices, and performing ascetic practices.
>
> [21] This is a difficult mode of life—it cannot be given up; it is similar to that of animals and birds; it involves collecting what one needs for that day and eating acrid and bitter food. Having embarked on this splendid path far away from wicked men and undertaken the forest life, a Brahmin never comes to ruin.
>
> [22] To move around with animals, to dwell with them alone, and to sustain oneself just like them—that is the visible token of heaven.

PENANCES

Student Breaking His Vow

4 [1] Now, if a student in some way breaks his vow, eats meat, or has sex with a woman—in all tribulations, [2] let him put wood in the sacred fire within the house; spread sacred grass around it; complete the rites up to the Agnimukha; and offer oblations of ghee in the fires, saying:

> It was done by Lust. Lust does it. To Lust belongs all this. To him who makes me do this, Svāhā!
>
> It was done by Mind. Mind does it. To Mind

belongs all this. To him who makes me do this, Svāhā!
It was done by Passion. Passion does it. To Passion belongs all this. To him who makes me do this, Svāhā!
It was done by Blindness. Blindness does it. To Blindness belongs all this. To him who makes me do this, Svāhā!
It was done by Evil. Evil does it. To Evil belongs all this. To him who makes me do this, Svāhā!
It was done by Wrath. Wrath does it. To Wrath belongs all this. To him who makes me do this, Svāhā! (cf. MNU 424–9)

[3] The rites beginning with the Jaya offering until the giving of a fine cow are well known. [4] Then he remains to the west of the sacred fire wrapped in a black antelope skin with its hairy side out and neck turned towards the east.

[5] At daybreak, he should crawl out through the hind part of the skin; go to a sacred ford; bathe in the standard way; while standing in the water, control his breath sixteen times, reciting the Aghamarṣaṇa hymn; perform the other well-known rites up to the worship of the sun; and return to his teacher's house.

[6] He should know that this is equal to participating in the bath that concludes a horse sacrifice.

Aghamarṣaṇa

5 [1] Next, we will explain the procedure of the Aghamarṣaṇa, an unsurpassed means of purification.

[2] The person should go to a sacred ford; bathe; wear clean clothes; erect an altar at the water's edge; wet his clothes with one handful of water; and, filling his hand once with water and facing the sun, perform his private vedic recitation with the Aghamarṣaṇa hymn. [3] He recites it one hundred times in the morning, one hundred times at midday, and one hundred times in the afternoon—or an unlimited number of times. [4] After the

stars have risen, he should eat a dish prepared with one handful of barley.

[5] In seven days he is freed from secondary sins causing loss of caste committed intentionally or unintentionally; and in twelve days from all sins except these—killing a Brahmin (A 1.19.15 n.), having sex with the wife of an elder, stealing gold, and drinking liquor. [6] In twenty-one days he rises above even these, he conquers even these.

[7] 'He rises above all. He conquers all. He obtains the fruits of all sacrifices. He becomes a man who has bathed in all the sacred fords. He becomes a man who has completed the vows for studying all the Vedas. He becomes a man known to all the gods. He purifies a row of people (A 2.17.21 n.) by just looking at them. And all his activities are successful'—so says Baudhāyana.

Barley Dish

6 [1] If what he has done weighs heavily on his conscience, after the stars have risen he should get a handful of barley cooked for his use. [2] Let him not offer any portion of it in the sacred fire; [3] at this rite no Bali offering is made. [4] He should consecrate the barley before it is cooked, while it is being cooked, and after it is cooked, reciting these formulas:

> [5] You are barley. You are the king of grains, sacred to Varuṇa. Mixed with honey, you take away all sins, and the seers have proclaimed you the means of purification.
>
> Barley, you are ghee, you are honey, you are indeed water and immortality. May you cleanse me of all my sins, of every evil deed I have done.
>
> Barley, cleanse me of what I have said, of what I have done, of evil thoughts I have had; cleanse me of bad luck and misfortune.
>
> Defilement from eating what has been touched by dogs or pigs or sullied by crows or leftovers

(A 1.3.27 n.), and disobedience to my parents
—cleanse me, O Barley, of all that.
The heinous crime against the king, together
with grievous sins causing loss of caste, as
well as offences against children and the
aged—cleanse me, O Barley, of all that.
Stealing gold, breaking my vow, officiating at
the sacrifices of people for whom it is forbidden to officiate, and defaming Brahmins
—cleanse me, O Barley, of all that.
Eating food given by a group of people, by
prostitutes, Śūdras, and thieves, or by people
impure on account of a birth or death, or
food given at an offering to ancestors or to a
recently deceased person—cleanse me, O
Barley, of all that.

[6]While the barley is being cooked, he should guard it by reciting: 'Homage to Rudra, the lord of creatures! The sky is appeased'; the passage: 'Unfurl your strength like a net spread out . . .'; the five refrains:

The fiend-slaying gods seated in the east led by
Fire—may they guard us, may they aid us!
To them, homage! To them, Svāhā!
The fiend-slaying gods seated in the south led
by Yama—may they guard us, may they aid
us! To them, homage! To them, Svāhā!
The fiend-slaying gods seated in the west led by
Savitṛ—may they guard us, may they aid us!
To them, homage! To them, Svāhā!
The fiend-slaying gods seated in the north led
by Varuṇa—may they guard us, may they aid
us! To them, homage! To them, Svāhā!
The fiend-slaying gods seated in the zenith led
by Bṛhaspati—may they guard us, may they
aid us! To them, homage! To them, Svāhā!
(TS 1.8.7.1);

and the two formulas: 'Do not hurt us in our children . . .'; and 'The Brahman-priest of the gods . . .'

[7]When it is cooked, let him eat a little of it, after purifying himself and serving it on a plate. [8]He should offer it in his self, reciting:

> The gods born from the mind, united with the mind, of keen wisdom, and sons of wisdom—may they guard us, may they aid us! To them, homage! To them, Svāhā! (TS 1.2.3.1)

[9]A man desiring wisdom should do this for three nights. [10]By drinking it for six nights, a sinner becomes purified of his sins; [11]by drinking it for seven nights, a man is purified of killing a Brahmin, having sex with the wife of an elder (A 1.6.32 n.), stealing gold, and drinking liquor; [12]and by drinking it for eleven nights, a man erases even sins committed by his ancestors.

[13]'Indeed, by drinking for twenty-one nights a gruel made with barley seeds excreted by cows, a man even sees the divine hosts, he sees the lord of the divine hosts; he sees learning; he sees the lord of learning'—so says Lord Baudhāyana.

Kūṣmāṇḍa Rite

7 [1]'A man who considers himself to be in some way impure should make an offering with the Kūṣmāṇḍa formulas. [2]A man who ejaculates his semen in any place other than the vagina* becomes equal to a thief, equal to a murderer of a Brahmin (A 1.19.15 n.). [3]He is freed from any sin short of murdering a Brahmin (TA 2.8.1–3).'

[4]Now, a man who has ejaculated his semen in any place other than the vagina except in sleep, or even a blameless man who wants to purify himself, [5]should get the hair of his head, beard, and body shaved and his nails clipped on a new-moon or a full-moon day. Following the rules laid down for a student, he observes a vow [6]for a year, for a month, or for twenty-four, twelve, six, or three days. [7]He should not eat meat, engage in sex, or sit on anything above the floor, and recoil from uttering an untruth.

[8] Living on milk is the primary rule. Or else, eating only a barley dish, he should perform the twelve-day arduous penance (B 2.2.38). Alternatively, he may beg for almsfood. [9] On these sorts of occasions Kṣatriyas take barley gruel, and Vaiśyas curd.

[10] In the morning, after putting wood into the sacred fire as prescribed for a cooked oblation and spreading sacred grass all around the fire, he completes the rites up to the Agnimukha and then makes offerings of ghee into the sacred fire, reciting these three passages: 'O gods, whatever offence we have committed against the gods . . .'; 'Whatever debt I have contracted without gambling . . .'; and 'May he give you the fullness of life on every side . . .' [11] He should offer ghee at each verse.

[12] He makes four offerings of ghee with the Sruva spoon, reciting: 'The strength in the lion, the tiger, the panther . . .'; and makes offerings of ghee reciting the four 'Returner' verses: 'O Fire, O Returner, return to us with fullness of life . . .'; 'O Fire, O Aṅgiras, may your returns be a hundredfold . . .'; 'Return again with strength . . .'; and 'Return with wealth, O Fire . . .' Firewood in hand, he remains at the place meant for the patron of the sacrifice and worships the fire, reciting the twelve-verse hymn: 'We announce to the Fire common to all men . . .' [13] Reciting the verse,

> If I have ever committed a sin by thought or word, free me from all that, you, whom I have praised, for you know the truth, Svāhā! (TA 2.6.2)

he puts a piece of wood into the sacred fire and gives the priestly fee.

[14] The rites from Jaya to the giving of a cow as the priestly fee are well known. [15] Only one person performs the fire services.

[16] At the setting up of the sacred fires, on the other hand, full oblations of ghee are offered, while reciting: 'O gods, whatever offence we have committed against the gods . . .'; 'Whatever debt I have contracted without gambling . . .'; and 'May he give you the fullness of life on every side . . .' [17] One who is going to perform the daily fire sacrifice after making these oblations should use the Ten-hotra text. One who is going to perform a

new-moon or a full-moon sacrifice after making these oblations should use the Four-hotra text. One who is going to perform a seasonal sacrifice after making these oblations should use the Five-hotra text. One who is going to perform an animal sacrifice after making these oblations should use the Six-hotra text. One who is going to perform a Soma sacrifice after making these oblations should use the Seven-hotra text.

[18] It is stated, moreover: 'Let him make an offering with these Kūṣmāṇḍa verses at the start of any rite. Purified in this manner, he will attain the world of the gods' (TA 2.7.5). So states a Brāhmaṇa text.

Lunar Penance

8 [1] Next, we will explain the rules of the lunar penance. [2] On the fourteenth day in the fortnight of the waxing moon he should fast. [3] He should get the hair of his head, beard, and body shaved and his nails clipped—or just get his beard shaved—and, wearing a new set of clothes and speaking the truth, enter the fire hall.

[4] A fire should be brought to that place for him a single time, or it may be produced by twirling the fire-drills (B 1.14.18 n.). [5] A student friend of his should be at hand to carry out his directions. [6] He eats sacrificial food for the duration of the vow.

[7] After putting wood in the sacred fire and spreading sacred grass all around it, he completes all the rites up to the Agnimukha and offers in the fire portions of the cooked food—[8] to Fire; to the lunar day on which the offering is made; to the lunar mansion together with its deity; the fifth to the moon, reciting the verse: 'Here indeed did they recognize . . .'; the sixth to heaven and earth; the seventh to the day and the night; the eighth to Rudra; the ninth to the sun; the tenth to Varuṇa; the eleventh to Indra; and the twelfth to the All-gods. [9] Tradition, moreover, records further oblations to the cardinal directions together with their respective deities and to the wide expanse of mid-space together with its deity.

[10] After he has made the offering to Fire who makes the offering flawless, reciting: 'Being born, it becomes ever new . . .', he

serves the remainder of the sacrificial oblation into the Kaṃsa bowl or the Camasa vessel; pours sauces fit for sacrifice over it; and eats fifteen regular-size lumps—[11] the first, saying 'You are for the out-breath!'; the second, saying 'You are for the in-breath!'; the third, saying 'You are for the inter-breath!'; the fourth, saying 'You are for the up-breath!'; and the fifth, saying 'You are for the link-breath!' When he eats only four lumps, he eats the first reciting the first two formulas; when he eats only three lumps, he eats the first reciting the first two and the second reciting the second two; when he eats only two lumps, he eats the first reciting the first two and the second reciting the last three; and when he eats only one lump, he eats it reciting all the formulas.*

[12] He then drinks water, saying,

> You are the waters heard by the gods. Refresh my life. Refresh my out-breath. Refresh my in-breath. Refresh my inter-breath. Refresh my sight. Refresh my hearing. Refresh my mind. Refresh my speech. Refresh my body. Refresh my limbs. Refresh my offspring. Refresh my house. Refresh my men. Refresh me together with my men. May my men never go thirsty (TS 3.1.8.1)

and afterwards makes additional offerings of ghee, reciting these seven texts:

> May my out-breath, in-breath, inter-breath, up-breath, and link-breath become purified. May I become the radiant, free of dust and evil! Svāhā!
>
> May my speech, mind, sight, hearing, taste, smell, semen, intelligence, intentions, and desires become purified. May I become the radiant, free of dust and evil! Svāhā!
>
> May my head, hands, feet, sides, back, belly, thighs, penis, sexual organs, and anus become purified. May I become the radiant, free of dust and evil! Svāhā!

May my outer and inner skin, flesh, blood, fat, marrow, sinews, and bones become purified. May I become the radiant, free of dust and evil! Svāhā!
May my (bodily constituents of) sound, touch, visible appearance, taste, and smell become purified. May I become the radiant, free of dust and evil! Svāhā!
May my (bodily constituents of) earth, water, fire, wind, and space become purified. May I become the radiant, free of dust and evil! Svāhā!
May my (body) made of food, breath, mind, intelligence, and bliss become purified. May I become the radiant, free of dust and evil! Svāhā! (cf. MNU 440–56)

[13] The rites from the Jaya offering to the giving of a fine cow are well known. [14] He worships the sun reciting the solar verses, and the moon reciting the lunar verses. [15] He recites softly, 'Keep awake, O Fire . . .', as he goes to sleep; [16] and 'You, O Fire, are the guardian of vows . . .', as he wakes up.

[17] Let him not speak with women or Śūdras, or look at urine or faeces. [18] Should he happen to see such filth, let him recite softly: 'My mind was out of control, and my sight was wayward. The sun is the best of the celestial lights. May you, O Consecration, forsake me not!' (TS 3.1.1.1–2).

[19] On the first day of the fortnight of the waning moon, he eats fourteen mouthfuls. [20] In this manner he decreases his food by one mouthful a day until the new moon. [21] No food is taken on the new-moon day. [22] Then, on the first day of the fortnight of the waxing moon, he eats one mouthful, and two on the second day. [23] In this manner he increases by one mouthful a day until the full moon. [24] On the full-moon day, he offers an oblation of cooked food to the fire, to the lunar day on which it is offered, and to the lunar mansions together with their respective deities. [25] Having first made an offering to the lunar mansion Abhijit

that comes before Śroṇa,* as well as to its deity, he should give a cow to Brahmins.

[26] What has been described above is the lunar penance with its middle like that of an ant. When it is done in the opposite way, its middle is like that of a barley grain.*

[27] When a sinner performs either of these, he become purified of all his sins causing loss of caste. [28] They say that this may be performed to obtain any type of wish; [29] by this a man obtains whatever he wishes. [30] It is by means of this that in ancient times the seers purified themselves and accomplished their goals. It procures wealth, merit, sons, grandsons, cattle, long life, heaven, and fame, as well as everything one desires. [31] A man who recites this obtains the splendour of the lunar mansions, as well as union with and residence in the same world as the sun and the moon themselves.

Vedic Recitation while Fasting

9 [1] Next, we will describe the procedure of reciting the complete Veda while fasting. [2] The performer should be dressed in clean clothes or a bark garment [3] and try to procure food fit for a sacrifice or water and fruits.

[4] Setting out from the village towards the east or the north, he should apply a coat of cowdung on and sprinkle with water a quadrangular area of ground the size of a cow's hide (B 1.10.1 n.); draw auspicious lines on it; and sprinkle the area with water. He should then put firewood into the fire, spread Kuśa grass around it, and offer oblations to these gods: 'To Fire, Svāhā! To Prajāpati, Svāhā! To Soma, Svāhā! To All-gods. To Svayambhu. To Ṛg-verses. To Yajus-formulas. To Sāman-chants. To Athavan-formulas. To Faith. To Intelligence. To Wisdom. To Prosperity. To Modesty. To Savitṛ. To Sāvitrī. To the Guardian of the Abode. To Assent.'

[5] After making these offerings, he should start reciting from the very beginning of the Veda and continue the recitation without interruption. [6] During the recitation he should neither talk nor pause. [7] Should he talk or pause during the recitation, let him control his breath three times and start reciting from

the exact point where he left off. [8]If he cannot remember* a passage, he should recite a passage he knows for as long as he fails to remember,* substituting Ṛg-verses for Ṛg-verses, Yajus-formulas for Yajus-formulas, and Sāman-chants for Sāman-chants; [9]he may recite the Brāhmaṇa text connected with and the deity and metre of the forgotten passage.

[10]He should recite the Vedic Collection twelve times. If he has recited the Veda during forbidden times, angered his elders (A 1.6.32 n.), or done forbidden things, this recitation cleanses him of all that. The Veda he possesses becomes purified and cleansed. [11]If he recites more than that, the results accumulate. [12]By reciting the Vedic Collection twelve more times, he obtains the world of Uśanas. [13]By reciting the Vedic Collection an additional twelve times, he obtains the world of Bṛhaspati. [14]By reciting the Vedic Collection a further twelve times, he obtains the world of Prajāpati. [15]Should he recite the Vedic Collection one thousand times without eating, becoming Brahman and free from stain, he becomes Brahman.

[16]If he lives on almsfood for one year, he obtains divine vision. [17]By living on barley for six months, on water and barley meal for four months, on fruits for two months, or on water for one month, or fasting completely for twelve days, he obtains the power to disappear suddenly; he purifies his relatives—seven before him, seven after him, with himself as the fifteenth; and he purifies those alongside whom he eats (A 2.17.21 n.).

[18]This, they say, is the ladder of gods. [19]By means of this, evidently, the gods obtained their status as gods, as also the seers their status as seers. [20]Now, there are just three times when this sacrifice can be started: at the time of the morning or the midday Soma pressing, or during the night's last watch sacred to Brahman (B 2.17.22 n.). [21]It was Prajāpati who disclosed this to the seven seers. The seven seers disclosed it to Mahājajñu, and Mahājajñu to Brahmins.

Justification of Penance

10 [1]We* have explained the Law pertaining to the social classes and the Law pertaining to the orders of life.

[2] Now, when a man here commits foul actions or acts wrongly, officiates at sacrifices of people for whom it is forbidden to officiate, accepts gifts from people from whom it is forbidden to receive gifts, eats food given by people whose food it is forbidden to eat, or indulges in forbidden activities—[3] there is a debate as to whether such a man is required to perform a penance or not.

[4] Some argue that an act can never be wiped out. [5] But he is indeed required to do so, [6] as it is stated, 'After offering the Punaḥstoma sacrifice, he gets to participate again in the Soma sacrifice.' [7] Now, they also quote: 'A man who offers a horse sacrifice overcomes all sins, he overcomes even the murder of a Brahmin' (SB 13.3.1.1); [8] and, 'A heinous sinner (A 1.3.25 n.) should offer the Agniṣṭut sacrifice'.

[9] The expiations for such a man are softly reciting prayers (A 1.15.1 n.), austerity, ritual offering, fasting, and giving gifts. [10] Upaniṣads; the beginnings of the Vedas; the conclusions of the Vedas (*vedānta*); the Hymn-Collections of all the Vedas; the 'Honey' verses; Aghamarṣaṇa hymn; Atharvaśiras; Rudra hymn; Puruṣa hymn; the Sāmans called Rājana, Rauhiṇi, Bṛhat, Rathantara, Puruṣagati, Mahānāmnī, Mahāvairāja, and Mahādivākīrtya; any of the Jyeṣṭha Sāmans; Bahiṣpavamāna Sāman; Kūṣmāṇḍa verses; Pāvamānī verses; and the Sāvitrī verse—these are the purificatory texts. [11] To do the following in accordance with the rules of fasting: living on milk alone; eating only vegetables; eating only fruits; eating only roots; living on gruel made with one handful of barley; eating gold; eating ghee; and drinking Soma juice—these are the cleansing activities. [12] All mountains; all flowing rivers; sacred lakes; sacred fords; dwellings of seers; cow-pens; sacred grounds; and temples—these are the appropriate places. [13] Practising non-injury; speaking the truth; refraining from theft; bathing at dawn, noon, and dusk; obedience to elders; chastity; sleeping on the floor; wearing a single garment; and fasting—these are the austerities. [14] Gold; cow; garment; horse; land; sesame seeds; ghee; and food—these are the gifts. [15] One year; six months; four months; three months; two months; one month; twenty-four days; twelve days; six days; three days; a day and night; and one day—these are the lengths of time.

[16]When no specific penance has been prescribed, people may perform these, [17]the heavier penances for grave sins and the lighter penances for minor sins. [18]The arduous penance (B 2.2.38), the very arduous penance (B 2.2.40), and the lunar penance (B 3.8) are expiations for all types of sins.

BOOK FOUR

Controlling the Breath as a Penance

1 [1]We will describe separately the penances meant for different offences, both the heavier penances and the lighter ones.

[2]Let a man prescribe whichever is suitable for a particular case—heavier penances for severe offences and lighter ones for minor offences.

[3]A man should control his breath several times in accordance with the rules given in authoritative texts for sins committed through his sexual organ, feet, hands, mind, speech, hearing, skin, smell, or sight.

[4]Alternatively, when he has committed transgressions through his sight, hearing, skin, smell, or mind, he is purified by controlling his breath three times.

[5]When someone eats the food given by a Śūdra or has sex with a Śūdra woman, for each such offence he should control his breath seven times a day for seven days. [6]When someone consumes forbidden or unfit food, forbidden drink, or improper food; sells forbidden goods with the exception of honey, meat, ghee, sesame oil, spices, salt, or inferior food; or commits other similar offences, he should control his breath twelve times a day for twelve days. [7]When someone commits a sin—except a grievous, non-grievous, or secondary sin causing loss of caste—, he should control his breath twelve times a day for half a month. [8]When someone commits a sin—except a grievous or non-grievous sin causing loss of caste—, he should control his breath

twelve times a day for twelve times twelve days. [9] When someone commits a sin—except a grievous sin causing loss of caste—, he should control his breath twelve times a day for twelve half-months. [10] When someone commits a grievous sin causing loss of caste, on the other hand, he should control his breath twelve times a day for one year.

Offences Regarding Marriage

> [11] A man should give his daughter in marriage while she still runs naked (G 18.23 n.) to a man of good qualities who has maintained his vow of chastity, or even to a man lacking good qualities; let him not hold back a girl who has started to menstruate.
>
> [12] If a man does not give his daughter in marriage within three years after she has reached puberty, he undoubtedly incurs a guilt equal to that of performing an abortion (A 1.19.15 n.).
>
> [13] That is the case if there is no suitor; but if there are suitors, then he incurs that guilt each time. Manu has declared that he becomes guilty of a grievous sin causing loss of caste at each of her menstrual periods.
>
> [14] For three years a girl who has reached puberty should heed her father's orders. But after that, in the fourth year, she may choose a husband of equal station. If a man of equal station is not found, she may even turn to a man lacking good qualities.
>
> [15] If a virgin has been forcibly abducted but has not been married with the recitation of ritual formulas, she may be given in marriage to another man in accordance with the rules; she is in every respect like a virgin.
>
> [16] If the husband dies after a girl has been given away or after the nuptial offering has been

made, and she returns home after going away, she may be given in marriage again following the procedure of a second marriage, provided she is still a virgin.

Marital Offences

17 If a man does not have sexual intercourse for three years with his wife who menstruates, he incurs a guilt equal to that of performing an abortion (A 1.19.15 n.).

18 If a man does not have sexual intercourse with his wife after she has taken the bath that concludes her menstrual period when she is nearby, his ancestors will lie during that month in her menstrual discharge.

19 One who does not have sex with his wife during her season (A 2.1.17 n.), and one who has sex with her outside her season, as also one who deposits his semen in a place other than the vagina (B 3.7.2 n.)—they all incur the same guilt.

20 When a wife suppresses her menstrual periods* out of antipathy towards her husband, he should bring her to the middle of the village, declare her to be an abortionist, and drive her away from his house.

21 If a man does not have sexual intercourse with his virtuous and disciplined wife after she has taken the bath that concludes her menstrual period, for that transgression he should control his breath one hundred times.

Yogic Practice and Control of Breath

22 Seated with purificatory grass in hand, he should control his breath and recite the purificatory texts, the Calls, the syllable OṂ, and the daily portion of the Veda.

[23] Constantly practising Yoga, he should control his breath repeatedly, generating the most extreme heat of austerity up to the very tips of his hair and nails.

[24] The suppression of breath generates wind; fire arises from wind; and fire gives rise to water. By these three, therefore, he is purified internally.

[25] By Yoga one obtains knowledge. Yoga is the mark of the Law. All good qualities are rooted in Yoga. Therefore, one should constantly practise Yoga.

[26] The syllable OṂ is the beginning and end of the three Vedas. The syllable OṂ and the Calls constitute the eternal Veda.

[27] When a man is constantly devoted to the recitation of OṂ, the seven Calls, and the three-footed Gāyatrī verse, no danger will ever befall him.

[28] When someone recites the Gāyatrī together with OṂ, the Calls, and the Śiras formula while controlling his breath, it is called the control of breath.

[29] Controlling the breath sixteen times every day while reciting the Calls and the syllable OṂ cleanses even an abortionist (A 1.19.15 n.) within one month.

[30] The best austerity begins with this. This is the mark of the Law. And to wipe out all sins, this is the most excellent means.

Purificatory Texts

2 [1] We will describe individual penances meant for various types of offences, both the heavier penances and the lighter ones.

[2–3] Let a man prescribe whichever is suitable for a particular case—heavier penances for severe offences and lighter ones for minor offences. Let him prescribe penances in accordance with the rules given in authoritative texts.

[4] A man who has intended to accept, as also a man who has actually accepted, gifts [from someone from whom it is forbidden to accept gifts] should recite the four Taratsamandī verses.

[5] When someone has eaten unfit food or food given by unfit persons, the way to remove his sin is to wash himself while reciting the Taratsamandī verses.

[6] Next, I will declare an alternate procedure for expiating the murder of a Brahmin (A 1.19.15 n.), a procedure by which a man is freed also from every type of grievous sin causing loss of caste.

[7–8] During twelve nights, living on milk and controlling his breath, he should recite softly the purificatory texts, the Calls, the syllable OṂ, and the Aghamarṣaṇa hymn. Alternatively, he becomes pure by bathing and then remaining in his wet clothes for three nights, subsisting on nothing but air.

[9] Even if a man has habitually engaged in forbidden practices over and over again, he is freed from all sins by worshipping with the Vāruṇī verses.

[10] Now, a student who has broken his vow of chastity should put firewood into the sacred fire on the night of the new moon, perform the preliminary rites of a Darvīhoma, and make two offerings of ghee, saying: 'O Lust, I am a man who has broken his vow of chastity! I am a man who has broken his vow of chastity, O Lust! To Lust, Svāhā! O Lust, I have done wrong! I

have done wrong, O Lust! To Lust, Svāhā!' [11] After making this offering, he should join his palms together and, turning somewhat sideways, worship the fire, saying:

> May the Maruts pour upon me, may Indra and Bṛhaspati, and may this fire pour upon me long life and strength. May they make me live long. (TA 2.18)

The Maruts, indeed, give him back the vital breaths, Indra the strength, Bṛhaspati the lustre of vedic knowledge, and fire everything else. He is made whole in his body and lives his full life span. Let him then address the gods repeating the formulas three times; 'for the gods', it is stated, 'are triply true' (TS 3.4.10.5).

> [12] When a man feels that he is in some way stained by a secondary sin causing loss of caste, he is freed from all sins by making a fire offering according to the above procedure.

[13] When someone, moreover, has consumed unfit food or forbidden drink or food, or performed a sinister rite, whether it is done deliberately or not, and when someone deposits his semen in a Śūdra woman or in a place other than the vagina (B 3.7.2 n.), he becomes purified by bathing while reciting the Ablinga and Vāruṇī verses. [14] Now, they also quote:

> Whether he has consumed unfit food or forbidden drink or food, performed rites that are against the Law, and even committed deliberately sins comparable to sins causing loss of caste—he is cleansed of all that, and even of every sin causing loss of caste.
>
> [15] Or he may fast for three nights, bathe three times a day, and recite the Aghamarṣaṇa hymn while controlling his breath. Manu has declared this to be equal to taking part in the bath that concludes a horse sacrifice.

[16] It is also said:

> This purificatory procedure has been displayed of old, purified by which one passes beyond evil deeds. Purified by that spotless means of purification, may we pass beyond evil and adversity.

Penances for Secret Sins

3 [1] We will describe specifically the penances for secret sins—what should be done when people who are collected and controlled commit mistakes.

[2] For all sins causing loss of caste, a man should sip water while reciting all the Calls preceded by the syllable OṂ. [3] When he sips water the first time, he gladdens thereby the Ṛgveda. When he sips water the second time, he gladdens thereby the Yajurveda. And when he sips water the third time, he gladdens thereby the Sāmaveda. [4] When he wipes his lips the first time, he gladdens thereby the Atharvaveda. And when he wipes his lips the second time, he gladdens thereby the Itihāsa-Purāṇa. [5] When he sprinkles water on his left hand, and when he applies water to his feet, head, heart, nostrils, eyes, ears, and navel, he gladdens thereby plants and trees, as well as all the deities. Therefore, a man is freed from all sins by just sipping water.

[6] Alternatively, he may offer eight pieces of firewood in the fire, saying:

> You are the expiation of sins committed against the gods, Svāhā!
> You are the expiation of sins committed against human beings, Svāhā!
> You are the expiation of sins committed against the forefathers, Svāhā!
> You are the expiation of sins committed against myself, Svāhā!
> You are the expiation of sins that we have committed during the day and the night, Svāhā!

You are the expiation of sins we have committed while asleep or awake, Svāhā!
You are the expiation of sins that we have committed knowingly or unknowingly, Svāhā!
You are the expiation of each and every sin, Svāhā! (cf. VS 8.13; TS 3.2.5.7)

[7] By making offerings with these eight formulas, one is freed from all sins. [8] Now, they also quote:

> Aghamarṣaṇa, Devakṛta, Śuddhavatī, Taratsama, Kūṣmāṇḍa, Pāvamānī, Virajā, Mṛtyulāṅgala, Sāvitrī verse, the Calls, and the Rudras wipe out the great sins.

4 [1] We will describe specifically the penances for secret sins—what should be done when people who are collected and controlled commit mistakes.

[2] When a man recites three times the Aghamarṣaṇa hymn: 'The right and the truth . . .', while standing in water, he is freed from all sins. [3] When a man recites three times the verse, 'The spotted bull has come . . .', while standing in water, he is freed from all sins. [4] When a man recites three times the verse: 'As one released from the stake . . .', while standing in water, he is freed from all sins. [5] When a man recites three times the verse, 'The goose seated in the light . . .', while standing in water, he is freed from all sins. [6] Or else, when a man recites the Sāvitrī verse three times, first foot by foot, then half-verse by half-verse, and finally the entire verse, while standing in water, he is freed from all sins. [7] Or, when a man recites the Calls three times, first individually and then collectively, while standing in water, he is freed from all sins. [8] Or, when a man recites just the syllable OṂ three times while standing in water, he is freed from all sins.

[9] One should not impart this Treatise of Law to someone who is not one's son or pupil or who has not lived with him for at least one year. [10] The fee is one thousand, or ten cows with a bull, or the teacher's kindness.

RITES TO OBTAIN WISHES

Preliminary Purifications

5 [1] Now I will proclaim the rites of the Ṛg-, Sāma-, Yajur-, and Atharva-vedas by which a man will quickly obtain his heart's desires.

[2] He should perform the rites only after purifying his body by the soft recitation of prayers, burnt offerings, oblations, and restraints. He will not attain success otherwise.

[3] When he is about to engage in the soft recitation of prayers, make burnt offerings and oblations, and practise restraints, a Brahmin should first get his head and beard shaved and his nails clipped on an auspicious day and under an auspicious lunar mansion during the fortnight of the waxing moon.

[4] Let him bathe at dawn, noon, and dusk; guard himself from anger and untruth; not speak with women or Śūdras; remain chaste; and eat only food fit for sacrifice.

[5] Let him pay homage to cows, Brahmins, ancestors, and gods and refrain from sleeping during the day; and, engaged in the soft recitation of prayers, in making burnt offerings and oblations, and in practising restraints, let him remain standing during the day and seated during the night.

[6] When during twelve days a man successively eats only during the daytime for three days and during the night for three days, eats food given unasked during three days, and lives on air during three days, that is the arduous penance sacred to Prajāpati.

[7] When a man eats one day during the daytime and the next day during the night, the following

day eats what is given unasked, and lives on air the last day, and repeats this three times, it is called the arduous penance of children.

[8] When someone eats a single mouthful of food a day during the first three three-day periods according to rules given above and lives on air during the final three days, it is called the very arduous penance.

[9] When a man lives on water during those three-day periods and lives on air during the final three days, this third type should be known as penance beyond the very arduous penance, which is highly purifying.

[10] When a man drinks only hot milk, hot ghee, and a hot decoction of Kuśa grass during the three three-day periods respectively, and lives on air during the final three days, it is called the hot-arduous penance.

[11] When a man subsists on cow's urine, cowdung, milk, curd, ghee, and a decoction of Kuśa grass for one day each, and on the final day lives on air, tradition calls that the Sāntapana penance.

[12–13] He takes the cow's urine with the Gāyatrī formula, the cowdung with the formula 'Perceived by the smell . . .', the milk with the formula 'Swell up . . .', the curd with the formula 'Of Dadhikrāvan . . .', the ghee with the formula 'You are the sheen . . .', and the decoction of Kuśa grass with the formula 'Aroused by god Savitṛ . . .' He mixes one part of cow's urine, half that amount of cowdung, three parts of milk, two parts of curd, one part of ghee, and one part of the Kuśa decoction. This is the Sāntapana penance; it purifies even a Śvapāka.

[14] When a man subsists one day each on cow's urine, cowdung, milk, curd, and ghee for five

days, he is purified by these five products of the cow.

[15] When a man, self-controlled and vigilant, lives without eating for twelve days, that arduous penance is called Parāka; it effaces all sins.

[16] When a man lives one day each on cow's urine and so forth for a total of seven times three days, vedic savants call that arduous penance the Great-Sāntapana.

[17] When a man observes two fasts during the two fortnights, increasing the food eaten by one mouthful during the fortnight of the waxing moon and decreasing by one mouthful during the fortnight of the waning moon, the traditional texts call it the lunar penance.

[18] When a Brahmin eats four lumps of food in the morning with a collected mind and four lumps after sunset, he is performing the lunar penance of children.

[19] When a man, self-controlled, eats eight lumps of food fit for sacrifice at noon each day for one month, he is performing the lunar penance of ascetics.

[20] When a Brahmin eats eighty times three (240) lumps of food fit for sacrifice during one month in any manner whatsoever, he attains the same world as the moon.

[21] As the moon, when it rises, removes the fear of darkness from the world, so a Brahmin, when he performs the lunar penance, removes the fear of sin.

[22] When a man subsists on rice alone for one day, on oil-cake for three days, on watered buttermilk for five days, and on barley water for seven days, and lives on air for one day, it is the Tulāpuruṣa penance that destroys sins.

[23] Living on barley gruel, as also a seven-day fast, wipes out the sins of embodied beings within seven days—this was discovered by wise men.

[24] By remaining in wet clothes during the fortnight of the waxing moon in the lunar month December–January, by living in the open air during the same fortnight in August–September, and by exposing himself to the sun during the same fortnight in May–June, a Brahmin is freed from all sins except those that cause loss of caste.

[25] Cow's urine, cowdung, milk, curd, ghee, and a decoction of Kuśa grass when mixed with barley water is the highly purifying Brahmakūrca.

[26] When a man fasts on new-moon days and eats only sesame seeds on full-moon days, within the course of one year he will be freed from sins committed during the fortnights of the waxing and waning moon.

[27] Subsisting on almsfood obtained from Brahmins who perform the daily fire sacrifice purifies a man in one month, whereas subsisting on almsfood obtained from Yāyāvaras (B 3.1.1) purifies him in ten days, and from forest hermits in five days.

[28] Subsisting on food obtained from a man who keeps provisions sufficient for a single day purifies a man in one day. A man who subsists by drinking water given by a person living the Kāpotā life (B 3.2.15) is purified in three days.

[29] A man should recite three times the Ṛg-, Yajur-, and Sāma-vedas or just one of these Vedas from beginning to end while fasting. That is an exceptional means of purification.

30 If, however, someone wants to finish it fast, let him live on air during daytime and spend the night standing in water until daybreak. That is equal to the arduous penance sacred to Prajāpati (B 4.5.6).

31 By reciting the Gāyatrī verse eight thousand times at sunrise, a man is freed from all sins, provided he is not a murderer of a learned Brahmin.

32 A man who distributes food, speaks the truth, and is full of compassion to creatures is far better than any man purified by the above mentioned restraints.

6 1 The Rudra verses accompanied by the Mādhuchandas hymns, the Gāyatrī verse together with the syllable OṂ, and the seven Calls should be recited; they wipe out sins.

2 The Mṛgāra, the Pavitreṣṭi, the Trihavis, and the Pāvamānī, together with the Vaiśvānarī, are the offerings that wipe out sins.

3–4 Listen further to this other secret that I will disclose. A man is freed from all sins except the grievous sins causing the loss of caste by washing himself while reciting the purificatory verses (B 3.10.10), by reciting softly the eleven Rudra verses, by making oblations of ghee while reciting the purificatory verses, and by giving gold, a cow, and sesame seeds.

5 When a man eats barley gruel cooked in cow's urine together with liquid cowdung, curd, milk, and ghee, he is instantly freed from sin.

6 A man who fathers a child from a Śūdra woman, as also a man who has sexual intercourse with a woman with whom sex is forbidden—both are freed from their sins in seven days by this method.

[7]It is also the remedy for consuming semen, urine, or faeces and for eating unfit food, as well as for a younger brother who establishes his sacred fire, performs the Soma sacrifice, or gets married before his older brother.

[8]A man is thus freed from all his sins, even if he has committed a very large number of them, provided they do not entail loss of caste—that is the judgement of virtuous men.

[9]This procedure, which is based on the authority of the vedic tradition, is declared to be that by which the likes of Bharadvāja attained the same nature as Brahman.

[10]When a Brahmin performs this rite with a tranquil heart, he obtains whatever his heart desires.

7

[1]When a Brahmin has turned away from sinful acts and practises meritorious deeds, his rites will succeed even without practising the above restraints.

[2]Upright Brahmins, therefore, purified by upright activities, accomplish whatever they have set their minds on.

[3]Thus a wise man should practise these restraints until such time as he achieves the purity of his body.

Gaṇa Oblation for Securing Wishes

[4]Having purified himself by these restraints and fasted for three nights, he should commence the rite by which he seeks to achieve success.

[5–7]Kṣmāpavitra, Puruṣa hymn, Mṛgāra verses, the two Gaṇas* called Aṃhomuca, Pāvamānī verses, Kūśmāṇḍī verses, and Vaiśvānarī verses—by offering ghee and rice in the sacred fire at dawn, noon, and dusk for seven days while reciting these formulas, as he remains silent, eating food fit for sacrifice, and controlling his senses and actions, and by gazing into a pot full of water placed at a cross-roads while reciting 'Into the lion my . . .', a man is freed from all sins, even from grievous sins causing loss of caste.

[8] He is freed also from the sins he has heaped up unintentionally in his old age, youth, and childhood, as well as in his previous births.

[9–10] When, at the conclusion of that rite, he feeds Brahmins with milk-rice mixed with ghee and, after they have eaten, presents them with cows, land, sesame seeds, and gold—that Brahmin, his sins burnt up like a kindling stick, becomes purified and ready to perform rites for securing wishes, as also rites such as the establishment of the sacred fires.

8 [1] If a man performs this rite for someone else either through excessive greed or through carelessness, he becomes tainted with sin and perishes as if he had drunk poison.

[2] A Brahmin who performs this rite for the sake of his teacher, father, mother, or himself shines forth like the sun. Therefore, one may perform this rite for them.

[3] The Creator made the Thousand-eyed god pure by means of this purificatory rite, as also Fire, Wind, Sun, Moon, Yama, and the other gods.

[4] Whatever holy name there is in this world, a name such as 'Brahmin' known across the three worlds, the Creator made it by means of this purificatory rite.

[5] This secret of Prajāpati was the first rite to be created for destroying sins. Thousands of other purificatory rites were produced after that.

[6] A man who offers this Gaṇa oblation for a year, for half a year, for a season, for a fortnight, or for a day purifies his ten ancestors and his ten descendants.

[7] And, while he is still on earth, he will become known to the gods in heaven as a man of meritorious deeds; and, as a man who has performed meritorious deeds, he will also rejoice in heaven like a god.

[8] If a Brahmin is unable to offer all these eight Gaṇa oblations, he should offer at least one of them, and it will destroy his stains.

[9] When someone's children or pupils offer the eight Gaṇa oblations, through the agency of these individuals, whom he has bought by his instruction, he is also freed from sin.

[10] When someone is unable to perform them himself, he may pay some people to offer these oblations with the desire of destroying his sins; an embodied man should not torment himself.

[11] Money is donated to secure the success of even proper rites. In some rites it frees a man without debt from his sin.

[12] Freed from the surging ocean of sin by this rite, a man should consider himself purified and competent to perform rites successfully.

[13] And when, freed from the torrent of all sins, someone undertakes any rite, it will become successful effortlessly for that man with a purified body.

[14] When someone teaches this ceaselessly, recalls it, or even listens to it, he will be freed

from all sins and become exalted in the world of Brahman.

15 A man should recite softly for twelve days those formulas by which he seeks to secure his wishes, eating once a day at night rice mixed with ghee, milk, and curd.

16 To secure one's wishes, one should offer the oblation together with ghee in the fire ten times at dawn, noon, and dusk, before he recites those formulas.

That concludes the Baudhāyana Dharmasūtra

The Dharmasūtra of Vasiṣṭha

THIS Dharmasūtra has been handed down as an independent treatise unconnected to any Kalpasūtra. Traditionally, Vasiṣṭha has been associated with the Ṛgveda. Like Gautama, this text is divided into chapters, reflecting the practice of later Smṛtis. Probably because it did not have the benefit of an ancient commentary, this Dharmasūtra does not have a strong manuscript tradition and contains some very corrupt passages. Stenzler's first edition (1883) was based on only five manuscripts, and in the Preface to the second edition (1914) he confesses that he was able to find only one additional manuscript. It is likely that the original text of Vasiṣṭha ended after the 24th chapter. The commentary of Kṛṣṇapaṇḍita was written in Benares in the middle of the nineteenth century and is of little value.

CONTENTS

KNOWLEDGE OF LAW

1 [1] Next comes the desire to know the Law for the sake of attaining the highest goal of man.* [2] Now, a man who knows the Law and follows it is a righteous man (*dhārmika*). [3] Such a man becomes pre-eminent in this world and wins heaven after death.

SOURCES OF LAW

[4] The Law is set forth in the Vedas and the Traditional Texts (A 2.15.25 n.). [5] When these do not address an issue, the practice of cultured people (Va 6.43; B 1.1.5–6) becomes authoritative. [6] Now, a cultured man is free from desires. [7] For something to be the Law, it must not have a tangible motive (A 1.12.8–11 n.).

Geography and the Law

[8] The region east of where the Sarasvatī disappears, west of Kālaka forest, north of Pāriyātra mountains, and south of the Himalayas is the land of the Āryas; [9] or else, north of the Vindhya mountains. [10] The Laws and practices of that region should be recognized as authoritative everywhere, [11] but not others found in regions with Laws contrary to those.* [12] According to some, the land of the Āryas is the region between the Ganges and Yamunā. [13] According to others, vedic splendour extends as far as the black antelope roams. [14] The Bhāllavins, moreover, in their *Book of Causes** cite this verse (B 1.2.11):

> [15] Vedic splendour extends only as far as the black antelopes roam east of the boundary river and west of where the sun rises.
>
> [16] What men who have a deep knowledge of the three Vedas and are learned in the Law declare

to be the pure and purifying* Law, that, undoubtedly, is the Law.

Regional Law

17 When there are no specific rules in vedic texts, Manu has said that one may follow the Laws of one's region, caste, or family.

SINS

List of Sinners

18 A man who is asleep when the sun rises or sets, or has bad nails or black teeth; a man whose younger brother gets married before him or who gets married before his older brother; a man who marries a younger sister whose older sister remains unmarried or an older sister whose younger sister is already married; a man who has extinguished his sacred fires or forgets the Veda—these are sinners.

Grievous Sins Causing Loss of Caste

19 They teach that there are five grievous sins causing loss of caste: 20 having sex with the wife of an elder (A 1.6.32 n.), drinking liquor, murdering a Brahmin, stealing gold from a Brahmin, and associating with outcastes 21 either through vedic instruction or through marriage. 22 Now, they also quote:

> When someone associates with an outcaste—not, however, by officiating at his sacrifices, by teaching him, or by contracting a marriage with him—but by travelling in the same vehicle or sitting on the same seat as he, or by eating together with him, he himself becomes an outcaste within a year. (B 2.2.35 n.)

Secondary Sins Causing Loss of Caste

23 Throwing away one's fires, assailing one's elder, being an

infidel, obtaining one's livelihood from infidels, and selling Soma—these are secondary sins causing loss of caste.

MARRIAGE

Number of Wives

[24] According to the order of the classes, a Brahmin may take three wives, a Kṣatriya two, and a Vaiśya and a Śūdra one each. [25] According to some, one may even marry a Śūdra woman just as one marries others but without the recitations of ritual formulas. [26] One should not do so, [27] for it results in the certain decline of one's family and the exclusion from heaven after death.

Types of Marriage

[28] There are six types of marriage: [29] Brahma, Divine, Seer's, Gandharva, Kṣatriya, and Human. [30] When a girl is given to a suitor after pouring water, it is a 'Brahma' marriage. [31] When during the course of a sacrifice a man adorns a girl and gives her to the officiating priest as he performs the ritual, they call it a 'Divine' marriage. [32] When a girl is given for a cow and a bull, it is a 'Seer's' marriage. [33] When a man in love has sex with a woman in love of a similar station, it is the 'Gandharva' marriage. [34] When a man forcibly abducts a girl, violently putting down opposition, it is the 'Kṣatriya' marriage. [35] When a man negotiates a price and purchases a girl for money, it is the 'Human' marriage. [36] Purchase is pointed out in this passage: 'Therefore, the groom should give one hundred cows together with a chariot to the bride's father' (A 2.13.11). [37] And in the chapter on seasonal sacrifices it is said: 'When a woman has been purchased by her husband and afterwards has affairs with other men. . . .'* [38] Now, they also quote:

> Lost knowledge comes back again; but when the family is lost, everything here is lost. Even a horse gets honour on account of its family line. Therefore, people marry wives from distinguished families.

GOVERNANCE BY BRAHMIN AND KING

[39] The three classes shall abide by the instructions of the Brahmin. [40] The Brahmin shall proclaim their duties (*dharma*), [41] and the king shall govern them accordingly.

Taxes

[42] Governing in accordance with the Law, however, the king may take in taxes a sixth part of their wealth, [43] except from Brahmins. [44] Indeed, it is said 'From them he takes as his share a sixth part of their sacrifices and good works' (cf. G 11.11); [45] 'The Brahmin makes the Veda rich; the Brahmin rescues from misfortune. Therefore, the Brahmin is not to be fed upon; Soma is his king' (SB 5.4.2.3); [46] and 'After death, moreover, he prospers'.

SOCIAL CLASSES

2 [1] There are four classes: Brahmin, Kṣatriya, Vaiśya, and Śūdra. [2] Three classes are twice-born: Brahmin, Kṣatriya, and Vaiśya (A 1.1.16–18). [3] Of these—

> The first birth is from the mother and the second at the tying of the Muñja-grass girdle. At the latter birth, the Sāvitrī verse is his mother, while the teacher is said to be his father.

The Teacher

[4] The teacher is said to be the father because he imparts the Veda. [5] They likewise quote: 'A Brahmin man clearly has two kinds of semen, the one located above the navel and the other located below the navel and going downward. By means of the semen above the navel children are born to him when he initiates Brahmins, when he teaches them, when he officiates at their sacrifices, and when he makes them good people. By means of the semen going downward from the navel, on the other hand,

the children of his loins are born. About a vedic scholar and savant, therefore, they never say, "You have no children"' (B 1.21.13).

[6] Hārīta also quotes:

> A child can perform no rites at all until the Muñja-grass girdle is tied around him, for he is equal to a Śūdra with respect to conduct until he is born through the Veda—

[7] except rites connected with offering water, saying Svadhā, and ancestors.

> [8] Now, vedic knowledge came up to the Brahmin and said: 'Guard me; I am your treasure. Do not disclose me to a man who is envious, crooked, or uncontrolled. Thus I shall wax strong.
>
> [9] 'A man you know to be pure, alert, wise, and chaste, a man who will not become hostile towards you under any circumstance—only to such a man should you disclose me as to a guardian of your treasure.'
>
> [10] The man who drills his ears with the truth, making him free from pain and conferring immortality upon him—that man he should consider as his father and mother, and at no time should he show hostility towards him.
>
> [11] When Brahmins do not honour in thought, word, or deed the teacher who taught them, just as they are of no use to their teacher, so their learning will be of no use to them.
>
> [12] As a fire burns up dry grass, so the Veda burns a man who requests it without showing any respect. Let him never disclose the Veda to such a man, who fails to honour him according to his ability. (= Yāska, *Nirukta*, 2.4)

Occupations

[13]A Brahmin has six occupations: [14]studying the Veda and teaching, offering sacrifices and officiating at sacrifices, giving and receiving gifts. [15]A Kṣatriya has three occupations: [16]studying, offering sacrifices, and giving gifts. [17]The Law specific to him is the protection of his subjects by the use of weapons; he should obtain his livelihood by this means. [18]The very same are the occupations of a Vaiśya, [19]and in addition agriculture, trade, animal husbandry, and lending money on interest. [20]To serve these classes is the invariable means of livelihood for Śūdras.

Hair Dressing [21]Each may wear his hair according to the fixed practice of his family, or all may let their hair hang loose with the exception of the topknot.

Occupations in Times of Adversity [22]Those who are unable to sustain themselves through the Law proper to their class may resort to the livelihood of the class immediately below theirs [23]but never to that of a class above theirs.

Trade [24]When someone assumes a Vaiśya livelihood and lives by trade, he should not deal in rocks,* salt, precious stones, hemp cloth, silk, linen, skins, [25]all types of dyed cloth, [26]prepared foods, flowers, fruits, roots, perfumes, condiments, water, plant extracts, Soma, weapons, poison, meat, milk, milk products, iron, tin, lac, and lead. [27]Now, they also quote:

> By selling meat, lac, or salt, a Brahmin falls
> from his caste immediately; and by selling milk,
> he becomes a Śūdra in three days.

[28]He may not sell the following: among domestic animals, those that are one-hoofed or furry; all wild animals, birds, and animals with fangs or tusks; [29]among grain, they mention sesame. [30]Now, they also quote:

> If a man uses sesame for any purpose other
> than eating, anointing, and giving as a gift,
> reborn as a worm, he will plunge into a pile of
> dog shit together with his ancestors.

[31] Or else, people may freely sell sesame if they have tilled the ground and grown it themselves; [32] and for that purpose he should plough the land before breakfast, using a pair of uncastrated bulls whose noses have not been pierced. [33] When ploughing in the summer, he should give them water to drink.

> [34] The plough accompanied by stout ones, provided with a fine share, and with a handle for the drinker of Soma—it digs up a cow, a sheep, a plump maid, and a swift horse for the chariot. (VS 12.71)

[35] 'The plough accompanied by stout ones'—accompanied by virile ones, namely, by men and oxen; 'provided with a fine share'—provided with a good looking ploughshare, for its ploughshare is good looking and with the ploughshare it digs up, that is, pierces deep; 'and with a handle for the drinker of Soma'—for Soma reaches him, and that is the handle; 'it digs up a cow, a sheep' as well as goats, horses, mules, donkeys, and camels; 'a plump maid'—beautiful, good looking, in the flower of her youth.*

[36] For how can the plough dig that up unless he sells the grain.

[37] He may barter condiments for condiments of greater or lesser value, [38] but never salt for condiments. [39] He is permitted to barter sesame, rice, cooked food, knowledge, and human beings.

Lending on Interest [40] Brahmins and Kṣatriyas shall not engage in usury. [41] Now, they also quote:

> When a man acquires grain at the going rate of interest and lends it at a higher rate, he is an usurer and is denounced by vedic savants.
>
> [42] Usury and abortion (A 1.19.15 n.) were once weighted on a balance. The abortionist rose to the top, while the usurer trembled. (cf. B 1.10.23)

[43] Or else, they may freely lend on interest to people who neglect their ritual duties or to wicked people. [44] The interest on gold is double the principal, on grain triple the principal. [45] The rule with respect to grain applies to condiments, [46] as well as flowers, roots, and fruits. [47] The interest on articles measured by weight is eight times the principal.* [48] Now, they also quote:

> Two, three, four, or five per cent a month is laid down in traditional texts, and he may charge these rates of interest according to the order of the classes.
>
> [49] When the king dies, however, the interest on loans ceases to accrue. The principal begins to accrue interest when the new king is anointed.
>
> [50] Listen to the rate of interest laid down by Vasiṣṭha for moneylenders: five Māṣas for twenty (G 12.29 n.). In this way the Law is not violated.

Brahmins and Learning

3 [1] Brahmins who are not learned, who do not teach, or who do not maintain the sacred fires become equal to Śūdras. [2] On this point they cite a verse of Manu:

> When, without studying the Veda, a twice-born man strives after other matters, he quickly sinks to the level of a Śūdra in this very life together with his descendants. (M 2.168)
>
> [3] A man ignorant of the Veda cannot be a Brahmin, and neither can a trader, an actor, a man taking orders from a Śūdra, a thief, or a physician.
>
> [4] The king should punish a village from which Brahmins who do not keep to their vows or study the Veda obtain almsfood, for such a village is giving sustenance to a thief.

[5] Even if people who do not keep to their vows or study the Veda and who use their caste only to make a living come together in their thousands, they are incapable of constituting a legal assembly (Va 3.20).

[6] When fools, befuddled by darkness, make a pronouncement without knowing the Law, that sin, compounded a hundredfold, engulfs those who proclaim it.

[7] When three or four experts in the Veda proclaim something, it should be recognized as the Law, not what others say, be they in their thousands.

[8] Offerings meant for gods or ancestors should always be given only to a learned Brahmin, for what is given to one who is not a learned Brahmin reaches neither the gods nor the ancestors.

[9] Even if a learned man lives far away, while a fool lives in one's own house, one should give a gift to the learned man; one does not incur the sin of neglecting a Brahmin when the man is a fool.

[10] One does not incur the sin of neglecting a Brahmin when the man is a fool and bereft of vedic knowledge, for one does not offer an oblation in the ash ignoring a blazing fire.

[11] An elephant made of wood, a deer made of leather, and an uneducated Brahmin: all these three are so only in name.

[12] Those kingdoms in which ignorant men eat what ought to be eaten by the learned will experience a drought or a great calamity.

Treasure-Trove [13] If someone finds a treasure whose owner is unknown, the king may take it after giving one-sixth to the finder. [14] If, however, the treasure is found by a Brahmin devoted to the six occupations proper to him, the king should not take it.

Killing an Assailant [15] When someone kills an assailant, they say that the killer incurs no guilt. [16] Now, they also quote:

> An arsonist, a poisoner, a man brandishing a weapon, a robber, and a man who seizes one's land or abducts one's wife—these six are called assailants.
>
> [17] A man may kill an assailant who attacks with the intent to kill, even if he is deeply versed in Vedas including the Vedāntas; it does not make him a Brahmin killer.
>
> [18] When someone kills even a man learned in the Vedas and born in an illustrious family who is trying to kill him, it does not make him a murderer of a learned Brahmin; there wrath recoils on wrath.

Persons Who Purify Others [19] An expert in the three Nāciketa fire altars; a man who maintains the five sacred fires (A 2.17.22 n.); a man who knows the three 'Bird' verses; an expert in the four types of sacrifices (A 2.17.22 n.); a man who knows the White Yajur Veda; a man who knows the six Vedic Supplements (A 2.8.10–11); a son of a woman given in marriage according to the 'Brahma' rite (Va 1.30); a man who knows the Sāma Veda; a man who sings the Jyeṣṭha Sāman; a man who knows both the mantra and the liturgical portions of the Veda (p. xxiii); a man who studies the Laws; a man in whose family nine generations of ancestors on both the father's and mother's side are known to have been learned Brahmins; learned men; and bath-graduates (A 1.30.9 n.)—these are persons who purify those alongside whom they eat (A 2.17.21 n.).

Legal Assembly

> [20] Four men, each proficient in one of the four Vedas; one exegete; one who knows the Vedic Supplements (A 2.8.10–11); one legal scholar;

and three leading men belonging to three different orders of life—these constitute a legal assembly with a minimum of ten members.

Definition of Teacher [21]The man who initiates a person and teaches him the entire Veda is called 'teacher'; [22]whereas someone who teaches just a section of the Veda is called 'tutor', [23]as also someone who teaches the Vedic Supplements.

Taking up Arms

[24]A Brahmin or a Vaiśya may take up arms to defend himself and to prevent the mixing of classes. [25]A Kṣatriya, on the other hand, should do so all the time, because it is incumbent upon him to protect the people.

PURIFICATION

Purification of Persons

[26]Having washed his feet and his hands up to the wrists and seated on his haunches facing the east or the north, he should sip water three times without making any sound and using the part of the hand sacred to Brahman, that is, the line above the base of the thumb (B 1.8.14–16 n.); [27]wipe his lips twice; [28]rub water on the cavities of his head (G 1.36 n.); [29]and pour water on his head and on his left hand. [30]He should not sip water while he is walking, standing, lying down, or stooping.

[31]A Brahmin is purified by water free of bubbles or froth and reaching the heart; [32]a Kṣatriya by water reaching the throat; [33]a Vaiśya by water taken into the mouth; [34]and a woman or Śūdra by water merely touching the lips (A 1.16.2 n.). [35]Even water from a crevice may be used if it is sufficient to slake the thirst of a cow, [36]but not water contaminated with colouring, perfume, or condiments, or collected in a foul place.

[37]Saliva spattering from the mouth does not make a person impure if it does not touch his body. [38]After sleeping, eating, sneezing, drinking, crying, or bathing, and after putting on a garment, he should sip water over again even if he had already

sipped water, [39] as also after touching a hairless part of the lips. [40] No taint is created by the hair of the moustache getting into the mouth.

> [41] Bits of food sticking between the teeth are like the teeth themselves, as also whatever is in the mouth. One becomes purified by simply swallowing them.
>
> [42] Even when someone pours water for others to sip and drops splash on his feet, they do not make him unclean; they are said to be the same as the ground.
>
> [43] If a person touches something unclean while handling food, he should lay that food on the ground, sip some water, and continue with his activity once again.

Purification of Things

[44] Whenever a person has a doubt regarding the purity of something, he should sprinkle some water on it.

> [45–7] Wild animals killed by dogs; a fruit made to fall by a bird; what has been passed around by children or handled by women; goods displayed for sale so long as they have not been spoilt by gnats and flies landing on them; impurities in the mouths of women; water collected on the ground sufficient to slake the thirst of cows—having enumerated all these, Prajāpati declared them to be pure.

[48] Anything stained with an impure substance is purified when the stain and smell are removed with earth and water (G 1.42 n.). [49] Articles made of metal are to be scrubbed with ash; earthenware is to be fired; wooden implements should be scraped; and cloth is to be washed. [50] Stones and gems are purified like metal; [51] conch shells and mother of pearl like gems; [52] bone like wood; [53] and ropes, cane, and leather like cloth. [54] Articles made of

fruits are purified by rubbing them with cow's hair, [55] and those made of linen by rubbing them with a paste of yellow mustard.

[56] The purity of a piece of land is restored by sweeping, smearing with cowdung, scraping, sprinkling water, and by scattering clean soil, depending on the degree of defilement. [57] Now, they also quote:

> Digging, burning, scraping, and trampling by cows—by these four means, and fifthly by smearing with cowdung, a piece of land is purified.
>
> [58] A woman is purified by her menstrual flow, a river by its current, brass with ash, and earthenware by being fired again.
>
> [59] Earthenware that has come into contact with liquor, urine, faeces, phlegm, pus, tears, or blood cannot be purified by being fired again.
>
> [60] The body is purified by water, the mind by truth, the spirit by knowledge and austerity, and the intellect by knowledge.

[61] Gold is cleaned with just water, [62] as also silver. [63] Copper is cleaned with an acidic cleanser.

Parts of Hand for Sipping

[64] The base of the little finger is the part of the hand sacred to the gods; [65] the middle of the fingers is the part sacred to the seers; [66] the tips of the fingers is the part sacred to human beings; [67] the middle of the palm is the part sacred to Fire; [68] and the part between the forefinger and the thumb is sacred to the ancestors (B 1.8.14–16 n.).

EATING ETIQUETTE

[69] He should pay homage to his meals morning and evening, by saying 'I am delighted!'; [70] at an ancestral offering, by saying 'I have eaten well!'; [71] and at a rite for prosperity, by saying 'It is perfect!'

SOCIAL CLASSES

4 [1]The four classes are distinguished by their origin and by specific sacramentary rites. [2]There is also the vedic passage:

> His mouth became the Brahmin; his arms were made into the Kṣatriya; his thighs are the Vaiśya; and from his feet the Śūdra was born. (RV 10.90.12)

[3]'He created the Brahmin with the Gāyatrī metre, the Kṣatriya with the Triṣṭhubh metre, and the Vaiśya with the Jagatī metre; whereas the Śūdra he created without the use of any metre.'* This passage points out that the Śūdra is not to undergo any sacramentary rite.

[4]Speaking the truth, refraining from anger, giving gifts, not killing living creatures, and fathering children—these are common to all classes.

MEAT AND HOSPITALITY

[5]The treatise of Manu states: 'An animal may be killed only on the occasion of paying homage to ancestors, gods, or guests.'

> [6]When offering the honey mixture (A 2.8.8), at a sacrifice, and during rites for ancestors and gods—only on these occasions, Manu has declared, should an animal be killed.
>
> [7]Without killing a living creature you can never obtain meat; and killing living creatures does not get you to heaven. Killing an animal at a sacrifice, therefore, is not a killing.*

[8]'He should, moreover, cook a big ox or a big male goat for a Brahmin or a Kṣatriya who comes to his house. In this way they show him hospitality' (SB 3.4.1.2).

OBSERVANCES AT THE DEATH OF A RELATIVE

Funerary Rites

[9] When those who are two years or older die, they are to be offered libations of water, and their death creates a period of impurity; [10] according to some, this is true from the time a child has teethed.

[11] After cremating the body, they should go away without looking back and enter a place of water. [12] On uneven days they should pour libations of water with both hands facing the south. [13] The south, clearly, is the direction of the ancestors. [14] After returning home, they should remain seated on mats fasting for three days. [15] If they are unable, they should live on food that they have purchased or has been given to them unasked.

Periods of Impurity after Death and Birth

[16] After a death, a ten-day period of impurity is enjoined on those belonging to the same ancestry (A 2.14.2 n.). [17] Relatives up to the sixth degree, it is said, fall under the category of common ancestry, [18] and in the case of married women, up to the second degree. [19] Others should perform the funerary rites of married women; and such women should perform them for those people.*

> [20] The very same rule regarding impurity
> applies also to a birth for those who desire per-
> fect purity.

[21] Alternatively, it applies only to the mother and the father, [22] or, according to some, only to the mother, because the birth results from her. [23] Now, they also quote:

> At a birth there is no period of impurity for the
> man, unless he comes into contact with her.
> One should know that the impure element there
> is the vaginal discharge, and that does not
> occur in the man.

[24] If during that period another arises, they become pure at the

end of the time remaining from the first period of impurity; [25] but if only one day remains, then at the end of two days; [26] and if it happens on the morning after the conclusion of the first period, then at the end of three days.

[27] A Brahmin becomes pure after ten days, [28] a Kṣatriya after fifteen days, [29] a Vaiśya after twenty days, [30] and a Śūdra after a month. [31] Now, they also quote:

> When a man eats the food of a Śūdra who is in a state of impurity caused by a death or a birth, he will go to hell and take birth in the womb of an animal.
>
> [32] If a Brahmin accepts an invitation and eats at the house of an outsider during the ten days of impurity cased by a death, when he dies he will be reborn as a worm and eat the faeces of that man.

[33] 'Such a man', it is said, 'becomes purified after reciting a vedic collection of hymns for twelve months or twelve fortnights without eating' (B 3.9).

[34] When a child less than two years old dies or when there is a miscarriage, the period of impurity of those belonging to the same ancestry (A 2.14.2 n.) lasts for three days; [35] according to Gautama, they become pure immediately (cf. G 14.44). [36] When someone living in a distant region dies and the news arrives after ten days, the period of impurity lasts for one day. [37] According to Gautama, when a man who has established his sacred fires dies while he is away on a journey, they should perform his final obsequies anew and then purify themselves as if they had actually disposed of the corpse.

[38] If someone touches a sacrificial post, a pyre, a cemetery, a menstruating woman, a woman who has just given birth, and sordid men (A 1.21.12–19), he should enter water submerging his body and head under water.

WOMEN

Dependence on Men

5 [1]A woman cannot act independently; she is under the authority of the man. [2]'A woman who is neither a girl running naked (G 18.23 n.) nor in her menstrual period', it is stated, 'is ambrosia.' [3]Now, they also quote:

> Her father takes care of her in her childhood;
> her husband takes care of her in her youth; and
> her son takes care of her in her old age. A
> woman is not fit to act independently.

[4]The penance for her being unfaithful to her husband has been declared in the secret penances:

> [5]For month after month their menstrual flow
> washes away their sins. (Va 28.4)

Menstruation

[6]A menstruating woman remains impure for three days. [7]She should not apply collyrium on her eyes or oil on her body, or bathe in water; she should sleep on the floor and not sleep during the day; she should not touch the fire, make a rope, brush her teeth, eat meat, or look at the planets; she should not laugh, do any work, or run; and she should drink out of a large pot or from her cupped hands or a copper vessel. [8]For it is stated: 'Indra, after he had killed the three-headed son of Tvaṣṭṛ, was seized by sin, and he regarded himself in this manner: "An exceedingly great guilt attaches to me". And all creatures railed against him: "Brahmin-killer! Brahmin-killer!" He ran to the women and said: "Take over one-third of this my guilt of killing a Brahmin." They asked: "What will we get?" He replied: "Make a wish." They said: "Let us obtain offspring during our season, and let us enjoy sexual intercourse freely until we give birth." He replied: "So be it!" And they took the guilt upon themselves. That guilt of killing a Brahmin manifests itself every month. Therefore, one should not eat the food of a

menstruating woman, for such a woman has put on the aspect of the guilt of killing a Brahmin' (TS 2.5.1.2–5).

[9] Now, they say: 'One should never accept collyrium or oil from such a woman, because for women that is food' (TS 2.5.1.6); and 'Therefore, people feel disgust towards her and her condition, thinking "Let her not come near!" '

> [10] People in whose homes there are menstruating women, people who do not maintain the sacred fires, and people in whose family there hasn't been a vedic scholar—all these are equal to Śūdras.

GOOD CONDUCT

6 [1] Good conduct is the highest Law for all—that is certain. A man steeped in vile conduct comes to ruin in this world and the next.

[2] Whether it is austerities, vedic learning, daily fire sacrifices, or gifts to priests—nothing will rescue a man of vile conduct who has gone astray.

[3] The Vedas do not purify a man bereft of good conduct, even if he has studied them together with the six supplements (A 2.8.10–11). The vedic lore forsakes him at the time of death, like birdlings a nest when they have grown their wings.

[4] Like a pretty wife to her husband who is blind, what happiness can all the Vedas together with the supplements and sacrifices bring to a Brahmin who is bereft of good conduct?

[5] The vedic lore cannot rescue from his wickedness a deceitful man living by deceit. When even a couple of syllables are learnt properly, that Veda purifies the man, like clouds in the autumnal month.*

[6] For a man of evil conduct is the object of contempt in the world. Woes follow him all the time; afflicted with sicknesses, his life is cut short.

[7] Through good conduct flourishes righteousness; through good conduct flourishes wealth; through good conduct he obtains success; and good conduct erases inauspicious marks.

[8] Even if he lacks auspicious marks, a man of good conduct, full of generosity (B 1.10.4 n.) and free from envy, will live a hundred years.

[9] A man who knows the Law should eat, void urine and excrement, and engage in sexual activity in great secrecy. Likewise, what he says and thinks, as well as his wealth and age, should be kept well concealed.

Excretion

[10] He should void both urine and excrement facing the north during the day and the south during the night. In this way his allotted span of life will not be diminished.

[11] If a man urinates in the direction of a fire, the sun, a cow, a Brahmin, the moon, or water, it will destroy his intelligence.

[12] He should not pass urine in a river, on a road, on ash, on cowdung, on a field that has been ploughed or sown with seed, on a grassy patch, or in a shady spot offering shelter.

[13] When he is standing in the shade, when it is dark, or when he fears for his life, a Brahmin may do it day or night facing any direction he wants.

Purification

[14] He should perform rites with water that has been drawn out (G 9.10 n.), [15] but he may bathe even with water that has not been drawn out.

> [16] A Brahmin should fetch some sandy earth (G 1.42 n.) from the bank of a river.
> [17] Earth from under water, a temple, anthill, or a mound over a rat-hole, and earth left behind by someone after his purification—he should not take these five types of earth.
> [18] Tradition lays down one application of earth on the penis, three on the left hand, and two on both hands; and five applications on the anus, ten on the left hand, and seven on both hands.
> [19] This is the purification for householders. It is twice that much for students, three times for forest hermits, and four times for ascetics.

Food

> [20] A sage's meal is eight mouthfuls, a forest hermit's sixteen, a householder's twenty-two, and a student's an unlimited quantity.
> [21] A man who has set up the three ritual fires, a draught ox, and a student—these three are able to do their tasks only if they eat. They cannot do them if they do not eat (A 2.9.13; B 2.13.7–8).

[22] These restrictions apply to vows, penances, sacrifices, vedic recitations, and religious observances.

Brahmin and Śūdra

> [23] Discipline, austerity, self-control, liberality, truthfulness, purity, vedic learning, compassion, erudition, intelligence, and religious

faith—these are the characteristics of a Brahmin.

[24] Bearing long grudges, envy, mendacity, reviling Brahmins, slander, and ruthlessness—these should be recognized as the characteristics of a Śūdra.

[25] Those who are tranquil and self-controlled, whose ears are ever occupied with listening to the Vedas, who have mastered their senses, who refrain from killing living creatures, and who close their hands when they are offered gifts—they are the Brahmins who have the capacity to redeem others.

[26] Some are worthy to receive gifts because of their vedic learning, and others because of their austerities. Among all men worthy of receiving gifts, the most worthy is the man into whose stomach the food of a Śūdra has never entered.

[27] If a Brahmin dies with the food of a Śūdra in his stomach, he will be reborn as a village pig or in the family of that Śūdra.

[28] For a man whose body is nourished by the food of a Śūdra does not find the celestial path, even though he recites the Veda, offers sacrifices, and is constantly engaged in the soft recitation of prayers (A 1.15.1 n.).

[29] If a man has sex after eating the food of a Śūdra, however, his sons will belong to the man who gave the food, and he will not attain heaven.

[30] A man who rises to recite the Veda and comes from a good family; who is perfectly tranquil, devoted to performing sacrifices, and afraid of sin; who has vast knowledge and is patient with women; who is righteous, protects cows, and wears himself out with penances—such a man, they say, is worthy to receive gifts.

> [31–2] As milk, curd, ghee, or honey poured into an unbaked pot is lost because the pot was so weak, and both the pot and those delicacies perish, so when an ignorant man accepts a cow, gold, a garment, a horse, a piece of land, or sesame seeds, he is reduced to ashes like a piece of firewood.

Rules of Good Conduct

[33] He shall not make a noise by cracking his joints or striking his nails; [34] tap an eating bowl with his nails; [35] drink water from his cupped hands; [36] splash the water with his foot or hand; [37] splash water on to water; [38] or pluck fruits by throwing brickbats [39] or other fruits at them.

[40] He should not become a cheat or a hypocrite, [41] or learn the language of barbarians. [42] Now, they also quote:

> 'He should not be fickle in anything he does, whether it is with his hands, feet, eyes, speech, or body'—that is the view of cultured people.
>
> [43] Those Brahmins, in whose families the study of the Veda together with its supplements is hereditary, and who are able to adduce as proofs express vedic texts (G 3.36 n.), should be recognized as the cultured.
>
> [44] When no one knows whether he is good or bad, learned or ignorant, virtuous or vile, he is indeed a Brahmin.

ORDERS OF LIFE

7 [1] There are four orders of life: [2] student, householder, forest hermit, and wandering ascetic. [3] After studying one, two, or all the Vedas, a man who has not violated his vow of chastity may live in whichever of these he prefers.

Student

[4]Student—he should serve his teacher until death [5]and, when the teacher dies, the sacred fire; [6]for it is stated, 'The fire is your teacher' (SG 2.3.1).

[7]He should be restrained in his speech [8]and eat every fourth, sixth, or eighth mealtime (A 1.25.10 n.). [9]He should beg for almsfood [10]and obey his teacher. [11]He should wear all his hair matted, or just the topknot.

[12]He should wait upon his teacher, walking behind him if he is walking, standing by if he is seated, and sitting if he is lying down. [13]He should recite his lesson only when he is called upon to do so. [14]He should announce everything he has received to the teacher and eat with his permission.

[15]He should refrain from sleeping on a bed, brushing his teeth, washing his body, applying collyrium on his eyes or oil on his body, wearing shoes, or carrying an umbrella. [16]He should remain standing during the day and seated at night, [17]and bathe three times a day.

Householder

8 [1]Householder—after bringing his anger and excitement under control and taking the final bath with the permission of his teacher, he should select for his wife a woman who does not belong to a lineage with the same ancestral seer (A 2.11.15 n.), who has not experienced sex before, who is younger than he and belongs to the same class as he, [2]and who is not related within four degrees on the mother's side or six degrees on the father's side. [3]He should kindle the nuptial fire.

Hospitality [4]He should not turn away a guest who arrives in the evening. [5]A guest should not remain in his house without being given to eat.

> [6]When a Brahmin who has come to someone's
> house seeking a place to stay is given nothing to
> eat, he leaves taking with him all the good
> works of that man.

> [7] A Brahmin who spends one night, according to tradition, is called a guest. He is called 'guest' because his stay is brief.*
>
> [8] A Brahmin who lives in the same village or comes for a social visit is not a guest. Whether he comes at the proper time or not, a guest should not remain in his house without receiving food.

Sacrifices [9] A man who is generous (B 1.10.4 n.) and without greed, should neither live without the sacred fires if he has the means to establish them, [10] nor fail to offer the Soma sacrifice if he has the means to offer it.

Duties [11] He should be intent on privately reciting the Veda, offering sacrifices, and begetting offspring. [12] He should honour anyone who comes to his house by rising up to meet him, offering him a seat, and giving kind greetings and unstinting praise; [13] and all creatures by giving them food according to his ability.

> [14] A householder alone offers sacrifices; a householder performs austerities. Of all the four orders, the householder is the best.
>
> [15] As all rivers and rivulets ultimately end up in the ocean, so people of all the orders ultimately end up in the householder.*
>
> [16] As all living beings live dependent on their mothers, so all mendicants live dependent on the householder.
>
> [17] When a Brahmin always carries water with him (B 1.7.1), always wears the sacrificial cord (A 1.6.18 n.), always recites the Veda privately, avoids the food of outcastes, has sexual intercourse with his wife during her season (A 2.1.17 n.), and offers sacrifices according to the rules, he does not fall from the world of Brahman.

Forest Hermit

9 [1] Forest hermit—he should wear matted hair and a garment of bark or skin. [2] He should not enter a village [3] or step on ploughed land. [4] He should gather uncultivated roots and fruits; [5] observe chastity; [6] be full of patience; [7] and when guests come to his hermitage, honour them with almsfood of roots and fruits.

[8] He should only give and never receive, [9] and bathe at dawn, noon, and dusk. [10] After establishing the hermit fire (G 3.27 n.), he should maintain the sacred fire. [11] After continuing in this manner for six months, he should live homeless and without a fire at the foot of a tree.

[12] He should make offerings to gods, ancestors, and men. He will thus attain an endless heavenly abode.

Wandering Ascetic

10 [1] Wandering ascetic—he should depart after giving the gift of safety to all creatures. [2] Now, they also quote:

> When a sage wanders about after giving the gift of safety to all creatures, no creature poses a threat to his own safety.
>
> [3] When, however, someone gives up the active life without giving the gift of safety to all creatures, as also when he accepts donations, he brings to ruin the past and future generations of his family.
>
> [4] Let him abandon all ritual activities; the Veda alone let him never abandon. By abandoning the Veda he becomes a Śūdra; therefore let him never abandon the Veda.
>
> [5] The Monosyllable OṂ is the highest Veda; the control of breathing is the highest austerity. Eating almsfood is better than fasting; and compassion far excels the distribution of gifts.

[6] A wandering ascetic should be shaven-headed, free from

selfish yearning, and without possessions. [7]He should go randomly to seven houses to beg for almsfood [8]at a time when smoke is not rising from the kitchens and the pestles have been laid aside (B 2.11.22 n.).

[9]He should wrap himself with a single piece of cloth, [10]or cover his body with an antelope skin or with a garment of grass nibbled by cows.

[11]He should sleep on the ground [12]and not keep a fixed residence, [13]staying in the outskirts of a village, in a temple or an abandoned house, or at the foot of a tree. [14]He should apply his mind to the cultivation of knowledge, [15]living always in the wilderness [16]and never walking within sight of village animals.

> [17]Freedom from rebirth, indeed, is secure for a man who always lives in the wilderness; has brought his senses under control and put an end to all sensual pleasures; focuses his mind on contemplating the Highest Self; and looks upon everything dispassionately.

[18]He should display neither the emblems* of his state nor his way of life [19]and, although he is not mad, give the appearance of being mad. [20]Now, they also quote:

> Liberation is not achieved by a man who takes delight in verbal sciences and in captivating the folks, has his heart on food and clothes, and loves beautiful residences.
>
> [21]He should never try to get almsfood by interpreting portents or omens, by displaying his knowledge of astrology or somatomancy, by giving advice, or by participating in debates.
>
> [22]Let him neither be disheartened when he does not receive nor elated when he does. Let him take only as much as would sustain his life, free from attachment even to the few articles in his possession.
>
> [23]Hut, water, clothes, tripod (B 2.17.11 n.),

house, seat, food—a man who is not attached
to these has surely won liberation.

[24] Morning and evening he should eat only what he obtains from a Brahmin household, avoiding honey and meat [25] and without eating until he is full.

[26] Alternatively, he may live in a village, [27] abandoning crooked and dishonest ways, homeless and resolute. [28] Let him not become sensually attached to anything. [29] Let him look upon everyone dispassionately, desisting from either causing harm or doing favours to any creature.

Virtues Common to All Orders

[30] To refrain from slander, envy, pride, egotism, disbelief, dishonesty, praising oneself, running down others, hypocrisy, greed, perplexity, anger, and jealousy is regarded as the Law common to all orders of life. [31] A Brahmin who wears a sacrificial cord, carries a water pot, is pure, and avoids the food of Śūdras will not fail to win the world of Brahman.

DISTRIBUTION OF FOOD AND RECEPTION OF GUESTS

Guests

11 [1] Six individuals are worthy to receive the welcome water (G 5.32 n.): [2] an officiating priest, a bridegroom, a king, a paternal uncle, a bath-graduate, and a maternal uncle.

[3] Morning and evening, he should offer in the fire a portion of the food he has cooked as an oblation to the All-gods; [4] make a Bali offering to the house deities; [5] give the first portion to a vedic scholar or a student; and immediately thereafter make an offering to his ancestors. [6] After that he should give food to the guests according to their relative eminence; [7] among those of his household, to the young women, the children, the elderly, the youngsters, and the women who have recently given birth; [8] and finally to other members of his family. [9] He should throw some food on the ground for dogs, Cāṇḍālas, outcastes, and crows;

[10] and give leftover (A 1.3.27 n.) or fresh food to a Śūdra. [11] The householder and his wife should eat what remains.

[12] If a guest arrives after he has made the offering to the All-gods, he should cook a fresh meal using all the normal ingredients. He should prepare an exquisite meal for that guest. [13] For it is stated:

> A Brahmin guest enters a house as the fire common to all men. Through him they obtain rain, and through rain food. So people call the reception of such a guest a rite to avert evil. (cf. KaU 1.7)

[14] After giving food to that guest, he should pay him homage [15] and follow him as he leaves up to the village boundary or until he gives him leave to return.

Ancestral Offerings

[16] He should offer oblations to the ancestors after the fourth day in the fortnight of the waning moon. [17–18] Having issued invitations to the Brahmins the day before, he should feed ascetics or virtuous householders who are not too old, do not follow bad occupations, and are vedic scholars, and who neither have been his pupils nor are living with him as pupils; or he may even feed his pupils who possess fine qualities, [19] but avoid people who go naked, suffer from white leprosy, are impotent or blind, have black teeth, suffer from black leprosy, or have bad nails. [20] Now, they also quote:

> If, however, a man who knows the Veda is afflicted with bodily defects that defile those alongside whom he eats, Yama has proclaimed him faultless; he undoubtedly purifies those alongside whom he eats (A 2.17.21 n.).
>
> [21] At an ancestral offering the leftovers should not be removed until the end of the day, for streams of nectar ooze from them, which are drunk by the departed who have not been offered libations of water (B 2.15.12 n.).

[22] One should not clean up the leftovers until the sun has set; rich streams of milk flow from them meant for the departed who get their share with difficulty.

[23] Both the leftovers and the fallen fragments, Manu has declared, are undoubtedly the share of one's own family members who have died before initiation.

[24] Fragments fallen on the ground and the smearings and water scattered on the sacred grass he should offer as food to the spirits of those who have died young or without offspring.

[25] With perverse minds the demons surely wait for their chance nearby when someone offers food to the ancestors without using both hands.

[26] Let him, therefore, not keep either hand empty as he serves the food; or let him stand holding the food plate until both kinds of remnants have been produced.*

[27] He should feed two at an offering to the gods and three at an offering to ancestors, or one at either offering. Even a rich man should not indulge in feeding a larger number.

[28] A large number is detrimental to five things: offering proper hospitality, doing things at the right place and the right time, carrying out purifications, and finding Brahmins of quality. Therefore, he should refrain from feeding a large number.

[29] Or else, he may feed a single Brahmin who has mastered the Veda, is endowed with learning and virtue, and is free of any unfavourable bodily marks (Va 11.19).

[30–1] How can an offering to the gods be made at an ancestral offering where just one man is fed?

Taking some from all the prepared food and putting it in a bowl, he should place it in a temple and then continue with the ancestral offering. He should throw that food in the fire or give it to a student.

[32] The ancestors will eat as long as the food is warm, the diners eat in silence, and no comment is made about the quality of the oblation.

[33] No comment must be made on the quality of the oblation until the ancestors have been sated. After the ancestors have been sated, they should say 'The oblation was exquisite!'

[34] If an ascetic invited to an offering to the ancestors or gods refuses to eat meat, he will go to hell for as many years as the number of hairs on that animal's body.

[35] Three things purify an ancestral offering: a daughter's son, the midday, and sesame seeds. Three things they commend for it: purification, not being angry, and avoiding haste.

[36] During the eighth part of the day the sun moves slowly; this period is known as 'midday'; and anything given to ancestors at this time becomes inexhaustible.

[37] If someone engages in sexual intercourse after offering or eating at an ancestral oblation, his ancestors eat his semen during that month.

[38] A child born from such a union after offering or eating at an oblation to the ancestors does not acquire knowledge and is born with a brief life span.

[39–40] When a son is born, his father, grandfather, and great-grandfather hover around him, as birds around a fig tree, saying: 'He will present ancestral offerings to us with honey, meat, vegetables, milk, and milk-rice pudding during the rainy seasons and the Maghā constellation' (A 1.6.18 n.).

[41] The ancestors rejoice at a son who extends the family line, is diligent in presenting ancestral offerings, and devoted to gods and Brahmins.

[42] When someone offers food to his ancestors at Gayā, they rejoice, just as farmers rejoice at well-ploughed fields; in him his ancestors are blessed with a true son.

[43] He should make ancestral offerings on the full-moon days of July–August and November–December and on the ninth day of the fortnight of the waning moon in the four lunar months between November and March. [44] When extraordinary materials or Brahmins or an extraordinary place is at hand, however, rules regarding the proper time do not apply.

Sacrifices

[45] A Brahmin has the obligation to establish the sacred fires. [46] And he should offer the full-moon and the new-moon sacrifices, the sacrifices of the first fruits, the seasonal sacrifices, the animal sacrifices, and the Soma sacrifices; [47] for this is specifically enjoined and is also acclaimed as a debt. [48] It is stated: 'A Brahmin is born carrying three debts—of sacrifice to the gods, of offspring to the ancestors, and of studentship to the seers. That man is free from debts who has offered a sacrifice, fathered a son, and lived as a student' (cf. TS 6.3.10.5).

THE STUDENT

Time of Initiation

[49] One should initiate a Brahmin in the eighth year from conception, [50] a Kṣatriya in the eleventh year from conception, [51] and a Vaiśya in the twelfth year from conception.

Insignia

[52] A Brahmin's staff should be of Palāśa wood, [53] a Kṣatriya's of banyan wood, [54] and a Vaiśya's of Udumbara wood. [55] A Brahmin's staff should reach the hair of the head, [56] a Kṣatriya's the forehead, [57] and a Vaiśya's the nose. [58] A Brahmin's girdle should be made of Muñja grass, [59] a Kṣatriya's of a bowstring, [60] and a Vaiśya's of hemp thread. [61] A Brahmin's upper garment should be the skin of a black antelope, [62] a Kṣatriya's the skin of the spotted Ruru antelope, [63] and a Vaiśya's the skin of a cow or a male goat. [64] A Brahmin's garment should be white and unblemished, [65] a Kṣatriya's dyed madder, [66] and a Vaiśya's dyed yellow or made of silk. [67] Or else, people of all classes may wear undyed cotton garments.

Begging

[68] A Brahmin should request almsfood placing 'Madam' at the beginning, [69] a Kṣatriya placing 'Madam' in the middle, [70] and a Vaiśya placing 'Madam' at the end (A 1.3.28–30 n.).

Time Limit for Initiation

[71] For a Brahmin the time for initiation does not lapse until the sixteenth year, [72] for a Kṣatriya until the twenty-second year, [73] and for a Vaiśya until the twenty-fourth year. [74] After that time they become excluded from the Sāvitrī; [75] and no one should initiate them, teach them, officiate at their sacrifices, or enter into marriage alliances with them.

[76] A man who is excluded from the Sāvitrī should perform the Uddālaka penance: [77] for two months he should live on barley gruel, for one month on milk, for a fortnight on curd, for eight days on ghee, for six days on food received unasked, and for three days on water; and he should fast for a day and night. [78] Alternatively, he may participate in the ritual bath that concludes a horse sacrifice; [79] or he may perform the Vrātyastoma sacrifice.

THE BATH-GRADUATE

Proper Conduct

12 [1] Next, we will describe the observances of a bath-graduate (A 1.30.4 n.). [2] He should not beg for anything except from the king or a pupil of his. [3] If he is racked by hunger, however, he may beg for a little something—a ploughed or unploughed piece of land, a cow, a goat, or a sheep, and in the last place gold, grain, or food. [4] The directive, however, is that a bath-graduate should not languish because of hunger.

[5] He should not have sex with a menstruating woman, [6] with a pre-pubescent girl, [7] or with an inappropriate woman. [8] Let him not carry tales from one family to another (G 9.53 n.). [9] He should not step over a rope to which a calf is tied [10] or look at the sun at sunrise or sunset.

[11] He should not urinate or defecate in water, [12] or spit into it. [13] He should void urine and excrement with his head covered and after spreading some grass unfit for ritual purposes on the ground, facing the north during the day and the south during the night, and sitting down facing the north during the twilights. [14] Now, they also quote:

> Bath-graduates should always wear a lower and an upper garment and two sacrificial cords (A 1.6.18 n.), and carry a staff and a pot filled with water.
>
> [15] Purity, it is said, is brought about by water, hand, stick, and fire. Therefore, he should clean the water pot with his hand using water; [16] for Manu, the Lord of creatures, has proclaimed this to be the encircling with fire (B 1.6.2).
>
> [17] After he has answered a call of nature, a man with a sound knowledge of the rules of purification should sip some water.

[18] He should eat his food facing the east. [19] He should silently swallow the whole lump, pushing it into the mouth with his thumb [20] without making any sound.

[21] He should engage in sexual intercourse with his wife during her season (A 2.1.17 n.), avoiding the days of the moon's change (A 1.26.14 n.) [22] and not having intercourse in unusual positions. [23] Now, they also quote:

> If a man performs the sex act in the mouth of
> the woman he has married, during that month
> his ancestors will feed on his semen. All bizarre
> sexual practices are against the Law.

[24] It is, moreover, stated in the Veda of the Kāṭhakas: '"May we lie with our husbands even when we are going to give birth the following day." This is the wish granted to women by Indra' (cf. Va 5.8).

[25] He should not climb trees; [26] go down into wells; [27] blow on a fire with his mouth; [28] or pass between a Brahmin and a fire, [29] between two fires, [30] or between two Brahmins—or he may do so after receiving their permission. [31] He should not eat in the company of his wife; in the Veda of the Vājasaneyins it is stated: 'His children will lack manly vigour' (SB 10.5.2.9). [32] He should not point out a rainbow using the name 'Indra's bow' (*indradhanus*); [33] instead, he should call it 'jewelled bow' (*maṇidhanus*; cf. A 1.31.16; G 9.19–24; B 2.6.11–19).

[34] He should avoid stools, footwear, or tooth cleaners made with Palāśa wood (A 1.32.9 n.); [35] and not eat food placed on his lap [36] or on a chair.

[37] He should carry a bamboo staff [38] and wear a pair of gold earrings. [39] Outdoors, he should not wear a necklace, except one made of gold. [40] He should avoid casinos and fairs (A 1.3.12 n.). [41] Now, they also quote:

> To deny the authority of the Vedas, to vilify the
> seers, and to act contrary to the rules in any
> matter is to destroy one's self.

[42] He should not go to a sacrifice unless he has been chosen to officiate; but if he does, he should return keeping his right side towards it (A 1.7.2 n.). [43] He should not set out on a journey when the sun is seen over the trees,* [44] get into an unsafe boat, [45] or cross a river by swimming.

[46] If he gets up in the last watch of the night, he should recite the Veda and not go back to sleep. [47] At the time sacred to Prajāpati* a Brahmin should perform some religious observance.

Annual Course of Study

13 [1] Next, the commencement of the annual course of vedic study. It takes place on the full moon day of July–August or August–September. [2] He should kindle the fire and offer whole rice grains in it, [3] saying: 'To the gods! To the seers! To the Vedas!' [4] He should get Brahmins to say 'May there be well-being!', feed them with curd, and then begin the study of the Veda.

[5] He should continue the study for four and a half or five and a half months (A 1.9.1–3 n.). [6] Outside that period, he should study the Veda during the fortnights of the waxing moon. [7] If he wants to, he may study the Vedic Supplements (A 2.8.10–11).

Suspension of Vedic Recitation

[8] Vedic recitation is suspended [9] when it thunders during twilight; [10] at the morning and evening twilights; [11] in places where there is a corpse or a Cāṇḍāla; in towns—[12] or, if he wishes, he may recite it there after smearing an area with cowdung and drawing a line around it—; [13] near a cemetery; [14] when he is lying down; [15] and when he has accepted anything at an ancestral offering. [16] In this connection, they cite this verse from Manu:

> Even after accepting fruits, water, sesame seeds, foodstuffs, or anything else given at an ancestral offering, vedic recitation is suspended; a Brahmin's hand, tradition says, is his mouth. (B 1.21.8–10 n.)

[17] Vedic recitation is suspended when he is running; when there is a foul smell and the like; in a barren area; [18] when he has climbed a tree; [19] in a boat and an army encampment; [20] after eating, as long as his hands are wet; [21] when the sound of a lute is heard;

[22] on the fourteenth day of every fortnight; on new-moon days; on the eighth day of every fortnight; at the ancestral offerings on the eighth day after the full moon; [23] when he is seated with his legs stretched out, cross-legged, or leaning against something; [24] near his elders (A 1.6.32 n.); [25] on the night that he engages in sexual intercourse; [26] while wearing the clothes he had on when he had intercourse, unless they have been washed; [27] in the outskirts of a village; [28] after vomiting; [29] and after voiding urine or excrement.

[30] The recitation of the Ṛgveda and the Yajurveda is suspended when the recitation of the Sāmaveda is heard (G 16.21 n.). [31] Vedic recitation is suspended when he has indigestion; [32] when lightning strikes; [33] when there is an earthquake; [34] and during an eclipse of the moon or the sun.

[35] When a strange sound comes from the sky or there is an earth slide on a mountain, and when it rains stones, blood, or dust, vedic recitation is suspended until the same time the next day. [36] When meteors fall and lightning flashes at the same time, the suspension lasts for three days; [37] if they happen separately, for that day; [38] and if they occur out of season, until the same time the next day; [39] when his teacher dies, for three days; [40] when his son, pupil, or wife of his teacher dies, for a day and a night.

Salutation

[41] He should rise up and greet an officiating priest, a father-in-law, or a paternal or maternal uncle who is younger than himself; [42] the wives of those whose feet he is obliged to clasp and of his teacher; [43] and his parents.

[44] To a person who knows how to greet, he should say, 'I am so-and-so, sir!' [45] A person who does not know, however, [he should greet without using his name: A 1.14.23 n.]. [46] When returning a greeting, he should lengthen the last vowel of the name of the person he is greeting to three morae. If it is a diphthong '*e*' or '*o*' subject to euphonic combination, it is pronounced '*āy*' and '*āv*'; thus '*bho*' becomes '*bhāv*'.*

Falling from Caste

[47] A father should be forsaken when he becomes an outcaste, whereas a mother is never an outcaste to her son (A 1.28.9 n.). [48] Now, they also quote:

> A teacher is ten times more eminent than a tutor (B 1.11.28 n.); a father is a hundred times more eminent than a teacher; and a mother is a thousand times more eminent than a father.
>
> [49] One should first reprimand a wife, sons, or pupils who have become involved in sinful activities, and only thereafter should one forsake them. If someone forsakes them otherwise, he himself becomes an outcaste.

[50] A man should disown an officiating priest or a teacher who neglects to officiate at sacrifices or to teach the Veda; if he does not, he becomes an outcaste.

[51] They say that a son born to an outcaste becomes an outcaste himself, but not a daughter, [52] for she betakes herself to an outsider. [53] One may marry such a girl without taking a dowry.

Precedence

> [54] When his teacher's teacher is near by, he is expected to treat him as he does his own teacher. He should treat his teacher's son as he does the teacher himself—so states a vedic text.

[55] A Brahmin must not accept weapons, poison, or liquor as gifts. [56] Knowledge, wealth, age, kinship, and occupation are deserving of respect, [57] each preceding one being more respectable than the one that follows.

[58] Old people, children, the sick, people carrying heavy loads, women, people riding on vehicles—when someone meets these, he should give way to them, the ones mentioned later taking priority over the ones mentioned earlier. [59] If a king and a bath-graduate meet, the king should give way to the bath-graduate.

[60] All should give way to a bride being taken to her husband's house.

[61] Some straw, a place on the floor, fire, water, a welcome that is joyful and ungrudging are never wanting in the house of a good man.

FOOD

Unfit Food

14 [1] Next we will describe food that is fit and food that is unfit to be eaten (A 1.16.16 n.). [2] The following are unfit to be eaten: food given by a physician, a hunter, a harlot, a law enforcement agent, a thief, a heinous sinner (A 1.3.25 n.), a eunuch, or an outcaste; [3] as also that given by a miser, a man consecrated for a sacrifice, a prisoner, a sick person, a man who sells Soma, a carpenter, a washerman, a liquor dealer, a spy, an usurer, a leather worker, [4] a Śūdra, [5] a man who bears arms, [6] a lover of a married woman and a husband who countenances it, [7] an arsonist, [8] or one who does not execute those who deserve the capital punishment; [9] food announced publicly: 'Who will eat this?'; [10] food given by a corporate body or by a courtesan. [11] Now, they also quote:

> Gods do not eat the food of a man who keeps dogs, who is married to a Śūdra woman, who is controlled by his wife, or who lets his wife's lover remain in his house.

[12] He may accept the following from even such people: firewood, water, fodder, Kuśa grass, popped rice, food given unasked, vehicles, shelter, Śapharī fish, millet, garlands, perfumes, honey, and meat. [13] Now, they also quote:

> For the sake of his teacher, to save his wife, and to honour gods or guests, a man may accept gifts from anyone, but never to satisfy himself.

[14] He should not refuse the food of a man who hunts with bow and arrow, [15] for it is stated: 'During a sacrificial session lasting a

thousand years, Agastya went hunting; and he had sacrificial cakes made with the choice meat of excellent animals and birds.' [16] In this connection, moreover, they cite these verses of Prajāpati:

> Almsfood brought and handed over even by an evildoer, in the opinion of Prajāpati, is suitable for eating, so long as it has not been previously announced.
>
> [17] In particular, the food given by a generous man (B 1.10.4 n.) should be eaten, even if he is a thief, but never that given by a man who performs sacrifices for a lot of people and initiates a lot of people.
>
> [18] If a man spurns such food, his forefathers will not eat from him for fifteen years and the sacred fire will not convey his oblations.
>
> [19] Almsfood given by physicians, hunters, surgeons, fowlers, eunuchs, and unchaste wives is not to be accepted even if it is given unasked.

[20] Leftover food (A 1.3.27 n.) from anyone other than one's teacher is unfit to be eaten, [21] as also one's own leftovers, and food that has come into contact with leftovers [22] or with a garment, hair, or insects. [23] If he wants, however, he may eat it after removing the hair or the insect from it, sprinkling it with water, strewing some ash over it, and getting it verbally declared as suitable. [24] In this connection, moreover, they cite these verses of Prajāpati:

> Gods invented three means of purification for Brahmins: being unaware that something is impure, sprinkling it with water, and getting it verbally declared as suitable.
>
> [25] When food is touched by crows or dogs during a divine procession, marriage festivities, or while sacrifices are in progress, it should not be thrown away.
>
> [26] After extracting from it the defiled portion of

food, the rest should be purified, liquids by straining them and solids by sprinkling them with water.

[27] When something is touched by a cat's mouth, it undoubtedly remains pure.

[28] Food that has gone stale, looks revolting (G 17.13 n.), makes a person uneasy, has been cooked again, or is raw or undercooked is unfit to be eaten. [29] If he wants, however, he may eat such food after pouring some curd or ghee over it. [30] In this connection, moreover, they cite these verses of Prajāpati:

A Brahmin should not eat anything that drips from someone's nails, whether it is ghee or oil; Yama has declared that it is impure and equal to eating cow's meat.

[31] Oils, salt, or sauces served with the hand are of no service to the giver, while the eater devours guilt.

[32] These should never be served with the hand or with an iron utensil.

Forbidden Food

[33] If someone eats garlic, onions, mushrooms, Gṛñjana onions, Śleṣmāntaka fruits, tree resins, or red juices flowing from incisions on tree barks (G 17.33 n.), he should perform the very arduous penance (B 2.2.40). [34] He should not drink* the milk of cows in heat or whose calves have died, [35] or of cows, buffaloes, or goats during the first ten days after giving birth; [36] or water collected at the bottom of a boat. [37] He should refrain from eating wheat cakes, fried grains, porridge, barley-meal, oil-cake, oil, milk-rice, or vegetables that have turned sour, [38] as also preparations made with milk and barley-meal.

[39] Among animals with five claws, the porcupine, hedgehog, hare, tortoise, and Godhā monitor lizard may be eaten (A 1.17.37 n.), [40] as also, among domestic animals, those that have teeth in only one jaw, with the exception of the camel (G 17.28 n.).

[41]These are forbidden to be eaten:* among fish, the Ceṭa, the Gavaya, the porpoise, the alligator, and the crab, [42]as also grotesque fish and snake-head fish; [43]Gaura bison, Gayal oxen, and Śarabha, [44]as also animals not specifically indicated; * [45]milch-cows, draught oxen, and animals whose milk-teeth have not fallen.

[46]It is stated in the Veda of the Vājasaneyins that the milch-cow and the draught ox are pure and can be eaten (A 1.17.31 n.). [47]Regarding the rhinoceros and the wild pig, however, there are conflicting opinions.

[48]Among birds, the following are forbidden: birds that feed by scratching with their feet, web-footed birds, Kalaviṅka sparrow, Plava heron, Haṃsa goose, Cakravāka goose, Bhāsa vulture, crow, Pārāvata dove, Kurara osprey, Sāraṅga cuckoo, white dove, Krauñca crane, Krakara partridge, Kaṅka heron, vulture, falcon, Baka egret, Balāka ibis, Madgu cormorant, Ṭiṭṭibha sandpiper, Māndhāla flying fox, nocturnal birds, woodpecker, sparrow, Railātakā bird, Hārīta pigeon, Khañjarīṭa wagtail, village cock, parrot, Śārika starling, Kokila cuckoo, and carnivorous birds, as well as those living in villages.

ADOPTION

15 [1]A man comes into being through blood and semen* with his mother and father as the cause. [2]His father and mother have the power to give for adoption, to sell, or to abandon him.

[3]No one should give for adoption or adopt an only son, [4]for he is intended to continue the family line for his ancestors. [5]A wife should neither give a son for adoption nor adopt a son except with her husband's permission.

[6]When someone is going to adopt a son, he should summon his relatives; inform the king; in the middle of the house make an offering of ghee in the fire, reciting the Calls; and then take in adoption only someone whose relatives do not live far away, that is, someone with relatives close by. [7]If, however, a doubt arises, he should keep the person whose relatives live far away as if he were a Śūdra,* [8]for it is stated: 'By means of one he saves a multitude.'

[9] If, after adopting a son, a natural son is born to a man, the adopted son inherits one-quarter of the estate, [10] unless he is devoted to performing rites to secure prosperity.

EXCOMMUNICATION FROM AND READMISSION TO CASTE

[11] A man who has divulged the Veda or officiated at a Śūdra's sacrifice, and those who have fallen from the rank of the highest class—for them the rite of overturning the water pot should be performed. [12] A slave, a son from a wife of a lower caste, or a relative of a lower class lacking good qualities should fetch a broken pot from a heap of unusable pots; spread on the ground some Darbha grass or Lohita grass with their tips cut off; and overturn the pot filled with water with his left foot for that person. [13] And his relatives, their hair dishevelled, should touch the man who overturned the pot. [14] They may then return home as they wish, turning their left side towards that place (A 1.7.2 n.). [15] From that time onwards they should not let him participate in their religious activities. [16] Those who let him participate become his equals.

[17] Outcastes who have performed the penance, however, may be readmitted. [18] Now, they also quote:

> One should walk in front of those who are being readmitted displaying revelry and laughter, and behind those who are being excommunicated displaying grief and lamentation.

[19] A person who has assaulted his teacher, mother, or father may be readmitted through the compassion of these people or by performing an expiation.

This is how such people are readmitted. [20] They should fill a gold or clay pot with water from a holy lake or a river and pour it over him while reciting the verses 'Waters, you are refreshing . . .' [21] The discussion about the birth of a son gives all the rites to be performed upon the readmission of a person who has been bathed in this manner.*

KING

Legal Procedure

16 [1]Next, the legal procedure. [2]The king or his minister should run the court proceedings. [3]When there is a legal dispute between two parties, he should not take one side.

[4]An offence is determined according to social position; with regard to people of the lowest caste, there can be no offence. [5]He should treat all creatures equally. An offence is determined according to social position in the case of the first two classes, and lastly according to knowledge.*

Property Rights

[6]He should, moreover, protect what he has won, [7]as also the property of royal children [8]and minors (G 2.34 n.). [9]When they have reached the legal age (G 2.34 n.), however, it should be handed over to them.

> [10]Written evidence, witnesses, and possession
> are, according to traditional texts, the three
> types of evidence for claiming title to a prop-
> erty. In this way an owner may reclaim a
> property that had previously belonged to him.

[11]Space must be reserved for the road in a field through which a road runs, as also space for turning a cart. [12]Along newly built houses and other similar structures one should allow a passage three feet wide.

[13]When there is a dispute regarding a house or a field, the testimony of neighbours provides the proof. [14]When neighbours provide contradictory evidence, written documents provide the proof. [15]When conflicting documents are produced, the proof is based on the testimony of aged inhabitants of the town or village and that of guilds. [16]Now, they also quote:

> Ancestral property, what is bought, a pledge,
> things received by a wife at her wedding, a gift,
> what one receives for conducting a sacrifice,

property of reunited coparceners, and the eighth, wages.

[17] Any of these is lost to the owner when it is used by someone else continuously for ten years. [18] But they also quote a verse to the contrary:

> A pledge, a boundary, property of minors, an open deposit, a sealed deposit, women, and the property of the king or a vedic scholar are not lost to the owner by being used by someone else.

[19] Abandoned property belongs to the king. [20] If it is not abandoned, the king, together with ministers and city folk, should administer the property.

Royal Entourage

[21] Is a king, shifty like a reed, better off surrounded by vulture-eyed courtiers? [22] Or is he better off without an entourage of vulture-eyed courtiers? [23] He should surround himself with an entourage of vulture-eyed courtiers, but he should not be a vulture surrounded by vulture-eyed courtiers.* [24] For it is the courtiers who bring to light crimes [25] such as theft, robbery, and oppression. [26] At the outset, therefore, he should make enquiries of his courtiers.

Witnesses

[27] Next, witnesses. [28] Vedic scholars, handsome men, people of good character, people who do good works, and people who speak the truth—these may act as witnesses. [29] Or else, anyone at all may act as witnesses for anyone. [30] For women he should get women to act as witnesses; for twice-born men, twice-born men of equal standing; for Śūdras, Śūdras; and for the lowest caste people, men of the lowest birth. [31] Now, they also quote:

> A son is not obliged to repay the following [debts of his father]: what he owed as a surety or promised idly, debts he incurred gambling

or drinking, and unpaid portions of fines or taxes.

[32] Speak the truth, O witness! Your ancestors hang in suspense awaiting your statement, in accordance with which they will soar up or come crashing down.

[33] When a man bears false witness, he will end up naked, shaven-headed, and blind; racked with hunger and thirst; and going to his enemy's house with a begging bowl to obtain almsfood.

[34] When he gives false testimony concerning virgins, he slays five; concerning cattle, he slays ten; concerning horses, he slays a hundred; and concerning a man, he slays a thousand (G 13.14 n.).

[35] [verse corrupt and untranslatable]*

[36] A man may tell a lie at a marriage; during a sexual encounter; when his life is at stake; when there is a risk of losing all his property; and for the sake of a Brahmin. These five types of lies, they say, do not entail loss of caste.

[37] If during a trial someone gives evidence that is partial to one side either to help a relative or for money, he will cause the ancestors of both his spiritual lineage (A 2.17.4 n.) and his natural family, even those who are in heaven, to fall.

SONS

17 [1] 'A debt he pays in him and immortality he gains, the father who sees the face of his son born and alive' (AB 7.13).

[2] 'Eternal are the worlds of those men who have sons. A sonless man has no world'—so states a vedic text (cf. AB 7.13).

[3]And there is the curse: 'May our enemies be childless!' (RV 1.21.5). [4]There is also the vedic saying: 'Through offspring, O Fire, may we attain immortality' (RV 5.4.10).

> [5]Through a son one gains the worlds; through a grandson one attains eternal life; and through the son's grandson one gains the crest of the sun.

To Whom Belongs a Son

[6]People are in disagreement, some saying: 'A son belongs to the husband of the woman,' and others: 'A son belongs to the man who fathered him' (A 2.13.5 n.). [7]And they produce evidence in support of both positions:

> [8]Even if a bull fathers a hundred calves on someone else's cows, the calves belong to the owner of cows; the bull has spilled his semen in vain.
>
> [9]Diligently guard this progeny of yours, lest strangers sow their seeds in your field; in the transit to the next world, a son belongs to the man who fathered him. Otherwise a husband makes this progeny of his worthless for himself.
>
> [10]If one among many brothers of the same father has a son, then through that son they all become men who have sons—so states a vedic text.
>
> [11]If one among many wives of the same husband has a son, then through that son they all become women who have sons—so states a vedic text.*

Types of Sons

[12]Only twelve types of sons are recorded in the Purāṇas. [13]The first is a son sired by the husband himself on his own wife whom he has married according to the proper rites.

[14] Failing that, a *son begotten on his wife* after she has been duly appointed is the second.

[15] The third is an *appointed daughter*. [16] 'A brotherless girl', it is stated, 'goes back to her male ancestors and returning gains the status of a son.' [17] On this there is a verse:

> I will give you in marriage the brotherless girl
> adorned with finery with the provision that the
> son she bears will be my son.

[18] The fourth is a *son of a remarried woman.* [19] A 'remarried woman' is one who, after leaving the husband of her youth and consorting with others, returns to his house again. [20] A 'remarried woman' is also one who, after leaving a husband who is impotent, an outcaste, or mad, or after her husband is dead, finds another husband.

[21] The fifth is a *son of an unmarried woman.* [22] They say that a child born of lust to an unmarried woman in her father's house is the son of his maternal grandfather. [23] Now, they also quote:

> When someone's unmarried daughter bears a
> son from a man of the same class, through that
> child his maternal grandfather gets a son. He
> should make funeral offerings to that grand-
> father and inherit his estate.

[24] The sixth is a *son born in secret* at home. [25] These types of sons, they say, are heirs and relatives; they rescue one from great danger.

[26] Now, among the sons who are relatives but not heirs, the first is the *son received with the marriage.* [27] When one marries a pregnant woman, that is the son received with the marriage.

[28] The second is a *son given in adoption*, [29] that is, given for adoption by his parents.

[30] The third is a *purchased son.* [31] This type is described in the story of Śunaḥśepa: [32] 'There was a king Hariścandra. He purchased the son of Ajīgarta Sauyavasi.'

[33] The fourth is a *son given in adoption by himself.* [34] This type is described in the story of Śunaḥśepa: [35] 'Śunaḥśepa, when he was tied to the sacrificial post, praised the gods. The gods released

him from his bonds. The officiating priests said to him: "Let him be my son." He did not acquiesce to them. Then they said: "Let him be the son of whomever he chooses." The Hotṛ priest of that sacrifice was Viśvāmitra, and Śunaḥśepa made himself his son.'*

[36] The fifth is a *son who has been abandoned*, [37] that is, a son who is adopted after he has been abandoned by his parents.

[38] The sixth, they say, is simply the *son from a Śūdra wife*. These types of sons are relatives but not heirs. [39] Now, they also quote: 'When there is no heir belonging to the first group of six, then the latter may inherit the estate.'

Partitioning of the Estate

[40] Next, the partitioning of the estate among brothers. [41] [It should be delayed] until the childless wives bear sons. [42] The oldest son should take a double share [43] and one-tenth of the cows and horses. [44] The youngest son gets the goats, the sheep, and the house. [45] The middle son gets the iron and the household goods. [46] The daughters should share the mother's wedding gifts.

[47] If a Brahmin has sons from wives of Brahmin, Kṣatriya, and Vaiśya classes, [48] the son of the Brahmin wife should take a triple share, [49] the son of the Kṣatriya wife should take a double share, [50] and the others should get equal shares.

[51] If one of them has contributed his own earnings, he should take a double share. [52] Those who have entered another order of life do not receive any shares, [53] as also those who are impotent, mad, or outcastes. [54] The impotent and the mad should be maintained.

Levirate

[55] The wife of a deceased man should sleep on the floor for six months, observing her vow and eating food without salt or condiments. [56] After the completion of the six months, she should bathe and make a funeral offering to her husband. Then the father or the brother should assemble the elders (A 1.6.32 n.) who taught or performed rites for the deceased person and his relatives and get them to appoint her for levirate. [57] One should

not appoint a widow who is deranged, barren,* or sick, [58] as also one who is very old—[59] the age-limit is sixteen years from puberty. [60] Nor should she be appointed if the man with whom she should cohabit is sickly.

[61] At the time sacred to Prajāpati (Va 12.47 n.), the man should approach her like a husband, without laughing together and without maltreating her verbally or physically. [62] She should be given precedence in food, clothing, bathing, and lotions.

[63] A son born to a widow who has not been appointed, they say, belongs to his biological father, [64] whereas if she has been appointed, the son belongs to both the males involved in the appointment. [65] An appointment is invalid if it is made through greed for the estate of the deceased, [66] although, according to some, one may appoint her after imposing a penance.

Time of Marriage for Girls

[67] After she attains puberty, a girl shall wait for three years. [68] After three years, she should find herself a husband of the same class as she. [69] Now, they also quote:

> If due to her father's negligence a girl here is given in marriage after her proper time has elapsed, she, who was made to wait, brings ruin to her giver, like a teacher's fee that is paid after the time has passed.
>
> [70] Out of fear that she should menstruate, a father should give a girl in marriage while she still goes about naked (G 18.23 n.), for if she remains in his house after puberty her father becomes guilty of a sin.
>
> [71] As many menstrual periods a girl has while men of equal class are asking for her hand in marriage and she herself is willing, so many foetuses do her parents kill—so states the Law.
>
> [72] If, after a girl has been betrothed with words and the pouring of water but before she is given in marriage with the recitation of ritual

formulas, the bridegroom dies, the girl belongs to her father.

[73] If a virgin has been forcibly abducted but has not been married with the recitation of ritual formulas, she may be given in marriage to another man in accordance with the rules; she is like a virgin in every respect.

[74] If the husband dies after a young girl has been given in marriage with the recitation of ritual formulas and if she is still a virgin, she may be given in marriage again.

Missing Husband

[75] The wife of a man who has gone to a distant land should wait for five years. [76] After the lapse of five years she may go to her husband. [77] If, however, she is unwilling to go to a distant land for religious or financial reasons, she may act as if he were dead. [78] Accordingly, a Brahmin woman should wait for five years if she has offspring and for four years if she does not; a Kṣatriya woman should wait for four years if she has offspring and for three years if she does not; a Vaiśya woman should wait for three years if she has offspring and for two years if she does not; and a Śūdra woman should wait for two years if she has offspring and for one year if she does not.

[79] After that time [she may go to one of the following]: one who shares the same property as her husband, one who is born from the same parents, one who belongs to the same ancestry (A 2.14.2 n.), one who belongs to the same distant ancestry,* and one who belongs to the same lineage (A 2.11.15 n.). Among these each preceding is more honourable than each following. [80] She should not, however, go to a stranger when a member of her family is available.

Alternate Heirs

[81] In the absence of an heir belonging to the first six types of sons

(Va 17.13–25), people belonging to the same ancestry or those taking the place of sons (Va 17.26–38) should divide the estate of the deceased; [82]in the absence of these, the teacher and the resident pupil should take the estate; [83]and in their absence, the king. [84]The king, however, should not take the estate of a Brahmin; [85]the property of a Brahmin is dreadful poison.

> [86]Poison is not truly poison, they say; the true poison is the property of a Brahmin. Poison kills just one man, while a Brahmin's property kills even his sons and grandsons.

[87]He should hand it over instead to virtuous men versed in the triple Veda.

MIXED CLASSES

18 [1]A child sired by a Śūdra man on a Brahmin woman, they say, becomes a Cāṇḍāla; [2]on a Kṣatriya woman, a Vaiṇa; [3]and on a Vaiśya woman, an Antyāvasāyin. [4]A child sired by a Vaiśya man on a Brahmin woman, they say, becomes a Rāmaka; [5]and on a Kṣatriya woman, a Pulkasa. [6]A child sired by a Kṣatriya man on a Brahmin woman, they say, becomes a Sūta. [7]Now, they also quote:

> You can know by their actions all those who have been secretly conceived and who are tainted with the attributes arising from relationships in the inverse order of class, because they are devoid of virtue and good conduct.

[8]Children sired by Brahmins, Kṣatriyas, and Vaiśyas on women of one, two, or three classes below the man's become Ambaṣṭhas, Ugras, and Niṣādas, respectively. [9]Children sired by a Brahmin on a Śūdra woman are Pāraśavas. [10]They say that a Pāraśava is neither fully alive nor fully a corpse. [11]According to some, Śūdras are a cremation ground. [12]Therefore, one should not recite the Veda in the vicinity of a Śūdra. [13]Now, they also quote these verses proclaimed by Yama:

Śūdras, people of evil conduct, are manifestly a cremation ground. Therefore, one should not recite the Veda in the vicinity of a Śūdra.

[14] One should not impart wisdom to a Śūdra or give him one's leftovers (A 1.3.27 n.) or the remnants of a sacrificial offering. One should not teach him the Law or prescribe to him a vow.

[15] A man who teaches him the Law or prescribes to him a vow will go to the dreadful hell called Asaṃvṛta.

[16] If ever a worm is found in someone's wound, he is purified by performing the Prājāpatya penance (B 4.5.6) and giving gold, a cow, and a garment as a sacrificial fee.

[17] After a man has performed the rite of building the fire altar, he should not cohabit with a Śūdra wife. [18] A wife belonging to the dark class is only for pleasure, not for the fulfilment of the Law.

KING

19 [1] To take care of creatures is the special duty (*dharma*) of a king, and he attains success by fulfilling it. [2] To give up fear and pity, wise men say, is truly for him a sacrificial session lasting until old age.* [3] Therefore, he should appoint a personal priest to carry out the obligations incumbent on a householder. [4] It is stated: 'When a Brahmin has been appointed as the king's personal priest, the kingdom prospers', [5] for thus both sets of duties are taken care of, [6] because he is unable to do both.*

Administrative Duties

[7] After enquiring into all the Laws specific to various regions, castes, and families, the king should make the four classes adhere to the Laws proper to them [8] and punish them when they

deviate from them. [9]The punishment for battery and the use of abusive language should be imposed in keeping with the place and time of the offence; the virtue, age, knowledge, and social position* of the parties; [10]and in accordance with precept and precedent.

[11]He should not damage trees that produce flowers and fruits, [12]but may cut them down to facilitate cultivation or for household needs.*

[13]He should secure the measures and weights. [14]Export is not permitted from the capital city. [15]Merchants may only export the selling price or the value of the merchandise. [16]During the two festive times, however, there is no crime and there should be no punishment.*

Ferries, Tolls, and Taxes

[17]For water transport, a boat should have ten oarsmen and two sets of equipment. [18]Each vessel should have its own drinking water supply. [19]It should carry a load of not more than one hundred men; [20]and one and a half times that many women.

[21]If the river's width is such that an arrow shot from the shore will land in the middle, then the toll is eight Māṣas (G 12.8); whereas if it lands beyond that, then the toll is a quarter Kārṣapaṇa. [22]When the water level is low, the toll is one Māṣa.* [23]The following are exempt from toll: vedic scholars, officials of the king, destitutes, wandering ascetics, children, old people, youngsters, and new mothers; [24]as also widows who have returned to their families, young women, and wives of servants. [25]If someone crosses a river swimming, he should pay one hundred times the toll (A 1.32.26 n.).

[26]There shall be no taxes on what is obtained from rivers, thickets, forests, cremation places, and mountains; [27]or else, people who gain a living in this manner may give something. [28]From artisans,* however, he should collect taxes every month.

Succession

[29]When the former king has died, he should give the requisites

for the occasion. [30] This provision entails the maintenance of his mother. [31] The king should also maintain the paternal and maternal uncles of the queen, [32] as also her other relatives. [33] The wives of the deceased king should receive food and clothing; [34] or, if they are unwilling, they may become wandering ascetics.

Taxes

[35] The king should maintain people who are impotent or mad, [36] because their estates go to him. [37] With reference to taxes, they also quote this verse of Manu:

> There is no tax when the sum is less than one Kārṣapaṇa, as also on craftsmen, children, and messengers; on what is received as alms or what remains after a robbery; and on vedic scholars, wandering ascetics, and sacrifices.

Criminal Justice

[38] A man is not considered guilty of theft simply by accompanying a thief, [39] but only if he is caught armed, carrying stolen property, or wounded; and, according to some, if he has misrepresented himself.* [40] If a guilty man is allowed to go free, the king should fast for one day [41] and his personal priest for three days. [42] If an innocent man is punished, his personal priest should perform an arduous penance (B 2.2.38) [43] and the king should fast for three days. [44] Now, they also quote:

> The murderer of a learned Brahmin rubs his sin off on the man who eats his food, an adulterous wife on her husband, a pupil and a patron of a sacrifice on the teacher, and a thief on the king.
>
> [45] Those people who have committed sins and have been punished for them by kings, however, go to heaven unsullied, just like virtuous men who have done good deeds.
>
> [46] When he sets free a culpable man, the sin falls

> on the king. If he has him executed, however, the king slays the crime with the Law.
>
> [47] The rule is that the king always becomes pure immediately when he carries out capital as well as non-capital punishments; the reason for this is simply time.

[48] In this connection they also quote a verse proclaimed by Yama:

> The stain of impurity* does not affect kings, as well as people performing vows and sacrificial sessions, for they are always seated on the throne of Indra and become one with Brahman.

PENANCES

Miscellaneous

20 [1] A penance should be performed for any offence not deliberately committed [2] and, according to some, even deliberately committed.

> [3] The elder (A 1.6.32 n.) disciplines those who are self-controlled and the king disciplines those who are wicked, whereas Yama, son of Vivasvat, disciplines those who commit sins secretly.

[4] Among these, a person who was asleep at sunrise should remain standing during the day reciting the Sāvitrī verse; [5] and a person who was asleep at sunset should remain seated during the night. [6] A man with bad nails or black teeth, on the other hand, should perform the arduous penance (B 2.2.38) for twelve days.

[7] A man whose younger brother has got married before him should perform the arduous penance for twelve days and get married, and then take her to himself;* [8] whereas a man who gets married before his elder brother should perform an arduous and a very arduous penance, hand his wife over to his brother,

and get married again, and then take her to himself. [9] A man who marries a younger sister whose older sister remains unmarried should perform an arduous penance for twelve days and get married, and then take her to himself. [10] A man who marries an older sister whose younger sister is already married should perform an arduous and a very arduous penance, hand his wife over to his brother, and get married again.

[11] We will explain below (Va 21.27) the penance for a man who has extinguished his sacred fire. [12] A man who has forgotten the Veda should perform an arduous penance for twelve days and once again learn the Veda from his teacher.

Grievous Sins

[13] A man who has had sex with the wife of an elder (A 1.6.32 n.) should tear out his penis together with the testicles and, holding them in his cupped hands, walk towards the south. And wherever he meets with an obstacle, he should stand at that spot until he dies. [14] Or else, he should shave his hair, smear his body with ghee, and embrace a heated column (A 1.25.2 n.). It is stated: 'He will be purified after death.' [15] The same applies for having sex with the wife of a teacher, son, or pupil.

[16] If someone has sex with a female elder (A 1.6.32 n.) of the family, a female friend, a female friend of an elder, or a degraded or outcaste woman, he should perform an arduous penance for three months. [17] The same applies for eating the food of a Cāṇḍāla or an outcaste. Afterwards he should be re-initiated; the shaving and other similar rites, however, are omitted. [18] On this point, moreover, they quote a verse of Manu:

> Shaving, girdle, staff, begging almsfood, and the vows—these are omitted in the rite of re-initiation. (M 11.152)

[19] If someone deliberately drinks an intoxicant that is not *surā* liquor* or inadvertently drinks *surā* liquor, he should perform an arduous and a very arduous penance and consume some ghee, and then he should be re-initiated. [20] The same applies to consuming urine, faeces, or semen.

[21] If a twice-born man drinks water that has remained in a liquor pot, he becomes purified in three days by drinking a decoction made with the leaves of lotus, Udumbara, wood-apple, and Palāśa.

[22] If a twice-born man drinks *surā* liquor repeatedly, however, he should drink the same liquor boiling hot. It is said, 'He will be purified after death.'

Murder

[23] We will explain the meaning of the term *bhrūṇahan*—'murderer of a Brahmin' (A 1.19.15 n.). By killing a Brahmin or a foetus whose gender cannot be determined one becomes a *bhrūṇahan*—a murderer of a Brahmin; [24] for foetuses whose gender cannot be determined grow to be males. That is why people offer oblations in the fire so as to produce a male child.* [25] A murderer of a Brahmin should kindle a fire and make the following offerings in it:

> [26] First: 'I offer the hair of my body to Death. I invest Death with the hair of my body.'
> Second: 'I offer my skin to Death. I invest Death with my skin.'
> Third: 'I offer my blood to Death. I invest Death with my blood.'
> Fourth: 'I offer my flesh to Death. I invest Death with my flesh.'
> Fifth: 'I offer my sinews to Death. I invest Death with my sinews.'
> Sixth: 'I offer my fat to Death. I invest Death with my fat.'
> Seventh: 'I offer my bones to Death. I invest Death with my bones.'
> Eighth: 'I offer my marrow to Death. I invest Death with my marrow.'

[27] Or else, facing the enemy unflinchingly, he may lay down his life in battle for the sake of the king or a Brahmin; [28] for it is stated: 'A criminal is purified when he remains undefeated three times.'

[29] It is said: 'For when confessed, a sin is made less' (SB 2.5.2.20). [30] Now, they also quote:

> By telling an outcaste 'You're an outcaste!', or a thief 'You're a thief!', a man by his speech becomes as sinful as they; and if his accusation is false, he becomes twice as sinful.

[31] If someone kills a Kṣatriya, he should perform for eight years the same penance* [as for killing a Brahmin]; [32] if he kills a Vaiśya, for six years; [33] and if he kills a Śūdra, for three years.

[34] If someone kills a Brahmin woman who is an Ātreyī (A 1.24.8–9 n.) or a Kṣatriya or a Vaiśya engaged in performing a sacrifice, [the penance is the same as for a Brahmin]. [35] We will explain who an Ātreyī is. They say that 'Ātreyī' is a woman who has bathed after her menstrual period, [36] for in her (*atra*) the future (*ī-*) offspring comes into being.

[37] For killing a Brahmin woman at a time other than after her menstrual period, the penance is the same as for killing a Kṣatriya man; [38] for killing a Kṣatriya woman, the same as for killing a Vaiśya man; [39] and for killing a Vaiśya woman, the same as for killing a Śūdra man. [40] If someone kills a Śūdra woman, he should perform the same penance for one year.

Theft

[41] When someone has stolen gold from a Brahmin, the thief should dishevel his hair and run to the king, saying, 'I am a thief, sir! Do punish me, lord.' The king should hand him a weapon made of Udumbara wood. With that the thief should kill himself. It is stated: 'He will be purified after death.' [42] Alternatively, he may shave his hair, smear his body with ghee, and get himself burnt from feet upward in a fire of cowdung. It is stated: 'He will be purified after death.' [43] Now, they also quote:

> Listen to how their bodies are—people who died a long time ago after engaging in various types of sinful activities and are now reborn in new bodies.
>
> [44] A thief becomes a man with deformed nails; a murderer of a Brahmin becomes a man with white leprosy; one who drinks liquor becomes a man with black teeth; and one who has sex with the wife of an elder (A 1.6.32 n.) becomes a man with skin disease.

Association with Outcastes

[45] When someone has established a ritual or matrimonial alliance with outcastes, he should give up any articles he may have received from them and cease associating with them. [46] 'He becomes purified by going towards the north and reciting a vedic Collection of Hymns without eating any food,' says the Veda. [47] Now, they also quote:

> A sinner is freed from his sin by mortifying his body, by austerity, and by reciting the Veda, as also by giving gifts.

So it is stated.

Illicit Sex

21 [1] If a Śūdra has sex with a Brahmin woman, he should be wrapped in Vīraṇa grass and thrown into a fire. The Brahmin woman's head should be shaved and her body smeared with ghee, and she should be paraded on a highway naked and seated on a black donkey. 'In this way,' it is stated, 'she becomes pure.'

[2] If a Vaiśya has sex with a Brahmin woman, he should be wrapped in tufts of Lohita straw and thrown into a fire. The Brahmin woman's head should be shaved and her body smeared with ghee, and she should be paraded on a highway naked and

seated on a yellow donkey. 'In this way,' it is stated, 'she becomes pure.'

[3] If a Kṣatriya has sex with a Brahmin woman, he should be wrapped in Śara grass and thrown into a fire. The Brahmin woman's head should be shaved and her body smeared with ghee, and she should be paraded on a highway naked and seated on a white donkey. 'In this way,' it is stated, 'she becomes pure.'

[4] The same punishment applies to a Vaiśya who has sex with a Kṣatriya woman [5] and to a Śūdra who has sex with a Kṣatriya or a Vaiśya woman.

Adultery

[6] If a wife has been unfaithful to her husband in her mind, she should spend three days eating barley or milk-rice and sleeping on the floor. At the end of the three days, the husband should make eight hundred offerings in the fire reciting the Sāvitrī verse and the Śiras formula while the wife remains immersed in water. 'In this way,' it is stated, 'she becomes pure.'

[7] If she has had an adulterous conversation with another man, she should do the same penance for one month. At the end of the month, the husband should make three thousand two hundred offerings in the fire reciting the Sāvitrī verse and the Śiras formula while the wife remains immersed in water. 'In this way,' it is stated, 'she becomes pure.'

[8] If she actually committed adultery, however, she should wear a garment smeared with ghee and sleep in a trough of cowdung or on a spread of Kuśa grass for one year. At the end of the year, the husband should make eight hundred offerings in the fire reciting the Sāvitrī verse and the Śiras formula while the wife remains immersed in water. 'In this way,' it is stated, 'she becomes pure.'

[9] If she commits adultery with an elder (A 1.6.32 n.), however, she cannot participate in her husband's ritual activities.

> [10] These four are to be abandoned: a wife who has sex with one's pupil, a wife who has sex with one's elder, especially a wife who tries to

kill her husband, and a wife who has sex with a degraded man.

[11] When a Brahmin woman drinks liquor, gods do not lead her to the world of her husband; bereft of merits, she meanders in this very world, becoming a leech or a pearl oyster living in water.

[12] When wives of Brahmins, Kṣatriyas, or Vaiśyas have sex with Śūdra men, they are purified by a penance only if they do not bear children, not otherwise.

[13] Women who have sex with men of a class lower than they should perform an arduous penance (B 2.2.38) followed by a lunar penance (B 3.8).

[14] Wives who are devoted to their husbands, vowed to truth and purity, however, attain worlds equal to those of their husbands; those who are unfaithful are born as jackals.

[15] Half his body* becomes outcaste when a man's wife drinks liquor. No expiation is provided for someone half of whose body has become outcaste.

[16] If a Brahmin inadvertently has sex with the wife of another Brahmin, he should perform an arduous penance if her husband has not abandoned his ritual duties, and a very arduous penance if he has abandoned his ritual duties. [17] The same applies to Kṣatriya and Vaiśya men.

Killing Animals

[18] If a man kills a cow, covering himself in its raw hide, he should perform an arduous or a very arduous penance for six months. [19] This is the procedure for those two penances.

[20] He eats during the daytime for three days and during the night for the next three days, subsists

> on what he receives unasked for three more days, and does not eat at all for the last three days. That is an arduous penance.
>
> [21] He drinks hot water for three days, hot milk for the next three days, and hot ghee for three more days, and subsists on air during the last three days.

That is a very arduous penance.* [22] In addition, he should give a gift of a bull and a cow. [23] Now, they also quote:

> Because of killing a spotted deer, a billy goat, and a bird, three diseases came into being in ancient times: jealousy, hunger, and old age. A man who kills them should perform a penance for ninety-eight days.

[24] If someone kills a dog, a cat, a mongoose, a snake, a frog, or a rat, he should perform an arduous penance for twelve days and give a little something as a gift. [25] If he kills a quantity of boneless animals equal in weight to a cow, however, he should perform an arduous penance for twelve days and give a little something as a gift. [26] In the case of animals with bones, on the other hand, the penance should be performed separately for each.

Miscellaneous

[27] If a man extinguishes his sacred fires, he should perform an arduous penance for twelve days and have the rite of establishing the sacred fires carried out over again. [28] If someone falsely accuses an elder of his (A 1.6.32 n.), he should bathe with his clothes on and seek forgiveness from that elder. 'He becomes pure', it is stated, 'by his forgiveness.'

[29] An infidel should perform an arduous penance for twelve days and abandon his infidelity. [30] Someone who receives subsistence from infidels, however, should perform a very arduous penance. [31] This explains the penance for a man who sells Soma.

[32] A forest hermit who violates his vow should perform an

arduous penance for twelve days and increase his austerities in a dense wood. [33]Mendicants violating in the same manner as hermits should perform a lunar penance (B 3.8) and undergo initiation in the manner prescribed in their respective texts.

Justification for Penance

22 [1]Now,* with regard to a man here who makes false statements, officiates at sacrifices of people for whom it is forbidden to officiate, accepts gifts from people from whom it is forbidden to accept, eats forbidden food, or does things that one ought not to do—[2]there is a debate as to whether such a person is required to perform a penance or not. [3]Some say that he is not required to do so, [4]arguing that an act can never be wiped out. [5]But he is indeed required to do so, because it is so prescribed in vedic texts; * [6]for example: 'A man who offers a horse sacrifice overcomes all sins, he overcomes even the murder of a Brahmin' (SB 13.3.1.1); [7]and, 'A heinous sinner (A 1.3.25 n.) should offer the Gosava or the Agniṣṭut sacrifice.'

General Penances

[8]The expiations for such a man are: softly reciting prayers (A 1.15.1 n.), austerity, ritual offerings, fasting, and giving gifts. [9]Upaniṣads, the beginnings of the Vedas, the conclusions of the Vedas [*vedānta*], the Hymn-Collections of all the Vedas, the 'Honey' verses, Aghamarṣaṇa hymn, Atharvaśiras, Rudra hymn, Puruṣa hymn, the Sāmans called Rājana and Rauhiṇī, Kūṣmāṇḍa verses, Pāvamānī verses, and the Sāvitrī verse—these are the purificatory texts. [10]Now, they also quote:

> The Vaiśvānarī sacrifice, the Vrātapatī sacrifice,
> and the Pavitreṣṭi sacrifice—a man who offers
> these once every season purifies ten ancestors.

[11]To do the following in accordance with the rules of fasting: living on milk alone, eating only fruits, living on gruel made with one handful of barley, eating gold, and drinking Soma juice—these are the cleansing activities. [12]All mountains, all rivers,

sacred lakes, sacred fords, dwellings of seers, cow-pens, and temples—these are the appropriate places. [13] One year, one month, twenty-four days, twelve days, six days, three days, and a day and night—these are the lengths of time.

[14] When no specific penance has been prescribed, people may perform these optionally, [15] the heavier penances for grave sins and the easy penances for minor sins. [16] The arduous penance (B 2.2.38), the very arduous penance (B 2.2.40), and the lunar penance (B 3.8) are expiations for all types of sins.

Sins of a Student

23 [1] If a student has sex with a woman, he should sacrifice a donkey dedicated to the fiends, offering it in an ordinary fire at a crossroad in the wilderness; [2] or he should offer an oblation of milk-rice to Nirṛti. [3] He should make offerings of it in the fire, saying: 'To lust, Svāhā! To the one who lusts after lust, Svāhā! To Nirṛti, Svāhā! To the divine fiends, Svāhā!'

[4] The same penance applies when he masturbates deliberately, sleeps during the daytime, or practises some other observance, until the time he returns home after completing his studies.

[5] If he has sex with an animal, he should give a gift of a white bull. [6] The culpability for having sex with a cow is spelt out in the rule about killing a Śūdra woman.

[7] A student breaks his vow if he takes part in a funeral, [8] except that of his parents.

[9] If a student is sick, he may freely eat all his teacher's leftovers as medicine (B 2.1.26 n.). [10] If a student dies while engaged in something ordered by his teacher, the teacher should perform three arduous penances (B 2.2.38).

[11] If a student eats meat as part of the leftovers of his teacher, he should perform an arduous penance lasting twelve days and finish his vow. [12] The same applies for eating food given at an ancestral offering or by someone tainted with the impurity of a recent birth or death. [13] Honey offered without being yearned for, it is stated in the Vājasaneyaka text, does not defile (cf. SB 11.5.4.18).

Suicide

[14] A man who commits suicide becomes a heinous sinner (A 1.3.25 n.); relatives of his belonging to the same ancestry (A 2.14.2 n.) desist from performing funeral rites for him. [15] A person who kills himself by means of a club, water, a clod of earth, a stone, a weapon, poison, or a rope, is a suicide. [16] Now, they also quote:

> If out of love a twice-born man performs the funeral rites for someone who has committed suicide, he should perform a lunar penance accompanied by a hot-arduous penance (B 2.2.37).

[17] We will describe the lunar penance below (Va 23.45).

[18] One who resolves to commit suicide should fast for three days. [19] It is said: 'A man who survives an attempt at suicide should perform an arduous penance for twelve days; fast for three days; and, always wearing clothes smeared with ghee and controlling his breath, recite three times the Aghamarṣaṇa hymn.' [20] Alternatively, he may recite the Sāvitrī verse following the same procedure; [21] or, having kindled his sacred fire, he should offer ghee while reciting the Kūṣmāṇḍa verses. [22] It is said: 'By means of this a man is cleansed of all except the grievous sins causing loss of caste (Va 1.19–20).' [23] He may, moreover, sip water in the morning, saying, 'May fire and wrath, and the lord of wrath, protect me'; focusing his mind on his sin, he should recite the Calls beginning with OṂ and ending with Truth, or recite the Aghamarṣaṇa hymn.

Contact with Impurity

[24] If someone touches a human bone with soft tissue attached to it, he remains impure for three days; [25] while if it has no soft tissue attached to it, he is impure for a day and night, [26] as also when he follows a corpse in a funeral procession.

[27] If someone passes between persons engaged in vedic recitation, he should fast for a day and night; [28] and the reciters

should stay away from home for three nights and sprinkle each other with water. [29]They should do the same for a day and night if a dog, a cat, or a mongoose passes quickly between them.

[30]If someone eats the meat of a dog, a cock, a village pig, a Kaṅka heron, a vulture, a Bhāsa vulture, a Pārāvata dove, a man, a crow, or an owl, he should fast for seven days until all the excrement is gone, then consume some ghee and undergo re-initiation.

> [31]A Brahmin who is bitten by a dog becomes purified by going into a river that flows into the ocean, controlling his breath one hundred times, and consuming some ghee.
>
> [32]These six means of purification are recommended for creatures: time, fire, purifying the mind, water, looking at the sun, and being unaware that something is impure.

[33]'If someone touches a dog, a Cāṇḍāla, or an outcaste,' it is stated, 'he becomes pure immediately by bathing with his clothes on.' [34]When people hear* the sound of an outcaste or a Cāṇḍāla, they should remain seated silently and without eating for three days. [35]'Or else,' it is stated, 'they become pure by reciting it* at least one thousand times.'

Miscellaneous

[36]The above provision spells out the penance for teaching reprehensible people and for officiating at their sacrifices. 'They also become pure', it is said, 'by giving up the fees they have received.' [37]This also spells out the penance for a heinous sinner (A 1.3.25 n.).

[38]If a man is guilty of murdering a Brahmin (A 1.19.15 n.), he should live on water for twelve days and observe a total fast for twelve more days. [39]If someone has falsely accused a Brahmin of a grievous or secondary sin causing loss of caste (Va 1. 19–23), he should repeat the Śuddhavatī verses for one month while

living on water [40] or participate in the ritual bath that concludes a horse sacrifice.

[41] This provision spells out the penance for sexual intercourse with a Cāṇḍāla woman.

Description of Penances

[42] Next, another procedure of the arduous penance, a modified form applicable universally:

> [43] Eating only in the morning on one day; eating only at night on the next day; eating only what is received unasked on the following day; observing a total fast on the next day; repeating the same series during the following two four-day periods—as a favour to Brahmins, Manu, the chief upholder of the Law, has proclaimed this 'Children's Arduous Penance' for children, old people, and the sick.

[44] Next, the procedure of the lunar penance:

> [45] On the first day of the fortnight of the waning moon a person should eat fourteen mouthfuls and complete the fortnight by reducing the food by one mouthful each day. In this manner, he should eat one mouthful on the first day of the fortnight of the waxing moon and complete the fortnight by increasing the food by one mouthful each day.
>
> [46] During that period he should sing Sāman verses or softly recite the Calls.
>
> [47] This month-long lunar penance has been acclaimed by seers as a means of purification. It is prescribed as the penance for all offences for which there is no specific penance.

24 [1] Next, the very arduous penance: [2] one should perform the arduous penance as given above—eating only in the

morning for three days, eating only in the evening for three days, eating what is received unasked for three days, and observing a total fast for three days—except that one should eat only what one can take in one mouthful. That is the very arduous penance.

[3] A very arduous penance during which one lives only on water is the penance beyond the very arduous penance.

[4] The observances during arduous penances are as follows. [5] Blessed Vasiṣṭha has said: 'He should shave the hair of his beard and head, except the eyebrows, eyelashes, and the top-knot; cut his nails; wear a single garment; eat food that is beyond reproach—food obtained by begging just once is beyond reproach—; bathe at dawn, noon, and dusk; carry a staff and a water pot; refrain from speaking with women and Śūdras; carry out faithfully the standing and the sitting—that is, remain standing during the day and seated during the night.'

[6] Now, a man should impart this Treatise on Law to no one other than a son or a pupil who has lived with him for at least a year. [7] The fee for teaching it is one thousand in cash, or ten cows and a bull, or obtaining the favour of the teacher.*

Secret Penances

25

[1] I will explain fully the purification of all sinners whose guilt has not been made public, sinners guilty of both major and minor sins.

[2] The penances given in the section on secret penances are meant for individuals who have established the sacred fires and are disciplined, elderly, and learned. Other people should follow the penances given above.

[3] Those who are constantly engaged in controlling their breath, reciting the purificatory formulas (Va 28.10), giving gifts, offering sacrifices, and the soft recitation of prayers will undoubtedly be free from sins causing loss of caste.

[4] Seated with purificatory blades of grass in

hand, he should control his breath repeatedly and recite the purificatory formulas, the Calls, the syllable OṂ, and the daily sections of the Veda.

[5] Always intent on yogic practice, he should control his breath repeatedly and thus practise the highest austerity up to the very tips of his hair and nails.

[6] By suppressing the breath air is generated, and from air, fire, and from fire, water. So he is cleansed internally by these three.

[7] Not by severe austerity, not by the daily recitation of the Veda, not even by sacrifice can a man attain the state that one obtains by the practice of Yoga.

[8] By Yoga one obtains knowledge. Yoga is the earmark of the Law. Yoga is the highest austerity. Therefore, he should always be engaged in yogic practice.

[9] A man who is always intent on reciting the syllable OṂ, the seven Calls, and the Gāyatrī with its three feet will never experience any danger.

[10] The syllable OṂ is the beginning and the end of the Vedas; all that consists of speech is OṂ. Therefore, one should repeat OṂ.

[11] The Monosyllable OṂ, which is the supreme Veda, traditional texts declare, is the best purifier.

[12] When all sins rise up in unison, the most effective purification is to recite the Gāyatrī verse ten thousand times.

[13] When someone recites three times the Gāyatrī verse together with the Calls, the syllable OṂ, and the Śiras formula while controlling his breath, it is called 'control of breath'.

26

[1] When a man duly controls his breath three times without tiring, that very instant the sins he committed during the previous day and night are destroyed.

[2] By controlling his breath while seated during the evening twilight a man wipes away the sins he committed during that day by thought, word, or deed.

[3] By controlling his breath while standing during the morning twilight, a man wipes away the sins he committed during that night by thought, word, or deed.

[4] Controlling one's breath sixteen times every day while reciting the Calls and the syllable OṂ purifies even a murderer of a Brahmin within a month.

[5] Even a man who has drunk liquor is purified by reciting silently Kutsa's hymn 'Burning away our evil . . .', the triple verse of Vasiṣṭha 'To welcome the Dawn . . .', the Māhitra hymn, and the Śuddhavatī hymn.

[6] Even a man who has stolen gold becomes instantly stainless by reciting silently the Asyavāmīya hymn and the Śivasaṃkalpa formulas.

[7] A man who has had sex with the wife of an elder (A 1.6.32 n.) is freed from his sin by reciting silently the hymn 'Of that pleasant and gray-haired Hotṛ priest . . .', the triple verse 'No anxiety, no danger . . .', and the Puruṣa hymn.

[8] Or else, he should recite the Aghamarṣaṇa hymn silently while immersed in water. Manu has declared it to be equal to bathing at the conclusion of a horse sacrifice.

[9] The sacrifice consisting of softly recited

prayers is ten times better than a sacrifice involving the immolation of an animal; reciting prayers silently is a hundred times better; and mental prayer, tradition says, is a thousand times better.

10 The four types of sacrifices with cooked food* together with the sacrifices ordained in the Veda are not worth a sixteenth part of a sacrifice consisting of softly recited prayers.

11 Only through softly recited prayers does a Brahmin attain final bliss, in this there is no doubt. Whether he does other things or not, he is said to be a Brahmin who is a friend to all.

12 People who softly recite prayers, offer fire sacrifices, meditate, live at sacred fords, or have bathed after the 'Head' vow*—their sins do not endure.

13 As a fire fanned by the wind and fed with offerings of ghee burns brightly, so a Brahmin given constantly to the soft recitation of prayers glows exceedingly bright.

14 People who always engage in private vedic recitation and constantly keep themselves pure, who softly recite prayers and offer sacrifices—they will never come to ruin.

15 A man who seeks purity, though he be standing in the midst of all sins, should recite the divine Gāyatrī at most one thousand times, one hundred times on an average, and ten times at a minimum.

16 A Kṣatriya should overcome his misfortunes through the strength of his arms, a Vaiśya and a Śūdra through wealth, and a Brahmin through softly recited prayers and fire sacrifices.

17 As horses without chariots and chariots without horses, so is austerity for a man with-

out knowledge and knowledge for a man not given to austerity.

[18] As food combined with honey or honey combined with food, so austerity and knowledge combined is a powerful medicine.

[19] When a Brahmin is united with knowledge and austerity and softly recites prayers every day, he does not become guilty of sin even if he constantly commits evil deeds.

27

[1] Even if a man has done a hundred crimes or more but remembers the Veda, the fire of the Veda burns up all that, like a fire the kindling wood.

[2] As a fierce fire burns up even green trees, so the fire of the Veda burns up his guilt caused by evil deeds.

[3] Even if he were to slaughter the whole wide world and to eat the food of anyone at all, no sin touches a Brahmin if he keeps the Ṛgveda in mind.

[4] Relying on the power of the Veda, one should not take pleasure in sinful deeds. It burns up only sins committed through ignorance or negligence, and not others.

[5] Take a sage who practises austerities in the wilderness eating roots and fruits, and someone who recites a single verse of the Ṛgveda—these two and their actions are of equal worth.

[6] One should strengthen the Veda by means of epics and Purāṇas; the Veda dreads a man of modest learning, fearing 'He will neglect me.'

[7] Reciting the Veda and carrying out the series of Great Sacrifices (B 2.11.1–8) every day according to one's ability quickly destroy sins, even grievous sins causing loss of caste.

[8] Every day a man should perform tirelessly the rites specifically enjoined on him by the Veda. By performing them according to his ability he attains his highest goal.

[9] By teaching sinful people, by officiating at their sacrifices, by contracting marriage alliances with them, and by accepting gifts from them, a learned Brahmin does not incur any guilt, for he is like the fire and the sun.

[10] When a doubt has arisen as to whether a particular food one has eaten is forbidden or not, I will describe the purification. Listen well as I explain it!

[11] Let a Brahmin drink a decoction of the Brahmasuvarcalā plant without salt or condiments for three days, as also a decoction of the Śaṅkhapuṣpī grass together with milk.

[12] He should boil Palāśa and wood apple leaves, Kuśa grass, and lotus and Udumbara leaves, and drink that water; he will be purified in just three days.

[13] Living one day each on cow's urine, cowdung, milk, curd, ghee, and water boiled with Kuśa grass, and observing a total fast for one day purifies even a man who has eaten dog meat.

[14] When a man subsists one day each on cow's urine, cowdung, milk, curd, and ghee for five days, he is purified by these five products of the cow.

[15] When a man consumes barley grains in accordance with the rules (B 3.6), he becomes visibly pure: if he has become pure, the grains remain white; whereas if he has not become pure the grains become discoloured.*

[16] For three days eating in the morning food fit for sacrifice, similarly for three days in the even-

ing, and for three days eating what is received unasked—that constitutes three fasts.

[17] If, on the other hand, someone wants to expedite it, he should subsist on air during the daytime and during the night remain standing in water until daybreak. This is equal to the Prājāpatya penance.*

[18] By reciting the Sāvitrī verse eight thousand times at sunrise, however, a man is freed from all sins, unless he has murdered a Brahmin.

[19] Even if someone has been a thief, drunk liquor, murdered a Brahmin, and had sex with a wife of an elder, he is freed from all sins causing loss of caste by simply studying the Treatise on Law.

[20] The arduous penance and the lunar penance destroy all sins, whether they are improper actions, improper sacrifices, or grievous sins.

[21] One should increase the food by one mouthful each day of the fortnight of the waxing moon, decrease it by one mouthful each day of the fortnight of the waning moon, and not eat at all on the new-moon day. This is the procedure of the lunar penance.

Purification of Women

28 [1] A woman is not polluted by a lover, a Brahmin by vedic rites, water by urine and faeces, and fire by the act of burning.

[2–3] Whether she has strayed on her own or has been expelled, whether she has been raped forcibly or abducted by robbers—a wife who has been defiled should not be forsaken; there is no law permitting the forsaking of a wife. One should wait for her to menstruate; she is purified by her menstrual period.

[4]Women possess an unparalleled means of purification; they never remain defiled, for month after month their menstrual flow washes away their sins.

[5]Women are first enjoyed by the gods Moon, Gandharva, and Fire, and only thereafter go to men; in accordance with the law therefore, they cannot be defiled.

[6]The Moon granted them purification; Gandharva, a sweet voice; and Fire, the capacity to eat anything. Women, therefore, are free from taint.

[7]There are three things in the world, people who know the Law declare, that cause women to fall from their caste: killing the husband, murdering a Brahmin, and getting an abortion.

[8]A calf is pure when it makes the milk to flow, a bird when it makes a fruit to fall, women in the act of love, and a dog when it catches a deer.

[9]Pure is the mouth of a goat and horse; pure the back of a cow. Pure are the feet of a Brahmin; but a woman is pure all over.

Purificatory Texts

[10]Next, I will declare the purificatory texts of all the Vedas by whose soft recitation or use in fire sacrifices people are undoubtedly purified.

[11–15]They are: Aghamarṣaṇa, Devakṛta, Śuddhavatī, Taratsama, Kūṣmāṇḍa, Pāvamānī, Durgāsāvitrī, Atīṣaṅga Sāman, Padastobha Sāman, Vyāhṛti Sāmans, Bhāruṇḍa Sāmans, Gāyatra Sāman, Raivata Sāman, Puruṣavrata Sāmans, Bhāsa Sāman, Devavrata Sāmans, Abliṅga, Bārhaspatya Sāman, Vāksūkta,

'Honey' verses, Śatarudrīya, Atharvaśiras, Trisuparṇa, Mahāvrata, Gosūkta, Aśvasūkta, the two Śuddhāśuddhīya Sāmans, the three Ājyadoha Sāmans, the Rathantara Sāman, the Agnervrata Sāman, the Vāmadevya Sāman, and the Bṛhat Sāman. When these are recited softly, they purify creatures, and, if someone so desires, he will acquire the memory of past lives.

Gifts

16 Gold is the firstborn of Fire; land is the daughter of Viṣṇu; and cows are the children of Sun. A man who gives gifts of gold, land, or cows obtains an eternal reward.

17 The cow, horse, gold, and land frustrate the donor when they see the outstretched hand of a Brahmin who is ignorant and neglectful of his rites.

18–19 On the full-moon day of April–May if someone gives to seven or five Brahmins black or white sesame seeds mixed with honey, saying, 'May the King of Law rejoice!', or expressing any other wish he may have in mind, that very moment all the sins he has committed during his whole life will be wiped away.

20 Listen now to the merit that is the reward for giving the skin of a black antelope to which the legs are still attached, after gilding the navel with gold and covering the skin with sesame seeds:

21 'Undoubtedly by that gift he has in fact given the four-faced earth, together with its caves filled with gold and with its mountains, forests, and groves.

22 'A man who places sesame seeds, gold, honey,

> and ghee upon a skin of a black antelope and gives it to a Brahmin overcomes all sins.'

29 [1] By giving gifts a man obtains all his wishes—[2] a long life and rebirth as a handsome vedic student.

[3] A man who refrains from causing injury to living beings goes to heaven. [4] By entering a fire, one attains the world of Brahman; [5] by keeping a vow of silence, one achieves prosperity; [6] and by living in water (B 3.9 n.), one becomes the lord of elephants.

[7] A man who gives until his store is exhausted becomes free from disease. [8] A man who gives water fulfils all his wishes. [9] A man who gives food gets a good eyesight and a keen memory. [10] A man who gives the gift of safety from all dangers becomes intelligent. [11] By allowing the use of cows, one gets the same reward as by bathing in all the sacred fords; [12] by giving beds and seats, one becomes the lord of a harem; [13] and by giving umbrellas, one gets a house. [14] A man who gives a house obtains a town. [15] A man who gives shoes obtains a vehicle.

[16] Now, they also quote:

> Whatever sin a man may have committed under the pressure of his occupation, he is cleansed from all that by giving a piece of land even as small as a 'cow's hide' (B 1.10.1 n.).
>
> [17] If a man gives a pot full of water to a Brahmin for use in sipping, after death he obtains complete immunity to thirst and is reborn as a man who drinks Soma.
>
> [18] Giving one thousand oxen capable of drawing carts to a most worthy recipient according to the rules is equal to giving a virgin in marriage.
>
> [19] Three, they say, are super-gifts: cows, land, and knowledge. The gift of knowledge is superior to all gifts and surpasses even those super-gifts.
>
> [20–1] This is the rule of conduct that grants endless rewards and awards liberation with the

release from the cycle of rebirth—a wise man who, free from envy, follows it, or a man, pure and self-controlled, who simply remembers or hears it with a trusting heart, sheds all his sins and rejoices in the very summit of heaven.

EXCELLENCE OF THE BRAHMIN

30 [1] Practise righteousness (*dharma*), not unrighteousness. Speak the truth, not an untruth. Look at what is distant, not what's near at hand. Look at the highest, not at what's less than the highest.

[2] A Brahmin is a fire, [3] because a vedic text states: 'A Brahmin is clearly a fire' (cf. SB 1.4.2.2; B 1.6.2 n.). [4] How can that be? [5] It is, moreover, stated in the vedic text of the Kāṭhakas: 'At this rite the altar is the body of the Brahmin occupying his seat; the sacrifice is his declaration of intent; the sacrificial animal is himself; the rope for tying it is his intellect; the offertorial fire is the mouth of the Brahmin occupying his seat; [the south fire] is his navel; the householder's fire is the fire of his stomach; the Adhvaryu priest is his out-breath; the Hotṛ priest is his in-breath; the Brahman priest is his inter-breath; the Udgātṛ priest is his link-breath; and the sacrificial vessels are his sense organs. A man who, knowing this, offers to the sense organ by means of the sense organs . . .'*

[6] Now, they also quote:

> An offering made in the fires that is the mouth of a Brahmin, fires that have been set ablaze by the kindling wood of the Veda, protects both the giver and that Brahmin himself and rescues them from sins.
>
> [7] Since it is not spilt or dropped, and does not fall on the offerer, an oblation offered in the mouth of a Brahmin is far better than the daily fire sacrifice.

[8]The fire is meditation, the firewood is truthfulness, the offering is patience, the Sruva spoon is modesty, the sacrificial cake is not causing injury to living beings, and the priestly fee is the arduous gift of safety to all creatures.

[9]As a man gets old his hair and teeth show signs of age. The yearning for life and wealth, however, show no sign of aging even as a man grows old.

[10]Yearning! Fools find it difficult to give it up. It does not weaken with age. It is a lifelong disease. A man who gives it up finds happiness.

[11]I pay homage to Śatayātu Vasiṣṭha, the son of Ūrvaśī by Mitra and Varuṇa!

That concludes the Vasiṣṭha Dharmasūtra

APPENDIX I

RITUAL VOCABULARY

1. Names of Rites, Priests, and Ritual Objects

Adhvaryu. One of the four principal priests at a vedic sacrifice. He belongs to the Yajurveda and is responsible for most of the sacrificial actions, including the offerings made in the sacred fire.

Āgnīdhra. The name of one of the assistants of the Adhvaryu, he maintains the fires. His seat is located to the west of the Utkara mound.

Agnimukha. This term refers to all the preliminary rites that precede the principal offering.

Agniṣṭoma. One of the seven types of Soma sacrifices (see G 8.20), it is considered the model for Soma sacrifices lasting one day.

Agniṣṭut. A Soma sacrifice of the Agniṣṭoma type.

Aptoryāma. One of the Soma sacrifices: Kane 1962–75, ii. 1206.

Aṣṭakā. The rite for ancestors offered on the eighth day after the full moon.

Atirātra. One of the seven types of Soma sacrifices (see G 8.20) performed over a day and a night.

Atyagniṣṭoma. A variation on the Agniṣṭoma with the addition of several rites.

Bali. The offering of cooked food to various deities, spirits, and animals.

Brahmaudana. A preparation of rice cooked during a ritual for the use of the officiating priests.

Camasa. A square ladle made of banyan wood and used for a variety of purposes in a sacrifice, including serving as a container or a drinking vessel for Soma.

Catuścakra. This is an optional rite to be performed on a new- or full-moon day. It is recommended for a person who has enemies. The sacrifice consists of four offerings. See *Śrautakośa*, i. 524.

Cātvāla. A pit dug outside the sacrificial arena (*vedi*) near its north-eastern corner. Earth dug from this pit is used for a variety of ritual purposes.

Cooked oblation (*pākayajña*). This is a general term for domestic rites involving the offering of cooked food. It is distinguished from vedic offerings called *haviryajña*.

Cooking fire. This is the ordinary kitchen fire in which the daily cooking is done. It is distinguished from the five sacred fires (A 2.17.22 n.).

Dadhigharma. A mixture of hot milk and curd poured into a warm pot and used as a libation at a Soma sacrifice.

Dākṣāyaṇa sacrifice. A modified form of the full-moon sacrifice performed to obtain a special wish, such as heaven, cattle, or children.

Darvīhoma. A simplified fire offering of ghee or curd made with a ladle named Darvī.

Dhruvā. A round spoon with a spout at the end and a long handle, somewhat similar to the Juhū. It belongs to the Sruc class and is used in making offerings into the fire.

Domestic fire (*aupāsana*). The fire in which domestic offerings (as opposed to vedic sacrifices) are made. This fire is established at marriage (G 5.7).

Dvādaśāha. A Soma sacrifice lasting twelve days.

Gharmocchiṣṭa. Gharma is the hot milk mixed with ghee used at a Soma sacrifice. Gharmocchiṣṭa is the drinking of the remnants of Gharma (after it has been offered in the fire) by the offerer.

Gosava. This is a one-day Soma sacrifice. It is recommended for people aspiring to sovereignty. See Kane 1962–75, ii. 1213.

Hall fire (*sabhya*). This fire is located in the hall where ritual gambling takes place and forms one of the five sacred fires of the vedic sacrifice (A 2.17.22 n.).

Hearth fire (*āvasathya*). This fire is located in the shed for guests and forms one of the five sacred fires of the vedic sacrifice (A 2.17.22 n.).

Horse sacrifice (*aśvamedha*). One of the most important vedic sacrifices, it is perfomed by a king to demonstrate his sovereignty and ritually to enhance his dominion. A horse is set free to roam at will for a whole year, during which time it is guarded by the king's troops. At the end of the year it is brought back and sacrificed.

Hotṛ. The priest belonging to the Ṛgveda and responsible for all the recitations during a sacrifice.

Householder's fire (*gārhapatya*). One of the three fires required for vedic sacrifices. It is located at the western end of the sacrificial arena in a round fire pit.

Iṣṭi. This is a class of sacrifices, of which the model is the new-moon sacrifice, requiring four priests. It is distinguished from other types, such as animal sacrifices and Soma sacrifices.

Iḍādadha. This is a sacrifice consisting of three offerings of cakes to

Fire, Indra, and Mitra-Varuṇa on the new-moon day. Described in *Śrautakośa*, i. 523–4.

Jaya. These are a set of ghee offerings called 'victorious' recommended for a person setting out for battle. See TS 3.4.4.1; *Śrautakośa*, i. 201.

Juhū. A round spoon with a long spout at the end and a long handle. It is held over the Upabhṛt and used to pour ghee into the fire. It belongs to the Sruc class and is made of Palāśa wood.

Jyotiṣṭoma. A Soma sacrifice lasting five days.

Kaṃsa. A bowl made of brass and used in sacrifices to hold the melted ghee.

Kuṇḍapāyinām Ayana. This is a *sattra* (sacrificial session) type of Soma sacrifice lasting a full year.

Mārjālīya. A mound of earth where sacrificial utensils are cleaned. It is located on the south side of the great sacrificial arena (*mahāvedi*) half inside and half outside with the entrance towards the north, that is, facing the arena.

Mṛgāra. A set of ten offerings forming part of the horse sacrifice: TS 7.5.22. See Mṛgāra verses in App. I.2.

Nāciketa. Bodewitz (1985, 8–10, 25) has shown that this term refers not to particular fires but to the building of a special fire-altar bearing the name of Naciketas, the central figure in the KaU.

Nirūḍhapaśubandha. Sometimes called simply Paśubandha, this is the sacrifice of a disembowelled animal. It is regarded as the model for all animal sacrifices. See Kane 1962–75, ii. 1107 f.

Offertorial fire (*āhavanīya*). One of the three sacred fires at a vedic sacrifice, it is located at the eastern end of the sacrificial area in a square fire pit. All offerings intended for the gods are placed in it. It is kindled by taking flaming pieces of firewood from the householder's fire (B 2.17.18).

Pāvamānī/Pāvamāneṣṭi. This is a triple oblation to the Fire 'that purifies'. See *Āpastamba Śrautasūtra*, 5.21.1–11.

Pavitreṣṭi. This is a sacrifice to 'Fire that purifies' performed on a new- or full-moon day to expiate any sin. See *Śrautakośa*, i. 594.

Punaḥstoma. This is a Soma sacrifice performed in a single day. It is prescribed for someone who has accepted too many gifts and feels as if he has swallowed poison.

Sacrificial session (*sattra*). This is a class of Soma sacrifices lasting more than twelve days.

Ṣaḍhotṛ. A subsidiary offering at an animal sacrifice using the six-hotṛ text: TA 3.6.

Sarvapr̥ṣṭhā. This is a sacrifice to Indra performed by a person seeking virility. See *Śrautakośa*, i. 635.

Sautrāmaṇī. A sacrifice at which *surā* liquor and a goat are offered. It is performed either as an independent rite or at the conclusion of a royal consecration. See Kane 1962–75, ii. 1224.

Seasonal sacrifices (*cāturmāsya*). These are sacrifices performed on the full-moon days that begin the seasons: Vaiśvadeva in the Spring, Varuṇapraghāsa in the Rainy Season, Sākamedha in the Autumn, and Śunāsīrīya on the fifth full-moon day after the Sākamedha.

Ṣoḍaśin. One of the seven principal types of one-day Soma sacrifice. Kane 1962–75, ii. 1204.

Soma. This is the name of a plant that was crushed to extract its juice. Soma juice was used in several types of Soma sacrifices.

Southern fire (*anvāhāryapacana* or *dakṣiṇāgni*). One of the three vedic fires, it is located to the south-east of the householder's fire in a half-moon-shaped fire pit. The southern fire was used for cooking the grain preparations used at a sacrifice.

Sruc. The common name for ladles, including Juhū, Upabhr̥t, and Dhruvā, used for pouring ghee into the sacred fire.

Sruva. Distinguished from the Sruc-type ladles, this is a smaller spoon used mainly for spooning out ghee or milk into the Sruc. The Sruva has a long handle at the end of which there is a small globular spoon without a spout. It is made of Khadira wood.

Traidhātavīya. A sacrificial rite to obtain a particular wish, this is recommended for people who wish to perform sorcery. Three cakes (from which it gets the name) are offered, the first made with rice, the second with barley, and the third again with rice.

Trihavis. It is described as a triple offering to ancestors in *Śāṅkhāyana Śrautasūtra*, 3.16.1. Govinda (on B 4.6.2), however, identifies it as Savaneṣṭi, which is an offering of a cake baked in eight potsherds to Fire, a cake baked in eleven potsherds to Indra and Fire, and a cake baked in twelve potsherds to the All-gods: see *Śrautakośa*, i. 760.

Ukthya. One of the seven principal types of one-day Soma sacrifice. See Kane 1962–75, ii. 1204.

Utkara. This is a small mound made with the earth dug up while preparing the sacrificial arena. It is located outside the north-eastern corner of the arena.

Utsargiṇām Ayana. A Soma sacrifice of the 'sacrificial session' type lasting one year. See *Śāṅkhāyana Śrautasūtra*, 13.20.

Upabhṛt. A spoon with a long handle somewhat similar to the Juhū and used in making offerings of ghee into the fire. It belongs to the Sruc class and is made of banyan wood.

Vaiśvānarī. A sacrifice to the 'Fire present in all men' generally cooked on twelve potsherds.

Vājapeya. A type of Soma sacrifice in which the number seventeen dominates. It was supposed to be offered by someone who desired lordship.

Viśvajit. A sacrifice at which a person gave away all his possessions as a sacrificial gift to the officiating priests.

Vrātapatī. An offering to the 'lord of the vow'. See *Āpastamba Śrautasūtra*, 9.3.24; 9.4.17.

Vrātyastoma. A Soma sacrifice performed in a single day. It is said to get its name from the fact that through this rite even people who have not performed their initiation at the proper time (i.e. Vrātyas) become as illustrious as a vedic savant.

Yajñakratu. According to Haradatta (on A 1.27.2), these are rites such as Soma sacrifices.

Yajñavāstu. A domestic rite of the Sāmaveda Brahmins at which a handful of sacred grass is sprinkled with ghee and thrown into the fire. See *Gobhila Gṛhyasūtra*, 1.8.26–9; Oldenberg 1886–92, ii. 37.

2. Names of Ritual Formulas and Texts

Abliṅga. See App. 1.3: 'Waters, you are refreshing.'

Aghamarṣaṇa. This is the hymn RV 10.190 used in a particular ritual to efface sins: see B 3.5.

Agnervrata Sāman. 'Fire is the crown, the peak, of the sky. Lord here of the earth, he quickens the seeds of the waters.' SV 1.27 (= RV 8.44.16). See Sāyaṇa on ĀrṣB 6.4.1.1.

Ājyodha Sāman (also called Ācyadoha, Ācidoha). 'The crown of the sky, the dispenser of the earth; Vaiśvānara, the fire born of Ṛta, the sage, the sovereign, the guest of men—the gods have begotten him as a cup for their mouths.' SV 1.67 (= RV 6.7.1). See Sāyaṇa on ĀrṣB 6.1.4.2.

Aṃhomuca. This consists of two sets of formulas. The first is: 'That body of yours to be striven after, O Indra and Varuṇa, with that free this person from tribulation. That strong, protecting, brilliant body of yours, with that free him from tribulation.' The second is: 'That disease of yours, O Indra and Varuṇa, that is in the fire—that disease of yours I appease hereby. That disease of yours, O Indra and Varuṇa, that is in the two-footed cattle, the four-footed, the cattle-yard, the houses, the waters, the plants, the trees—that disease of yours I appease hereby.' TS 2.3.13.1.

Āṅgirasa. For this verse, see App. 1.3: 'The goose seated in the light; . . .'

Aśvasūkta. The Sāman SV 1.122 (= RV 8.14.1; same verse is given under Gosūkta). See Sāyaṇa on ĀrṣB 2.1.9.

Asyavāmīya. See App. I.3: 'Of that pleasant and grey-haired Hotṛ priest . . .'

Atharvaśiras. Nandapaṇḍita (on Vi 56.22) identifies this as the verse beginning 'Brahmā arose as the first among gods.' See MuU 1.1.

Atīṣaṅga. This consists of the verses SV 2.47–9 (= RV 9.101.1–3). See Sāyaṇa on ĀrṣB 6.4.2.12–13.

Bahiṣpavamāna Sāman. This central chant of the Soma sacrifice contains nine verses: RV 9.11.1–3; 9.64.28–30; 9.66.10–12. For a description see Kane 1962–75, ii. 1169 f.

Bārhaspatya Sāman. This Sāman consists of SV 1.56 (= RV 1.40.3). See Sāyaṇa on ĀrṣB 1.7.2.

Bhāruṇḍa Sāman. According to Nandapaṇḍita (on Vi 56.13), this consists of the twenty-one verses beginning with RV 10.16.6. This verse, however, is not found in the SV.

Bhāsa Sāman. This consists of SV 1.470 (= RV 8.46.8). See Sāyaṇa on ĀrṣB 5.1.4.

Brahman's Heart. This passage is TA 10.28.

Brāhmaṇa. A vedic text distinct from the hymns and ritual formulas. Such texts are considered to contain injunctions, which are the source of *dharma*. See p. xxiii.

Bṛhat Sāman. This consists of SV 1.234 (= RV 6.46.1).

Calls (*vyāhṛti*). These are the names of the seven worlds in ascending order: *bhur* (earth), *bhuvaḥ* (mid-space), *svar* (sky), *mahar* (great), *janas* (people), *tapas* (austerity), *satya* (truth). The utterances are considered sacred and powerful. The first three are generally referred to as simply Calls, whereas all seven are called Great Calls (*mahāvyāhṛti*).

Devakṛta. The formulas contained in VS 8.13, variants of which are given in B 4.3.6: 'You are the expiation of sins committed against the gods . . .'

Devavrata Sāmans. Kṛṣṇapaṇḍita (on Va 28.13) identifies these as 'From untruth I go to truth . . .' (TB 1.2.1.15). Sāyaṇa (on ĀrṣB 6.3.5.2) gives a different identification.

Durgāsāvitrī. The verse RV 1.99.1.

Fiend-killing Sāmans (*rakṣoghna*). SV 1.124 (= RV 7.15.13). See Sāyaṇa on ĀrṣB 1.4.4. Besides this Govinda (on B 2.14.5) lists RV 6.16.43; 10.87.24–5; 8.23.15, 14, 13; 1.127.1 as forming part of these Sāmans. See also the formulas at B 3.6.6 (= TS 1.8.7.1).

Five-hotra text. This is TA 3.2.

Four-hotra text. This is TA 3.3

Gāyatra Sāman. This is the Gāyatrī verse sung in the Sāman manner. Sometimes other verses set in the Gāyatrī metre are used. See Eggeling, SB, iv. 178.

Gāyatrī. This term is used with two meanings. First, it is a type of metre with three octosyllabic feet. Second, it is another name for the Sāvitrī verse, which is set in the Gāyatrī metre.

Gosūkta. The Sāman SV 1.122 (= RV 8.14.1; same verse is given under Aśvasūkta). See Sāyaṇa on ĀrṣB 2.1.9.

Great Calls. See Calls.

Hiraṇyavarṇa verses. The four verses TS 5.6.1.1.

'Honey' verses (*madhvṛcaḥ*). The three verses RV 1.90.6–8, each containing the word 'honey' (*madhu*).

Jagatī. A vedic metre consisting of four feet of twelve syllables each.

Janas. See Calls.

Jyeṣṭha Sāman. Haradatta (on A 2.17.22; G 15.28) identifies this as SV 1.31 (= RV 1.24.15), while Govinda (on B 2.14.2) identifies it as SV 1.67 (= RV 6.7.1) and (on B 3.10.10) as SV 1.33 (= RV 10.9.4) and RV 1.115.1. Obviously, there is a lot of confusion regarding this Sāman.

Kṣmāpavitra. According to Govinda (on B 4.7.5), the six verses beginning: 'O Fire, lead us by a fair path to wealth . . .', TS 1.1.14.3–4.

Kūṣmāṇḍa. The four formulas TA 2.3.

Lunar verses. According to Govinda (on B 3.8.14), the three verses RV 10.85.19; 6.6.7; 1.84.15.

Mādhuchandas hymns. The ten hymns RV 1.1–10.

Mahādivākīrtya. The Sāman SV 2.803 (= RV 10.170.1). See Sāyaṇa on ĀrṣB 6.4.1.5–6.

Mahānāmnī. The verses contained in AA 4.

Mahar. See Calls.

Mahāvairāja. The Sāman SV 1.398 (= RV 7.22.1). See Sāyaṇa on ĀrṣB 6.1.6.15.

Mahāvrata. This is a Sāma-chant sung at a bawdy rite of the same name that takes place on the penultimate day of the Soma sacrificial session called Gavāmayana. This chant consists of several Sāmans: Gāyatra, Rathantara, Bṛhat, Bhadra (SV, ii. 460–2), Rājana. See Eggeling in SB, iv. 282–3. Nandapaṇḍita (on Vi 56.24) identifies it as SV 1.91.

Māhitra. The hymn RV 10.185.

Mānavī hymns. The hymns RV 8.27–31.

Mitra, verses addressed to. See App. I.3: 'The fame of Mitra, supporter of the people . . .'

Mṛgāra verses. These are the twenty-two formulas of the Mṛgāra offering contained in TS 4.7.15.

Mṛtyulāṅgala. The verse 'I know that immense Person, having the colour of the sun and beyond darkness. Only when a man knows him does he pass beyond death; there is no other path for going there', TA 3.13.1.

Padastobha. The Sāmans SV 2.578–80.

Pāvamānī. For these seven purificatory verses, see App. I.3: 'Whether near or afar . . .'

Puruṣa hymn. The creation hymn RV 10.90.

Puruṣagati Sāman. The verse 'I am the firstborn . . .', TB 2.8.8.1; see Sāyaṇa on ĀrṣB 6.1.6.18.

Puruṣavrata Sāmans. The first six verses or the first and fourth verses of the Puruṣa Hymn (RV 10.90). See Sāyaṇa on ĀrṣB.

Raivata. The Sāman SV 1.153 (= RV 1.30.13).

Rājana. The Sāman SV 1.318 (= RV 7.27.1). See Sāyaṇa on ĀrṣB 6.3.4.8. The same verse is used for singing the Rauhiṇi Sāman.

Rathantara. The Sāman SV 1.233 (= RV 7.32.22). See Sāyaṇa on ĀrṣB 6.1.6.10.

Rauhiṇi. The Sāman SV 1.318 (= RV 7.27.1). See Sāyaṇa on ĀrṣB 6.3.4.8. The same verse is used for singing the Rājana Sāman.

Raurava. The Sāman SV 1.511 (= RV 9.63.28). The same verse is used for singing the Yaudhājaya Sāman.

Retasyā. This is the verse TA 1.30.1 (= BU 6.4.5): 'I retrieve this semen that fell on earth today; into water or plants though it may have seeped. May I regain my virility, my ardour, my passion; let the fire and the fire-mounds each return to its place.' Hardatta (on G 23.20) cites another opinion, according to which the formula is TA 2.5.3.

Rudra verses. The eleven passages beginning: 'Homage to your wrath, O Rudra . . .', TS 4.5.1.

Sāman. A verse generally taken from the RV and sung to a particular melody. The Sāmans are contained in the Sāmaveda.

Sāmapavitra. 'With what riches will this splendid friend, waxing ever strong, come to us, with what mighty aid.' RV 4.31.1; SV 1.169.
Śatarudrīya. The hymn to Rudra found in VS 16.1–66.
Satya. See Calls.
Sāvitrī. The most sacred of ritual formulas: RV 3.62.10. See also Gāyatrī. Sometimes the term is used with reference to vedic initiation, because teaching this verse to the initiated boy forms a central part of that rite (see Va 11.74).
Seven-hotra text. TA 3.5.
Śiras formula. 'OṂ the Waters, the Light, the Taste, the Immortal, Brahman! Earth, Atmosphere, Sky! OṂ!' MNU 342.
Śivasaṃkalpa hymn. This is VS 34.
Six-hotra text. This is found in TA 3.6.
Solar verses. According to Govinda (on B 3.8.14), RV 1.50.10; 1.50.1; 1.115.1.
Śuddhāśuddhīya. The Sāman SV 1.350 (= RV 8.95.7). See Sāyaṇa on ĀrṣB 3.12.9.
Śuddhavatī. The three verses RV 8.84.7–9.
Surabhimatī verse. The verse 'Of Dadhikrāvan . . .' See App. I.3.
Svadhā. The exclamation accompanying the offering of an oblation to ancestors. See Svāhā.
Svadhā-containing Yajus. This is found in TB 1.3.10.2.
Svāhā. The exclamation accompanying the offering of an oblation to gods. See Svadhā.
Tapas. See Calls.
Taratsama. Same as the following.
Taratsamandī. The hymn RV 9.58.
Ten-hotra text. This is found in TA 3.1.
Triṣṭubh. A vedic metre of four feet with eleven syllables each.
Trisuparṇa. The verse containing the term *suparṇa* ('bird') three times: RV 10.114.4. This explanation is given by Haradatta on G 15.28; but commenting on A 2.17.22 he gives opinions that take it to be TB 1.2.1.27 or TA 10.48–50.
Vāksūkta. Kṛṣṇapaṇḍita (on Va 28.13) identifies this as 'The female mongoose, covered by the lips' found in the *Sāma-Mantra-Brāhmaṇa*, 1.7.15. See Oldenberg 1886–92, ii. 2, 84; *Gobhila Gṛhyasūtra*, 3.4.29.
Vāmadevya. The Sāman SV 1.169 (= RV 4.31.1). See Sāyaṇa on ĀrṣB 2.6.6.
Varuṇa, verses addressed to. See the following.
Vāruṇī verses. 'Hear this cry of mine, O Varuṇa . . .' and 'To you,

therefore, I go . . .' See App. I.3; B 2.7.9. Haradatta (on G 23.28), however, identifies them as RV 7.89.5; 1.25.19; 1.24.11, 14.

Vaṣaṭ. A ritual exclamation uttered by the Hotṛ priest at the conclusion of the sacrificial verse as the Adhvaryu priest puts the oblation into the sacred fire.

Virajā. The formulas contained in MNU 440–56. Some of these formulas are given in B 3.8.12.

Vṛṣākapi. The hymn RV 10.86.

Vyāhṛti Sāman. The five Calls *bhūh*, *bhuvaḥ*, *svaḥ*, *satyam*, and *puruṣaḥ* sung as Sāmans.

Yajus formula. A ritual formula in prose contained in the Yajurveda. These formulas accompany the ritual offerings into the fire.

Yajuḥpavitra. 'May the waters, the mothers, cleanse us. May they who cleanse the ghee cleanse us with ghee.' RV 10.17.10; TS 1.2.1.1

Yaudhājaya. The Sāman SV 1.511 (= RV 9.63.28). The same verse is used for singing the Raurava Sāman.

3. Formulas Cited in the Translations by the First Words

Note: Translations of TS are based on Keith 1914.

'Accept us, O guardian of the house. Be of kind entrance for us and free from ill. Grant to us what we seek from you.' TS 3.4.10.1.

'Aroused by god Savitṛ, I take you with the arms of the Aśvins, with the hands of Pūṣan. You are the spade. You are the woman.' TS 1.3.1.1.

'As one released from the stake; as a sweaty man cleansed from the filth by bathing; as ghee purified by a strainer; so may all the gods free me from sin.' TB 2.4.4.9.

'Blaze up, O Fire, dispelling my misfortune. Bring me cattle and grant me sustenance in every direction.' MNU 67–8.

'Being born, it becomes ever new. It goes in front of the dawns as the banner of the days. As it arrives, it apportions to the gods their portions. The moon stretches out a long life span.' RV 10.85.19; TS 2.4.14.1.

'Born beyond this firmament, may that bright light carry us beyond our enemies. To the Fire common to all men, Svāhā!' TS 4.2.5.2.

'Brahman was first born in the east. Vena [sun] has disclosed from the glittering boundary. He has disclosed its fundamental nearest forms, the womb of the existent and the non-existent.' AV 4.1.1; TS 4.2.8.2.

'Burning away our evil . . .' This is the hymn RV 1.97, whose seer is Kutsa Āṅgirasa.

'Do not hurt us in our children, our descendants, or our life. Do not hurt us in our cattle or our horses. Do not assail our heroes in anger, O Rudra. With oblations, let us serve you with honour.' TS 3.4.11.2–3.

'Fire has put back the sight; Indra and Bṛhaspati have put it back. And you two, O Aśvins, put back the sight into my eyes.' TS 3.2.5.4.

'Gazing, beyond the darkness, upon the highest light, we have come to the sun, god amongst gods, the highest light.' TS 4.1.7.4.

'Golden-coloured, pure, and purifying, in whom were born Kaśyapa and Indra; who have conceived Fire as a germ of varied colour—may these waters be gentle and kind to us. Those, in whose midst Varuṇa goes gazing on the truth and falsehood of men, dripping honey, pure, and purifying—may these waters be gentle and kind to us. Those in the sky that the gods make their food; those that are diffused manifold in mid-space; those that inundate the earth with their sap, the pure ones—may these waters be gentle and kind to us. With an auspicious gaze look upon me, O waters; with an auspicious body touch my skin. I invoke all you Fires that sit in the waters. Do you confer upon me radiance, might, and force.' TS 5.6.1.1–2. These are the four Hiraṇyavarṇa verses.

'Hear this cry of mine, O Varuṇa, and be merciful this day. Seeking for help, I call on you.' TS 2.1.11.6.

'Here indeed did they recognize the hidden bull of Tvaṣṭṛ, in the very house of the moon.' TB 1.5.8.1; RV 1.84.15.

'He who has arisen from the great ocean, glistening from the midst of the water; may that sun, the red-eyed bull, the sage, purify me with his mind.' TA 4.42.5.

'Homage to Rudra, the lord of the dwelling. In coming, in running away, in leaving, in departing, in returning, in journeying, I invoke him who protects.' TB 3.7.9.6–7.

'Into the lion my fury . . .' This is a rather long passage given in the *Baudhāyana Śrautasūtra*, 2.5, as a vedic text.

'Keep well awake, O Fire. Let us be glad. Guard us for prosperity, grant us to wake again.' TS 1.2.3.1.

'May he give you the fullness of life on every side, Fire here, the desirable. Let your breath come back to you. I drive away the disease from you . . .' This is a long recitation of seventeen verses contained in TA 2.5.

'May my speech be in my mouth, breath in the nostrils, sight in the eyes, hearing in the ears, might in the arms, and strength in the thighs. May all my members be uninjured. May your body be with my body. Homage to you. Harm me not.' TS 5.5.9.2.

'May the juices unite in you, may your strength, the might of him who overcomes the foe. Swelling up for immortality, O Soma, place in the sky the highest glories.' TS 4.2.7.4.

'May the Maruts pour upon me, may Indra and Bṛhaspati; and may this fire pour upon me long life and strength. May they make me live long.' TA 2.18.

'May we, O guardian of the house, obtain your fellowship in a friendship effectual, joyful, and proceeding well. Aid our wishes in peace, in action. Guard us always with blessings.' TS 3.4.10.1.

'Mitra draws people together, the wise one. Mitra supports the earth and sky. Mitra regards men without blinking. To the true one let us offer an oblation rich in ghee.' TS 3.4.11.5.

'No anxiety, no danger . . .' These verses are found in RV 10.126.

'O Fire, O Returner, return to us with fullness of life, with radiance, with gain, with wisdom, with offspring, with wealth.' TS 4.2.1.2.

'O Fire, O Aṅgiras, may your returns be a hundred; your movements, a thousand. With the increase of their increase, do you bring back for us what is lost; bring back to us wealth.' TS 4.2.1.3.

'Of Dadhikrāvan have I sung, the swift strong horse. May he make our mouths fragrant and lengthen our life.' TS 1.5.11.4; RV 4.39.6.

'Of that pleasant and grey-haired Hotṛ priest . . .' This is the rather long hymn RV 1.164 containing fifty-two verses.

'O gods, whatever offence we have committed against the gods . . .' These verses are contained in TA 2.3.

'Perceived by the smell, invincible, ever fertile, abounding in cow-dung, and the sovereign over all creatures, I invite her [the earth] here for prosperity.' MNU 110–11.

'Return again with strength. Return, O Fire, fatten with food and life. Guard us again on all sides.' TS 3.2.1.3.

'Return with wealth, O Fire, fatten with the stream, all-gaining on every side.' TS 3.2.1.3.

'Swell up, O Soma [moon], and may your strength be gathered from all sides. Become strong in the gathering of vigour.' TS 3.2.5.3.

'That bright eye rising in the east appointed by the god—may we see it a hundred autumns, may we live a hundred autumns.' TA 4.42.5.

'The Brahman-priest of the gods, leader of poets, sage of seers, bull of wild beasts, eagle of vultures, axe of the forests, Soma goes over the sieve singing.' TS 3.4.11.1.

'The fame of Mitra, supporter of the people, of the god, is eternal, true and most varied in fame.' TS 3.4.11.5.

'The goose seated in the light; the bright one seated in mid-space. The Hotṛ seated at the altar; the guest seated in the house. Seated among men, seated in the highest, seated in truth, seated in the firmament. Born of the waters, born of the cow, born of truth, born of the mountain, the great truth.' TS 1.8.15.2.

'The light by which the gods went up on high, as also the Ādityas, Vasus, and Rudras, by which the Aṅgirases attained greatness—with that light may the patron of the sacrifice attain prosperity.' TS 5.7.2.2.

'The purifier, the heavenly one . . .' This is a passage (*anuvāka*) with seventeen verses in TB 1.4.8.

'The rays carry you up—you the all-knowing god, the sun—for all to see.' TS 1.4.43.1.

'The resplendent face of the gods has risen, the eye of Mitra, Varuṇa, and Agni. He has filled the sky and earth, and the mid-space. The sun is the self of what moves and what stands still.' TS 1.4.43.1.

'The right and the truth . . .' This is the Aghamarṣaṇa hymn, RV 10.190.

'The spotted bull has come and reached again the mother and the father, faring to the heaven.' TS 1.5.3.1.

'The strength in the lion, the tiger, the panther . . .' These four verses are found in TB 2.7.7.1–2.

'To you, therefore, I go, praising you with my hymn. The sacrificer seeks this with his offerings. Be not angry here, O Varuṇa. Do not carry away our life, O wide ruler.' TS 2.1.11.6.

'To welcome the Dawn the inspired Vasiṣṭhas did first awaken with songs and praises . . .' This is the hymn RV 7.80 containing three verses.

'Unfurl your strength like a net spread out . . .' This is the passage (*anuvāka*) TS 1.2.14.

'Waters, you are refreshing. Further us to strength, to see great joy. The auspicious flavour that is yours, accord to us here, like eager mothers. To him may we come with satisfaction, to whose dwelling you quicken us, O waters, and propagate us.' TS 4.1.5.1. These are the Abliṅga formulas.

'We announce to the Fire common to all men . . .' This hymn is found in TA 2.6.

'Whatever blemish there is in me, Fire, all-knowing and swift-moving, has removed it.' TS 3.2.5.4.

'Whatever debt I have contracted without gambling . . .' This is a long recitation of thirteen verses contained in TA 2.4.

'Whether near or afar . . .' These are the seven Pāvamānī verses contained in RV 9.67.21–7.

'With that body of yours worthy of sacrifice, O Fire, come here and mount my body, procuring many riches, splendid and manly. Becoming the sacrifice, sit down at the sacrifice, your own abode. O All-knowing Fire, being born from the earth, come with your abode.' TB 2.5.8.8.

'With that purifier of a thousand streams with which the gods always cleanse themselves, may the purificatory verses cleanse me.' TB 1.4.8.6.

'You are the sheen! You are the radiance! You are the brilliance!' TS 1.1.10.3.

'You, O Fire, are the guardian of vows among gods and men, you who are to be invoked at the sacrifices.' TS 1.2.3.1.

'You, O Fire, with your favour take us across once more over every trouble. Be a broad, thick, and wide fortress for us, and health and wealth for our children and descendants.' TS 1.1.14.4.

APPENDIX II

NAMES OF GODS, PEOPLE, AND PLACES

Aditi. A female deity, the mother of several gods, including Varuṇa and Mitra. In later mythology she is made the mother of gods in general. Sometimes she is identified with the earth.

Āditya(s). Literally the son(s) of Aditi, the term in the plural refers to a group of gods, including some prominent ones such as Varuṇa, Mitra, and Indra. Early texts give their number as eight, but the Brāhmaṇas already show their number as twelve, which has remained the norm ever since. Together with the Vasus and the Rudras, they constitute the three major classes of gods. In the singular, the term Āditya refers to the sun.

Agastya. The name of an ancient sage, said to be the son of Mitra and Varuṇa. In a later myth he is said to have instructed the Vindhya mountains to remain bowed (not to grow taller) until he turns from southern India.

Agni. Fire and the god of Fire.

All-gods (*viśvedeva*). The name of a class of gods. In the later Dharma texts they are listed as ten in five pairs: Kratu and Dakṣa, Vasu and Satya, Dhuri and Locana, Kāla and Kāma, and Purūravas and Ārdrava. See Kane 1962–75, iv. 457.

Ambaṣṭha. A mixed social class consisting of offspring fathered by a man on a woman one class (*varṇa*) below him.

Aṅga. The name of the far eastern region of the Ganges plain, roughly corresponding to the western part of Bengal.

Āṅgirasa. The name of a class of priests closely associated with another group called Atharvan. The name is also used with reference to a group of sundry divine beings and is an epithet of several gods, especially the fire god Agni.

Antyāvasāyin. A child fathered by a Śūdra man on a Vaiśya woman.

Āraṭṭa. The name of a people and a region in the Punjab, in the north-western part of India. This region was outside the cultural area of Brahmanism and out of bounds to Brahmins.

Asaṃvṛta. The name of a hell: see Va 18.15; M 4.81.

Aśvins. Twin deities described as young, beautiful, fond of honey, and expert in medical knowledge. They are the physicians of the gods.

Aupajaṅghani. An ancient authority on Dharma cited by Baudhāyana (2.3.33) on inheritance.

Avanti. An area of western north-central India, corresponding to western Madhya Pradesh.

Āyogava. A child fathered by a man on a woman of the class (*varṇa*) immediately above his.

Bhāllavins. The adherents of an ancient school of teachers constituting a branch of the Sāmaveda. A Brāhmaṇa belonging to this branch is cited in the *Bṛhaddevatā*, 5.23.

Bharadvāja. An ancient seer to whom the composition of the sixth book of the Ṛgveda is ascribed.

Bhṛjyakaṇṭha. A mixed class considered to be the offspring of a Brahmin father and a Vaiśya mother.

Boundary River. This river is given in a verse of the Bhāllavins (B 1.2.12; Va 1.15) as the western boundary of the land of vedic splendour. Its identity is unclear, but it is probably the same as the Sarasvatī.

Brahman. This term is applied to the ultimate cosmic principle and, in the Vedas, especially to formulations of ultimate truth. In later times, it is used with reference to the creative principle and sometimes also the creator god.

Brahmaṇaspati. Literally 'the lord of brahman', the term is an epithet of Bṛhaspati.

Brahmin. The first of the four classes of ancient Indian society, generally associated with learning and ritual activities.

Bṛhaspati. A deity closely linked to the fire god and to sacred speech. Regarded as the priest of the gods and the source of wisdom, he is the lord of speech and eloquence. Later tradition identifies him with the planet Jupiter and ascribes to him, now considered a seer, texts of religious law and politics.

Cāṇḍāla. An outcaste person whose mere touch pollutes. He is considered the offspring of a Śūdra father and a Brahmin mother.

Dauṣyanta. A mixed class, considered as the offspring of a Kṣatriya father and a Śūdra mother.

Deccan. The region in India to the south of the Vindhya mountain range.

Dhanvantari. A god produced at the cosmogonic churning of the ocean, he is the physician of the gods and the divine author of medical science.

Dhīvara. A mixed class considered to be the offspring of a Vaiśya father and a Kṣatriya mother.

Eka. An ancient teacher of Dharma cited in A 1.19.7.

Gandharva. In the early vedic literature Gandharvas appear as a class of divine beings alongside the gods and the forefathers. They are associated with the Soma drink and are said to be fond of females. They are often associated with the celestial nymphs, Apsarases. In later literature, especially the epics, the Gandharvas are depicted as celestial singers and are associated with music.

Ganges. The major Indian river, of which the Yamunā is a tributary, flowing from the north-central plains into the Bay of Bengal.

Gayā. One of the most sacred places of pilgrimage located close to the modern city of Patna in Bihar.

Hārīta. The name of an ancient authority on Dharma cited frequently in the Dharmasūtras.

Indra. The most famous of the vedic gods, Indra is called the king of the gods. He is powerful and loves to drink Soma. His claim to fame is his victory over Vṛtra, a combat that is given cosmogonic significance. In the Vedas Indra is closely associated with rain, and prominence is given to his weapon, the Vajra, conceived of as the thunderbolt.

Janaka. Perhaps the most famous and prominent of the kings mentioned in the Upaniṣads. Videha is to the east of the Kuru-Pañcāla country, the home of the major figures of the Upaniṣads. Janaka, the king of Videha, represents the growing importance of the eastern regions from which the new religions of Buddhism and Jainism would emerge some centuries later.

Kālaka (lit., 'black forest'). The location of this forest is uncertain, but it must have been in the eastern reaches of the Ganges, possibly eastern Bihar or western Bengal.

Kaṇva. An ancient authority on Dharma cited by Āpastamba: see Kane 1962–75, i. 273.

Kāṇva. An ancient authority on Dharma cited by Āpastamba. This is also the name of a vedic branch to which Baudhāyana belonged (B 2.9.14): see Kane 1962–75, i. 273.

Karaṇa. A mixed class considered as the offspring of a Vaiśya father and a Śūdra mother.

Kāraskara. Name of a people and a region. Later literature places it somewhere in the Narmadā river valley in the Vindhya hills.

Kaśyapa. The name of an ancient sage, cited as an authority on Dharma by Baudhāyana (1.21.2): see Kane 1962–75, i. 274.

Kātya. An ancient authority on Dharma cited by Baudhāyana (1.3.46).

Kautsa. An ancient authority on Dharma cited by Āpastamba (1.19.4; 1.28.1).

Kṣattṛ. A mixed class considered to be the offspring of a Vaiśya father and a Brahmin mother.

Kṣatriya. The second of the four classes of ancient Indian society, generally associated with warfare and government.

Kukkuṭa. A mixed class said to be the offspring of a Vaiśya father and a Niṣāda mother.

Kuṇika. An ancient authority on Dharma cited by Āpastamba (1.19.7).

Kutsa. An ancient authority on Dharma cited by Āpastamba (1.19.7).

Magadha. An eastern region along the Ganges plain corresponding roughly to modern Bihar. It was the centre of the Aśokan empire.

Māgadha. A mixed class considered to be the offspring of a Vaiśya father and a Brahmin mother.

Mahājajñu. The name of an ancient teacher mentioned by Baudhāyana (3.9.21).

Māhiṣya. A mixed class considered to be the offspring of a Kṣatriya father and a Vaiśya mother.

Manu. The first man and the progenitor of all humans, he plays the central role in the Indian myth of the flood. Later legends make him also the first lawgiver, and an important collection of ancient Indian laws is ascribed to Manu.

Maruts. A group of gods connected with the wind and the thunderstorm, and thus associated with Indra's exploits. They are called the sons of Rudra and are often referred to in the plural as 'the Rudras'.

Maudgalya. An ancient authority on Dharma cited by Baudhāyana (2.4.8).

Mūrdhāvasikta. A mixed class considered to be the offspring of a Brahmin father and a Kṣatriya mother.

Nirṛti. A goddess who is the personification of evil and adversity.

Niṣāda. A mixed class considered to be the offspring of a Brahmin father and a Vaiśya mother.

Pāraśava. A mixed class considered to be the offspring of a Brahmin father and a Śūdra mother.

Pāriyātra. Probably a mountain range of the Vindhyas, the latter being substituted for Pāriyātra in the definition of the land of Āryas found in later texts (M 2.21).

Prajāpati. Literally 'lord of creatures', he is the creator god *par excellence* in the Brāhmaṇas and the Upaniṣads. He is the father of the gods and the demons (*asura*), as well as of all creatures.

Prānūna. I have not found any source that identifies this region.

Pulkasa. A mixed class considered to be the offspring of a Niṣāda father and a Vaiśya mother.

Puṇḍra. Appearing already in the AB 7.18 as a degraded people, they were probably located somewhere in Bengal or Bihar.

Pūṣan. Closely associated with the sun god, he is viewed as the one who knows the paths and conducts the dead safely to the world of the fathers.

Puṣkarasādi. An ancient authority on Dharma cited by Āpastamba (1.19.7; 1.28.1).

Rāmaka. A mixed class considered to be the offspring of a Vaiśya father and a Brahmin mother.

Rathakāra. A mixed class considered to be the offspring of a Vaiśya father and a Śūdra wife.

Rudra. Generally regarded as a storm god, Rudra has an ambivalent personality. He is fierce and feared. He is also a healer, the one who averts the anger of gods. In his benign aspect he is referred to as *śiva*, 'the benign one', an epithet that becomes the name of the later god Śiva, with whom Rudra is identified.

Rudras. In the plural, the term refers to a group of eleven gods, who, together with the Ādityas and the Vasus, constitute the three classes of gods. The Rudras are associated with the Maruts; both of these groups are ruled by Rudra.

Sādhyas. A group of somewhat ill-defined deities, said to occupy a region above that of the gods.

Sarasvatī. The most celebrated river of the vedic age (although its identity in the early period is not altogether certain), it is personified as a goddess. In the Brāhmaṇas she becomes identified with speech and the goddess of speech, and in later mythology Sarasvatī is the goddess of eloquence and wisdom. This river flowed between the Indus and Ganges river systems. Its disappearance in the desert became the focus of myths and folk tales.

Sauvīra. Name of a border people living probably in south-western Punjab near the Indus.

Savarṇa (lit., 'of the same class'). Offspring of a mother of the same class as the father or one class below him.

Savitṛ. An aspect of the sun god, this deity became famous because the celebrated Sāvitrī verse is addressed to him.

Sindh. The region around the southern reaches of the Indus river; today the area around Karachi in Pakistan.

Soma. A sacrificial drink pressed from a plant with apparently mind-altering qualities, it was personified as a god and later identified with the moon. Thus the term often simply means the moon.

Śūdra. The fourth and lowest of the four classes of ancient Indian society associated with service and servile functions within society. Some Śūdras may have been slaves.

Sūta. A mixed class considered to be the offspring of a Kṣatriya father and a Brahmin mother.

Surāṣṭra. The region of Kathiawar in south-eastern Gujarat.

Śvapāka. A mixed class considered to be the offspring of an Ugra father and a Kṣattr̥ mother.

Śvetaketu. The reference probably is to the son of Uddālaka Āruṇi, who figures prominently in the Upaniṣads. BU 6.2; CU 5.2; 6.

Tvaṣṭr̥. Described as a skilled workman, he is the father of Indra.

Ugra. A mixed class considered to be the offspring of a Vaiśya father and a Śūdra mother.

Upāvr̥t. A border land whose geographical location is uncertain.

Uśanas. The name of an ancient sage who becomes the domestic priest of the Asuras (demons) in their war with the gods. He is cited as an authority on Dharma.

Vaideha(ka). A mixed class considered to be the offspring of a Śūdra father and a Kṣatriya mother (see also Vaiṇa).

Vaiṇa. A mixed class considered to be the offspring of a Śūdra father and a Kṣatriya mother (see also Vaidehaka).

Vaiśya. The third of the four classes of ancient Indian society. Vaiśyas are the common people engaged in agriculture and trade.

Vaṅga. Bengal or its eastern regions.

Varuṇa. One of the great gods in the early vedic literature, he is viewed as the grand sovereign and upholder of the natural and moral order. He becomes increasingly associated with the waters and the west, and his residence comes to be located within the ocean.

Vārṣyāyaṇi. An ancient authority on Dharma cited by Āpastamba (1.28.2).

Vasus. A group of eight gods distinguished from the Ādityas and Rudras, although their general character and specific identities remain rather vague.

Vindhya. The major mountain range in north-central India dividing north India from the Deccan.

Viṣṇu. The great god of later Hinduism, who is a somewhat minor solar deity in the vedic literature. He is especially celebrated in his two human incarnations, Rāma and Kṛṣṇa.

Vrātya. The term is used in ancient literature to refer to groups of people, at least some of whom appear to have led a wandering or a nomadic life. Already in some vedic texts, however, the Vrātya is presented as a mysterious, powerful, and even divine person. In later times the term is used to refer to either mixed-caste people or to Brahmins who have not undergone vedic initiation.

Vṛṣaparvan. The name of a sage whose daughter entered into a dispute with the daughter of Uśanas.

Yama. The Indian god of death from the most ancient period of vedic mythology until contemporary times. In ancient myths he is called king and divine characteristics are ascribed to him, but he comes to be identified with death itself and many of the negative aspects of death become associated with Yama. Later myths associate him with judgment and punishment of the dead.

Yamunā. The major tributory of the Ganges river.

Yavana. A mixed class considered to be the offspring of a Kṣatriya father and a Śūdra mother: see p. xxxii.

APPENDIX III

FAUNA AND FLORA

COMMON fauna and flora that can be readily translated are not listed here; they are found in the Index.

Babhru (lit., 'deep- or reddish-brown'). The term refers to a type of mongoose, possibly the Ruddy Mongoose (*Herpestes smithi*), a variety of the common Indian mongoose (*Herpestes edwardsi*). Prater 1997, 102.

Badara. The jujube tree. *Zizyphus Jujuba.*

Baka. This term is applied to a wide variety of water fowl, including heron, ibis, stork, and the common flamingo. Dave 1985, 383–7, 408–9.

Balāka. Flamingo; the term is sometimes applied to other water fowl, such as the egret. Dave 1985, 409–21.

Balbaja. A type of coarse grass. *Eleusine Indica.*

Bhāsa. A species of vulture, identified by Dave (1985, 188) as the bearded vulture.

Black antelope: see Eṇa and Hariṇa.

Bṛhacchiras. 'Large-headed', a type of fish, although the reading is somewhat uncertain: B 1.12.8 n. Bühler identifies it as the Indian salmon (Māhsir).

Brahmasuvarcalā. Refers either to a variety of sunflower (*Heriantus*) or to *Clerodendron Siphonanthus.*

Cakravāka. The ruddy sheldrake called the Brahmani Duck. The fidelity of a mated pair to each other and their grief when separated is celebrated in Indian poetry and folklore.

Ceṭa. The identity of this fish or aquatic animal is uncertain. Kṛṣṇapaṇḍita (on Va 14.41) reads Āveṭa and explains it as Kumbhīra, the Ganges alligator. Given the other aquatic animals listed alongside at A 1.17.38–9 and Va 14.41–2, it is likely that this is also either an unusual fish or some type of amphibian.

Cilicima. A kind of fish also forbidden in the *Caraka Saṃhitā* (1.26.83; tr. i. 210). There it is described as full of scales, with red eyes and red lines on its body, resembling a Rohita fish, and generally moving 'on the ground' (probably, at the bottom of the water).

Darbha. A type of grass used for ritual purposes, most commonly the same as Kuśa; specifically the grass *Saccharum cylindricum.*

Sometimes, Darbha can mean simply a tuft or bundle, as in Va 21.2 *lohitadarbha* (Lohita grass).

Ḍerikā. A type of musk rat according to Haradatta (on A 1.25.13). It must have had some cultural importance, since killing it was considered a serious crime (B 1.19.6).

Ḍiḍḍika. Another type of musk rat. Govinda (on B 1.19.6) identifies it as Chuchundarī, a term occurring at M 12.65, where the commentator Govindarāja identifies it as Rājaduhitṛ, also a kind of musk rat.

Eṇa. The Blackbuck (also called Kṛṣṇasāra: M 2.23), an antelope with black hair on the back and sides and white under the belly: *Antilope cervicapra.* About 32 inches at the shoulder and weighing about 90 lbs., with horns 20–5 inches long. See Prater 1997, 270.

Gaura. The Indian bison, standing close to 6 feet at the shoulders: *Bos gaurus.* See Prater 1997, 243.

Gavaya. In Va 14.41 it is given as a type of fish. The name indicates that the fish (or probably its head) must have had the appearance of an ox or bison.

Gayal. A wild ox: *Bos gavaeus.*

Godhā. Often translated as 'iguana' (a lizard found exclusively in the Americas), this is clearly the Indian monitor lizard (see Lüders 1942; Jamison 1998), the smaller variety of which (called Talagoyā in Sri Lanka) is eaten.

Gṛñjana. An unidentified species of onion or garlic.

Haṃsa. The ruddy goose, most celebrated species of Indian goose. The term is often applied to other large geese and swans.

Hariṇa. An Indian antelope. According to Prater (1997, 270), Hariṇa is the female of Eṇa. But it appears from A 1.3.3 that Hariṇa is distinguished from Eṇa and may have been light brown in colour. There may have been some confusion here, since the male Eṇa is black, whereas the female is brown.

Hārīta. The green pigeon. Dave 1985, 251.

Kalaviṅka. A species of sparrow, identified as the 'village sparrow' by Vijñāneśvara on Y 1.174. According to Dave (1985), the word is used for blackbirds, magpies, and finches.

Kaliṅga. The east-central coastal region, corresponding roughly to modern Orissa up to the mouth of the river Kṛṣṇā.

Kaṅka. The name is used for several varieties of eagle, heron, and kite. Its feathers were used in making arrows. Dave 1985, 242. Fitzgerald (1998, 258) has argued that the term refers to a carrion-eating stork.

Kapiñjala. The Francoline partridge, called Cātaka in North India.

Karañja. The term *karañja* (also written *kalañja*) is not found in any Dharma text apart from Āpastamba (1.17.26), although it figures prominently in the exegetical rule 'Karañja Maxim' described in PMS 6.2.5.19–20. Commenting on this, Śabara gives an ancient food prohibition. '*Kalañja*, garlic, and onion should not be eaten.'

Khañjarīṭa. The yellow wagtail. Dave 1985, 103.

Kokila. The black Indian cuckoo (Koil), whose singing has made it famous in Indian poetry and folklore.

Krakara. The large imperial sand-grouse. Dave 1985, 265.

Krauñca. A species of large water bird, probably the common crane: Dave 1985, 312. Haradatta (on A 1.17.36) says that they travel in pairs, and Bühler identifies the bird as the red-crested crane now called Sāras.

Kruñca. The flamingo: Dave 1985, 313, 408. Haradatta (on A 1.17.36) says that these travel in flocks, and Bühler identifies the bird as the common crane now called Kulam or Kūñc.

Kuluṅga. A species of antelope.

Kurara. The osprey. Dave 1985, 185.

Kuśa. The most common of the sacred grasses (see Darbha) used for ritual purposes. *Poa cynosuroides.*

Lakṣmaṇa. A type of crane related to Vārdhāṇasa: see A 1.17.36. Dave 1985, 312.

Lohita. The reference is not altogether clear. The term is used for a variety of plants, but the reference here may be to a variety of rice. The term is used only at Va 15.12 and 22.2, where the meaning may be dried straw of the Lohita rice.

Madgu. The snake fish or a cormorant. Dave 1985, 372.

Mahāśakari. A kind of fish, although the reading is uncertain: B 1.12.8 n.

Māndhāla. A species of bat or flying fox.

Mṛdura. The identity of this aquatic species is unclear. Haradatta (on A 1.17.39) calls it Makara, a somewhat mythological sea animal often identified with the crocodile.

Muñja. A species of rush belonging to the sugar-cane family and reaching about 10 feet in height and used for basket weaving: *Saccharum Munja.* Its principal ritual use is in the manufacture of the girdle given to a Brahmin boy at his vedic initiation.

Mūrvā. A species of hemp used in the manufacture of bow strings and of the ritual girdle given to a Kṣatriya boy at his vedic initiation: *Sanseviera Roxburghiana.*

Naḷa. A kind of reed used for weaving baskets: *Arundo Tibialis* or *Karka*.

Palāśa. A variety of fig tree called Dhak with a beautiful trunk and abundant leaves: *Butea frondosa*. Incisions produce a red juice used as an astringent. The tree was viewed as sacred in ancient India and its wood used to make ritual implements.

Pārāvata. This name is applied to a variety of pigeons, including the blue rock pigeon, wood pigeon, and snow pigeon.

Pīlu. The tree *Careya arborea* (patana oak) growing in grassy expanses.

Plava. A coot or cormorant. Dave 1985, 372.

Pṛṣata. A spotted antelope or deer.

Railātakā. I have been unable to find any information on this bird.

Rājīva. Said to be a kind of lotus-coloured fish, or one with stripes (Medhātithi and Govindrāja on M 5.16).

Rohita. A kind of red fish said to feed on moss (*Caraka Saṃhitā*, 1.27.80) and called the most nutritious of fish (ibid. 1.25.38).

Ṛśya. The white-footed antelope called Nilgai (blue bull): *Boselaphus tragocamelus*. The male is dark in colour, reaching over 4 feet in height, and the female is light brown. Prater 1997, 272.

Ruru. A species of spotted antelope.

Sahasradaṃṣṭra (lit., 'with a thousand teeth'). Possibly a type of sheat fish.

Śaṅkhapuṣpī. A type of grass: *Andropogon aciculatus.* Govinda (on B 2.1.22) remarks that it grows mainly along the seashore.

Śapharī. A small glittering minnow that darts in the water.

Śara. A species of reed belonging to the sugar-cane family used for making arrows: *Saccharum Sara.*

Śarabha. Probably a kind of large antelope. In later literature a mythical beast of enormous strength. Haradatta (on A 1.17.29) calls it 'a wild deer with eight feet'; clearly he was guessing!

Sāraṅga. The name is applied both to the peacock and to the crested little bustard. Dave 1985, 328.

Śārika. A small brown bird commonly known as Maina (mynah) that can imitate human speech like a parrot. Dave 1985, 81.

Śatabali. A kind of fish identified with Rohita by Haradatta (on A 2.17.2), who says that it has a lot of bones.

Sidhraka. Appears to be a type of tree with strong and heavy wood used for making pestles for husking rice. I have not succeeded in identifying the tree.

Śleṣmāntaka. Also called Śleṣmāta and Śelu; the fruit of this small tree is about the size of a cherry. Called Bhokar in Marathi, it is used today for making pickles.

Snake-head fish (Sarpaśīrṣa). The identity is unclear, and the commentators are of no help. Possibly a kind of eel or water snake.

Suparṇa. A common name for any large bird of prey, especially the golden eagle. Dave 1985, 201.

Tamāla. The tree *Xanthochymus pictorius* with a very dark bark. Haradatta (on A 1.2.37) says that this tree is also known as Mūloda.

Ṭiṭṭibha. The name refers to a variety of plovers and lapwings. Dave 1985, 357.

Udumbara. A type of fig tree whose wood is used for ritual purposes: *Ficus glomerata*.

Vāraṇa. Identified by Dave (1985, 327) as the great bustard.

Vārdhrāṇasa (or Vārdhrīṇasa; lit., 'leather-snouted'). This sometimes refers to the rhinoceros, but in these texts it refers to a type of bird, probably a hornbill: Prater 1997, 159. At B 1.12.6, however, it is classified as a bird that scratches with its feet in searching for food, which would argue against a waterbird.

Varmi. A kind of fish, commonly known as Vāmi.

Vibhītaka. The tree *Terminalia Bellerica*, whose seeds were used as dice in gambling.

Vīraṇa grass. A fragrant grass: *Andropogon Muricatus.*

NOTES

The Dharmasūtra of Āpastamba

BOOK ONE

1.1–3 *accepted customary Laws . . . Vedas*: Āpastamba, more than any other author, points to generally accepted custom as the basis of Law (*dharma*). Here he puts the Vedas last, in contrast to the other three who place it first (G 1.1; B 1.1.1; Va 1.4). Āpastamba opens his *Gṛhyasūtras* (1.1.1) with a similar remark: 'Next, we take up the rites derived from practice (*ācārādyāni*).' He refers to customs over which there is common agreement also at A 1.7.31; 1.23.6. 'Those who know the Laws' are called elsewhere 'the cultured élite' (*śiṣṭa*: see the definition in B 1.1.5–6), that is, those who are both learned in the sacred traditions and steadfast in virtue, who are authorities both with regard to the correct language (Sanskrit) and in matters of proper conduct. 'Authority' (*pramāṇa*) has a technical meaning in Indian epistemology. It signifies a means or source of correct knowledge. Several such means are recognized, including perception, inference, and authoritative verbal testimony. Both the conduct of the cultured élite and Vedic revelation are such verbal testimonies, and therefore authoritative means of knowing the Laws. See p. xxxix.

1.10 *Sāvitrī . . . Vedas*: the purpose here is to show that no separate initiation takes place for studying the different Vedas.

1.14 *teacher . . . gathers*: a common strategy in these texts is to use phonetic similarities to establish etymological derivations, which in turn has the didactic purpose of explaining the 'deeper' meaning of a word, in this case 'teacher'. I give the Sanskrit within parenthesis to help the English reader to detect the phonetic link.

1.16–18 *gives birth . . . body*: The initiatory rite performed by the teacher is viewed as the second birth of the boy. It is because of this second birth that people belonging to the three upper classes (*varṇa*), who alone are entitled to vedic initiation, are called 'twice-born' (*dvija*): see G 1.8; 10.50.

1.28 *season*: an Indian season lasts approximately two months. See G 14.25 n.

1.32 *Brahman-killers*: there is a double entendre here, the term meaning both a murderer of a Brahmin and a man who has not kept the Veda 'alive' by neglecting vedic study and has thus 'killed' the

Veda, which is also called *brahman*. 'They are all', namely oneself, one's father, and one's grandfather; the same meaning below at A 1.2.5.

2.5 *cremation grounds*: this is an epithet used elsewhere with reference to Śūdras and other low-caste and outcaste people (Va 18.11–13) and indicates the impurity of such individuals.

2.19 *sin causing loss of caste*: for this category of sins, see A 1.21.7–20; G 21.1–3; B 2.2.1–11; Va 1.19–22.

2.22 *ritual food*: i.e. food that is ritually offered to gods or ancestors.

2.28 *not wash his body*: the period of studentship was viewed as a time of penance. Rites of passage generally involve separation from one's previous status, a liminal period sometimes involving seclusion, and finally the integration into the new status (van Gennep 1960). Vedic studentship was such a liminal period. Not washing oneself and keeping oneself dirty are some ways of expressing this liminality. The student is required to keep 'his body dirty, his teeth stained' (A 1.7.11; cf. G 2.13). These provisions stand in contrast to others that require a student to bathe frequently, indicating changing practices or that here 'bathing' is considered purely a ritual immersion and not 'washing' the body. People in periods of ritual impurity (*āśauca*), such as after the death of a family member, and menstruating women are also not permitted to wash themselves, since washing is a rite that expresses the recovery of purity: see Va 4.14; 5.6–7. The end of studentship, significantly, is signalled by a ritual bath (integration into a new status), after which the young graduate decorates his body and wears perfumes and garlands (A 1.8.2).

3.12 *casinos and fairs*: the meanings of *sabhā* and *samāja* are unclear, but I think they are technical terms rather than generic words translated by Bühler as 'assemblies and crowds'. I take the former in the sense of a gambling hall as used at A 2.25.12. The second probably refers to some sort of fair or spectacle that attracted crowds, something looked down upon by the third-century BCE emperor, Aśoka (Rock Edict 1). See Ghosh 1973, 56.

3.25 *degraded or heinous sinners*: these are technical terms for classes of sinful and/or socially ostracized people. The former are referred to at A 1.21.6 and probably defined under sins that make people sordid at A 1.21.12–19. Acts making someone a heinous sinner are given at A 1.24.6–9 and Va 23.14.

3.27 *leftovers*: the Sanskrit term *ucchiṣṭa* refers most frequently to the food left over after one has eaten. Such remnants are considered extremely impure and polluting. In an adjectival sense, however, the term refers to a person who is rendered impure by coming into contact with *ucchiṣṭa* food. Thus, after a meal a person remains *ucchiṣṭa* until he or she has performed the required purification. There are, however, other extended meanings of the term. Medhātithi (on M 4.80), an early commentator of Manu, isolates four possible meanings of *ucchiṣṭa*: (1) because of contact with the inside of the mouth while eating, the eater, the eaten food, and the plate from which one eats become *ucchiṣṭa*; (2) food left on the plate after someone has eaten off it is *ucchiṣṭa*; (3) as also what is left in the dish from which food has been served to someone; (4) food left in the pot after people have been served; and (5) a person is *ucchiṣṭa* after voiding urine or excrement and before purification. According to Medhātithi, the primary meaning of the term is (1), the pollution resulting from food and fingers coming into contact with the inside of the mouth. Some types of *ucchiṣṭa*, however, are good and can be eaten. Generally such leftovers belong to a person superior to oneself. Thus, a wife may eat the leftovers of her husband, a student the leftovers of his teacher, and everyone the leftovers of a sacrifice or an offering to a god (A 1.4.1–11; G 2.31–2). Eating what is left over after feeding guests and members of the household is often considered as a great virtue in a householder (A 2.8.2; B 2.5.18). See Malamoud 1972; Olivelle 1998.

3.28–30 *A Brahmin . . . at the end*: the set formula for requesting almsfood is: 'Madam, give food' (see B 1.3.16), which is how a Brahmin would say it. A Kṣatriya would say 'Give, Madam, food', and a Vaiśya, 'Give food, Madam'. The formula implies that it was the housewife who normally distributed food to students and mendicants. This type of public ritualized behaviour, as well as minute differences in the dress code, are constant reminders to oneself and to others of the class of society to which a person belongs and points to the centrality of the class (*varṇa*) system within ancient Indian society, at least in the eyes of our Brahmin authors.

4.8–10 *for a vedic text . . . from it*: for a discussion of these exegetical rules, see G 3.36 n.; p. xlii.

4.22 *forgo sleep*: the meaning is that a student should assist the teacher in preparing his bed and so forth, and go to sleep after the teacher. When he does this, he can be said to never sleep: see A 1.4.28.

4.27 *make him desist*: Bühler translates this as 'he may return home'. The Sanskrit term *nirvartayet*, however, has the meaning of restraining someone (so also Böhtlingk 1885*b*, 518), and the commentator Haradatta's observation that he should do this himself or get someone else like his father to do it also points to putting pressure on the teacher to abandon his former ways.

4.29 *A student . . . householder*: this hints at the possibility of a person remaining a student throughout his life, an institution recognized within the *āśrama* system: A 2.21.6; Olivelle 1993, 78–81.

5.25 *At times . . . forbidden*: for these occasions, see A 1.9.1—1.11.38 and parallels elsewhere.

6.4 *not wrong . . . bed*: it is understood that the student sleeps on the floor.

6.18 *wear one . . . arm*: the upper garment is simply a piece of cloth like a shawl formed into a loop. Wearing it in this manner is called *yajñopavīta* or simply *upavīta*. Later the upper garment worn in this manner became contracted to merely a cord, also called by those terms (B.1.8.5), a cord with which a boy was ritually invested at his initiation (p. xxx). This cord was made with three strings, each containing three threads twisted to form a single string (B 1.8.5). So each cord had nine threads. It became the practice especially for Brahmins to wear this sacred cord (also called *brahmasūtra*) at all times (B 2.3.1; Va 8.17), a distinguishing mark of Brahmins in India even today. Some recommend one such cord for students and a double cord (i.e. with six strings and eighteen threads) for a bath-graduate and a householder (B 1.5.2; Va 12.14). The upper garment (or the sacred cord) is worn over the right shoulder and under the left arm (a pattern called *prācīnāvīta*) at ancestral rites (B 2.10.1), and over the neck like a garland (a pattern called *nivīta*) in rites involving humans, such as sexual intercourse, sacramentary rites, and going to the toilet. Another mode of wearing it ('suspended or tied below') is given in B 1.8.10. Govinda explains this as tying it below the navel when engaged in activities such as applying oil on or massaging the body. See B 1.8.7–9; TS 2.5.11.1; Kane 1962–75, ii. 287–97.

6.32 *elder*: the Sanskrit term *guru* is frequently translated as teacher, but in these texts it has a much wider connotation. It includes the teacher, the specific word for whom is *ācārya* (A 1.1.14 n.), but frequently refers to other venerable people, such as parents, grandparents, uncles, and the like. I have translated *guru* generally as elder, unless the context clearly indicates the teacher. On the term *guru*, see Hara 1980.

7.2 *counterclockwise . . . clockwise*: walking around a sacred object or a revered person in a clockwise manner, that is, keeping one's right hand towards the object or person (technically called *pradakṣiṇa*) as a mark of respect has been a cultural constant in India from the most ancient to contemporary times. The counterclockwise procedure is used to indicate disrespect and in rites that are inauspicious (see Va 15.14).

8.22 *tooth cleaners*: in ancient India, as also in rural areas today, sticks cut from certain trees are used to brush the teeth. One end of the stick is crushed to form the brush.

8.26 *A pupil ceases . . . dolt*: I follow Böhtlingk's (1885*b*, 519) convincing argument. The commentator Haradatta has misunderstood this passage, and Bühler follows him in this laboured translation: 'That pupil who, attending to two (teachers), accuses his (principal and first) teacher of ignorance, remains no (longer) a pupil.'

8.29 *until . . . studies*: the commentator Haradatta and, following him, Bühler interpret the expression *ā nivṛtteḥ* to mean 'until he stops his wrong behaviour'. But in the very next sentence the term *nivṛtta* is used with a reference to the completion of studentship. The meaning is that the teacher has the authority to punish a pupil's infractions only while he is his student.

9.1–3 *After commencing . . . half months*: Rohiṇī (Aldebaran) is the fourth lunar mansion of the month. Under the first option, the period of study lasts five months. Under the second option, where the period is shortened to four and a half months, the start is delayed until the full moon of August–September or the conclusion is advanced. Cf. Va 13.5.

9.6 *rod's throw*: the term *śamyā* ('rod') refers to a stick (about one and a half feet long) used in preparing the sacrificial arena. A 'rod's throw' must have referred to a particular distance; the same expression is used in M 8.237, where three rod's throws and hundred arrow-lengths (about 600 feet) are juxtaposed. If the two distances are comparable, then one rod's throw should be about 200 feet.

10.1 *full-moon . . . season*: these are the full-moon days on which the seasonal sacrifices (*cāturmāsya*) are to be performed: February–March, June–July, and October–November.

10.7 *consecrated for a sacrifice*: prior to performing a sacrifice, the patron is ritually consecrated through a rite of initiation at which his head and beard are shaved. The provision of this rule refers only to such a shaving of the head, and not to the routine shaving of the beard.

10.28 *rite for a newly deceased person*: after death a person enters a liminal state (*preta*, 'ghost') in which the dead person is dangerous and impure. Rites (*ekoddiṣṭaśrāddha*) are performed for such newly deceased individuals at which Brahmins are fed. This period lasts until the rite (*sapiṇḍana* or *sapiṇḍīkaraṇa*) that formally transfers the deceased to the world of the ancestors is performed, usually on the twelfth day after death. On ancestral rites, see Kane 1962–75, iv. 334–551.

11.3 *gods who were originally humans*: the meaning of the expression *manuṣyaprakṛtīnāṃ devānām* is unclear, and the commentator Haradatta gives different possible interpretations, including gods who have human faces. He gives Nandi and Kubera as examples of gods who were formerly humans and became gods through severe austerities. A similar provision is found in G 16.34, where it reads simply 'sacrifice to humans' (*manuṣyayajña*). In explaining the latter passage, the commentator Haradatta refers to A 1.11.3, but Maskarin explains the term as simply referring to a get-together with friends (*mitramelaka*). But this can well be simply the feeding of guests that is part of the five 'great sacrifices': see B 2.11.1, 5, where the very term *manuṣyayajña* is used.

11.32 *hour*: i.e. a *muhūrta*, 48 minutes, the Indian equivalent of an hour. There are thirty *muhūrtas* in a day. Often the term *muhūrta* does not have a precise meaning of 48 minutes, but refers to a somewhat extended period of time or to a brief moment (see A 1.15.8; Friedrich 1993, 101). Thus *brāhma muhūrta* is the time of the morning sacred to Brahman (B 2.17.22 n.). Often *muhūrta* indicates an aupicious time when significant activities, such as marriage, are performed.

11.35 *outside the proper time*: the time for taking up a new section is the annual course of study described above, and that is done under the tutelage of a teacher. Only texts that have already been studied can be recited at other times. Study here refers principally to the proper method of reciting the vedic texts, with the correct accentuation, etc. Without that knowledge, which can be received only from a teacher, it is forbidden to recite a vedic text.

11.38 *legal assemblies*: the commentator Haradatta takes the term *pariṣad* here to mean legal texts (*dharmaśāstras*), which is unlikely. Bühler takes it to mean 'teaching and works of other Vedic schools', a meaning I have not found elsewhere. On legal assemblies, see G 28.49 n.

12.8–11 *accepted practice . . . vedic text*: for an explanation of these exegetical rules, see p. xli.

13.8 *During . . . syllable*: commands given by one priest to another during a sacrifice, as well as the assent to such commands, begin with OṂ. See TU 1.8.

13.10 *mutual agreement*: this appears to be a technical term for the ritual/legal obligations undertaken by both teacher and pupil when the latter ritually places himself under the former as his pupil. Such a compact requires the pupil to submit to a strict behaviour regimen and total obedience to the teacher, as described in the section on the student, A 1.2–7.

Triḥśrāvaṇa, Triḥsahavacana: the commentator Haradatta, as well as Bühler (1879–82) and Friedrich (1993) pass over these in silence. They clearly referred to some type of vedic texts or passages. I have been unable to identify them.

13.12, 15, 17 *subservience . . . play*: the meaning of the term *gati* is unclear. It is used a total of four times, three times in the negative phrase *na gatir vidyate* (A 1.13.12, 15, 17), and once positively *gatir eva tasmin* (A 1.14.5). The term appears to be used with a technical meaning by Āpastamba. A similar meaning is not attached to it in any other Dharmaśāstric text. The commentator Haradatta and, following him, Bühler take it to mean obedience. But the word for that is *śuśrūṣā*, which is used at A 1.14.6. So the two cannot be simply synonyms. Friedrich (1993) takes it to mean 'Weg', the way to heaven, and connects it with the paragraph on OṂ at A 1.13.6–9. I think he is mistaken. There appears to be a clear attempt here to distinguish a pupil's relationship to his teacher (*ācārya*) from that to other individuals who may teach him or occupy a position of authority. We see a similar distinction earlier at A 1.7.28–9, where also the teacher is distinguished from a temporary tutor appointed by the teacher and from older fellow students. It is likely that in such an academy more advanced students may have been given the task of instructing less advanced students, somewhat like graduate students acting as teaching assistants for undergraduate courses in modern universities. The term *gati* is probably also connected with the 'mutual agreement', that is, the ritual and legal contract between teacher and pupil referred to in the previous sentence (A 1.13.10). I think *gati* refers to this condition of being a pupil *vis-à-vis* the teacher, a condition that entails special privileges and obligations, such as eating a teacher's leftovers, massaging his feet, etc. It may be possible that *gati* is related to *anugamana* ('walking behind'), a term used with regard to the primary duty of a pupil: see A 2.4.26. Śabara (on PMS 6.2.6.21–2) uses the term *anugantavya* (the teacher 'to be followed') as a short-hand term for a pupil's duties. For want of a better term, I have translated it as 'subservience'.

13.16 *as also . . . students*: this extraordinarily brief (*vṛddhānāṃ tu*) aphorism of two words is extremely unclear. I think the commentator Haradatta's instinct to take *tu* ('but') as meaning 'and' (*ca*) is correct. I also think that the sequence of appointed tutors and older students found at A 1.7.28–9 is repeated here, and the term *vṛddhānām* (lit., 'of old people') refers to fellow students older than oneself. The commentator Haradatta gives three possible explanations, indicating that he is also merely guessing. Basically, according to his explanation, older students need not obey younger teachers. But the teacher was dealt with in A 1.13.10–12, and from A 1.13.13–15 the subject is tutors other than the teacher, tutors who may indeed have been older fellow students. Friedrich (1993) joins this *sūtra* with the preceding one and thinks that *tu* ('but') has somehow migrated into this from the previous *sūtra*. His translation of the two *sūtras* (1.13.14–15) does not make sense to me: 'Nicht aber gibt es den Weg von den alten.'

14.23 *use a pronoun*: the normal way to greet someone is: 'I, so-and-so [one's personal name], greet you.' But in these cases the personal name is omitted, and one simply says, 'I greet you'. See G 6.5; Va 13.44–6.

14.26–9 *He should ask . . . good health*: this is one more example of public and routinized assertion of class/caste distinctions (cf. A 1.3.28–30 n.). The first provision applies to Brahmins, and, since they are the target audience of these texts, the author does not mention them explicitly (p. xxxiv). The Sanskrit terms *kuśala* ('doing well') and *anāmaya* ('in good shape') have similar meanings, although the latter may have a physical meaning (not injured), given the military calling of Kṣatriyas.

15.1 *softly reciting prayers*: the common Sanskrit term *japa* has the technical meaning of 'murmuring' ritual formulas or texts, that is, articulating the words with the mouth and lips in such a way that they are audible only to oneself.

15.2 *water collected on the ground*: generally, this would be water in a lake or reservoir. But even 'water collected on the ground sufficient for cows to slake their thirst' (B 1.9.10) may be used for purposes of purification.

15.13–14 *When he is . . . to the ground*: in general, when a pure person sits on the same seat or couch as an impure person, the seat transmits the impurity from the latter to the former. Such a seat could be made by arranging a bed of straw properly. But when it is arranged haphazardly, it is not considered a seat. Likewise, when seats are directly on the ground and not raised up on legs, they are equivalent to the ground itself, which is always pure (A 1.16.15) and hence cannot spread impurity.

16.2 *water sufficient to reach his heart*: the issue is the quantity of water used for sipping. The largest amount is required by Brahmins, and this amount is characterized by 'sufficient to reach the heart'; possibly because one can feel the water going all the way into the chest. Here too some texts indicate a difference among the classes: Kṣatriyas become pure by sipping water sufficient to reach the throat, Vaiśyas with water taken into the mouth, and Śūdras and women by water touching the lips: B 1.8.23; Va 3.31–4.

16.7 *touch the organs*: one rubs water on the eyes with the thumb and ring finger, either simultaneously or one eye at a time; on the nostrils with the thumb and forefinger; on the ears with the thumb and little finger.

16.14 *touch water*: the Sanskrit term *upaspṛśet* is ambiguous. The commentator Haradatta explains that in some instances one should bathe, in others sip water, and in yet others merely touch water.

16.16 *not fit to be eaten*: the Dharma texts make a clear distinction between two types of food that should not be eaten. The first is 'unfit food' given the technical term *abhojya*, and the second is 'forbidden food', *abhakṣya*. The first type consists of food that one is normally permitted to eat, such as meat and rice, but that has been rendered unfit to be eaten because it has come into contact with something or someone impure. Thus, food in which one finds a hair or which has been licked by a dog is 'unfit' to be eaten. 'Forbidden food', on the other hand, are types of food that are never permitted, such as garlic and the meat of certain animals (see M 1.113; 5.1–26). Although the two terms are not used exclusively in this technical sense, we can detect a clear distinction between these two types of food that should not be eaten: see A 1.26.7.

16.21 *Food that . . . eaten*: not all food that becomes impure needs to be thrown away as 'unfit' to be eaten. Some, like the ones mentioned here, can be purified, generally by sprinkling it with water or mixing it with ghee, and then consumed.

16.24 *filth*: the Sanskrit term *amedhya*, like its quasi-synonym *mala*, may refer to any type of filthy substance. Most frequently, however, these terms refer specifically to substances that come out of the human body, such as urine, excrement, and phlegm. Sources often refer to twelve such substances: 'Oily exudations, semen, blood, fat, urine, faeces, snot, ear-wax, phlegm, tears, discharge of eyes, and sweat—these are the twelve impurities (*malas*) of men (M 5.135; Vi 22.81). See Olivelle 1998.

16.27 *mouse droppings or mouse parts*: Böhtlingk (1885*b*, 520) emends *mūṣakalāṅgam* to *mūṣakalaṅkam*. The translation then would be 'in which there are mouse droppings', eliminating mouse parts. Bühler (1886*b*) rejects this emendation.

17.7 *terrace*: the commentator Haradatta, whom Bühler follows, interprets the term *prāsāda* to mean a wooden platform.

17.31 *The meat . . . sacrifice*: I have been unable to trace this passage in the SB, which is the text normally referred to by Āpastamba as the text of the Vājasaneyins (White Yajurveda). But at SB

3.1.2.21 there is a discussion of the cow and the ox as containing the vigour of all other species of animals and a prohibition against eating their meat. But it cites a sarcastic saying by Yājñavalkya (the reputed author of the White Yajurveda) that he, for one, will eat it if it is tender!

17.36 *Vārdhrāṇasa cranes and Lakṣmaṇa cranes*: Haradatta and, following him, Bühler take Lakṣmaṇa as a qualifier of Vārdhrāṇasa. The translation would then be: 'with the exception of the Lakṣmaṇa variety of Vārdhrāṇasa cranes'.

17.37 *Animals with five claws*: this is an ancient and widespread rule forbidding the eating of animals with five nails or claws, with the exception of some. Here seven such exceptions are listed, whereas the standard rule contains only five exceptions. The general formulation of this rule is: 'The five five-clawed animals may be eaten', meaning that five-clawed animals other than those enumerated are forbidden. This is an example of the so-called *parisaṃkhyā* injunction, which is a prohibition couched as an injunction. Thus, the intent of the rule is to prohibit five-clawed animals, not to enjoin the eating of the five listed animals. Thus, someone may avoid eating *all* five-clawed animals, even those listed, without violating this injunction. The forbidding of animals with five 'nails' may indeed be a residue of a proscription of cannibalism, since human beings are among animals with five nails. See G 17.27; B 1.12.5; Va 14.39; M 5.17–18. For a detailed study, see Jamison 1998.

18.11 *as during . . . penitential act*: here I follow the compelling emendation suggested by Böhtlingk (1885*b*, 520) *yatra prāyaścittam* for *yatrāprāyaścittam*, although I recognize that the latter is the *lectio difficilior* and therefore has a greater claim to be the original. Bühler, following Haradatta, translates: 'He shall not eat in a house where (the host) performs a rite which is not a rite of penance, whilst he ought to perform a penance.' This appears to be rather far-fetched and convoluted, whereas the alternative is rather simple: one is not permitted to eat at the house of a man who has committed a sin and is in the process of performing the required penance.

18.23 *prior to . . . for a sacrifice*: the reference is to a Soma sacrifice. Part of the ritual process consists of the ritual purchase of the Soma plants to be used in the sacrifice. This rule forbids eating the food of a man consecrated for the sacrifice (see A 1.10.7 n.) before that purchase.

18.24–6 *Only after . . . remainder*: a similar provision is found in AB 2.9.

19.1 *debtor*: I follow the sensible emendation suggested by Böhtlingk (1885*b*, 520), reading *ṛṇaka* ('debtor') for *aṇika*, a term of very doubtful meaning interpreted by Haradatta as 'a man who learns the Veda from his son'.

19.15 *abortionist*: the Sanskrit term *bhrūṇahan* has two meanings: a killer of a foetus (abortionist) and a killer of a learned Brahmin. The VkhG (1.1), giving the definitions of eight types of Brahmins in terms of their learning, defines a *bhrūṇa* as a Brahmin who has mastered the Veda, set up the ritual fires, and offered a Soma sacrifice. See Kane 1962–75, ii. 131, 148 n., 334; iii. 612 n. 1161. The Dharma literature uses the term with both meanings. At G 21.9 it means an abortionist, while at B 1.18.13 it clearly refers to a murderer of a Brahmin. At other places, such as here and in most passages, it is impossible to tell which meaning is intended. Indeed, both meanings may be intended in many of these passages; Va 20.23, in fact, gives both definitions of the term.

20.9 *both worlds*: i.e. this world and the next.

21.12 *actions that make people sordid*: Āpastamba uses *aśuci* ('impure') eight times (1.21.12; 1.21.19; 1.29.14; 1.29.15; 1.29.17; 1.29.18; 2.12.22; at 1.2.29 it means filth). Certainly in six of these and in all likelihood also in a seventh (A 1.29.14), *aśuci* is used not as an adjective but as a substantive with reference to a type of sinner. The sins that create this state are called *aśucikara*, 'making someone *aśuci*'. Āpastamba does not know or does not recognize the distinction common in later literature between *mahāpātaka* and *upapātaka*, grievous and secondary sins causing loss of caste. He begins the section on sins by stating that 'social interaction with outcastes (*patita*) is not permitted, as also with degraded (*apapātra*) people' (A 1.21.5–6). Then he describes one group of sins which he calls *patanīyāni* ('causing loss of caste': A 1.21.7–11), and a second group of sins which he calls *aśucikarāṇi* ('causing someone to be *aśuci*: A 1.21.12–19). These two groups must correspond to the two categories of people in the introductory statement; an *aśuci*, therefore, is an *apapātra*, a degraded person with whom social interaction is forbidden. For similar use of this term, see G 9.11; 9.16; 16.46; 23.22; B 2.2.15; 2.2.23; 2.2.24. I have discussed this in detail in Olivelle 1998.

22.4 *cave*: This probably refers to the cavity of the heart: cf. KaU 1.14; 2.12; 3.1; 4.6–7; MuU 2.1.8, 10; 3.1.7.

22.6–7 *Follow what . . . without compare*: these two verses are very obscure and possibly corrupt. The translation is tentative.

24.1 *If someone . . . enmity*: although the person committing the crime is not identified, a Brahmin is clearly meant (p. xxxiv). Bühler's translation 'for the expiation of his sin' follows the commentator and is obviously wrong, as he himself acknowledges in a note on this passage. The motive for giving the cattle was to appease the vengeance of the murdered man's relatives, a common feature in ancient penal codes. This motive is stated also in B 1.19.1. See Lingat 1973, 64.

24.8–9 *foetus . . . period*: these two provisions are linked by the fact that in the first the foetus *may* be a male Brahmin and killing it would entail the murder of a Brahmin (see the reason given in Va 20.24 n.), whereas in the second the woman is in her fertile period and killing her is tantamount to killing a future Brahmin (cf. G 22.12–13). Here there is the added possibility that the woman is pregnant. A woman soon after her menstruation is called by the technical term *ātreyī,* which is given an interesting etymological spin in Va 20.35–6. For a detailed study of this provision, see Jamison 1991, 213–23.

24.23 *Law and profit*: these are technical terms for two of the three traditional spheres of human endeavour (*puruṣārtha*): Law/righteousness (*dharma*), profit/wealth/power (*artha*), and pleasure (*kāma*). When they are in conflict with each other, one is expected to choose the higher—profit over pleasure, and righteousness over both profit and pleasure. In each of these fields expert treatises were composed: the Dharmaśāstras for the first, treatises on government (Arthaśāstra) for the second, and texts on erotics (Kāmasūtra) for the third.

25.2 *metal column*: the meaning of the Sanskrit term *sūrmi* is not altogether clear. It is certainly a cylindrical object made of metal. Bühler, following the lead of Haradatta, translates it as a 'metal image of a woman'. The column may have been hollow, because at A 1.28.15 the criminal is said to enter it.

25.10 *every fourth mealtime*: two mealtimes a day are acknowledged for humans, morning and evening. Eating every fourth mealtime amounts to eating one day in the morning and the next day in the evening, thus skipping two mealtimes between meals.

26.8 *cooked oblation*: the procedure for cooked oblations (*pākayajña*) are given at the very beginning of most Gṛhyasūtras: see SG 1.1.

26.14 *moon's change* (parvan): this may refer simply to the new- and full-moon days; or else, to the new moon, the eighth day after the new moon, the full moon, and the fourteenth day after the full moon. See also B 1.21.22.

27.1 *great river*: generally defined as a river that flows into the sea (cf. B 1.11.41).

27.5 *winter and spring*: winter (*hemanta*) is the two months from mid-November to mid-January (the lunar months of Āgrahāyaṇa and Pauṣa), and spring is the two months from mid-January to mid-March (Māgha and Phālguna).

27.10 *decoction*: Haradatta interprets this term (*kaṣāya*) as referring to any intoxicating drink other than the type called *surā* (see Va 20.19 n.).

27.11 *serving a person of the black class*: according to some commentators, this refers to having sexual contact with a woman of the 'black class', i.e. Śūdra.

28.2–4 *There are . . . crime*: the text is somewhat elliptic and possibly corrupt: see Böhtlingk (1885*b*, 522) and Bühler's (1886*b*, 537) reply. In all likelihood, the statements following the direct quotation also form part of Vārṣyāyaṇi's opinion.

28.9 *to bring about male progeny*: the reading *putratvasya* is problematic and possibly corrupt. Haradatta's explanation is far-fetched and rightly rejected by Böhtlingk (1885*b*, 522), who offers the conjecture *putratve 'sya* with the translation: 'dabei, dass er Sohn wird, das er zur Welt gelangt u. s. w.' I think Böhtlingk's instinct is right, even if we do not accept his conjectural reading. The meaning appears to be that a mother undergoes many rites to ensure that a male child is born, and once born does numerous things to make sure that he grows into adulthood. The maternal link created by these activities cannot be ruptured completely under any circumstances (see Va 8.16).

28.18 *in the above manner*: the reference is to the penance described in *sūtra* 11.

29.14 *semen of a sordid man*: I take *aśuciśuklam* as a compound (see A 1.21.12 n.). Haradatta and Bühler (as also Böhtlingk 1885*b*, 523) take *aśuci* as an adjective; the translation then would be 'impure semen'. See Friedrich 1993, 135; Olivelle 1998.

29.18 *in accordance . . . committed*: this may refer to whether the sin was committed intentionally or not (A 1.29.2–4) and/or to the frequency of the sin (A 1.26.7).

30.4 *bath-graduate*: the term *snātaka* means 'one who has taken a bath', and specifically a student who after completing his studies has taken the ritual bath that signals the conclusion of studentship. It appears that Āpastamba distinguishes a bath-graduate from a mere student who has returned home, a subject he deals with at A 1.7.19 f. A bath-graduate is accorded special status and privileges (A 2.8.6; 2.27.21; G 6.24). It is clear that the title of bath-graduate attaches to an individual not merely between the conclusion of studentship and marriage, as generally believed by scholars, but also after marriage. Many of the provisions given under the topic of bath-graduate imply that he is married and is the head of a household (A 1.32.1–2; G 9.25).

30.9 *When there . . . prevails*: for the general rule that when there is a conflict between injunction in vedic (*śruti*) and traditional texts (*smṛti*) the former prevails, see p. xlii. The reason for inserting this statement here, according to Haradatta, is that a person who performs the daily fire sacrifice (*agnihotra*) should not go outside the village, because the Veda prescribes that rite is to be performed in the home. That rule takes precedence over the previous rule that requires a person to perform the normal twilight worship (*sandhyā*) outside the village.

30.15 *spreading something on the ground*: Haradatta says that one should spread grass or some such material on the ground and void urine or excrement on it and not directly on the ground (see B 1.10.10).

32.9 *Palāśa wood*: Palāśa (see Appendix III) is a sacred tree and its branches and wood are used for ritual purposes (see A 1.2.38). It should not be used for making the items listed in this prohibition, all of which come into contact with impure parts of the body. Cf. A 1.8.22 n.

32.11 *until nightfall*: Bühler, following the commentator Haradatta, translates: 'Let him be awake from midnight.' This translation is inaccurate: the particle *ā* means 'until' and not 'from' and *niśā* means 'night' and not 'midnight'. See Böhtlingk 1885*b*, 523.

32.15 *thinking . . . forbidden*: the reason for such a conclusion, according to Haradatta, is that the next day happens to be a day on which recitation is forbidden (see A 1.9–10).

32.16 *rest . . . something*: the meaning of *apaśśayīta* is unclear. Haradatta and Bühler take it to be an altered form of *apāśrayīta*, and I have followed their lead in taking it to be a Prakritic form. Böhtlingk (1885*b*, 523) rejects this and gives the conjecture *apaśayīta*, 'er lege sich abseits, in einiger Entfernung nieder'. The point of the prescription, however, is that he should *not* go back to sleep.

32.24 *This is how . . . Kumālana*: Haradatta gives the story behind this elliptic quote. A certain seer had two pupils, Dharmaprahrāda and Kumālana. Once the two brought two large bundles of firewood from the forest and threw them carelessly into the teacher's house. One of these hit the teacher's son and killed him. The teacher asked them who killed his son, and both denied responsibility. The teacher then summoned Death and asked him. Death did not want to give a direct answer and, weeping, indirectly pointed to Dharmaprahrāda as the guilty party by saying that the guilt fell 'not on Kumālana'. See A 2.12.21.

32.26 *crossing a river by swimming*: an obvious reason for this is the danger it poses: G 9.32. Another reason is given in Va 19.25: swimming across a river is a way to avoid paying the toll at a river crossing. A man who resorts to it is fined one hundred times the applicable toll.

BOOK TWO

1.4 *On new- and full-moon days*: literally, 'on the days of the moon's change' (A 1.26.14 n.), but here the reference is specifically to the new- and full-moon days: see SG 1.3.

1.7–12 *On the anniversary . . . every anniversary day*: my translation of this passage is based on the interpretation of the ambiguous expression *etasminn ahani* (lit., 'on that day') as referring to the day of the couple's marriage. This is Haradatta's interpretation, although he acknowledges that other commentators did not agree with him. At AG 3.8.7 the expression *etad ahar* ('that day') clearly refers to the wedding day, and I think the expression has the same meaning here. Friedrich (1993, 145) thinks that this expression refers to the 'days of the moon's change' of the *sūtra* 4; but that is unlikely because the term there (*parvasu*) is in the plural and, as Haradatta himself observes, unlikely to be referred to by a pronoun in the singular.

1.17 *in season*: the 'season' for the wife is the days of the month when she is fertile, which were thought to be the days immediately following her menstrual period. During that time a husband was obligated to have sexual intercourse with his wife. AG 3.9.1 recommends even days from the fourth day (that is, the day when the period of menstrual impurity ends with the wife's bath) to the sixteenth following the start of the menstrual flow.

1.18–19 *And if his wife . . . Brāhmaṇa passage*: the Brāhmaṇa passage referred to may be TS 2.5.1.5, where it is said that women obtained from Indra the gift of becoming pregnant after their period and of enjoying sex right up to the time of delivery. Accordingly, Haradatta is right to take *dāra eva* ('only regarding the wife') to mean *dāra eva sakāme sati*, 'only when the wife wishes'. The intent appears to be that a good man should eschew such intercourse, but if the woman wants it (women being viewed as unable to control their passions), he should oblige because of this vedic text. Cf. Va 5.8; 12.24.

3.14 *While . . . one day*: the final offering is described at A 2.4.8. According to Haradatta, the formula here is TA 10.67 (= MNU 465–6).

3.16–23 *first six . . . last four formulas*: these formulas are given in the TA 10.67 (= MNU 457–9), each formula ending with Svāhā: 1. To Fire; 2. To All-gods; 3. To Firm Earth; 4. To Firm Abode; 5. To Unshakable Abode; 6. To Fire who makes the offering flawless;

7. To Dharma; 8. To Adharma; 9. To Waters; 10. To Plants and Trees; 11. To Fiends and Divine Hosts; 12. To Home Deities; 13. To Hosts nearby; 14 To Lords of the Hosts nearby; 15. To All Creatures.

4.1–8 *With the ritual formula . . . at night*: these formulas are also found at TA 10.67 (= MNU 460–2), and all end with Svāhā: 1. To Love; 2. To Mid-space; 3. What stirs, bestirs, and moves, Bhāga by name—to that name; 4. To Earth; 5. To Mid-space; 6. To Sky; 7. To Sun; 8. To Moon; 9. To Constellations; 10. To Indra; 11. To Bṛhaspati; 12. To Prajāpati; 13. To Brahman. The last two are special: 14. Svadhā to Ancestors, to Gods Svāhā; 15. Hail to Rudra, Lord of Animals, Svāhā.

4.4. *seat of Brahman*: Haradatta explains that this is the centre of the house. Others explain it as the place where the Brahman priest sits, that is, to the south of the sacred fire.

5.11 *interrupting*: I follow Böhtlingk's (1885*b*, 524) interpretation. Bühler, following Haradatta, translates: 'He shall not contradict his teacher', which is also the interpretation of Friedrich (1993).

6.4 *one branch . . . Vedas*: Haradatta thinks the meaning is that the person has studied the Veda of his own branch, because that was the accepted meaning of the term *śrotriya* ('vedic scholar'). It is difficult to see how the Sanskrit expression *ekaikām* could be made to elicit that meaning. For vedic 'branch', see p. xxii.

7.2 *fire within the guests*: this may refer to the fire in the stomach thought to be responsible for digestion or to the breaths conceived of as fires: see B 2.12. For the other fires, see App. I.1.

7.6–10 *When a man . . . final bath*: here the various acts of hospitality towards a guest are equated with parts of a Soma sacrifice. Viṣṇu steps are the four steps a person offering the sacrifice takes at its conclusion. He recites a ritual formula at each step, and every formula begins with 'You are the step of Viṣṇu'. See Kane 1962–75, ii. 1083. Every sacrifice concludes with the final bath known as *avabhṛtha.*

8.3 *savoury dishes*: the meaning of *rasa* here and elsewhere is unclear. It can refer to any tasty beverages, spices, seasonings, or condiments, and thus to sweet or savoury foods.

8.10–13 *The Veda . . . principal texts*: this section appears to be somewhat out of context, the only connection being with *sūtra* 5 dealing with a man capable of reciting the Veda. This passage distinguishes the 'Veda' from its six supplements. The opponent objects, because, according to Haradatta, the ritual expositions contain material dealing with vedic rituals and should therefore be regarded as the 'Veda'. Thus the number of supplements should be five and not six. The author answers that supplementary texts cannot be given the same name as the principal, a doctrine articulated in the PMS 1.3.11–14.

11.14 *for a wife . . . supplementary*: the meaning appears to be that the wife who participated at the establishment of the husband's sacred fires must be present for all subsequent rites using those fires, effectively making it impossible for him to divorce her or to take another wife.

11.15 *lineage*: the term *gotra* refers to a family line that is connected to a single ancient teacher as a common ancestor. The definition of this relationship is quite vague and often confused in the literature: see Kane 1962–75, ii. 479–501. *Gotra* is connected to another ancient Indian kinship category called *pravara* based on having the same ancestral seer. Each *gotra* may have several *pravaras*. 'Connection of gotra and pravara may be stated thus: Gotra is the latest ancestor or one of the latest ancestors of a person by whose name his family has been known for generations; while pravara is constituted by the sages or in some cases the remote ancestor alone' (Kane, 1962–75, ii. 497). Two persons related through the one or the other are not permitted to marry each other.

12.10 *mixing . . . fires*: this may mean that one should not put a firebrand from a sacred fire into a common fire, or vice versa. Haradatta explains it as forbidding a person from bringing to one place fires burning in different places.

13.5 *A son . . . fathers him*: there was an intense debate in ancient India about the person to whom a son belonged. Some maintained that the husband of the mother, being 'the owner of the field', owned the son. The example for this position is a seed and a field. If one man plants a mango seed (i.e. his semen) in another man's field (i.e. wife), the mangoes produced from that tree belong not to the man who owns the seed but to the man who owns the field (M 9.42–3). This anxiety is revealed in the advice that a man should not marry a girl without brothers, because the girl's father may have secretly appointed her to bear sons for him, and thus owns the field (G 28.20). On the other hand, as this passage indicates (cf. G 18.9), when the protection of the wife is uppermost in the mind, the opposite view is maintained. Cf. Va 17.6–11.

14.2 *relative belonging to the same ancestry*: the Sanskrit term *sapiṇḍa* refers to a group of close relatives, but there is great controversy in the tradition with regard to both its meaning and the extent of the group covered. One interpretation takes *piṇḍa* (lit., 'round lump') to mean a bodily particle and *sapiṇḍa* to mean people who through birth have bodily particles in common. In general, the relationship extends to six generations before and after the father and five generations before and after the mother. Another interpretation takes *piṇḍa* to mean the balls of rice offered to ancestors and *sapiṇḍa* to mean people who are connected through these ancestral offerings. See B1.11.9. This subject is treated in detail by Kane (1962–75, ii. 452–78).

14.7 *black produce of the earth*: according to Haradatta, either black grains, such as beans, or iron.

14.8 *The chariot . . . father*: some connect this sentence with the previous one and translate: '. . . eldest son, as well as the father's chariot and the household furniture' (Friedrich 1993; Bühler 1879–82, i. 134 n. 8). I agree with Haradatta and Bühler that this is a separate sentence for two reasons. First, the syntax with the genitive *pituḥ* ('of/for father') coming as the second word followed by a further item and then by *ca* ('and') replicates the syntax of the next *sūtra* regarding the wife. Second, Āpastamba appears to refute this view about the share of the eldest son (*sūtras* 6–7) in *sūtras* 10–15, and the division of estate between husband and wife (*sūtras* 8–9) in *sūtras* 16–20.

14.10 *that*: the antecedent of this pronoun, though left unstated, is clearly *sūtras* 6–7: see the previous note.

14.13 *Experts . . . for a mate*: The argument is based on a fundamental principle of vedic exegesis that distinguishes injunctions, which alone are meaningful with regard to Law (*dharma*) from 'explanatory passages' (*arthavāda*) that do not have injunctive force (PMS 6.7.30). The latter type of passages are further subdivided into metaphor (*guṇavāda*), reiteration (*anuvāda*), and historical statement (*bhūtārthavāda*). Here Āpastamba puts the texts cited by the opponent into the second subdivision. For a detailed discussion of these exegetical principles, see Kane 1962–75, v. 1225–56. The passages quoted cannot be identified in any known vedic text.

15.1 *The above . . . families*: the meaning is that customs of a particular region and family are authoritative *vis-à-vis* people belonging to that region or family unless those customs go against vedic provisions, a principle stated above in *sūtra* 10.

15.5 *principal elder*: Haradatta defines as teacher, mother, and father: see A 1.6.32 n.

15.9 *They should . . . to do*: the deceased recognize that the water is offered to them through the recitation of the proper ritual formula: 'I offer this water to you, N. N.', stating the personal and family name. For the interesting comment about women as the repositories of traditional custom, see also A 2.29.11, 15.

15.25 *traditional teaching*: the reference is to the authoritative texts of the tradition called *smṛti* that are distinct from the Vedas: see p. xli.

16.1 *In ancient times . . . behind*: this is an old belief recorded in ancient vedic texts: SB 2.3.4.4. See Olivelle 1993, 37–41.

16.3 *In this rite . . . fire*: in the technical ritual vocabulary 'deity' (*devatā*) refers not directly to a god but to that with reference to which an offering is put in the fire (Kane 1962–75, v. 1207). So, the 'deity' can be an ancestor, a demon, or some other being. An ancestral offering is a meal, and the food is offered there in the mouth of the participating Brahmins, their mouths substituting for the offertorial fire in which offerings are normally placed.

17.4 *blood . . . pupillage*: for lineage, see A 2.11.15 n. Officiating at a sacrifice establishes a spiritual bond between the priest and the patron of the sacrifice. A pupil and teacher, likewise, become spiritually related.

17.21 *alongside whom they eat*: at a funerary offering the assembled Brahmins sit in one row on seats of sacred grass spread on the floor. An especially holy and learned Brahmin (see list in G 15.28) is viewed as transmitting his purity to those who sit on the same row as he. The inverse of such a man is a person who defiles those alongside whom they eat (G 21.11).

17.22 *four types . . . sacred fires*: the four types of sacrifices are: horse sacrifice, sacrifice of all possessions (Sarvamedha), human sacrifice (Puruṣamedha), and funeral offering (Pitṛmedha). But see Va 26.10 n. The five fires are the three used in vedic rituals: householder's, offertorial, and southern; as well as the hearth (*āvasathya*) and the hall (*sabhya*) fires. See App. I.1.

17.23–5 *An ancestral . . . eclipse*: the last *sūtra* is not found in some manuscripts, and Haradatta says that it was not recognized by northerners. He also thinks that it should come immediately after *sūtra* 23. The meaning appears to be that when the night falls after the start of an ancestral offering, it should be suspended until the next morning, unless there happens to be a lunar eclipse that night; in any case the participants have to fast until the entire rite is completed.

18.4 *forty-eight-year vow*: according to Haradatta, this is the studentship (*brahmacarya*) lasting forty-eight years (see A 1.2.12).

18.14–16 *He should have . . . the altar*: this appears to be an occult rite. Ancestors normally occupy the southern side. Thus, when the Brahmins are on the northern side, the performer will be able to see both. Haradatta thinks that it is the power of this rite that makes the normally invisible ancestors visible to the performer.

18.19 *Tiṣya*: also called Puṣya (γ, δ, and θ Cancri), it is the eighth in the sidereal monthly cycle of twenty-seven lunar mansions (*nakṣatra*), while Maghā (α, γ, ε, ζ, η, and μ Leonis) is the tenth.

20.1 *one measure each*: the term *droṇa* technically refers to a weight of approximately 21.25 lb. or 9.6 kg. The meaning appears to be that for each rite requiring sesame, such as food and anointing, such a quantity should be used if possible.

20.3 *Great King*: Haradatta identifies the god as Vaiśravaṇa, the patronymic of the god Kubera.

21.1 *four orders of life*: for a detailed study of this entire chapter, see Olivelle 1993.

21.6 *novice student*: two types of students are identified here: the novice student, who spends a number of years following his initiation at his teacher's house studying the Veda (dealt with in *sūtra* 3); and the permanent student, who lives with the teacher all his life (cf. A 1.4.29). The latter alone is considered an order of life (*āśrama*).

21.8 *From that very state*: that is, from the state of a novice student.

21.17 *said later on*: the exact meaning of *param* is unclear. Friedrich (1993, 193) takes it to mean 'the next order of life', namely, the forest hermit; but that is quite unlikely. Haradatta takes it as referring to the pain felt in the next world, but this expression generally refers to some topic dealt with in the text. I think the term refers to the later discussion (A 1.23.3–24.14) regarding the relative superiority of the orders of life where Āpastamba attacks the position of those who take the celibate orders to be the best.

22.16 *give one*: possibly to his wife who remains behind at home.

22.23 *sitting . . . bare ground*: Bühler (1879–82) and Friedrich (1993) interpret *anupastīrṇe* as a dual qualifying *śayyāsane*. The translation would then be: 'His seat and bed is uncovered.' But it is anomalous for a man who lives in the open air to have chairs and beds! I agree with Haradatta that *anupastīrṇe* is a locative going with an implied *deśe* ('on uncovered ground'). The meaning then is that he has his seat and bed on an uncovered piece of ground, that is, he sits and sleeps on bare ground.

24.13 *bodies . . . up above*: the seven ancient seers were believed to be visible in the night sky as the seven stars in the Big Dipper.

25.12 *of Vibhītaka seeds*: Haradatta and Bühler think that the dice were made of Vibhītaka wood. See, however, Falk 1986, 103. Falk also has the most detailed and up-to-date discussion of the ancient Indian game of dice.

26.6–7 *nine miles, couple of miles*: a *yojana* is approximately 9 miles or 14.5 kilometres, and a *krośa* is one-quarter of that, approximately 2.25 miles or 3.6 kilometres.

27.17 *blindfolded*: the Sanskrit *cakṣunirodha* is ambivalent. It may also mean to blind, a meaning favoured by Friedrich (1993, 203). But that is unlikely, because Dharma texts generally prohibit the corporal punishment of Brahmins.

The Dharmasūtra of Gautama

1.4 *When . . . option*: this is a basic principle of vedic exegesis. The standard example given in the exegetical literature is the fact that some vedic texts enjoin barley for ritual purposes and others rice, creating a conflict. So, a person may use either. But for there to be an option the injunction should have equal force. Since the Veda has greater authority than either traditional texts or custom, when an injunction in such a text or a custom is in conflict with a vedic prescription, then the latter has to be followed. See G 11.20; A 2.14.10; Kane 1962–75, v. 1250.

1.25 *bent . . . sacrificial post*: the sacrificial post, to which the animal to be immolated is tied, is cut from a tree with green leaves. It must not be crooked and must be bent towards a direction other than the south: Kane 1962–75, ii. 1110–12.

1.28 *If, while . . . down*: the complication created by Sanskrit sandhi makes the reading ambiguous: *ucchiṣṭo 'nidhāya* where the negative 'a' is elided and in manuscripts often left unmarked (no *avagraha*); thus the latter term may be read as a positive or a negative. The commentator Maskarin reads without the negative 'a' and interprets this to mean that one should place what is in the hand on the ground and then sip water. Haradatta, on the other hand, reads it with the negative 'a', but says that one should place any food on the ground but not other articles, such as clothes. See Bühler's long note to this passage.

1.36 *cavities of his head*: they are the eyes, ears, and nostrils: see A 1.16.7 n. Water is applied also on the chest above the heart: B 4.3.5.

1.43 *earth and water*: in ancient India soft earth, as well as other substances such as ash and cowdung, were used with water as cleansing agents, much like soap powders today. It was used on the body and to clean utensils. Other substances, such as ash and cowdung, were used for utensils made of different materials: B 1.14.5.

1.45 *In cases . . . Veda*: this applies to purifications carried out at a vedic ritual. Utensils used in a sacrifice, for example, are cleansed in the manner prescribed by vedic texts. See A 1.17.13; B 1.8.50.

1.48 *vital organs*: according to the commentators, these are the sense organs of the head, the same as the 'cavities of the head': G 1.36 n.

1.51 *The five . . . Truth*: this probably refers to the Vyāhṛti Sāman (see App. I.2).

2.9 *only after . . . some*: the ritual of the first shave (called *godāna*, 'gift of cow') is performed when the young man is 16 (see Pandey 1969). According to some, the daily bath is required only after this ceremony. See G 2.13, where the student is forbidden to bathe or clean his teeth, and A 1.2.28 n.

2.34 *legal age*: according to the commentators, the legal age is 16.

3.1 *He*: i.e. a student who has completed his vedic studies (see G 3.36 n.).

3.13 *rainy season*: the rainy season or monsoon lasts for about four months from June to October. This period, during which travel was difficult and sometimes dangerous, is generally considered holy in India. Wandering ascetics are not permitted to roam about during the rains and are required to set up a stable residence in one place, generally in or near a village from which they can obtain their almsfood.

3.27 *He kindles . . . recluses*: a hermit gives up the normal ritual fires he used as a common householder and sets up a new ritual fire. The procedure for setting up this fire appears to have been given in a treatise on that subject. Such a treatise in mentioned in B 2.11.14, and a procedure for setting up the hermit's fire is given in Vkh 2.1.

3.36 *single order of life*: the position that the householder's life is the only legitimate order for adults is expressed also in B 2.11.27. For an extensive study of this early view of conservative Brahmins, see Olivelle 1993, 83–91. Given that Gautama frequently refers to the orders of life (see p. xxxi), it is likely that his intent here is not to issue a blanket prohibition of the orders but to forbid any order other than a householder's for a student who has completed his vedic studies (see G 3.1n.).

express vedic texts: these are texts that are actually available and recited in various vedic branches. They are distinguished from vedic texts whose existence has to be inferred through the evidence of traditional texts or customs: see A 1.4.8–10 and p. xli.

4.26 *as also . . . woman*: the meaning is that a child of a Śūdra woman fathered by a man of a higher class, even though this does not constitute a reversed order, is nevertheless outside the Law.

5.30 *to a king and to a vedic scholar*: the Sanskrit lacks the word 'and' (*ca*) after *śrotriya* ('vedic scholar'), and because of this both Haradatta and Maskarin, as well as Bühler, takes 'vedic scholar' as qualifying the king. The translation would then be: '. . . to a king who is a vedic scholar'. I think this interpretation is unlikely, both because in these documents the term *śrotriya* always refers to Brahmins and because it is highly unlikely that somebody would slight a king simply because he is not considered to be learned.

5.32 *welcome water*: this consists of perfumed water with flowers and forms an integral part of the welcoming ceremony for important guests.

6.24 *extremely old people, the sick*: literally, 'those who are in the tenth decade of life' and 'those who deserve consideration'.

8.14 *Impregnation . . . initiation*: these are the rites of passage connected with birth, infancy, and childhood. The impregnation rite is performed soon after marriage to assure successful pregnancies. The quickening of a male foetus takes place in the third month of pregnancy to assure the birth of a boy (cf. Va 20.24 n.). The ritual parting of the wife's hair takes place in the seventh month of pregnancy to assure a safe delivery. The birth rite is performed for the newborn baby, and its naming ceremony is done on the tenth or twelfth day after birth. The first feeding with solid food takes place in the sixth month, and the tonsure, the first cutting of the baby's hair, between the first and seventh year. See Pandey 1969.

8.15 *four vows*: according to the commentators, the reference is to the special vows undertaken to study each of the four Vedas. Other vows are also associated with vedic study: see Bühler 1879–82, i. 216 n. 15.

9.7 *without a good reason*: the commentator Haradatta cites a verse giving the reasons for letting the beard grow: 'During his sixth and sixteenth year, during the year of his marriage, and when his wife is pregnant, he should refrain from using a razor.' See also G 16.3.

9.10 *drawn out*: this refers to water that has been drawn out of a well, pond, or river and kept in a pot (A 2.5.6; G 5.15). Such water should be strained with a cloth water strainer (Va 6.14). This rule applies only when one sips water from a pot; when one sips water at a pond or river, one may sip while standing.

9.21 *bhagāla in place of kapāla*: both Sanskrit terms mean 'skull'. *Kapāla* may well have been a more direct or coarser word, while *bhagāla* may have been a more polite way of referring to a skull.

9.53 *not carry . . . another*: the meaning of the term *kulaṃkula* is uncertain. The commentators give diverse opinions, indicating that they are simply guessing. Bühler, following Haradatta's lead, translates: 'Let him not be a stay-at-home.' The term occurs also at Va 12.8 and SG 4.12.11, where Oldenberg translates it as 'a wanderer from house to house'. But in the SG this term is given alongside 'reviler, slanderer, prattler', and I think in that context the term may mean 'carrying tales from one family to another'.

9.63–4 *livelihood . . . gods*: I think the commentators and Bühler have overinterpreted the expression *yogakṣema* (which I have translated 'livelihood') as 'obtaining what one does not have and securing what one has'. 'Gods' here refer to divine images. The meaning may be that a Brahmin in dire straits may go to a temple to obtain assistance from the temple funds, which technically are owned by the deity.

10.18 *cows or Brahmins*: this probably means that defeated warriors who debased themselves by calling themselves cows or Brahmins, both considered inviolable, are to be spared their lives.

10.21 *mounts*: this term may refer to horses, elephants, and/or chariots.

10.29 *he should . . . them*: the antecedent of 'them' is unclear. The commentator Haradatta takes it as referring to the subjects he is obliged to protect, while Maskarin thinks that it refers to his responsibility to collect taxes and duties.

11.16 *welfare*: for the expression *yogakṣema*, see G 9.63–4 n.

12.8 *fined a hundred*: the currency of payment is left unstated. The commentator Haradatta states that traditionally fines are calculated in terms of the copper Kārṣapaṇa (often called simply Paṇa), a coin with a weight of probably 9.33 gm. There are, according to Haradatta, twenty Māṣas to a Kārṣapaṇa (cf. G 12.22, 29), and four Kṛṣṇalas (another name for Raktikā) to a Māṣa (G 12.18). Coinage in India varied widely both geographically and over time; so it is impossible to determine with precision either the weight or the relative value of these coins.

12.29 *five . . . for twenty*: the meaning is that the monthly interest rate is five Māṣas for twenty Kārṣapaṇas (= 400 Māṣas; see previous note). Thus the monthly interest rate is 1.25 per cent, which converts to an annual rate of 15 per cent. The same rule is given in Va 2.50. The interest rates given in M 8.140 and Y 2.37 agree with this.

12.31 *If the loan . . . doubled*: this rule is called *dāmdupaṭ* in modern times. The total amount of interest payable on a loan can never exceed the loan. So, at any time the total amount payable by a debtor is twice the amount of the loan, that is, the loan plus 100 per cent in interest. See Kane 1962–75, iii. 419–24; Lariviere 1989, ii. 30, 59.

12.34–5 *The types . . . collateral*: the cyclical rate is often translated as 'compound interest', which is misleading. This is really simple interest but payable only at the end of the loan period together with the principal (see Lariviere 1989, ii. 59). The periodic rate is generally payable each month (G 12.29). The contractual rate is variable, either above or below the normal rate of interest, depending on the reliability of the person taking the loan. Manual labour is probably connected with indentured labour, the interest on the loan being deducted from the daily wages. On the question of debts in ancient India, see Kane 1962–75, iii. 414–61; Chatterjee 1971.

12.39 *There is . . . women*: the two commentators differ on the interpretation. Maskarin takes this to mean that even after ten years of use one does not gain ownership in these cases, whereas Haradatta takes the opposite view. In these cases, according to him, their use for even a shorter period of time establishes ownership. 'Women' here refers to slaves.

13.11 *execution of the Law*: the exact meaning of the expression *dharmatantra* is unclear. It occurs also in G 1.18.24, 32 and B 1.10.32. The commentators give different explanations at different places and are, therefore, untrustworthy. It is unlikely that it means different things in different places. I think *tantra* here means something like 'the working' or 'the execution'. Here the reference is to the execution of justice in a court of law, whereas at G 1.18.24, 32, the reference is to the performance of required rites, and at B 1.10.8 it may be either.

13.14 *slays*: here too the two commentators differ. According to Haradatta, the false witness kills the given number of animals or men with regard to whom he lied; that is, he should be subjected to the punishment for killing that many of the species. Maskarin thinks that this means he 'slays', that is, brings to ruin (or sends to hell) that number of his relatives. This view is supported by M 8.97.

14.9 *killed . . . Brahmins*: this is the interpretation of the commentators: cf. Y 3.27. But it could also mean 'killed by cows or Brahmins', and this provision is found also in Y 3.21.

14.20–1 *fellow reciter . . . fellow student*: the difference between *sahādhyāyin* and *sabrahmacārin* is unclear. I think the interpretations of the commentators are mere guesswork. The latter occurs frequently enough (A 1.7.29; 1.10.12; B 1.11.30; M 5.71) for us to be sure that it refers to a person who was a fellow student. This may explain the relatively short period of impurity, because theirs was merely a relationship formed in their student days. The former does not occur elsewhere, and I think indicates a closer relationship (hence the longer period of impurity), as that between people who regularly recite the Vedas together or who observe the annual course of study together.

14.25 *seasons*: there are five seasons in a year: spring, summer, rains, autumn, and winter; sometimes a sixth, the cool season, is added after winter.

15.15 *By offering . . . unlimited time*: this passage is not commented on by either Haradatta or Maskarin. In the absence of a critical edition of G, its authenticity cannot be determined.

15.18 *husband of a Śūdra woman*: that is, a Brahmin who has married a Śūdra woman.

16.21 *The recitation . . . is heard*: the reason for this, according to M 4.124, is the association of the Sāmaveda with deceased ancestors and hence with impurity.

17.13 *looks revolting*: the meaning of *bhāvaduṣṭa* is unclear. Bühler translates: 'naturally bad', which makes little sense. Both Haradatta and Maskarin give the identical explanation: 'food that is given contemptuously or that is offensive to the eater's mind'.

17.28 *animals . . . jaws*: Haradatta and Govinda (on B 1.2.4) give as an example the horse, while Maskarin's example is a man. In the Puruṣa Hymn (RV 10.90.10) also animals with teeth on both jaws are associated with the horse. Obviously, this cannot have a literal meaning and must refer to animals that have incisor teeth on both jaws, for example, horses, donkeys, and mules, as well as dogs, cats, and most carnivorous animals.

17.33 *red juices*: at TS 2.5.1.3–4 a mythological reason for this rule is given. A third of Indra's guilt of killing a Brahmin (Viśvarūpa, the son of Tvaṣṭṛ) was assumed by plants. This guilt became their sap, and the red sap has the colour of that guilt.

17.37 *killed for the sake of the Law*: that is, killed in a sacrifice.

18.6 *relative*: the commentators Haradatta and Maskarin take this to mean just a Brahmin, that is, a man of the same class or caste. But the term *yonisambandha* elsewhere refers to either blood relatives or relatives from the mother's side.

18.23 *before . . . clothes*: a girl is supposed to be given in marriage while she is young enough to be running about naked. Such a girl is given the technical term *nagnikā* ('naked girl') in later texts: see B 4.1.11; Va 17.70. A parallel development occurs in Sinhala, where a younger sister is called *naṅgi* (naked girl). Although such a girl's marriage is ritually and legally a true marriage, she would remain in her parent's home until puberty, when she will be taken ceremonially to her husband's home.

19 This entire chapter is the same as the corresponding chapter in B 3.10.

21.15–16 *A man . . . estate*: the reference here is to parents who have fallen from their caste.

22.2 *throw . . . three times*: Haradatta points out that, since he throws himself three times, the penance does not entail his death.

22.23 *eunuch*: the commentators themselves appear to have noticed the anomaly of inserting the eunuch in the middle of a passage on animals. Haradatta cites the opinion of some that the term *ṣaṇḍa* here refers to animals that have been castrated.

22.36 *other than a cow*: the cow is a sacred animal in India and is considered a mother, one reason being that we drink its milk. Sex with a cow, therefore, is equivalent to incest: see G 23.12.

23.25 *without skipping any*: the commentators explain that while he is gathering these withered fruits, he should not skip any in trying to find better ones. Bühler translates: 'avoiding (all other food)'.

28.32–3 *A natural son . . . lineage*: for definitions of these types of sons, see B 2.3.14–28.

The Dharmasūtra of Baudhāyana

BOOK ONE

1.1–4 *The Law . . . the third*: the reference here is to the three sources of the Law: cf. p. xli.

2.9 *The region . . . Āryas*: a similar definition is found twice in Patañjali's commentary on Paṇini (2.4.10; 6.3.109) and Va 1.8. Hultsch's second edition of B reads *kanakhalād*, 'from Kanakhala'. But this reading is supported only by two manuscripts. The evidence of Patañjali shows that the correct reading should be *kālakavanād*. The meaning of *ādarśa* is unclear. Bühler (on Va 1.8) takes it to mean a mountain range called Ādarśa. In all likelihood, however, the term is a secondary derivative of *adarśa*, 'non-seeing', and refers to the place where the sacred river Sarasvatī disappears in the Punjab. This place gets the name *vinaśana* ('perishing') in later texts: M 2.21.

3.10–15 *According to . . . each class*: in all these statements, the first refers to Brahmins, the second to Kṣatriyas, and the third to Vaiśyas.

3.11 *Gāyatrī . . . initiation*: the year in which people of the three classes are initiated is related to the number of syllables in each foot of the metre used in their initiation: Gāyatrī has eight, Triṣṭubh eleven, and Jagatī twelve. For the actual verses in these metres that a student is taught, see Kane 1962–75, ii. 302.

3.32 *in an exaggerated way*: I follow Böhtlingk (1885*c*) in translating the ambiguous word *antyaśaḥ*. The commentator Govinda and, following him, Bühler take it to mean 'too close', that is, standing too close.

3.47 *story of the young Āṅgirasa*: this story is found in M 2.151–3. The wise young Āṅgirasa taught his relatives who were old enough to be his father and addressed them as 'Little Sons'. The relatives complained to the gods, and the gods told them that Āṅgirasa had acted properly, because a man without knowledge is a child and the man who teaches him is his father.

4.7 *And when he performs his private . . . enters him*: this section is not found in the SB and is probably a later insertion for the sake of symmetry; there is, after all, no need to buy back the part that is already in him.

he may beg almsfood . . . of other rites: the text here appears to be corrupt and differs from the SB reading. It is left untranslated by Bühler. My translation is tentative. The SB reading makes better sense: 'Surely, by taking the final bath he conquers beggary, he conquers the hunger of his relatives and ancestors.'

He commits a sin . . . chastity: this verse is not found in the SB but is found in all the manuscripts of B.

5.10 *almsfood*: the difference is that 'uncooked food' consists of grain and other provisions, while almsfood is already cooked.

6.2 *Fire is said . . . grass*: the basis for the equation of these four items with fire is a passage in TB 3.7.3. It says that the daily fire sacrifice (*agnihotra*) should be offered in the fire. If a fire cannot be found, it should be offered in a male goat (nothing is said about the ear), because the goat is sacred to Fire (*āgneyī*); if a goat is unavailable, in the right hand of a Brahmin, because a Brahmin is the Fire in all men (*agni vaiśvānara*: see Va 30.2–7); and if a Brahmin is unavailable, in a clump of Darbha grass, because such a clump contains fire; and if Darbha grass is unavailable, in water, because water is all the gods.

firing the pot again: the reference is to cleansing the pot. Firing is one of the methods of cleansing an earthen pot that has become polluted (B 1.14.1).

6.13 *for fire . . . water*: the commentator Govinda explains that when someone controls his breath, heat (fire) is generated internally (B 4.1.23–4). At night the sun, which normally takes up (absorbs) water, enters the fire. So, with internal fire (Sun) the Brahmin can take up the water. The Brahmin, however, has already been compared to fire (B 1.6.2). Note the double meaning of 'take up': to draw water from a well or pond and to absorb water or to make it evaporate.

7.3 *While he . . . left hand*: the reason is that after toilet one pours water with the right hand and washes the private parts with the left hand, whereas in sipping one holds the pot in the left hand

and pours water into the right hand for sipping. The practice of using the left hand for unclean tasks made the left hand impure and inauspicious in Indian culture. Thus, one never uses the left hand for eating or for any sacred action.

7.19 *scripture . . . effect*: the commentator Govinda refers to TA 1.7.1 where a Ṛg verse is cited.

8.14–16 *He should sip . . . to seers*: water is taken into the right hand (B 1.7.3 n.), the hand is placed on the lips, and the water is sipped. The part of the hand placed on the lips, that is, the part through which water passes into the mouth, is given the technical term *tīrtha*, which literally means a ford in a river. Different parts are used depending on the ritual of which sipping is a part. See Kane 1962–75, ii. 315–16, 652–3.

8.30 *in the opposite way*: Bühler, following Govinda, takes the term *viparīta* as 'contrary to the rule'. But the same term is used elsewhere (B 1.8.8; 1.15.3) with the meaning of 'opposite', or doing something in an inverse manner. The meaning here appears to be that in the case of an earthen pot one sips water before placing it on the ground: cf. G 1.28; M 5.143.

8.48 *depending . . . nose*: I follow Böhtlingk's (1885*c*) interpretation, which I think is more appropriate. Bühler translates: '. . . semen, or a dead body, (but) are agreeable to the eye and the nose, shall be rubbed. . . .'

9.5 *sanctuary tree*: the word *caityavṛkṣa* is ambiguous. A *caitya* is some sort of a sacred area, especially a funerary mound, often demarcated by a wall or some structure. The tree commonly associated with such sanctuaries is the Bo tree (*Ficus religiosa*), although it is unclear whether Baudhāyana uses it with reference to Buddhist sanctuaries.

10.1 *cow's hide*: this probably refers to a particular measurement of land. Govinda takes it to mean an area that can contain a hundred cows. In Vi 5.183 'cow's hide' is defined as an area of land on which one man can subsist for a year, whereas the commentator Nandapaṇḍita (on Vi 92.4) defines it as an area 300 by 10 *hastas* (approximately 450 by 15 feet). But see B 3.9.4, where the area appears to be much smaller and the term taken literally.

10.4 *spirit of generosity*: the Sanskrit terms *śraddadhāna* and *śraddhā* are often taken as referring to 'faith'. But in the early literature these terms are closely associated with hospitality and generous giving. These verses oppose two types of givers, the one who gives in a spirit of generosity and the other who gives for other motives. 'Vacillation' (*śaṅkā*) in verse 8 is probably the opposite of generosity: one is hesitant to give. See also greed and envy as the opposites of *śraddhā* at Va 6.8; 8.9. For *śraddhā* as generosity, see Jamison 1996, 176–84; Hara 1979, 1992; Köhler 1973.

11.9–10 *one's great-grandfather . . . family line*: those belonging to the same ancestry (A 1.10.28 n.) are seven: oneself, three immediate ancestors, and three immediate descendants (all in the male line: see Note on the Translation). So, the great-grandson's son is excluded. These share an undivided oblation, because at the monthly ancestral offering rice balls are offered in common to father, grandfather, and great-grandfather. The son and grandson, together with oneself, are said to share an undivided oblation, probably because they will receive the monthly oblation from the great-grandson. But this passage is convoluted and possibly corrupt (Böhtlingk 1885*c*). Those belonging to 'the same family line' (*sākulya*) are more distant relatives to whom a common ancestral offering is not made, and they appear to be even more distant than those who 'belong to the same lineage', since their claim to an inheritance is more remote than that of the latter (B 1.11.11–12; M 9.187).

11.28 *one's teacher . . . three days*: the commentator Govinda has a different reading, according to which the impurity lasts for three days for the teacher, two nights and the intervening day for the tutor, and one day for a son of theirs. The teacher (*ācārya*) is defined in Va 3.21–3 as a man from whom one receives vedic initiation and learns the entire Veda, whereas a tutor (*upādhyāya*) is a person who teaches a section of the Veda or the Vedic Supplements.

11.34–5 *The same . . . sinner*: Bühler and Govinda take this to mean that the above provisions apply also when someone touches a menstruating woman. But the term *ṛtumatyām* is in the locative, and it is more likely that the rule of the three-day impurity applies to such a woman and during that period one should not touch her; the cited passage implies that touching here means having sexual intercourse.

12.1 *village animals*: the exact meaning of *grāmya* is unclear. It can mean animals that generally live in or around a village (as I have taken it) or specifically domesticated or tame animals (so Bühler). I think this provision does not refer to livestock, which can surely be eaten as indicated in the exception indicated in *sūtra* 4, but to other animals and birds, such as village pigs, cocks, and crows: see A 1.21.15; G 17.29; 23.5; Va 14.48; 23.30. At A 2.16.28 both village and wild animals are said to be fit for use in ancestral rites, while Va 14.47 refers to a debate whether non-village pigs can be eaten.

12.8 *Bṛhacchiras, Mahāśakari*: the reading appears to be corrupt with a large number of variants. The reading adopted in the edition is conjectural.

13.12 *Silk*: the term *tārpya* occurs in vedic texts (TS 2.4.11.6; SB 5.3.5.20: see Eggeling's note to this) and was obscure even to the early commentators, who explain it in various ways which are mostly educated guesses. It is likely that the term referred to a silk garment.

14.9 *skin*: the meaning of *vināḍa* (or *vināḷa*) is not clear. For the former, Monier-Williams (in his Sanskrit dictionary) gives the meaning 'leather bag' with just this reference. Govinda takes it to be a long sacrificial vessel made out of bamboo or cane. Cf. SB. 5.3.2.6.

14.18 *fires ascend . . . churning the fire-drills*: fire-drills consist of a wooden shaft twirled with a cord wrapped around it on a slab of wood with a depression in the middle. A new fire is produced by the friction caused by the churning of the shaft on the slab. The fire-drills are viewed as the womb of fire and are thought to contain the fire in a latent form. The sacred fire is sometimes made to 'ascend' the fire-drills through a special ritual. After this one's sacred fires are contained in the fire-drills and can be made to descend again through churning. For making the fires 'ascend' one's self, see B 2.17.26 n.

15.19 *the passageway . . . mound*: the Utkara is located outside the north-eastern corner of the sacrificial arena (see App. I.1). The performers go in and out along the western side.

15.20 *not been dedicated*: the meaning of *aprapanna* is unclear and the translation is tentative. Govinda does not comment on it, and Bühler leaves it untranslated. I take it that the wood should be brought in a special way into the sacrificial area and placed in the proper place beside the fire. The verb *pra-pad* with a similar sense of walking in the proper manner is found in adjacent *sūtras* 17 and 21.

15.31–2 *If he sees . . . my austerity*: the two ritual formulas are taken from TS 3.1.1.2–3. There the text explains the use of these formulas by saying that when a consecrated man sees filth (probably faeces), his consecration leaves him, as do his dark complexion and beauty; the ritual formula prevents them from leaving. Likewise, when rain falls on him, the heavenly waters, if unappeased by this formula, will destroy his force, might, and consecration. *Sūtra* 32 is missing in both Govinda and Bühler.

19.8 *crime*: Bühler (here and in the parallel at M 8.18–19) interprets *adharma* as the guilt of an unjust decision. This is clearly the sense of G 13.11. But here and in Manu, I think, *adharma* refers to the crime of which the man is accused; if he is not punished properly part of the guilt of the man's crime falls on the king and the court. A similar statement is made in the case of a king who fails to kill a thief who comes to him with a club: B 2.1.16–17; A 1.25.4–5; G 12.43–5.

19.9 *designated*: this is a technical term (*uddiṣṭa*) for a witness listed in the plaint (N 1.147–8; Vi 8.12) and distinguished from those not so listed. At N 1.129 these two types are called *kṛta* (appointed) and *akṛta* (not appointed).

19.13 *lack humanity*: the meaning of *mānuṣyahīna* is unclear. Bühler translates it as 'destitute of human (intellect)'. Govinda interprets it to mean a man without relatives.

21.8–10 *When someone . . . his mouth*: a Brahmin may either accept grains and provisions or actually eat at an ancestral offering. Even in the former case, he has to suspend recitation, because a Brahmin's hand (accepting provisions) is equal to his mouth (eating food): cf. B 1.6.2 n. For the time taken to digest food completely, see B 2.2.36.

21.13 *A Brahmin*: the reason for introducing this seemingly extraneous point is that the provision of *sūtra* 12 applies also to the death of one's teacher, because he is one's spiritual father. The commentator Govinda remarks that the three-day suspension applies only to a student who has not returned home, because a ten-day period of impurity is the norm when one's father dies.

BOOK TWO

1.24 *fails . . . instruction*: the term *saṃskṛte* is unclear. Both Bühler and I follow Govinda's explanation.

1.26 *all the leftovers*: the great medieval theologian Vijñāneśvara (commenting on Y 3.282) cites this passage and interprets 'all' (*sarvam*) to mean food items such as meat and garlic that are normally forbidden to students. When he is sick he may eat these so long as they are his teacher's leftovers; but for the contrary view see Va 23.11.

2.8 *child of a Śūdra*: Bühler translates this as 'becoming thereby her son'. Govinda takes it to mean a man who gives himself up for adoption by a Śūdra. I prefer Govinda's interpretation because all the other sins enumerated are avoidable actions (see the statement in *sūtra* 9 'When people have done any one of these') that cause loss of caste, whereas being born of a Śūdra woman is beyond the control of the child.

2.35 *When someone: . . . a year*: this verse is found in Va 1.22 and M 11.181. Most commentators agree with the interpretation given in my translation, including Vijñāneśvara who cites it in his commentary on Y 3.261. It is also supported by the reading of Vi 35.3–5. According to this interpretation, by doing the four exempted activities one becomes an outcaste immediately rather than after the lapse of a year. Govindarāja and Sarvajñanārāyaṇa, commenting on M 11.181, think that one becomes an outcaste within a year by officiating at their sacrifices, etc., and *not* by travelling with them in the same vehicle and other similar activities. See Böhtlingk 1886*a*, 144; 1886*b*.

2.41 *The third type*: the meaning of 'third' is unclear, and Govinda gives several different explanations, which are mere guesses. It could be that the first two are *arduous penance* and *very arduous penance*. The *hot-arduous* (37) and that of women and children (39) may be simply variants of the first and thus to be subsumed under it.

3.14 *by himself*: this is meant to exclude a son born through levirate (B 2.3.17).

3.18–19 *He has two fathers . . . stumble*: this indicates that persons other than the dead man's brother were permitted to father children for him. This is the only way that the child could have two different lineages and patrimonies, because brothers have the same lineage. In the verse, moreover, the son from such a union is said to make offerings to six ancestors, which is possible only if the biological father and the leviratic father belong to two different families. Ancestral offerings are made to the father, grandfather, and the great-grandfather; these will be different only if the two fathers are not brothers. See G 18.6–7.

3.50 *If it is . . . so forth*: Govinda explains: when a Brahmin woman has sex with a Vaiśya she performs the penance beyond the very arduous penance, and with a Kṣatriya, the very arduous penance, whereas a Kṣatriya woman having sex with a Vaiśya performs the arduous penance.

4.5 *The Moon . . . taint*: Va 28.5–6 indicates that these three deities grant these boons to the woman after enjoying her prior to her marriage, a point repeated by Vijñāneśvara commenting on Y 1.71. 'Purification' here may refer to her menstrual flow regulated by the lunar cycle (B 2.4.4). This verse occurs also in Varāhamihira's *Bṛhatsaṃhitā* in the eulogy of women (74.7), where the final phrase reads: 'Women, therefore, are like a gold ornament.'

4.15 *given above*: Govinda refers to B 2.4.12, but the reference is found within the quoted verse and, therefore, must refer not to Baudhāyana but to the original from which the quotation is taken. As Bühler notes, this is a significant piece of evidence for the existence of metrical works on Law at a very early period, distinct from floating verses containing age-old wisdom (Lariviere 1989, ii, p. xi).

4.22 *ritual fire*: in Sanskrit, simply *agni* (fire), probably referring to the domestic fire (*aupāsana*), which is different from the three vedic fires (see App. I.1).

4.26 *Now, they . . . no gifts*: this dialogue is part of a quarrel between two young women, Devayānī and Śarmiṣṭhā, each trying to show that her father is superior to the other's. The full story is found in the *Mahābhārata* 1.73–8.

5.15 *goodly portion*: Govinda takes *agra* ('goodly portion') as a technical term referring to a specific quantity of food: *grāsa* ('mouthful') is a lump the size of a peahen egg; four mouthfuls make a *bhaikṣa* ('almsfood'); four almsfoods make one *puṣkala*; and four *puṣkalas*, one *agra*.

7.8 *Let him . . . text*: Govinda and Bühler take this to be an incomplete sentence: 'If he gets tired by controlling . . . text, (*let him recite the Sāvitrī*).'

7.14 *uninterrupted . . . nights*: the performer will not die before the completion of his full life span. There may also be a cosmological meaning: the twilight worship ensures the rise of the sun each day and the regular sequence of days and nights.

9.6 *god Bhava . . . Great God*: these are all names of Śiva.

9.7 *Vighna . . . Lambodara*: these are all names of Ganeśa, the son of Śiva.

9.10 *Keśava . . . Garutmat*: the first twelve are the well-known names of the major Indian god Viṣṇu. The next four are the names of his wife, Śrī. Garutmat is another name for Garuḍa, the bird that acts as Viṣṇu's mount.

9.11 *Yama . . . Audumbara*: these are the different names of Yama, the god of death.

9.14 *Seers . . . Kāṇḍas*: the seers who discovered the Vedas are divided into Brahman, Divine, and Royal. For seers by learning, see A 1.5.5–6. Janas, Tapas, and Satya are three of the seven worlds: see under Calls in App. I.2. 'Kāṇḍas' probably refer to the internal divisions of the vedic texts. For the seven seers, see A 2.24.13 n.

Kāṇva . . . Vasiṣṭha: all these are individuals to whom major texts of the vedic tradition are ascribed. Baudhāyana, Āpastamba, Hiraṇyakeśin, Āśvalāyana, Śaunaka, and Vasiṣṭha are the authors of texts on ritual and Law. Yājñavalkya is responsible for the so-called White Yajurveda and figures prominently in the BU.

11.7 *repeated death*: the meaning is not altogether clear, but the implication is that a person subject to this type of death would die a second or third time after his natural death on earth. This idea is important because it is probably related to the development of the pivotal doctrines of later Indian religion: rebirth and *karma*. The concept of re-death does not exist in the early vedic literature, and its use is limited almost exclusively to the late vedic texts. For a discussion of this concept and the possible location of its origin, see Witzel 1989, 201–5. In his recent treatment of this topic, Bodewitz (1996, 36) claims that the concept of repeated death 'introduced together with its solution and with emphasis on this solution, reflects the reaction of the ritualists to attempts made by non-ritualists to devalue the ritualistic claims. These ritualists probably tried to refute the opinion of other circles that ultimately the merits become exhausted in heaven.'

11.9–10 *In the absence . . . offering*: this is an interpolation that appears to have migrated from its natural place within Baudhāyana's refutation of this novel doctrine at B 1.11.29. Excluding this interpolation, the passage B 1.11.1–25 contains the view proposed by an opponent (*pūrvapakṣa*). The terse expression *adr̥ṣṭatvāt* ('because of the fact it is not seen') refers to the absence of an explicit vedic text to back the interpretation offered by the opponents: see A 1.4.8–10 n.; G 3.36 n.; Olivelle 1993, 89. The entire section on the orders of life appears to be a parenthetical digression; Baudhāyana returns to the topic of the householder in the next section.

11.22 *He should go . . . put away*: the meaning is that a religious mendicant should go to beg when people have already finished their meals. In this way he does not become a burden on householders. It also means that he eats their leftovers (A 1.3.27 n.).

11.27 *no offspring is produced in the others*: the argument here is that the Veda enjoins all men to father children. Since that is precluded in all but the householder's order, the Veda implicitly prohibits the others.

11.28 *Kapila, the son of Prahlāda*: Kapila is well known as a sage and a renouncer in ancient Indian literature. This passage appears to ascribe the authorship of the 'orders of life' to him, calling him a demon and the son of a well-known demon king, Prahlāda. See Olivelle 1993, 98–9.

12.1 *offerings to the vital breaths*: the five breaths that reside in the body are often conceived of as fires. Offerings to these breaths are seen as an internalized substitute for the daily fire offering (*agnihotra*) of ordinary Brahmins. For a detailed study, see Bodewitz 1973.

14.3 *secret texts*: the meaning of *rahasya* is uncertain. Govinda takes it to mean sections of the Āraṇyaka. The Upaniṣads are also referred to as 'secrets': Olivelle 1996, pp. lii–liii.

15.9 *rules . . . full moon*: the reference is probably to the Gṛhyasūtra of Baudhāyana, where these rules are given at 2.11.

15.12 *supplicants for morsels*: these are distant ancestors, as well as those who do not normally receive offerings. They receive only fragments from or the leftovers of the main offerings. See Va 11.21–4.

17.1 *renunciation*: the term *saṃnyāsa*, common in later texts, appears here for the first time in the Dharma literature. This term specifically refers to the process and procedure whereby a man abandons his family, ritual fires, and possessions. See Olivelle 1981. The entire rite described here is probably a later addition and resembles the ritual accounts of medieval handbooks (*paddhati*).

17.11 *staffs, sling*: the plural 'staffs' indicates the triple staff carried by some types of ascetics (see Olivelle 1986, i. 35–54). It was made by tying together three thin bamboo reeds. Other ascetics carried a single bamboo staff (B 2.18.1). Sometimes the staff is confused with the tripod, also made with three sticks, and used to carry the water pot. The sling was similar to a macramé pot-hanger and was used to carry the water pot.

17.19 *Brahman*: here the term may well refer either to the syllable OṂ or to the Veda, or to both: see B 2.17.40.

17.22 *time sacred to Brahman*: Govinda defines this as the final period (about one hour and twelve minutes) of the last watch (three hours) of the night. 'Time' here is *muhūrta*: see A 1.11.32 n.

17.23 *spine of the sacrificial arena*: that is, along the middle of the arena from east to west.

17.26 *Deposits . . . himself*: in this rite, the new renouncer internalizes the sacred fires. From now on he will carry them in the form of his breaths. See B 1.14.18 n; 2.18.8; A 1.11.32 n.

18.15–19 *Now, with reference . . . medicine*: this entire section is somewhat obscure, and Govinda himself does not appear to have fully grasped its meaning. It probably refers to some special observances, especially dietary restrictions, relating to the study of an Upaniṣad or a secret text.

18.23 *brahman . . . response*: the word *brahman* here refers to the syllable OṂ. The 'response' is a technical term referring to the reply uttered by the Adhvaryu priest in reponse to the invitation (*āhāva*) of the Hotṛ priest.

18.27 *Brahman-bowl*: the meaning is unclear. It may refer to the begging bowl or to the body of the ascetic, or to both.

BOOK THREE

2.2 *six Nivartaṇas*: a Nivartaṇa is an area of land approximately 10,000 square yards.

2.11 *With respect . . . Saṃprakṣālanī*: this passage is obscure and possibly corrupt. Govinda, and following him Hultzsch (1st edn. of B, p. 84), think that this ascetic cultivates grains, which goes against the whole point of washing and turning over the dishes to indicate that he has nothing for the next day. The name is said to be derived from *saṃprakṣāl* ('to wash') and the prefix *ni* of *ni-ubj* ('to turn over').

2.13 *Pālanī*: I follow the reading adopted by Hultzsch in his first edition of B; the meaning agrees with the second name *ahiṃsikā*, a life given to non-injury. In the second edition Hultzsch adopts the reading *phālanī*.

3.9 *Unmajjakas*: this may be a reference to a type of ascetic who spent much of his time standing in water up to the neck: see *Rāmāyaṇa* 3.6.3.

3.18 *Brahma-anchorites*: the meaning is unclear. It may mean either that the rules are meant for anchorites who are Brahmins or for anchorites who seek union with Brahman.

3.20 *first*: the meaning is that he should offer hospitality, including food, to the guest before he himself eats.

7.2 *A man . . . vagina*: both Govinda and Sāyaṇa (on TA 2.8.1–3) take *ayoni* (lit., 'non-vagina') to mean 'an improper vagina' and interpret the passage as forbidding sex with a Śūdra woman. But at B 4.2.13 and A 1.26.7 having sex with a Śūdra woman is distinguished from depositing semen in a 'non-vagina'. The meaning may well include masturbation, nocturnal emission (which is the meaning in *sūtra* 4), anal intercourse, and oral sex (see Va 12.23). Commenting on A 1.26.7, Haradatta explains 'non-vagina' as discharging semen in water.

8.11 *When he eats only four . . . all the formulas*: these contingencies arise because the number of lumps eaten is reduced by one every day. Thus on the twelfth day of the fast he eats four lumps, the next day three lumps, and so on.

8.25 *Abhijit, Śroṇa*: the 28th lunar mansion is called Abhijit (α, ε, and ζ Lyrae) and was placed between the Uttarāṣāḍhā (21st; ζ and σ Sagittarii) and Śroṇā (or Śrāvaṇā, 22nd; α, β, and γ Aquilae), spanning the fourth quarter of the former and the first quarter of the latter. Its presiding deity is Brahmā. Cf. TB 1.5.2.3.

8.26 *What has been . . . barley grain*: the lunar penance described here begins on the day after the full moon with a meal of fourteen mouthfuls. The food is decreased until the new moon, when there is a total fast, and increased until the full moon. Thus the ends are larger and the middle narrower, like an ant. The opposite method is to begin on the new moon with a fast, increasing the food until the full moon and then decreasing again until the new moon. Here the two ends are narrow and the middle large, like a barley grain.

9.8 *remember*: this indicates that the person recited the Veda from memory and did not read from a manuscript.

10 This entire chapter is almost identical with G 19.

BOOK FOUR

1.20 *suppresses her menstrual periods*: Govinda explains that this is done through medications and other such means.

7.5–7 *Gaṇas*: the name Gaṇa (lit., 'host' or 'multitude') probably refers to groups of verses. Here the first Gaṇa contains four formulas, and the second eight. The entire rite is also called Gaṇa. The reason may be because this rite contains numerous offerings using several groups of verses set in numerous metres, a point stressed by Govinda.

The Dharmasūtra of Vasiṣṭha

1.1 *Next . . . goal of man*: the wording here is so similar to the opening *sūtras* of the PMS (1.1.1–2) that it is unlikely to be accidental.

1.8–11 *The region . . . contrary to those*: the reading of these passages, especially *sūtra* 11, is probably corrupt, and the translation is tentative.

1.14 *Book of Causes*: the meaning of *nidāna* is unclear. The commentator Kṛṣṇapaṇḍita take it to mean a treatise on various regions of India. It is more likely, as Bühler has noted, that the reference is to an ancient work of the Bhāllavins cited in the *Bṛhaddevatā*, 5.23.

1.16 *pure and purifying*: I follow Böhtlingk's (1885*a*) conjecture *pavanaṃ pāvanaṃ* for *pavane pāvane*. Bühler translates: 'for purifying oneself and others'.

1.37 *When a woman . . . men*: this statement is found in the chapter on seasonal sacrifices of MS (1.10.11) and KS (36.5). The rest of the statement reads: 'she undoubtedly commits a falsehood (or 'cheating': *anṛta*).'

2.24 *rocks*: Böhtlingk (1885*a*, 482) proposes changing *aśma* ('rock') to *apaṇya* ('not to be traded') as in G 7.8, because rocks are permitted to be traded in B 2.2.29. I prefer to keep the traditional reading and take *na kadācana* ('never') of the previous *sūtra* as continuing into this. Rocks are, indeed, forbidden in M 10.86. See Bühler's (1885) response to Böhtlingk, and the latter's further response (Böhtlingk 1886*a*).

2.35 *The plough . . . her youth*: this passage has probably been incorporated here from an old commentary or an exegetical text (*nirukta*): see Böhtlingk 1885*a*, 482; 1886*a*, 145; 1886*b*, 526; Bühler 1885. The meaning is that by ploughing the fields a man obtains wealth, which in turn provides the resources to purchase cows, sheep, maids, and the like. The point of this citation, as the very next *sūtra* indicates, is to show that the Veda permits the sale of grain, for that is the only way to purchase these items.

2.44–7 *The interest on gold . . . the principal*: the meaning is not altogether clear. This may refer to the general rule that the total interest on a loan cannot exceed the principal: see G 12.31n. Here, however, that rule applies only to gold, whereas the interest on other kinds of property may exceed that amount.

4.3 *He created . . . any metre*: although this particular passage cannot be traced to any existing vedic text, the connection between the social classes and specific metres in which the vedic hymns are set is common: see TS 7.1.1.4–6 (where the Śūdra is associated with the Anuṣṭubh); Smith 1994, 58–82.

4.7 *Without killing . . . not a killing*: the argument here appears to be as follows. You cannot get meat (required for sacrifice) without killing, and killing is a sin which will not get you to heaven. But offering a sacrifice *does* take you to heaven. So, killing for a sacrifice cannot really be a killing.

4.19 *Others should . . . people*: the same passage is found in PG 3.19.42–3. The meaning is that the funeral of a married woman is performed not by her own blood relations but by her husband or her in-laws. And married women participate in the funerals of her in-laws. Cf. G 14.36.

6.5 *like clouds in the autumnal month*: the month is September–October when the normal rainy season is over. The simile is somewhat obscure. The meaning probably is that a few good clouds in this month can still produce rain, so a couple of syllables learnt well can purify a man.

8.7 *because his stay is brief*: here we have a phonetic etymology of 'guest' (*atithi*) derived by combining '*a*' from *anitya* ('brief') and '*tithi*' from *sthiti* ('stay'). See A 1.1.14 n.

8.15 *As all rivers . . . householder*: the meaning of 'end up in' (*yānti saṃsthitim*) appears to be as follows. The existence of rivers depends on their connection with the ocean: it provides them initially with their water and into it they finally merge. Similarly, the existence of people in other orders depends on the householder in a variety of ways: they obtain food from householders, and new recruits are either householders or their children (see M 3.77–8). In a more pregnant sense, however, they end up with the householder, because in the rebirth process they end up as the semen of the householder through whom they receive their new birth (BU 6.2.9–13).

10.18 *emblems*: these are the staff, the begging bowl, and the like. Displaying them invites honour and adulation from ordinary people. An ascetic is expected to live incognito and even to invite ridicule by acting as if he were mad or a simpleton.

11.26 *Let him . . . produced*: the meaning of the verse is not altogether clear. It appears that he should use both hands in serving the food, left hand holding the bowl and the right hand the spoon. The two kinds of remnants may refer to the remnants in the bowl he is holding and the remnants in the plates of the Brahmins who are eating (A 1.3.27 n.). The meaning then is that he should remain standing with the bowl ready to serve until the Brahmins have finished their meal.

12.43 *sun is seen over the trees*: the reference is to late afternoon when the sun can barely be seen over the treetops.

12.47 *time sacred to Prajāpati*: this is the same as the time sacred to Brahman: B 2.17.22 n.

13.46 *When returning . . . bhāv*: in addressing a person the vocative case is used. Frequently, the vocative ends in 'a', e.g. Devadatta. Then the final syllable is lengthened. But in words whose stem forms end in 'i' or 'u' (e.g. Hari, Bandhu) the vocatives end in 'e' and 'o': Hare, Bandho. When these come before a vowel they are changed to Haray and Bandhav. The final syllables of such words are prolated, e.g. Harāy and Bandhāv.

14.34 *He should not drink*: the aphorism does not contain these words, but they are clearly implied within the context of the topic dealing with forbidden items of food and drink.

14.41 *These are forbidden to be eaten*: these words (see previous note) are missing in the aphorisms but are clearly implied.

14.44 *not specifically indicated*: the meaning is not altogether clear. It appears to say that one is not permitted to eat an animal that is not explicitly permitted, even though it may not be in the list of forbidden animals.

15.1 *blood and semen*: it was generally believed that the father contributes the semen and the mother the blood (often identified with menstrual blood) to the formation of the foetus.

15.6–7 *take in adoption . . . a Śūdra*: the meanings of the Sanskrit compound words *adūrabāndhava* and *dūrebāndhava* are not altogether clear. Bühler takes them to mean 'a not remote kinsman' and 'a remote kinsman', respectively (they are then 'descriptive determinative' compounds: *karmadhāraya*). The meaning would then be that a person should adopt a boy who is not a distant but a close relative of his. Wezler (1998), however, has convincingly demonstrated that the terms *adūra* and *dūra* refer to the proximity or distance not in terms of kinship but with reference to geography and that the compounds are 'possessive', *bahuvrīhi*: 'a person whose relatives are near by *or* far away'. The reason for this provision is that an adoptive parent should not take the biological parent's words regarding the boy's ancestry and qualities at face value but should check with other relatives of the child for their accuracy. This would not be possible if the boy's relatives live in a distant region. The expression 'someone with relatives close by' (*bandhusaṃnikṛṣṭam*) appears to be an old gloss on the previous expression 'someone whose relatives do not live far away' (*adūrabāndhavam*), a gloss that found its way into the text.

15.21 *The discussion . . . manner*: the meaning is that a person who is readmitted should be treated like a newborn. All the sacramentary rites (G 8.14 n.) should be performed for him.

16.4–5 *An offence . . . knowledge*: these two *sūtras* are evidently corrupt (Böhtlingk 1885*a*, 485). I think Bühler's translation is off the mark. I take the crucial expression *yathāsanam* to mean 'according to rank or social position'. The translation, however, is tentative.

16.21–3 *Is a king . . . courtiers*: these three *sūtras* are obscure and probably corrupt. I have followed the conjectures and interpretation offered by Böhtlingk (1885*a*, 485), because they at least make some sense, even though I am sceptical that Böhtlingk has discovered the original readings or meaning. A comparison between courtiers and vultures is also made in verse 118, Book 1, of the *Pañcatantra*. For a variant reading from a later citation of a similar passage ascribed to Śaṅkha-Likhita in a medieval text, see Kane 1962–75, i. 104 n. 108.

16.35 This verse is corrupt and makes no sense. Bühler omits it without explanation.

17.10–11 *If one among many brothers . . . a vedic text*: variants of these provisions occur also in M 9.182–3 and Vi 15.41–2. The connection between the two verses is not altogether clear. The second clearly refers to a polygamous marriage. Wezler (1998) disagrees with Jolly's suggestion that the former may refer to a polyandric marriage of several brothers to a single wife, as exemplified in the marriage of the five Pāṇḍava brothers in the *Mahābhārata*. Wezler suggests that when one brother has a son all his other brothers also become 'men who have sons' because through that son they all are freed from the debt to their father of bearing a son to continue the line. Likewise, the common wives are relieved of the burden of bearing a son for their common husband. At a linguistic level, moreover, a man can claim 'I have a son' when his father gets a grandson, just as a woman can claim 'I have a son' when the husband gets a son.

17.31–5: *This type . . . his son*: the story of Śunaḥśepa is told in the AB 7.13. King Hariścandra was childless. He made a vow to Varuṇa and received a son, Rohita, whom he was obliged to sacrifice to Varuṇa. Rohita ran away and Varuṇa brought a sickness upon Hariścandra. Rohita purchased Śunaḥśepa, the son of Ajīgarta Sauyavasi, as a substitute (this is an example of a purchased son). Śunaḥśepa saved himself from being sacrificed by praising the gods and gave himself to Viśvāmitra as his son.

17.57 *barren*: I follow Bühler's (on B 2.4.10) suggestion that the reading *avaśā* ('not barren') here should be changed to *vaśā* ('barren').

17.79 *same distant ancestry*: the term *samānodaka* means a set of relatives connected by the offering of water to the same ancestors. This relationship, according to some sources, extends up to the fourteenth degree.

19.2 *lasting until old age*: Bühler translates the expression *jarāmarya* as 'life-long'. Bodewitz (1973, 155 n. 2), commenting on the same expression used with reference to the daily fire sacrifice (*agnihotra*), has shown that 'having old age as its limit (*maryā*) is the only tenable' meaning. Eggeling's translation (at SB 12.4.1.1)—'ensuring death in old age'—is clearly inaccurate.

19.6 *both*: that is, the ritual duties incumbent on the king as a householder and the royal duties connected with good government. His personal priest becomes his *alter ego* and carries out his ritual duties, while he himself attends to governmental affairs.

19.9 *social position*: Bühler translates the term *sthāna* (lit., place) as 'the seat (of the injury)', meaning that different sorts of punishment would be meted out depending on what part of the body was injured. This interpretation is supported by M 8.124 where *sthāna* is used with the meaning of an area of the body. But I think 'social position' is more in keeping with the rest of the statement, and in very similar contexts the same term is used with this meaning in Kauṭilya's *Arthaśāstra*, 2.9.9; 2.10.5; 2.27.15.

19.12 *or for household needs*: Führer's edition of Va joins this phrase with *sūtra* 13. I follow Lakṣmīdhara, *Kṛtyakalpataru*, *Vyavahārakāṇḍa*, 504, and Caṇḍeśvara, *Vivādaratnākara*, 284, in joining the phrase with *sūtra* 12. Their reading clearly makes better sense. I also adopt their reading *gārhasthyāṅge* (or *-āṃśe*) in place of this edition's *gārhasthyāṅgānām*. Caṇḍeśvara explains this phrase as *gṛhasthakarma* ('householder's activities') or *gṛhasthopakaraṇa* ('householder's implements'). The meaning appears to be that trees may be cut down to provide wood for household needs. Given the first provision allowing trees to be cut down for cultivation, the meaning also may be that they can be cut down to build houses.

19.14–16 *Export . . . punishment*: this passage is probably corrupt. I have followed, by and large, the reading found in Lakṣmīdhara and Caṇḍeśvara (see previous note). The meaning, nevertheless, is still not completely clear. They read *nirhāra* for *nīhāra* (lit., 'fog') in this edition. Even though I have kept the latter as the *lectio difficilior*, I take it to be a variant of the former. I take its meaning to be the exporting of merchandise, a meaning attested to in M 8.399, rather than tax or duty, as assumed by Bühler. I take these two *sūtras* to mean that from the capital city merchants are not permitted to export their merchandise (possibly what they have imported into the city). They may take away only the sale price (*argha*) or the original value (*mūlya*) of the merchandise. Commentators explain the 'two festivals' as the birth of a son to the king and the festival of Indra. The translation, however, is very tentative. My reading of the text, on which the translation is based, is somewhat of a hybrid, but that is inevitable when the text is as corrupt as this: 14. *adhiṣṭhānān na nīhāraḥ*; 15 *sārthānām arghamānamūlyamātraṃ naihārikaṃ syāt*; 16 *mahāmahayoḥ tv anatyayḥ syād abhayaṃ ca.*

19.17–22 *For water . . . one Māṣa*: this section is exceedingly corrupt and some readings of Führer's edition make no sense. Bühler has left several such passages untranslated. I have had the benefit of the reading found in Caṇḍeśvara, *Vivādaratnākara*, 645, and his detailed commentary on it. On the whole, I think Caṇḍeśvara is right in taking the passage as referring to ferries and tolls. For Māṣa and Kārṣapaṇa, see G 12.8 n. The meaning is that to cross a large river the toll is 8 Māṣas, for a narrower river a quarter Kārṣapaṇa (= 5 Māṣas), and when the water is low, 1 Māṣa. My translation is based on the following somewhat hybrid reading: 17. *saṃyāne daśavāhavāhinī dviguṇakāriṇī syāt*; 18. *pratyekaṃ prapāḥ syuḥ*; 19. *puṃsāṃ śatāvarārdhavāhaṃ vahet*; 20. *adhyardhāḥ striyaḥ syuḥ*; 21. *taro 'ṣṭau māṣāḥ śaramadhyāyā aśaramadhyāyāḥ pādaḥ kārṣāpaṇasya*; 22. *nirudakas taro māṣyaḥ.*

19.28 *artisans*: I follow Bühler and the commentator in taking *udvāha* to mean artisan, although I am unsure about this meaning.

19.38–9 *A man . . . misrepresented himself*: the text is somewhat obscure. I have followed the interpretations of Lakṣmīdhara, *Kṛtyakalpataru*, *Vyavahārakāṇḍa*, 542, and Caṇḍeśvara, *Vivādaratnākara*, 331.

19.48 *stain of impurity*: I read *aghadoṣa* (found in the parallel in M 5.93) in place of *adya doṣa* in Führer's edition.

20.7 *take her to himself*: that is, the older brother should take the younger brother's wife as his own. The commentator notes that this is done only ritually, after which the wife is taken back by her husband.

20.19 *surā liquor*: often *surā* is used as a generic term for liquor. Here, however, it appears to refer to a specific type of intoxicant. M 11.95 distinguishes three types of *surā* made from molasses, rice, and a particular flower. The commentator Kullūka (on M 11.95) lists nine types of liquors called *madya*, which are distinguished from the three types of *surā*.

20.24 *That is why . . . child*: the rite called *puṃsavana* ('quickening a male child') is performed during the third month of pregnancy (G 8.14 n.). The argument here is that a foetus without developed sexual organs will turn out to be a male through the power of this rite and, therefore, aborting such a foetus is equivalent to murdering a Brahmin (always assumed to be male, because the murder of a female does not carry the same sanction: see Va 20.37). See A 1.24.8–9 n.

20.31 *the same penance*: the text here is evidently defective. Before this one should expect a penance for killing a Brahmin. Such a penance lasting twelve years is given in other texts: see A 1.24.10–20; G 22.4–6; B 2.1.2–3.

21.15 *Half his body*: the wife is considered a half of the husband's self or body: SB 5.2.1.10.

21.21 *very arduous penance*: this penance is elsewhere called 'hot arduous penance' (*taptakṛcchra*). See B 2.2.37. For another description of the very arduous penance, see B 2.2.40.

22.1 The entire chapter 22 is almost identical with G 19 and B 3.10, where notes are given.

22.5 *vedic texts*: the wording here makes it likely that the passage found in B 3.10.6 and G 19.7 has been omitted in the manuscripts of Va.

23.34 *people hear*: this, in all probability, cannot be taken literally. The commentator Kṛṣṇapaṇḍita and Bühler think that this applies when they are reciting the Veda.

23.35 *it*: Kṛṣṇapaṇḍita and Bühler take this to be a reference to the Gāyatrī verse.

24.7 *the teacher*: it appears very likely that at one time the text of Vasiṣṭha ended here. The final six chapters are probably later additions and are composed in the metrical style of the later Dharmaśāstras: see Bühler 1879–82, ii, p. xxii.

26.10 *four . . . cooked food*: this verse is identical with M 2.86 where most commentators interpret the four as four of the five so-called Great Sacrifices, excluding vedic recitation (B 2.11.1–6). Bühler takes them to mean four of the five sacrifices listed in M 3.73–4.

26.12 *'Head' vow*: the meaning is unclear. The same expression occurs in MuU 3.2.10 and may refer to some type of head-shaving connected with studying a particularly sacred text.

27.15 *if he has . . . discoloured*: the reference possibly is to excrement. After eating barley, if one's excrement contains white barley seeds then he is pure, if they are discoloured, he remains impure.

27.17 *Prājāpatya penance*: this is the same as the normal arduous penance (B 2.2.38).

30.5 *sense organs*: this appears to be a broken citation.

INDEX

In several significant areas, this Index groups related terms under a single broad topic. Accordingly, all animals are listed under *animals*, apart from birds and fish, which are listed separately; everything relating to ascetic life styles, under *ascetic institutions*; all bodily parts and fluids, under *body*; all matters relating to death and funerary practices, under *death*; directions, such as north and south, under *directions*; all grasses, under *grasses*, and all plants and trees, under *trees*; all items of food, under *food*, all deities, under *god*; matters relating to civil and criminal law, under *king*; issues relating to Law (*dharma*), under *Law*; all kinship terms and relatives, under *kinship*; all metallic substances, under *metal*; mother and father, under *parents*; names of regions, under *regions*; everything relating to sacrifices, under *sacrifice*; all social divisions and castes, under *social classes*; all divisions of day and night, under *time*; everything relating to the Veda, including vedic texts and formulas, under *Veda*; cities, towns, and the like, under *village*. The numbers refer to the internal divisions of the Dharmasūtras as described in the Note on the Translation (p. xliv).

abortion **A 1**: 19.15; 21.8; 24.8; 28.21; **G** 17.11; 20.1; 21.9; 24.6–9; **B 1**: 10.23; **B 4**: 1.12–13, 17, 20, 29; **Va** 2.42; 20.23–4; 28.7
actress **B 2**: 4.3
adversity, time of **A 1**: 20.11; **A 2**: 4.25; **G** 7.1–25; 9.67; **B 1**: 3.41–2; **B 2**: 5.7; 18.18; **Va** 2.22
Agastya **Va** 14.15
age **G** 6.20; **Va** 13.56
  one **A 2**: 15.2, 20
  five **G** 1.6
  seven **A 1**: 1.21
  eight **A 1**: 1.19, 22; **G** 1.5; **B 1**: 3.7; **Va** 11.49
  nine **A 1**: 1.23; **G** 1.6
  ten **A 1**: 1.24
  eleven **A 1**: 1.19, 25; **G** 1.11; **B 1**: 3.8; **Va** 11.50
  twelve **A 1**: 1.19, 26; **G** 1.11; **B 1**: 3.8; **Va** 11.51
  sixteen **A 1**: 1.27; **G** 1.12; **B 1**: 3.12; **Va** 11.71; 17.59
  twenty-two **A 1**: 1.27; **G** 1.12; **B 1**: 3.12; **Va** 11.72
  twenty-four **A 1**: 1.27; **G** 1.12; **B 1**: 3.12; **Va** 11.73
  eighty **G** 6.10
  counted from conception **A 1**: 1.19; **G** 1.7; **B 1**: 3.7; **Va** 11.49–51
  legal **G** 10.48; **B 2**: 3.36; **Va** 16.9
  seniority **A 1**: 14.9, 14, 21; **A 2**: 6.7; 17.10
agriculture **A 2**: 10.7; 16.14; **G** 10.5; **B 1**: 10.28, 30; 18.4; **B 3**: 2.2–4; **Va** 2.19; 19.12
  agricultural land **A 1**: 9.7; **G** 12.19–26, 28
  farmers **A 2**: 28.1; **G** 10.24; 11.21; **Va** 11.42
Ajīgarta Sauyavasi **Va** 17.32
ancestors **A 1**: 2.5; 19.13; 20.6; **A 2**: 4.5; 5.18; 17.8; 24.3; **G** 3.29; 4.29–33; 5.3, 9; 11.27; 15.22; 17.4; 27.17; **B 1**: 4.7; 8.16; 19.11–12; **B 2**: 2.26–7; 5.2–4, 18; 11.15, 33; 16.5, 7–8; **B 3**: 6.12; **B 4**: 1.18; 3.6; 5.5; 8.6; **Va** 2.7, 30; 3.68; 4.10; 10.3; 11.37, 48; 12.23; 14.18; 15.4; 16.32, 37; 17.16; 22.10
  see also death, kinship, parents
ancestral offering **A 1**: 10.28; 11.26; 13.1; **A 2**: 5.16; 15.11–18; 16.1–28; 17.1–25; 18.1–19; 19.17–20; 20.1–2; **G** 8.18; 10.53; 14.39; 15.1–30; 16.47–8; **B 1**: 5.12; 7.5; 8.8; 11.4; 15.3, 6; 21.2; **B 2**: 3.16, 18–19; 10.6; 11.1, 3; 13.6; 14.1–12;

milk **A 1**: 17.22; **G** 17.24; **B 1**: 12.11
for slaughter **G** 7.13
snake **G** 1.59; 22.25; **Va** 21.24
with teeth in one/both jaws **G** 17.28; 28.5; **B 1**: 2.4; **B 2**: 2.29; **Va** 14.40
tiger **B 3**: 3.6; 7.12
tortoise/turtle **A 1**: 17.37; **G** 15.15; 17.27; **B 1**: 12.5; **Va** 14.39
tusked **Va** 2.28
village **B 1**: 12.1; **Va** 10.16
wild **A 2**: 16.28; **B 3**: 2.19; **Va** 2.28; 3.45–7
wolf **B 3**: 3.6; howling **A 1**: 10.19; 11.33
worm **B 1**: 11.37–8; **B 2**: 2.26; **Va** 2.30; 4.32; 18.16
areca nut **B 1**: 8.39
arrow **A 1**: 15.19; **B 1**: 7.7; **Va** 14.14; 19.21
arsonist **G** 15.18; **Va** 3.16; 14.7
artisan **G** 10.31, 60; 11.21; 15.18; 17.7; **B 1**: 9.1; 10.24; **Va** 19.28
artist **G** 6.16
Ārya **A 1**: 3.40; 12.6, 8; 20.7–8; 21.13, 17; 23.6; 26.7; 28.13; 29.1, 9; **A 2**: 3.1, 4; 10.11; 25.13; 26.4; 27.8–9, 14–15; **G** 6.11; 9.65, 69; 10.59, 65–6; 12.2–4; 22.5; **B 1**: 10.20; **B 2**: 2.18; 6.31
ascetic institutions:
Ahiṃsakā **B 3**: 2.13
Cakracara **B 3**: 1.1–26; 2.1–19
Dhruvā **B 3**: 1.7; 2.7–10
forest hermit **A 2**: 21.1, 18–21; 22.1–24; 23.1–2; **G** 3.2, 26–35; **B 2**: 11.12, 14–15; 17.6; **B 3**: 3.1–22; **B 4**: 5.27; **Va** 6.19–20; 7.2; 9.1–12; 21.32; classification **B 3**: 3.1–9; clothes **A 2**: 22.1, 17; **G** 3.34; **Va** 9.1; food **A 2**: 9.13; 22.2–4, 24; 23.1–2; **G** 3.26, 28, 31, 35; **B 2**: 11.15; 13.7; 18.13; **B 3**: 3.3–14; hermitage **Va** 9.7; treatise on **B 2**: 14; **B 3**: 3.16–18
Kāpotā **B 3**: 1.7; 2.15; **B 4**: 5.28
Kauddālī **B 3**: 1.7; 2.5–6
Pālanī **B 3**: 1.7; 2.13
Śālīna **B 2**: 12.1; 17.3; 18.4; **B 3**: 1.1–26; 2.1–19
Saṃprakṣālanī **B 3**: 1.7; 2.11
Samūhā **B 3**: 1.7; 2.12
Ṣaṇṇivartinī **B 3**: 1.7; 2.1–4
Siddhecchā **B 3**: 1.7; 2.16
Śiloñchā **B 3**: 1.7; 2.14
Vanyā **B 3**: 1.8; 2.18–19
Yāyāvara **B 2**: 12.1; 17.3; 18.4; **B 3**: 1.1–26; 2.1–19; **B 4**: 5.27
ascetic/mendicant **A 1**: 18.31; **A 2**: 21.1, 7–17; 26.14; **G** 3.2, 11–25; 12.38; 14.44; 18.16; **B 1**: 19.13; **B 2**: 11.12, 16–26; 13.7; **B 3**: 3.5–7; **B 4**: 5.19; **Va** 6.19–20; 7.2; 10.1–31; 11.17–18, 34; 19.23, 34, 37; 21.33
begging/food **A 2**: 21.10; **G** 3.15–16; **B 2**: 18.4–15; **Va** 10.8–9, 21–2
clothes **A 2**: 21.11; **G** 3.18–19; **B 2**: 17.44; **B 3**: 2.17
naked **A 2**: 21.12
procedure of renunciation **B 2**: 17.1–41; **Va** 10.1
renouncer (*saṃnyāsin*) **B 2**: 18.14; **B 3**: 2.17
rules **B 2**: 17.42–4; 18.1–27; **Va** 10.6–29
ash **A 2**: 15.16; **G** 9.15, 40; **B 1**: 10.27; 14.5; **B 2**: 6.16; 12.6; **Va** 3.10, 49, 58; 6.12; 6.31–2; 14.23
astrology/astronomy **A 2**: 8.11; **G** 11.15–16; **B 2**: 2.16; **Va** 10.21
auspicious/inauspicious **A 1**: 13.9; 31.12; **A 2**: 4.23; 29.7; **G** 8.23; 9.66; 11.17; 20.11; 27.8; **B 2**: 6.34; **B 3**: 9.4; **B 4**: 5.3; **Va** 6.7–8
austerity **A 1**: 5.1; 12.1–2, 5; **A 2**: 24.8, 14; **G** 3.26; 19.11, 15; 23.27; 26.12; **B 1**: 10.6, 33; **B 2**: 5.1; 11.15, 34; 13.9; 16.3; **B 3**: 3.12, 20–1; 10.9, 13; **B 4**: 1.30; **Va** 3.60; 5.2; 6.23, 26; 8.14; 10.5; 20.47; 21.32; 22.8; 25.5, 7–8; 26.17–19; 27.5
axe **A 2**: 22.15

balance **Va**: 2.42
bald people **A 2**: 17.21; **G** 15.18, 30; 17.18; 21.11
Bali offering **A 1**: 12.15; **A 2**: 3.12, 15–23; 4.1–9; **G** 2.4; 5.9; **B 2**: 5.11; 11.1, 4; **B 3**: 6.3; **Va** 11.4

staff **A 1**: 2.38; **G** 1.22–6; **B 1**: 3.15; **Va** 11.51–7; 20.18
teaching householder's duties **A 1**: 2.7
vedic instruction **A 1**: 1.13, 31; 2.4, 8; 5.23; 30.1–3
student returned home **A 1**: 7.15–18, 31; 8.1; 10.7; 13.5; **A 2**: 5.4; **B 2**: 2.16
bath-graduate **A 1**: 8.7; 30.1–5; **A 2**: 8.6–7; 14.13; 27.21; **G** 2.49; 6.24; 8.16; 9.1–74; 15.28; 27.24; **B 1**: 5.1–15.32; **B 2**: 5.10–21; 6.1–42; 14.2; **Va** 3.19; 11.2; 13.59
rules of conduct **A 1**: 8.2–5; 14.7–9; 18.9–8; 29.6–23; 31.1–23; 32.1–29; **B 1**: 5.1–13; 6.7–42; **Va** 12.1–47; 13.1–61
Śūdra **A 1**: 1.4, 7–8; 3.41; 5.16; 16.22; 17.1; 26.4, 9; 27.11; **A 2**: 2.6; 3.4–11; 6.9–10; 17.21; 26.15; 27.8–10, 14–16; **G** 4.21; 6.11; 9.11; 10.42, 50; 12.1–7, 13, 15; 13.3; 14.5, 24; 16.19; 20.1; **B 1**: 6.9; 8.22–3; 10.20, 24; 16.1–5, 13; 17.3–7, 13–14; 18.5; 19.2–6; 20.13–15; 21.15; **B 2**: 2.6–8; 3.49, 52; 5.11–12; 7.15; **B 3**: 6.5; 8.17; **B 4**: 5.4; **Va** 1.24; 2.1, 6, 27; 3.1–3, 34; 4.2–3, 27–31; 5.10; 6.23–32; 10.4; 11.10; 14.4; 15.7; 16.30; 17.78; 18.1–18; 21.1–5, 12; 24.5; 26.16
black **A 1**: 27.11; **B 2**: 2.11; **Va** 18.18
cooks **A 2**: 3.3
food of **A 1**: 18.13–14; **A 2**: 18.2; **G** 17.5; **B 2**: 3.1; **B 4**: 1.5; **Va** 4.31; 6.26–9; 10.31
greeting **A 1**: 14.29; **G** 5.42; 6.10
killing **A 1**: 24.3; 25.13; **G** 22.16; **B 2**: 1.10; **Va** 20.33, 39–40; 23.6
occupations of **G** 7.22–3; 10.50–65; **B 1**: 18.5; **Va** 2.20
sacrificing for **G** 20.1; **Va** 15.11
seizing property from **A 1**: 7.20–1; **G** 18.24
serving **B 2**: 2.6, 11; **Va** 2.20
teaching the Law **A 2**: 29.11–12
wife **G** 15.18; 28.39; **Va** 17.37
woman **A 1**: 9.11; 18.33; **G** 4.26; 15.18; 25.7; **B 2**: 3.29; **B 4**: 1.5; 2.13; 6.6; **Va** 1.25
see also social classes
sun **A 1**: 27.10; 30.20; 31.19–20; **A 2**: 6.2; 22.13; **G** 2.11–12; 9.12; 25.9; 26.12; **B 1**: 1.14; 8.40; **B 2**: 6.10; 7.21; 11.31; 18.7; **B 3**: 2.8; 5.2; 8.7; **B 4**: 5.24; 8.2–3; **Va** 6.11; 11.36; 17.5; 27.9; 28.16
eclipse **A 1**: 11.30; **G** 16.22; **Va** 13.34
halo **A 1**: 11.31; **G** 16.16
looking at **G** 23.22; **Va** 23.32
northern course **A 2**: 20.3; 23.5
solstice **B 2**: 4.23
southern course **A 2**: 23.4; **G** 16.2
sunrise **A 1**: 5.18; 31.18; **A 2**: 12.14, 22; **G** 23.21; **B 1**: 2.12; **B 2**: 6.10; 7.12–15; **B 3**: 1.13; **B 4**: 5.31; **Va** 1.15; 12.10; 20.4; 27.18
sunset **A 1**: 4.15; 31.3, 18; 32.8; **A 2**: 12.13, 22; **G** 23.21; **B 1**: 6.10; **B 2**: 6.3, 10; 7.13–15; 17.18; **B 4**: 5.18; **Va** 11.22; 12.10, 43; 20.5
world of **B 3**: 8.30
worship **G** 26.13; **B 2**: 1.28; 8.12; 17.39; 18.11; **B 3**: 4.5; 8.14
Śunaḥśepa **Va** 17.31–5
Śvapāka **B 4**: 5.12–13
Śvetaketu **A 1**: 5.6; 13.19
sweeping **A 2**: 3.15; 4.23; **B 1**: 9.11; 10.1; **B 2**: 12.2; **B 3**: 2.12; **Va** 3.56
swimming **A 1**: 32.26; **G** 9.32; **B 2**: 6.26; **Va** 12.45; 19.25
swing **A 1**: 31.14; **B 2**: 6.14
sword **G** 14.12; **B 1**: 1.13

taste **B 1**: 8.17; 9.10; **B 4**: 1.3
teacher **A 1**: 1.11–13, 15; 3.43–5; 4.1–4; 5.7; 6.13; 10.15–17; 26.11; 32.10; **A 2**: 5.11; 6.1–2; 8.6–7; 21.6; 27.21; **G** 2.50; 5.26–7; 10.4; 11.31–2; 14.28; 15.14; 17.4; 20.2, 6, 14; 21.12; **B 1**: 4.7; 11.13, 28; 18.13; 21.22; **B 2**: 5.9; 11.13; 13.6; 18.15–16, 19; **B 3**: 4.5; **B 4**: 8.2; **Va** 2.3–12; 7.4–14; 8.1; 13.48, 50, 54; 14.13, 20; 15.19; 19.44; 20.12; 23.9–11
assisting **A 1**: 6.1; **B 1**: 3.35–5
conduct towards **A 1**: 1.15; 2.19–21; 3.15, 31–4, 43–5; 4.1–4, 22–9;

umbrella **A 1**: 7.5; **G** 2.13; 10.58; **B 1**: 3.24; 5.6; **Va** 7.15; 29.13
uncle, *see* kinship
usury, *see under* moneylender
Ūrvasī **Va** 30.11
Uśanas **B 2**: 4.26; **B 3**: 8.12
utensils/implements **A 1**: 17.9–13; **A 2**: 22.15–17; **G** 28.7; **B 1**: 13.21–32; 14.1–10
  bone **G** 1.31 **B 1**: 8.45; **Va** 3.52
  clay **A 1**: 17.9; **G** 1.29; **B 1**: 8.30, 34; 11.41; 14.1–3; **B 2**: 17.24; **Va** 3.49, 58–9; 15.20
  copper **Va** 5.7
  horn **B 1**: 8.46
  iron **B 3**: 3.10; **Va** 14.32; 17.45
  ivory **B 1**: 8.46
  metal **A 1**: 17.11; **G** 1.29–30; **B 1**: 8.27; 14.4–7
  stone **G** 1.30; **B 1**: 8.44; 14.8; **B 2**: 2.29; 17.24; **B 3**: 3.10; **Va** 3.49; 13.35
  wooden **A 1**: 17.12; **G** 1.29; **B 1**: 8.31, 35; **Va** 3.49, 52

Vaiśya **A 1**: 1.4, 19, 27; 2.36–8; 3.2, 6, 30; 5.16; **A 2**: 2.6; **G** 1.11–12; 4.20; 10.42; 12.8–14; 14.3, 24; **B 1**: 3.9, 17; 5.9; 6.9; 8.23; 16.1–4; 17.3–8; 18.4; 19.2; 20.13–15; **B 2**: 1.21; 3.50; 5.11; **B 3**: 7.9; **Va** 1.24; 2.1–2; 3.24, 33; 4.2–3; 11.51–73; 17.47, 78; 18.1–9; 21.2–5, 12, 17; 26.16
  greeting **A 1**: 14.23, 27
  guest **A 2**: 4.18
  killing **A 1**: 24.2; **G** 22.15, 18; **B 2**: 1.9; **Va** 20.32, 34, 38–9
  occupations of **A 2**: 10.7; **G** 6.18; 7.7, 25; 10.49; **B 1**: 10.2–22; 18.4; **B 2**: 4.18–19; **Va** 2.18–19, 24
  see also social classes
Varuṇa **G** 25.9; **B 1**: 6.8; **B 2**: 7.9, 19; 8.3, 9; **B 3**: 6.5–6; 8.7; **Va** 30.11
Veda **A 1**: 1.3; 4.5–8; 5.7; 12.2, 9, 11; 13.22; 21.8; 32.1; **A 2**: 5.14; 8.10–13; 14.11–12; 23.10, 12; **G** 1.1–2, 45; 5.20; 9.72; 11.19; 13.21; 20.1; 26.24; **B 1**: 1.1, 13, 16; 4.2, 7; 18.2; **B 2**: 11.31; 16.7, 13; 17.15; 18.24–6; **B 3**: 1.26; **B 4**: 1.26; **Va** 1.45; 2.8, 12; 3.19–22; 6.3–5, 25; 7.3; 12.41; 15.11; 27.1–8; 30.6
  abandoning **A 2**: 21.13; **G** 25.7; **Va** 10.4
  Abliṅga **A 1**: 26.7; **B 2**: 7.2; 17.37. **B 4**: 2.13; **Va** 28.11–15
  Aghamarṣaṇa **G** 19.12; 24.10–11; **B 2**: 8.11; 17.37; **B 3**: 4.5; 5.1–7; 10.10; **B 4**: 2.7–8, 15; 3.7; 4.2; **Va** 22.9; 23.19, 23; 26.8; 28.11–15
  Agnervrata Sāman **Va** 28.11–15
  Ājyadoha Sāmans **Va** 28.11–15
  Aṃhomuca **B 4**: 7.5–7
  Āṅgirasa **A 1**: 2.2
  Aśvasūkta **Va** 28.11–15
  Asyavāmīya **Va** 26.6
  Atharvan formulas **B 3**: 9.4
  Atharvaśiras **G** 19.12; **B 3**: 10.10; **Va** 22.9; 28.11–15
  Atharvaveda **A 2**: 29.12; **B 4**: 3.4; 5.1
  Atīṣaṅga Sāman **Va** 28.11–15
  Bahiṣpavamāna Sāman **G** 19.12; **B 3**: 10.10
  Bārhaspatya Sāman **Va** 28.11–15
  Bāruṇḍa Sāman **Va** 28.11–15
  Bhāsa Sāman **Va** 28.11–15
  Bird verses **Va** 3.19
  Brahman's Heart **B 2**: 7.8
  Brāhmaṇa text **A 1**: 1.10, 11; 3.9, 26; 7.6, 7, 11; 10.8; 12.1, 3, 7, 10, 13; 17.28; **A 2**: 13.5; **B 2**: 11.7; **B 3**: 7.18; 9.9
  Bṛhat Sāman **G** 19.12; **B 3**: 10.10; **Va** 28.11–15
  Devakṛta **B 4**: 3.7; **Va** 28.11–15
  Devavrata Sāman **Va** 28.11–15
  Durgāsāvitrī **Va** 28.11–15
  explicit vedic text **A 1**: 4.8; **A 2**: 8.12; **B 1**: 1.6; **Va** 6.43
  'Fiend-killing' Sāman **B 2**: 14.5
  forgetting **G** 21.11; **Va** 1.18; 20.12
  Four-hotra text **B 3**: 7.17
  four Vedas **G** 28.49; **B 1**: 1.8; **Va** 3.20
  Gāyatra Sāman **Va** 28.11–15
  Gosūkta **Va** 28.11–15
  Hiraṇyavarṇa **B 2**: 7.2; 17.37
  'Honey' verses **A 2**: 17.22; **G** 15.28; 19.12; **B 2**: 14.2, 5; **B 3**: 10.10; **Va** 22.9; 28.11–15